THE CRISIS

THE CRISIS

The President, the Prophet, and the Shah —
1979 and the Coming of Militant Islam

DAVID HARRIS

Little, Brown and Company
New York   Boston

Little, Brown and Company
Time Warner Book Group
1271 Avenue of the Americas, New York, NY 10020
Visit our Web site at www.twbookmark.com

First Edition

Photo credits — Page 1: Seal of the United States, former American embassy, Tehran, 2004, SIAVASH. Page 7: Jimmy Carter, president of the United States, 1976, © Owen Frankin/Corbis; Grand Ayatollah Ruhollah Khomeini, 1979, © Abbas/Magnum; Mohammad Reza Pahlavi, shah of Iran, 1960, © Bettmann/ Corbis. Page 93: The shah leaves Iran for the final time, January 16, 1979, © Patrick Shauvel/Corbis Sygma. Page 147: Rally in Tehran, 1979, © Abbas/Magnum. Page 197: Unidentified American hostage, first week of November, 1979, © Bettmann/Corbis. Page 277: Desert One, April 26, 1980, © Abbas/Magnum. Page 363: Presidential debate, October 28, 1980, © Bettmann/Corbis. Page 425: Freed hostages arrive in Germany, January 21, 1981, © Bettmann/Corbis.

Library of Congress Cataloging-in-Publication Data
Harris, David.
   The crisis : the president, the prophet, and the Shah — 1979 and the coming of militant Islam / David Harris. — 1st ed.
      p. cm.
   Includes bibliographical references and index.
   ISBN 0-316-32394-2
   1. Iran Hostage Crisis, 1979–1981.   2. United States — Foreign relations — Iran.   3. Iran — Foreign relations — United States.   4. United States — Foreign relations — 1977–1981.   5. Islam and politics — Iran.   6. Khomeini, Ruhollah.   7. Iran — Politics and government — 1979–1997.   I. Title.

E183.8.I55H37   2004
327.73055'09'047 — dc22   2004005901

10   9   8   7   6   5   4   3   2   1

Q-FF

Designed by Interrobang Design Studio

Printed in the United States of America

CONTENTS

––––––––

PROLOGUE

PROLOGUE

THE ANNIVERSARY IS NOT MUCH BY TEHRAN standards.

Crowds of a million were once run-of-the-mill along the six-lane Ayatollah Taleghani Avenue — just west of its intersection with Shahid Moffatah, a four-lane street named in the old days, decades before the Revolution, in honor of the American president Franklin Roosevelt. Barely five thousand will show up today to officially remember what once happened here. Nonetheless, the Iranian ceremony will far surpass the response in the United States, where there will be no notice paid at all.

In first light, before Tehran starts its daily churn and the inevitable automotive stampede breaks out, the place looks derelict — a neglected half block on the north side of Taleghani, east of the University of Tehran, just south of the soccer stadium. This stretch of the boulevard is shadowed by ten- and twelve-story buildings and an innocuous stretch of eight-foot-tall stone wall topped with razor wire and slathered with spray-painted slogans and political graffiti. The wall's three chained and locked gates lead to a two-story rectangular building that looks as if it has been vacant for a very long time. Set back from the street on a circular drive and only visible through the iron grillwork of the front gates, the reinforced concrete structure is faced with the same narrow yellow brick used to highlight California tract houses in the 1950s and equipped with security bars on all the ground-floor windows. No traffic goes in and out. Aside from the statue of the US Marine on the front porch and the small seal of the United States on the building's face that looks as though someone took a hammer to it with malicious intent, there is no hint this structure once housed the nerve center of the twenty-six-acre American embassy compound.

Today, a speakers' platform has been erected on scaffolding along the wall out front with banners attesting to the faithful's duty to resist the United States. Twenty-four years ago, during the birthing of the Islamic Republic of Iran, after the uprising that chased the Iranian monarchy into exile, this then embassy, known forever after as *Laneye Jasusi*, the Den of Spies, was seized by a group of some three hundred Iranians calling themselves Muslim Students Following the Line of the Imam and held, along with more than fifty captured American diplomats, for the next 444 days, despite all the American efforts to bring its hostages home. On most of those days, this stretch of Taleghani Avenue was a front-page dateline for every newspaper in the world — the backdrop for a series of events so central that they were soon universally shorthanded as just "the Crisis," with no need of further explanation; a location so familiar to so many that it was sufficient to say "the embassy" and everyone knew what and where you were talking about. In front of the Den of Spies almost a quarter century later, that 444-day obsession has been reduced to rote and ritual. Traffic barriers at each end of the block separate off enough space to dwarf this poor excuse for a crowd, most of them schoolchildren born long after the Revolution and now bussed in for the ceremony, relatively oblivious of the history they will celebrate.

The Crisis felt like an end while it was happening, but it was also just the beginning. And it is that beginning that haunts the memories along Taleghani Avenue.

Here, the era of Muslim statehood was introduced to the modern world, as was open religious conflict with the Americans and the dominance of Iran by its clergymen. Here, the posture of the United States began to pivot — deflected onto a far more belligerent course by its very first head-on collision with aroused Islam. When the dust cleared, both countries were left with governments they might never have had otherwise, headed in directions few had foreseen. Here, the communal antagonism — Islam versus America — that eventually collapsed the World Trade Center and punctured the Pentagon on September 11, 2001, came out of the closet. Here, the template for our most urgent present tense was first outlined in the sand and the opening battle of America's Islamic war was joined, though no more than a few rifle shots were ever exchanged.

And here, as in all the far more military engagements to follow, both sides lost.

This is their story.

PART ONE

COMMENCEMENT

· 1 ·

$\mathcal{F}$OR THE AMERICANS, OF COURSE, IT ALL BEGAN
with the shah of Iran, the "best friend" the United States had on the Persian
Gulf in those days.

He was referred to as "HIM" in minutes of the embassy's staff meetings —
short for "His Imperial Majesty," which was in turn short for "His Imperial
Majesty, *Aryamehr Shahanshah*, King of Kings, Light of the Aryans, Shadow
of the Almighty, and Vice Regent of God." In addition, the Iranian newspapers he allowed to publish described HIM as "beloved of the nation" and
"the focus of the universe," characterizations he both read and believed. His
actual given name was Mohammad Reza Pahlavi and in the fall of 1978 he
was about to celebrate his fifty-ninth birthday. He had been shahanshah for
the last thirty-seven years and now, for the first time in a long time, sitting in
his palace looking out over the disorder of Tehran, he had doubts about just
how much longer his reign would last.

Heretofore, Mohammad Reza Pahlavi had always at least looked the shah's
part — seeming, according to one western journalist, "exactly like the person

he was: rich beyond counting, handsome, alert, virile . . . self-possessed . . . a monarch among mortals. . . . That he considered himself superior to other men [was] unstated but obvious." Despite being half a foot shorter than his six-feet-four-inch father, Reza — founder of the Pahlavi dynasty, who was said to have inspired physical terror with just a glance or a twitch of his shoulders — Mohammad Shah made up for it by projecting a surety about his role that was almost mystical. He thought of himself as the soul of his people, the incarnation of a 2,500-year-old monarchy stretching all the way back to Cyrus the Great and the very first of the world's empires. And in western eyes, at least, he so embodied this ancient kingship that he was rarely even referred to by the names Mohammad or Pahlavi, but simply as "the shah of Iran."

HIM was perhaps the only leader from his part of the world who could have passed for a European had he wanted. His thick silver hair was brushed back in waves, he was trim and fit from a lifetime of tennis, horseback riding, and skiing — invariably tan, with a face that was all nose and black eyebrows framing gray eyes, the cheeks set off by deep creases, his forehead twice as long as his chin. *Handsome* was often used to describe him, in no small part for his ability to exude an elegance and noblesse oblige mastered at the best of Swiss preparatory schools. Fluent in English and French, he was the first shah in modern memory to speak a language other than Turkic or Farsi. His aura was always unruffled — a regal equanimity secretly assisted by his continuous consumption of small doses of the sedative Valium.

By the time his reign reached its last turning point in the fall of 1978, of course, the shah's face was internationally familiar. He appeared on the celebrity pages of the day, often seated with other royalty, usually escorting Farah, the shahbanou, his queen and third wife, on state visits or to the slopes at Saint Moritz in the height of the season. Just as often, his image flashed on the evening news: wearing one of his $6,000 suits, leading the oil producing nations' escalation of energy prices at Geneva, or, wearing sunglasses and a military uniform slathered with gold braid, overseeing maneuvers of his fledgling navy on the Straits of Hormuz. His comings and goings were tracked in the western gossip columns. His picture had been taken with Marshall Tito of Yugoslavia and General de Gaulle of France and every American president since Dwight D. Eisenhower. He was even mentioned in the chorus of a song by the Rolling Stones.

Inside Iran, of course, his kingship was everywhere. When streets were widened into modern boulevards, they were regularly renamed Pahlavi and decorated with obelisks honoring the shah or his father or both. His picture was posted on street corners and in shop windows. His birthday was a state occasion. His SAVAK security police arrested and tortured people who said unfavorable things about him. He had his father, Reza, officially renamed "Reza the Great" and interred his remains in a massive tomb surrounded by lawn and policed with a permanent honor guard. His Imperial Majesty's half-million-man army was trained to shout *"Javid shah,"* long live the shah, and did so regularly in his presence. Thousands of citizens were mustered to line his way when he made public appearances.

Despite a somewhat phobic response to crowds, HIM appeared at these events in full regalia and played his role to the hilt. Offstage, he was quite often, according to one acquaintance, "shy, sulky, and eminently fragile." The American ambassador since 1977, William Sullivan, witnessed the shah assuming his role: "With a sigh the shah straightened his tunic," Sullivan remembered, "stood up, and . . . from the gracious, easy, smiling host with whom I had been talking, he transformed himself suddenly into a steely, ramrod-straight autocrat. This involved not only adjusting his uniform and donning dark glasses but also throwing out his chest, raising his chin, and fixing his lips in a grim line. When he had achieved this change to his own satisfaction, he thrust open the door . . . and stalked out across the few remaining steps to the reviewing stand."

Since circumstances had not allowed a coronation when he took the throne in 1941, the shah staged one in 1967. The ceremony featured the legendary Peacock Throne, encrusted with gold and jewels. The shah wore a pearl-embroidered silk cape, a gold girdle with an emerald the size of a chicken egg for a buckle, and the "all-conquering" sword of the dynasty, its sheath covered with diamonds, emeralds, and rubies. He carried a solid-gold scepter, and his crown, originally designed for his father's coronation in 1926, included 3,380 diamonds, 368 pearls, 5 emeralds, and 2 sapphires.

The shah kept a bust of his late father in the anteroom of his office at his palace on the slopes of the Alborz Mountains in north Tehran. The palace was actually several buildings spread about in a leafy park, where the temperature was often five or ten degrees cooler than the baking south side of Tehran on the slopes below. Most of the palace had been built 160 years earlier, then renovated by Reza. The shah's work was largely done in the three-story Sahebgharanieh Palace, and his living quarters were in the newer Niavaran

Palace. By the standards of European monarchs — with whom he compared himself — the palace was visibly small-time, the size of the gatehouse at a place like Versailles. The shah had commissioned drawings for a new palace of dimensions suitable to a monarch such as himself, to be located even farther up the slope, but in the fall of 1978 it remained in the planning stage.

His current office in the Sahebgharanieh was a large salon with pink velvet walls and tall windows overlooking the leafy park in both directions. The plaster on the walls and ceilings was embedded with tiny fragments of mirror so the room sparkled. It was also decorated with gold plate at every turn: gold phones, gold cigarette boxes studded with jewels, gilt chandeliers, gold ashtrays, thread made of gold in the "Versailles-kitsch" furniture, gold-plated fixtures in his private lavatory. The office had the modern accoutrements of political power as well, with charts displayed, radios deployed, and an illuminated map board for quick reference. His desk was the final seat of authority for a nation of some 34 million, the second-largest petroleum exporter in the world. And, for the last decade, his personal power there had been closer to absolute than that of any other head of state on the planet. The shah truly ruled.

His Imperial Majesty had always lived like a man on the come: endless energy, everything going his way, engaged in what seemed to be an American men's magazine fantasy. Seeking to escape the cold winters in Tehran yet stay at home, he used state funds to develop Kish Island from what had been a sand spit in the Persian Gulf into a resort complex that included a palace, an airstrip, and all the infrastructure to allow the shah to rule while on vacation. Since the shah loved to ride but Kish Island was too warm to keep horses for much more than several weeks at a time, his horses were flown in and out by military transport. Besides water skiing, the shah's family liked to go out in the helicopter, piloted by HIM, hover over the water, and jump out one by one — a kind of portable diving board. Then the shah would give up the controls to his copilot and join them in the drink.

When the shah flew to Saint Moritz in his executive jet, he often piloted the plane himself. Sometimes a second jet came along to haul the baggage. In either case, his dogs — as many as six of them, in various sizes — flew with the shah. In Iran, he entertained himself by flying single-engine planes at treetop level in the Alborz and around the ten-thousand-foot-tall dome of Mount Damavand looming over Tehran. In addition to his Iranian palaces, he kept a home in England and another in Switzerland, where he often skied in restricted areas and along the lips of precipices. Whenever he visited any-

where, it was always behind a shield of dark-suited SAVAK state security police. He often had a gaggle of courtiers from his homeland in tow as well.

Upon arrival in Saint Moritz each year, the shah's caravan from the airport customarily split — the shahbanou, the dogs, and most of the rest of the
crowd driving on to the royal villa while he proceeded into town to the Suvretta House hotel. There, with SAVAK occupying the lobby and the hallway
outside a luxury suite, he was presented with a blond, wide-mouthed European woman for sex play. During the sixties, most of these playmates were
either Lufthansa stewardesses or very expensive prostitutes, scouted and
procured by members of his court with titles like "Adjutant to His Imperial
Majesty" or "the Shah's Special Butler." Those looking to rise in the court often did so by finding HIM women. Back in Iran, a small palace was reportedly reserved for these trysts. The prostitutes he used were contracted
through the legendary Madame Claude's whorehouse in Paris and flown in
for several-week shifts. A member of the court acted as advance man and patiently taught the women how to curtsy in order to appropriately greet the
shah when he arrived. Aside from sex, HIM reportedly liked to spend his
time with these women talking about himself.

Though the aristocracy had been abolished by his father, Reza, the shah
had reintroduced a court largely without titles. And those who joined it did
very well by themselves. "The [shah's] court," a CIA report in the 1970s observed, was "a center of licentiousness and depravity, of corruption and influence peddling." His half sister alone amassed a $500 million fortune. All
of the royal family drew benefits from the more than $1 billion in assets of
the Pahlavi Foundation. The shah's personal physician became one of the
largest landholders in Iran. The shah's special butler ended up with a monopoly on the export of Iranian caviar as well as a real estate fortune. "There
was an atmosphere of overwhelming nouveau-riche, meretricious chi-chi
and sycophancy," a European visitor to the court remembered. "There was
an overheated, overstuffed atmosphere in those super-deluxe mini palaces
in the imperial compound which left one gasping for air."

When worried or perplexed, Mohammad Pahlavi often sat silently at his desk
in his office, endlessly twisting a lock of his hair. He thought often of his father.
Their last contact had been thirty-four years ago, through a scratchy gramo-
phone voice recording Reza made shortly before his death in South Africa,
where the British had exiled him. On the vinyl disk he shipped to his son, the
ferocious Reza's only parting advice to HIM had been to "fear nothing."

By now, the shah had lost the recording and was having a very hard time following his father's dictum. "You're always afraid," he admitted to a British television interviewer early in 1978. "Something might go wrong. So you're constantly afraid. It's not physical fright. Or moral fright. It's a reasoned fright."

And that fall, all of the Shah's worst "reasoned" fears seemed to be coming true. On any given day, he could see wisps of smoke from a burning barricade down below in Tehran or hear far-off rifle shots as his army attempted to control the crowd that invariably came flooding down some major avenue, wearing black, tens of thousands strong, women and children at the front, exhorted by mullahs shouting "*Allah-u akbar,*" God is great, or "*Marg bar shah,*" death to the shah.

Though considered an abomination by much of Iran's Islamic faithful, the shah was actually devout after his own fashion, largely abstaining from alcohol and rarely missing his prayers. HIM was a Shiite Muslim, like most Iranians, a follower of the Koran and the prophet Muhammad's son-in-law, Ali ibn Abi Talib, the First Imam. When still the crown prince, the shah had even studied a little with a mullah, a fact he had to conceal from his zealously secular father. The shah's religious devotion was rooted in a series of three mystical experiences he had as a child.

The first came in May 1926, several weeks after his father Reza's coronation, when Mohammad, not yet seven years old, officially became heir to the throne, and the Pahlavi name — taken from the Farsi word for *heroic* — was first attached to the family. The new prince was infected with typhoid fever and delirious for weeks. The western doctor Reza summoned offered only faint hope that the boy would survive, and at that point Reza broke down in tears. It was the only time anyone had ever seen him cry. As he did so, the seemingly incoherent crown prince had a vision of Ali, the First Imam.

"Ali had with him his famous two-pronged sword," he remembered, "which is often seen in paintings of him. He was sitting on his heels on the floor, and in his hands he held a bowl containing liquid. He told me to drink, which I did." The next day, the crown prince's fever broke.

The future shah's second vision came later that summer, after the typhoid was behind him. His family, including his mother and sisters, was making their customary excursion to a favorite spot in the Alborz above Tehran. The trail was steep, and the young Mohammad was sharing a horse with a military officer when the horse slipped and Mohammad was thrown headfirst into a jagged rock and knocked out cold. When he came to, the crowd around him expressed amazement that he hadn't even a bruise on his head. The prince explained that "as I fell I had clearly seen one of our saints, named Abbas, and that I had felt him holding me and preventing me from crashing my head against the rock." Eventually Reza learned of the claim and gave his son a severe tongue-lashing for engaging in such mumbo jumbo. Mohammad didn't argue, but he didn't change his mind about having seen Abbas either.

A few weeks later, the six-year-old crown prince had his third and final vision while on a walk near his father's Shimran Palace. Out of nowhere, clear as day, he saw the legendary Twelfth and Final Imam, the Mahdi, whom Shiite Muslims expect to reappear and transform the world. "Our path lay along a picturesque cobbled street," the shah remembered. "Suddenly I clearly saw before me a man with a halo around his head — much as some of the great paintings, by western masters, of Jesus. As we passed one another, I knew him at once. He was the [Twelfth] Imam . . . the descendant of Muhammad who . . . disappeared but is expected to come again. . . . I asked my guardian: 'Did you see him?'

"'Who?' he inquired. 'No one was here.'"

The crown prince was so sure of his vision that he dismissed his guardian's response and never doubted he had seen the Twelfth Imam that afternoon on the cobblestones.

The faith those visions inspired sustained the second of the Pahlavi shahs. They also left HIM with a belief for most of his life that he was under divine protection. "I have felt that there is a Supreme Being who is guiding me," he explained. "I am driven — or perhaps I should say supported — by another force."

The shah's sense of benevolent destiny had only been reinforced by his brushes with death over the following years. In 1948 alone, the young monarch escaped death or even injury twice in crashes while out flying his Gypsy Moth stunt plane. Both incidents were thought by HIM to have been little "miracles."

Even more convincing to him were the two assassination attempts he survived. The first was on February 4, 1949, when the shah, dressed in formal uniform, led a ceremonial procession at the University of Tehran. A man broke out of the crowd with a six-shot pistol and started firing from barely ten feet away. The first three shots passed through HIM's hat without even singeing his hair. The fourth entered near his ear and passed out near his nose, a clean cheek wound that would hardly leave a scar. The shah sensed that the fifth shot would be aimed at his heart and twisted his body before the assassin fired. The bullet entered his shoulder but hit nothing vital. As the assassin started to fire his final round, the gun jammed. At that point, the shah's security detail shot the assailant dead. "My life was miraculously spared," HIM later maintained. "Even . . . the most eminent doctors of Koranic law called my survival a 'true miracle.'"

The second assassination escape, described by the shah as "another miracle," happened on April 10, 1964. As the shah entered the palace, automatic weapons fire broke out behind him. A man with a machine gun was loose on the palace grounds. The first Imperial Guardsman to intercept the gunman was shot dead. So was the second, but he managed to empty his machine gun into the assassin before collapsing. By then the shah had reached his office. Still firing, the assassin stumbled after him. Several bullets passed through one wall, whizzing past the shah's ear and into the chair in which he usually sat. The assassin was finally subdued without reaching the office door.

The decade following that last divine rescue had been the shah's best, during which he emerged as a global figure, fueled by a messianic sense of mission and entitlement and controlling an enormous influx of oil wealth with which to make his dreams come true. Through most of it, he had assumed his life was charmed.

But in the fall of 1978, when the outcome was still at issue and his fate up for grabs, the shah, faith aside, was unsure that his divine protection continued to work.

Martial law and strict curfews had been in effect for almost the entire two months since the shah had returned from his summer vacation on the Caspian Sea, but no one paid much attention to his ban on public gatherings. Hundreds, perhaps thousands, of demonstrators had already died at the hands of his troops, to little effect. Major intersections around the city now featured sandbagged gun emplacements, including one on the avenue then known as Takht-e Janshia, outside the American embassy, but the shah's army would still soon be forced to cede de facto control of the entire southern half of the city to the uprising against him.

Besides the ghost of Reza, the shah looked to two women as his emotional anchors.

The first was his twin sister, Ashraf. In Iran she was called "the Black Panther." According to a 1976 CIA report, Princess Ashraf had "a near legendary reputation for financial corruption and for successfully pursuing young men." The CIA also described her business practices as "often verging on if not completely illegal." After the Revolution, the Iranian government would eventually sue her for $3 billion she allegedly stole from the country's public coffers.

In Iran it was widely thought — by people of all classes and political persuasions — that Ashraf was her brother's backbone and that without her, he would be lost. The Soviet dictator Stalin, after having to negotiate with Ashraf face-to-face when she was still a young woman, said that if the shah "had ten like [her], he would have no worries at all." For Ashraf's part, one of her former lovers later wrote, her brother "was the light of her life, the apple of her eye, the blood that flowed in her veins. She loved him with a passion that was both possessive and unsharing. [The shah] was one half of the symbiotic whole of which the Princess was the other." This was a truth Ashraf did not deny. "Always," she admitted, "the center of my existence was, and is, Mohammad Reza Pahlavi."

She had been the second one born of the two, about an hour later on October 26, 1919. Reza had been up in the forests near the Caspian when the news of the twins' birth reached him. Known as Reza Khan then, he was still six years from becoming royalty, just the leading military commander of the previous dynasty, suppressing an insurrection that had proclaimed itself the Republic of the Jungle. He rode back to Tehran at once when he got the news. These were Reza's third and fourth children by three different wives, but for him, it was the son — his first — that mattered. The home the twins were born into was made of mud bricks and located at the end of a narrow alley called Greasy Lane, just off Tatooville Street. The neighborhood featured open sewers and crumbling real estate, but Reza's was one of the better houses, with a ten-foot-tall wall around it, and leased for roughly fifty dollars a year.

Throughout their rise from low-rent Greasy Lane to the Peacock Throne, Ashraf shadowed her twin brother as much as possible. She would sometimes sit in on the late-morning conversations about statecraft between the crown prince and Reza, and was considered by some the more apt pupil of the two children. When Reza left for exile, Ashraf was the only one of the royal siblings to stay behind in Iran with the new shah. "I thought he would need me," she explained.

Thirty-seven years later, she was serving as her brother's representative on the United Nations Commission on Human Rights. To call her controversial would be a considerable understatement. The crowds surging through the streets of Tehran in the fall of 1978 proclaimed Ashraf a "whore," and even the shah's supporters thought her a Jezebel. In any case, she was political bad news inside Iran, and eventually the shah had to act accordingly.

In September 1978, shortly after the imposition of martial law, the shah asked his twin to leave; she was too much of a target to be in Iran any longer. After what must have been a terribly poignant moment between them, the shah's twin acceded to his wishes and joined the migration. Most of Ashraf's fortune was already in the West, so she just cleaned out her Tehran palace and moved to her homes in New York, Paris, and the French Riviera. She and her brother would talk regularly on the phone, but His Imperial Majesty would still miss her dearly.

The other woman to whom HIM turned was Farah, the shahbanou. She was his third wife, though unlike his father's — who were concurrent — the shah's wives were consecutive, his first and second divorced for their failure to produce a male heir. The shah met Farah — young and quite beautiful, with dark Persian eyes — in 1958 at a reception in the Iranian embassy in Paris, where she had been studying architecture. He was freshly divorced and on the hunt for a third wife to bear a crown prince. Her father was an Iranian army general. They met once more back in Iran the following year and then they — he forty, she twenty-one — were married. Eleven months later, Crown Prince Reza was born, assuring that the shah would not have to look for a fourth wife.

Farah was every bit as "modernized" as her husband and played an activist shahbanou, with a liberal edge. She backed the arts and museums. She toured the underside of Iran, remote, impoverished, and anything but modern. "I saw the problems," she remembered, "while His Majesty saw the achievements. In bed, we would compare notes. I would report about what was going on in the regions I had just toured. His Majesty would try to dismiss my report as exaggerated or one-sided. At times he would tell me that such minor problems were *des accidents de parcours,* or the heritage of the past, and that all would be well in a few years' time. Sometimes, however, he would get impatient and edgy. 'No more bad news, please!' His Majesty would command. And I would, naturally, change the subject."

The shahbanou had none of her sister-in-law's political baggage. "Farah did everything with style and with courtesy," a journalist who covered her observed. "She was relaxed and convivial and far less snobbish than most of the Shah's family [and] emerged as a warmhearted, rather cultured figure who was much easier at her role than the Shah with his. She was visibly interested in social programs . . . and she managed to develop a reputation for compassion." She was rarely targeted in the chanting of the Tehran crowds and when she was, they only mentioned her jokingly, in a slogan proclaiming that once the shah was dead, Farah would become the American president Jimmy Carter's wife.

By the fall of 1978, many of the battalion of liveried footmen at the Pahlavis' palace had abandoned their posts, as had much of the court. The palace's public rooms, with panoramic mirrors, marble floors, seemingly endless Persian rugs, and gilded red velvet chairs, were now almost always empty. Only the shahbanou remained, and the two of them often dined alone by candlelight, since the city's power grid functioned only intermittently. The shah could have used the palace's generator to keep the lights on, but he was worried that the sight of the palace all lit up would provoke more attacks. Just getting across town was a military exercise. Many state ministries had effectively ceased functioning. Occasionally a few old court cronies came by to play gin rummy with HIM, but that was about all the social contact he had. When His Imperial Majesty used the palace's huge reception room, he often huddled by a portable kerosene heater, since the palace's supply of heating oil had been disrupted by strikes.

Tugging at his hair, staring out the window, the shah took on an increasingly petulant tone. "Everything is at an end," he whined to one visitor. "Nothing will be the same again. It is like a beautiful crystal vase that is broken for good; repair it and it will still show the cracks." For a moment, the self-pity in the room was thicker than the rug.

The shah's newfound vulnerability could be credited as much to the weight of a secret he'd been keeping as to the disorder outside his palace grounds. In addition to everything else, Mohammad Reza Pahlavi had cancer, a stage two lymphoma, and had been concealing his affliction for the past four years. Even the shahbanou hadn't learned of it until 1977.

In April 1974, when the shah was waterskiing at Kish Island on the Persian Gulf, he had noticed a swelling under his left rib cage. When HIM returned to Tehran and his Iranian physician determined the spleen was enlarged, a well-regarded hematologist was summoned from Paris and told the lie that he would be examining one of the officers in the shah's court. Having been sworn to secrecy, he was ushered into a room in the palace and found the shah, accompanied by his personal Iranian physician and favorite pet, an enormous Great Dane. After a routine physical exam, the French doctor also took blood samples and aspirated some bone marrow. It was the bone marrow that gave the shah's illness away. He had five times the normal amount of lymphoid cells, a common indicator of either chronic lymphocytic leukemia or a lymphoma presenting itself with those same symptoms.

Before informing the shah, the French doctor first shared his conclusions with the shah's Iranian physician. The Iranian trembled a bit, then asked the Frenchman not to use the words *leukemia* or *cancer* when speaking with the shah. HIM was not, as a rule, told bad news. He didn't like it and it wasn't good for him. As a result, the Frenchman told his patient he had a blood condition called Waldenstrom's macroglobulinemia. No one would call it cancer to His Imperial Majesty's face for another four years.

When the Frenchman returned in September 1974, he found the shah's spleen even further enlarged and ordered him to begin taking chlorambucil, a mild chemotherapy drug, to stabilize his condition. But the shah was a less than diligent patient and didn't take his medicine. As a consequence, in February 1975, the French doctor and a colleague were summoned to the Dolder Grand Hotel in Zurich, where the shah was staying for a series of meetings with representatives of nations seeking a way to tap into Iran's avalanche of oil wealth. HIM was in a suite, again with his Iranian doctor and his Great Dane. His spleen was now dangerously swollen. The shah made light of his doctors' worry. He was skiing regularly and felt great. They told him to stop skiing and take an increased dose of the chlorambucil. The shah agreed to the latter.

From then on, every four to six weeks, one of the French doctors flew to Tehran and collected samples to help track the course of the disease and the effect of the medication. The samples were filed with the French laboratory under the name and national identification number of one of the doctors' relatives. Finally, in 1977, when the shahbanou was in Paris, the French doctors thought they ought to tell her what was going on. With Farah, they were more direct and actually used the word *cancer* in their description of her husband's condition.

"I cried all night long," she later recalled. "I could not bear the thought of returning to Tehran and facing him. What would I tell him?"

In Paris she tried to convince the doctors to be as frank with the shah as they had been with her, and henceforth, the doctors at least made a concerted effort to impress upon their patient the seriousness of his situation. While still officially calling his disease Waldenstrom's macroglobulinemia,

His Imperial Majesty's doctors now frequently used terms like *lymphoma* with him.

The shah's response to this expansion of description was absolute passivity. Never once did he inquire what any of these new terms meant or ask for any more information about the condition from which he was supposed to be suffering. "For a long time it was just this act," Farah explained. "Sometimes I thought, Maybe he knows but doesn't want me to know. . . . My husband just said we mustn't tell anybody. . . . So for a long time we went on like this, not mentioning it to each other. It was strange for me. . . . I thought, How come . . . he's not curious?"

While stifling in many ways, the shah's avoidance and denial made it at least easier to keep his secret. None of the major intelligence organizations operating in Iran — neither the British, the French, the Israelis, the Russians, nor the Americans — had discovered his illness. The CIA station in the American embassy had picked up little hints but had not pursued them. The closest the embassy came to raising a warning flag was a cable sent to the State Department on July 26, 1978, by the foreign service officer filling in for Ambassador Sullivan, who was on home leave:

"For the last three weeks Tehran and Isfahan . . . have been awash with rumors re the Shah's health," the cable reported. "At every social occasion, Embassy officers and I have received anxious inquiries from Americans, Iranians, and other diplomats. . . . The rumors range from terminal malignancy, Leukemia, simple anemia to having been wounded in the arm or shoulder. . . . Our own sources indicate that there is no doubt the Russians in fact are spreading the stories. . . . To the best of our knowledge the Shah is fine."

· 2 ·

———

THE CLOSEST THING IN HIS LIFE TO A PRECEDENT for the kind of psychological reconstruction the shah faced at age fifty-nine had been his adolescence. The ages twelve to twenty-two, taking him from child to adult, were Mohammad Reza Pahlavi's crucible, a period that began and ended with a sudden transformation. Together, those two surges of change still dominated the Shah's emotional topography.

The first took place in 1931, when Reza and the Pahlavi dynasty had been ruling for five years. Following his model, Atatürk's revolution in Turkey, Reza's mission had been to "modernize" Iran. He began with his own family. The first Pahlavi — having barely taught himself to read as an adult — wanted his heir to have an education comparable to those of any other "modern" statesman. Until his teenage years, the young Mohammad had been schooled at the palace by a French governess and then in a special military school created by the shah to educate his sons. Thanks to his governess, the twelve-year-old crown prince was already fluent in French, the language in which he would be most comfortable throughout his life. As Mohammad's manhood approached, Reza decided the time had come for a more formal education. The school Reza selected for his eldest son was Le Rosey, one of Switzerland's foremost international schools for children of the wealthy and aristocratic. Mohammad and one of his younger brothers would be accompanied by two other Persians their age and two adult Iranian teachers to watch over them and continue their Persian education. Mohammad Reza Pahlavi would thus become the first shah ever educated outside of Iran.

His 1931 journey to school was daunting, the departure from home traumatic, and his prospects lonely — though the crown prince already lived at a certain distance from his family. He had been separated from his mother and siblings since Reza's coronation and his own designation as heir to the throne, living in a separate building in the palace compound, watched over by his governess and his own Turkic butler. His father called him "sir" and always used the formal plural tense with him rather than the more intimate singular. His mother addressed him as *"Vala Hazrat,"* Your Majesty. He visited with her an hour each day. He reserved a half hour late in the morning for his father, when they often discussed affairs of state. He also ate lunch and dinner with his father and his ten half and full siblings. Among his brothers and sisters, Mohammad was always served first.

On the opening leg of his voyage to Le Rosey, the crown prince departed in a fishing boat from the recently renamed port of Pahlavi on the Caspian Sea. The boat ferried him to a Soviet steamer lying off the coast. In turn, the ship carried him to Baku, capital of Soviet Azerbaijan. Then it was by train through the Soviet Union to Warsaw and by German train to Berlin and on to Switzerland. It would be almost five years before he saw Iran and his father again.

His first year abroad was spent prepping for Le Rosey's entrance exams, after which the thirteen-year-old future shah was accepted for study and began his education in earnest. On his first day, he got into a fistfight with one of the American students and was soundly beaten. Afterward, the shah offered the American his hand and ended up on good terms with a number of the two dozen or so United States citizens in the student body. One of his American classmates, Richard Helms, would go on to become director of the CIA and then United States ambassador to Iran.

Only a satisfactory, if diligent, student, the future shah excelled at track and field, and was chosen captain of Le Rosey's championship soccer team. He arrived there a Persian and left a young European in style and outlook. The shah later called his years at the Swiss school "the most important of my whole life."

Considering his son's western education complete, Reza summoned Mohammad home in 1936 to enter Iran's new military academy, and the crown prince found Iran as transformed as he was. Reza had "modernized" at a fierce pace in his boy's absence. He built the army into the most important force in the nation; he subdued the rebellious tribes; he replaced the Islamic legal system with a secular one, modeled somewhat on that of France in form and procedure; he partially rewrote the Persian language to eliminate Arabic words that had become embedded in it over the previous ten centuries; he banned the wearing of the veil and led the way by publicly parading all the women of his family barefaced and in Parisian dresses; he banned the turbans traditionally worn by mullahs; he banned a number of religious celebrations; government troops forcibly shaved the beards the mullahs grew as part of their religious practice; he required all Iranians to register for an identification card and, contrary to previous custom, to identify themselves with a western-style family name, as Reza had done in adopting Pahlavi; he banned the traditional dress of wide trousers and loose shirts and required many classes of workers to wear western-style clothes; he founded Iran's manufacturing industry; he brought electricity to the country for the first time; and he built a trans-Iranian railroad, linking the Persian Gulf to the Caspian Sea.

The crown prince, now seventeen, was stunned at the initial results. "It was like visiting a different country," he later recounted. "I recognized nothing. . . . My father had razed Teheran's old walls. Streets were paved and asphalted. The city had begun to take on the look and style of a European capital. I saw it all at first as if in a dream. . . . We drove in an open car through the streets. . . . Thousands of young people lined our route, tossing flowers. . . . The welcome was overwhelming, and surely one of the most moving experiences of my life."

The end of Mohammad Pahlavi's extended adolescence came abruptly in September 1941. The future shah had graduated from the Iranian military academy, taken an officer's commission, married his first wife — the sister of Egypt's King Farouk — and settled in as crown prince. Then his world turned on its ear. The Europe of his school days became engulfed in World War II, and the British and their Soviet allies suspected that Reza was a German sympathizer, despite his official neutrality. Accordingly, the allies decided to split authority over Iran — with the Soviet Union taking the northern segment for the duration of the war and the British, Tehran and south. To impose that decision, a British invasion force landed on the Gulf and marched on Tehran, establishing its rule along the way. On September 14, Reza called his son to him.

Reza's mind was made up, he said. He wasn't going to stay around and take orders from some "little English captain." The British had to be presented with a royal presence they could swallow. It was perhaps the only way to save the Pahlavi dynasty. He was going to abdicate in favor of his heir.

On September 16, Reza's letter of abdication was read to the Majlis, the rubber stamp parliament that had named him shah in the first place. According to one historian, "many deputies were crying, a few had even fainted. Most were . . . in a state of shock." Reza's letter went on to name Mohammad Reza Pahlavi as his successor. This assumption of the throne was endorsed by the Majlis, and then the new shah arrived to address the delegates. A now jubilant crowd in the square outside literally carried him into the building on their shoulders. His speech received a standing ovation, and Mohammad Reza Pahlavi, not quite twenty-two, was now shahanshah, Light of the Aryans, Shadow of the Almighty, and Vice Regent of God.

Ambivalent, the British had agreed to allow Reza's son to stay enthroned as a figurehead while they ran the country until the war was over. The occupiers had insisted, however, that Reza himself go into an exile of their choosing, far from Iraq. Reza waited at his palace with his bags packed until word of the Majlis approval of Mohammad reached him; he then left with two of his wives and almost a dozen children in tow, without waiting to say goodbye to his oldest son. Mohammad Pahlavi would never see his father again.

Reza wanted to go to Canada or Latin America, but the British took him to India instead. Then, unwilling to let him off the boat there, they took him to exile on the island of Mauritius and then on to Johannesburg, South Africa, where, after sending his son a recording of his final advice, he died in 1944.

Mohammad occupied Reza's royal office immediately upon returning to the empty palace, but for several days he could not bring himself to sit in his father's chair.

Despite Reza's modernizing, the Tehran HIM Mohammad Pahlavi had inherited in 1941 was still a splatter of one-story mud-brick dwellings fielding almost as many automobiles as paved roads. That would change. By the late 1970s, Tehran boasted concrete high-rises, pavement everywhere, televisions, and cars so thick traffic never quite unclogged. The shah had built dams and even nuclear power plants. He had built steel mills. He had built acres and acres of petrochemical plants. He had broken up and redistributed feudal landholdings, even confiscated property that endowed mullahs and mosques. He had given women the right to hold office in his government. He had nationalized the oil industry. He had even promulgated a law giving industrial workers the right to buy shares in the companies for which they worked, though he usually ignored the fact that it had rarely been enforced. Indeed, he once bragged to the Chinese about how "socialist" Imperial Iran was.

And, he pointed out, it was all part of a vision that *he* had brought to his people, not someone else. When still a schoolboy at Le Rosey, he had dreamed of being king and allowing "each peasant to amass a little fortune," and as shahanshah, he claimed he had been aggressively doing just that. To prosper, he explained, "our nation . . . had no alternative but to completely alter the archaic order of society and to structure its future on a new order compatible with the vision and needs of the day. This required a deep and fundamental revolution."

His Imperial Majesty dubbed this reconfiguration of his country the "White Revolution," to contrast it to the Red of the communists and the black of the mullahs. If the nation stayed backward, it would, he believed, exist in perpetual slavery to the whims of the great powers. So he made it modern with a capital *M* and bragged on his accomplishments. He spent Iran's flow of oil money lavishly. Tehran was now twenty times as large as it had been when he assumed the throne. Workers who would have spent their lives as peasants, sharecropping in the remote countryside, now flowed to the cities to find employment manufacturing machine parts or mixing plastic or laying pipelines or driving cement trucks. Where once the society had been hidebound and isolated, now Hollywood movies circulated, dubbed in Farsi. Discos flourished. Wealthy suburbs sprouted all over north Tehran. Iranian tourists swarmed around Europe and the United States. The bazaar peddled Sony and Westinghouse and Toshiba. All the major international carriers serviced the Tehran airport.

To make his vision happen, the shah had first had to construct his rule out of the political wasteland. That alone required some twenty years and a lot of outside help. During the first decade of his reign, Iran was governed by an approximation of the country's short-lived 1906 constitution, which had been reinstalled by the British before they ended their occupation in 1946. Under it, the shah had been declared constitutional titular head of state and commander in chief of the armed forces in a government balanced by the popularly elected Majlis and a prime minister — a system in which power was shared by a number of competing political parties. Then, in 1951, the leftist prime minister, Mohammad Mossadeq, convinced the Majlis to nationalize the Iranian oil industry, heretofore a British monopoly. Political tensions grew exponentially over the next two years until riots erupted in the streets between contending political factions. In August 1953, the shah dismissed Mossadeq as prime minister. According to a plan worked out with the CIA's Tehran station chief and the American ambassador — who were worried Mossadeq would take the country communist — the shah and his second wife went into hiding at one of his mountain retreats while an army officer delivered the prime minister's dismissal.

When that messenger was arrested by Mossadeq, the shah fled, piloting a twin-engine plane out of the Iranian mountains to Iraq. After two days in Baghdad, visiting Shiite holy sites, he traveled by commercial airliner to Rome. Then, in what was thought one of the great "intelligence victories" of the early Cold War, the CIA station chief put together a cadre of army monarchists who, backed by street mobs hired with American money and troops loyal to the shah, seized the government, arrested Mossadeq, and invited HIM to come back home and take the near absolute power that typified the rest of his reign. Henceforth the shah would operate with the armed forces, the secret police, and the Americans as a political base. Iran's new arrangement also featured a rubber-stamp Majlis and a prime minister to run a government over which the shah had final veto. HIM later told the CIA station chief, "I owe my throne to God, my people, and to you."

And he made the most of it. When Mohammad Pahlavi first assumed the throne at the tolerance of the British, the shah's views on issues had been officially referred to as "royal comments," then, as his power accumulated, they became "guiding points," then "royal instructions," and now "auspicious commands" to which everyone either had to salute or explain their reluctance to do so to the men from SAVAK, *Sazman-e Ettela'at Va Amniyat-e Keshvar,* the Iranian Organization for State Intelligence and Security. The organization had been founded as part of the initial American aid package. Its American designers meant for the organization to handle the shah's internal and external intelligence needs and act as his "eyes and ears." Its development amounted to a kind of Cold War pilot project, a model to be repeated elsewhere when the time came. "The CIA . . . went all out," a former SAVAK executive remembered. "It took charge and became deeply involved in every aspect of SAVAK's daily operations."

Once SAVAK got rolling, those daily operations were stunningly brutal. The organization's Third Division, for example, charged with combating domestic subversion, specialized in interrogations. Among their methods were pulling out suspects' fingernails, dangling heavy weights from suspects' testicles, dipping suspects in hot oil, attaching electrodes to suspects' genitals and administering shock treatments, suspending suspects upside down, beating suspects on their soles until their feet were reduced to bloody stumps, raping wives in front of husbands, raping husbands in front of wives, penetrating suspects with bottles (both broken and unbroken), penetrating suspects with electric cattle prods, disfigurement of suspects, and forcing water down suspects' throats. No official figures exist, but by the late 1970s, somewhere between 10,000 and 100,000 Iranians had been subjected to these techniques.

Employing 6,000 agents at the organization's largest, SAVAK used as many as 100,000 secret informants in its domestic intelligence gathering. Wives were recruited to spy on their husbands, sons on fathers, friends on friends. By the mid 1970s, it was widely believed that the shah's "eyes and ears" were everywhere and that no place was safe from them. To keep that fear alive, the shah's police conducted some 500,000 "interviews" between 1970 and 1975 in which suspects were questioned and detained for a day or a week or a month, just to get a taste of what would be out there waiting for them next time. The issues raised in these "interviews" were often as trivial as failing to use the shah's proper title and showing His Imperial Majesty's photograph insufficient respect.

"Particularly in the late 1960s and early 1970s," Ambassador Sullivan noted, "there was a sort or reign of terror in Iran. . . . All political activity was suspect. Not only the Communists and the Islamic extremists, but also the Social Democrats, the old aristocracy, and the regional political leaders. . . . Student organizations were especially watched and infiltrated. SAVAK informants were myriad. . . . Most prominent politicians, many westernized families, and persons from all over the realm were affected by it. There were mysterious disappearances, murders in the prisons, and the generalized use of torture."

Thanks in no small part to this approach, Mohammad Reza Pahlavi was the only monarch in the twentieth century to grow from window dressing to absolute power. And Iran, he pointed out over and over again, was the biggest beneficiary.

*   *   *

His Imperial Majesty expected to be adored for what he'd done, but he wasn't. Tehran was full of young men who had been torn out of the rural peasantry and the traditional life of interlaced family and clans, and thrown into concrete housing blocks or swarming tenements, never making enough money to go much further but now cut off from all the institutions that had given their life definition. They were lost and adrift, angry at the plutocracy, resentful of their fate, and often genuinely offended by the sensibilities of the New Iran, with its half-naked women and alcohol. Increasingly they turned to the mosque and the mullahs for consolation and guidance. Religious revival had swept much of the country in the mid-1970s, driven by Iranians alienated from their new circumstances and intent on recapturing their roots in the teachings of the Prophet.

The preeminent hero among all those Iranians who detested the shah and his rule was a seventy-seven-year-old Islamic cleric and self-proclaimed imam living in Iraqi exile, Grand Ayatollah Ruhollah Khomeini, also known among his followers as "the Smasher of Idols," "the one who humbles Satan," "the Sole Hope of the Downtrodden," and "the exalted Chief." He had begun referring to himself with the title imam, or leader, in 1977. For their part, the Americans would simply dub Khomeini "the ayatollah" after he suddenly emerged as the universal household image of the incomprehensible fanaticism that seemed to have ambushed their country. But that was later. In the fall of 1978, Ruhollah Khomeini was still virtually unknown, just a Persian wild card in exile, loosely tracked by a few people at the State Department and the CIA but otherwise all but invisible outside of Iran.

The image of the ayatollah that would come to dominate American television ratings, however, was already full-blown. As always, it was a head shot, framed in black — the color of both the robe he wore and the perfectly wound turban on his head, signifying his status as a sayyid, a direct descendant of the prophet Muhammad. Among the Iranian mullahs, Khomeini had a long-standing reputation as a distinguished turban winder — never sloppy, always clamped firmly in place, completely capturing the ayatollah's gray hair. The black of his sayyid's turban further resonated in his eyebrows, two obsidian hedges that almost joined across his forehead, separated only by the creases of his seemingly perpetual scowl. One French reporter who covered the ayatollah daily for more than a year claimed he had never seen him smile. Khomeini would eventually order all photographs of himself with a lighthearted expression removed from circulation.

Not surprisingly, the imam's mouth usually appeared in his images as little more than a grim line surrounded by a thick silver beard that spread over his chest. The imam's whiskers, full in the fashion of the faithful, were as close to foppery as Khomeini got. The beard, described by him as "the cherished friend of my face," was well washed, thoroughly combed, and regularly perfumed with the Christian Dior cologne Eau Sauvage. Still, the imam's eyes — though they were hardly visible — dominated all the rest, beard included: two dark implosions lurking on either side of his nose, like dead stars, emitting nothing yet throbbing with energy that seemed to burrow back into his head. Those eyes made Khomeini seem even more silent than he already was.

The imam had spent almost all of his fourteen-year enforced absence from Iran in the holy Shiite city of Najaf, among the Mesopotamian lowlands in Iraq, four hundred miles southwest of Tehran. It was here in 661 AD that Ali, Muhammad's son-in-law and cousin, the rightful inheritor of the caliphate of all Islam, had been stabbed by an assassin and, after lingering for two days, died and entered the Shiite pantheon as the First Imam. Those who continued to refuse to accept Ali's rival as caliph were known as *Shiat al Ali,* "followers of Ali," or Shiites. By the fall of 1978, they made up some 15 percent of the world's Muslims, and Najaf, a hundred miles south of Baghdad, was now a city of 150,000, and renowned as an ongoing center of Shiite theology. It welcomed a constant flow of religious scholars and students. A pilgramage to Najaf was one of the two most sacred Shiite journeys.

Khomeini was not a conspicuous presence in Najaf, despite the fact that everyone knew he was there. Though wealthy through the tithes of his followers, the ayatollah lived in a simple three-room brick house with his wife, Batul, who had been ten years old when they were married forty-six years earlier and whom he'd never supplemented with any of the additional wives he was allowed under Islamic law. He was reportedly devoted to her. His daily routine began with a simple breakfast of goat cheese and bread, though on many days he fasted. His floors were covered with layers of rugs, but he owned virtually no furniture. He had a servant and a cook, both of them also secretly in the pay of SAVAK. Every evening, he listened to Radio Baghdad and then the BBC Persian service. Mullahs from all over Iran visited him regularly.

Sometimes, however, Khomeini closed the door to his room and disappeared into prayers that lasted days. His seven-year-old daughter had died years earlier while he was submerged in such a prayer, and he had reportedly refused to be interrupted to even acknowledge her passing or attend her funeral. Isolation fit him like a second skin. From the time when the imam was a boy he had always taken great pleasure in walking alone and staring into the distance for hours on end. He now believed that a lifetime of such solitary meditation and ecstatic religious immersion had brought him closer to the word of the Prophet than almost anyone else. This belief was shared by many of the pilgrims who sought him out.

In Najaf he was most often seen publicly at the gold-domed holy shrine for Ali, a hub of the city's life. During the day, the shrine hummed with activity, overrun by a sea of people that included, according to one contemporary observer, "pilgrims, preachers, soothsayers, undertakers, healers, dervishes, luminaries, exorcists, water-bearers, dispellers of charms, casters of leeches, vendors, Iraqi and Iranian secret police agents easily recognized by their light-colored Dacron suits and dark sunglasses, *talabehs,* temporary concubines, opium and hasheesh pushers, reciters of the Holy Book, barbers, removers of unwanted hair from female faces, interpreters of the astrolabe and part-time butchers ready to cut the throat of a sacrificial lamb for a modest fee." The imam held sway there in the late evening, usually 10:00 p.m., when all the daily business had left.

The crowds who came to hear him, faithfully counted by the Iraqi secret police, usually numbered between three and four thousand, all assembled to hear the wisdom of the old man with the seemingly bottomless eyes. They came because he was one of only a half dozen grand ayatollahs, the highest living founts of Shiism, holier than the day was long. The many Iranians among them came because they knew they could hear things said freely by the imam that SAVAK banned on the other side of the border. They came because they yearned for meaning and he offered it.

The ayatollah opened with a prayer, and it was quickly apparent in the imam's manner that his favorite among the 999 names for Allah was "the Avenger." The old man's ferocity was unrelenting, and he preached a rigorous brand of faith. "Perdition begins with but a small step," he warned, "a tiny step that can be dismissed as insignificant. Man moves towards Hell step by step. All of those who were lost did not become corrupt all of a sudden — with a giant leap. . . . They began with tiny insignificant steps and were soon beyond salvation. . . . There is a devil in every man, corrupting him little by little."

But no one was more corrupted than the shah. The grand ayatollah had issued a fatwa — a declaration of Islamic law obliging Muslims to act — against His Imperial Majesty the year before, and Khomeini prefaced his fatwa

not with the name of Allah the Merciful, the Compassionate, as was traditional, but with the name of Allah, Punisher of Tyrants, yet another of his
999 identities. This man Pahlavi was Taghut, the imam warned — literally
"the Rebel," one of the names of Satan. Pahlavi and his father and his Jezebel
sister were trying to destroy Islam, Khomeini preached. They had taken Iran
away from the law of the Prophet and sold the country to the Americans and
the Israelis. These Pahlavis had made Iran a tool of the West, of the unfaith-
ful, of the plutocrats. Among the synonyms the imam used for His Imperial
Majesty were *leech, dog,* and *lackey.* It was now, he repeated, the obligation of
all good Shiites to bring HIM down.

"The Shah says that he is granting liberty to the people," Khomeini railed.
"Hear me, you pompous toad! Who are you to grant freedom? It is Allah
who grants freedom. It is Islam which grants freedom. . . . What do you
mean by saying 'We have granted you freedom'? What has it got to do with
you anyway to grant anything? Who are you anyway?"

Most of the imam's 10:00 p.m. sermons were taped, and master copies were
smuggled into Iran for reproduction and distribution. These copies were
played at mosques or at meetings in private homes. During 1978, according
to SAVAK, there were at least one hundred thousand such cassettes in circulation inside Iran. Despite a long-standing legal prohibition against even the
public mention of Khomeini's name in a favorable manner, his denunciations of the shah were readily available in the Tehran bazaar, labeled as simply "a religious sermon."

When the imam was done with his lesson for the day, he left the Shrine of
Ali quickly and was driven through Najaf to his house by a disciple in an old
van. The younger of Khomeini's two sons, Ahmed, forty-two, stayed behind
at the shrine for another hour, talking with small groups and collecting
names. Until just a year before, that had been the task of the imam's older
son, Mostafa, but Mostafa, forty-four, had died suddenly of a heart attack.
The imam still carried the weight of that loss. Mostafa, he explained, had
been "the light of my eyes." The imam's grief, however, was hard to distinguish against the background of his Shiite faith, woven as it was out of martyrdom and betrayal and loss and mourning.

Later — in the first frantic days after this heretofore obscure Persian holy
man had thrown America into a crisis that would dominate its politics for
the next year and a half and doom Jimmy Carter's presidency — Vice Presi-

dent Walter Mondale would turn to Harold Brown, the secretary of defense, sitting next to him at one of several daily White House meetings on Iran, and ask somewhat plaintively, "What the hell is an ayatollah anyway?"

The secretary would have no idea.

Ayatollah, literally "sign of Allah," was the highest of Shiism's ranks, reserved for those whose piety and understanding had been recognized as extraordinary by the consensus of those who already held the title, though no formal chain of command existed by which they were finally approved. All had been through the equivalent of a high graduate degree program in the "science of Islam" and all had written at least two theses, not unlike those required for a PhD. After that, they pursued their faith as the consensus surrounding them built to ayatollah status. The number of ayatollahs fluctuated, but in the fall of 1978, there were at least several hundred of them active in Iranian Shiism. Only grand ayatollahs — the half dozen ayatollahs recognized by all the rest to be yet another cut above — outranked them, and only ayatollahs, grand and otherwise, could command the faithful.

It was a role to which Ruhollah Khomeini seemed born.

His ancestry was full of mullahs, starting at least with his great-grandfather — who had migrated from northeastern Iran into the state of Kashmir in India during a brief eighteenth-century Persian expansion to the east. Henceforth, even when the ayatollah's ancestors returned to Iran and settled in the town of Khomein, their home there would be known as "the house of the Indians."

In Kashmir the great-grandfather ran a small madrassa and published one, almost unread, book of theological discursions. His son, the future imam's grandfather, left Kashmir for Najaf. He then emigrated back to Iran, settling in Khomein, where he was eventually acclaimed an ayatollah and married the daughter of another ayatollah, whose dowry made Khomeini's family temporarily well off. The economy of Khomein faltered, however, and by the time Ruhollah's father, Mostafa, was head of the household, the family had been reduced to sharecropping to supplement his scanty tithes.

The Khomein into which Ruholla was born in November 1900 — an oasis of some three thousand souls in the badlands between the Zagros and the Alborz mountain ranges — was, in Farsi parlance, *akhar-e-khat,* the end of the line. "Nobody with any alternative home would choose to live here," one Middle Eastern journalist observed. "Little more than [a] big village with a bazaar where local peasants exchange their produce for a limited range of necessities, [metropolitan] Khomein [centered on a] semi-derelict and often deserted mosque . . . built around a courtyard, at the center of which stood a rectangular pond of green, stagnant water. The mosque's dome had lost many of its turquoise-blue tiles and the only form of life it supported often consisted of a half dozen lean pigeons who had built . . . a nest . . . in the main prayer chamber. On Thursday evenings the mosque would be visited by the poor, the desperate, and the forgotten ones of this world. Women would tie pieces of cloth to the long dead tree standing by the pond. Some would weep, others would pray. . . . Skinny goats and sheep . . . roamed the streets . . . in search of anything that could be nibbled at — from discarded watermelon skins to pieces of cardboard and old newspapers."

Ruhollah was a most uncommon name in Khomein. It literally means "the spirit of Allah," and some Muslims considered its use sacrilegious, since it was also used as another name for Jesus Christ, whom Muslims accepted as a prophet, though not as the son of God.

Six months after Ruhollah's birth, Mostafa was killed in a fight following a dispute with two bailiffs representing an absentee landlord over what was remembered as "an unjust sharing of the crops." His body was found dumped by a road with six stab wounds in his chest. Mostafa, like his grandfather before him, had been educated in Najaf before returning to Khomein. Though only in his early thirties, he had already achieved some religious renown, judging from the memorial services held for him as far away as Tehran and Esfahan. He had a local reputation for spending most of the *khums* due him — both as a mullah and as a sayyid — on charity, thereby exacerbating his own and his family's poverty. At the time of Ruhollah's birth, thirty family members — brothers, sisters, husbands, wives, sons, daughters, aunts, uncles, and cousins — lived together in the crumbling, virtually windowless "house of the Indians."

As with the shah and as would be the case with Jimmy Carter, the loss of his father was transformative for Ruhollah, even though he was too young to even remember him. After the murder, peasants in Khomein wondered whether the infant was somehow responsible. It was possible, they said, that the baby Ruhollah was *bad-quadam,* "ill omened." Such superstitious conclusions were often made about infants born immediately before disasters, especially sudden, violent ones. It was pointed out that Mostafa had been killed with six stabs, one for each month of Ruhollah's life. As a result, the baby was somewhat shunned.

Ruhollah soon lost daily contact with his mother as well. She had been two months pregnant with another child, her sixth, when Mostafa was slain, and felt she had to give the young Ruhollah to an older aunt who lived across town under much better circumstances and could afford a wet nurse to suckle the infant. Henceforth, Ruhollah's aunt and uncle would raise him. In effect, he had been orphaned by the age of one.

Some of the imam's acolytes would point out years later that the Prophet too had been an orphan and gone to live with his uncle and aunt, but in the immediate moment in Khomein, it was only noted that the circumstance gave Ruhollah a far more comfortable upbringing than his siblings, with whom he attended the *maktab* (primary school). The future imam memorized the entire Koran by age six and as a teenager played on the village soccer team, though apparently not particularly well. He also worked with his family in the barley fields outside of town and was present at some family celebrations but not all. Otherwise, Ruhollah wandered alone in the desert outside of Khomein — even though brigands controlled much of the countryside — before returning to long solitary hours spent writing poems about what he saw out there.

His boyhood ended abruptly in 1917 at age sixteen when Khomein was ravaged by a typhoid epidemic that felled his aunt and then his mother. His aunt had bequeathed her nephew a small nest egg to pay for his religious schooling, and with that, Ruhollah left Khomein the following year and never returned, except to pass through on the way to somewhere else. Henceforth, Islam would be his family.

Ruhollah now moved to the holy city of Qom to study in a madrassa under the tutelage of a master theologian. His student days in Qom were a time of great ferment in Iran. The previous regime of shahs was shaky. The populist Republic of the Jungle uprising seeking to split off a bolshevized Islamic state along the Caspian coast that had been crushed by Reza Khan — soon to be Pahlavi — was still much talked about, though for most of his first decade as an aspiring theologian, Ruhollah had little time for politics. Besides the faith, his passion in those early years in Qom was poetry, which he wrote under the pen name Hindi, "the Indian": "It is spring . . . ," one of his poems went:

The bride of the garden stands naked and trembling
Like an old beggar woman chased off the street.

A moment's oblivion, the ingratitude of one moment
Leads to a terrible lesson for those who forget God.
Hindi, knowing all this, remembers at every breath
Not the beauty of the blossoms, but He who made them so.

Politics, however, soon intruded on Hindi's quietude. By 1926, when Reza seized the throne and founded the Pahlavi dynasty, Ruhollah had begun to teach philosophy classes at the Madrassa Faizieh. It was a trying time to be one of the faithful. When Reza's "modernization" hit full swing, theological refugees from Tehran and Mashhad began to stream into Qom with stories of abuse at the hands of the shah's troops. Soon turbans were banned, and the faithful were being waylaid on the street and having their beards cut. Some mullahs and seminary students were being shanghaied into the army; others were being shot or run over and left to rot by the side of the road. Some simply disappeared.

Such "modernization" was impossible not to take personally. In Qom Ruhollah stayed mostly in his room, prepared to flee at any moment to a shrine down the block and take sanctuary from the roving army press gangs. Even this might be insufficient: In Mashhad, the shah's troops had fired cannons into the Shrine of the Eighth Imam and hanged the group of clergy who had occupied it in protest. When he had to travel between Qom and Arak for a friend's funeral, Ruhollah took mules over the mountains rather than travel on the roads patrolled by the shah's troops — moving only after dark, wrapped head to toe in a blanket. When he had to travel to Tehran — the most unsafe place in Iran for the faithful — in order to negotiate his marriage to the then nine-year-old Batul with her father, a distinguished sayyid ayatollah there, Ruhollah disguised himself with a Turkish hat and even trimmed his beard.

By then Ruhollah was well-known in Islamic circles as his ayatollah's best student, a budding expert on Islamic law, and, in a somewhat rare combination of specialties, a scholar immersed in Shiite mysticism and ecstatic meditation as well. Ruhollah was now a full-blown mullah, one of the *ulama,* literally "the scientists," those who had mastered the "science of Islam" and who, like all such, could be supported out of the *khums,* the voluntary tithe all Muslims were required to pay to maintain the clergy, support the descendants of the Prophet, and propagate the faith.

In 1932, in response to Reza Shah's orders that everyone register with his government and adopt a last name, Ruhollah registered as Ruhollah Mostafavi, or "Ruhollah related to Mostafa." He also, like many Persian men of action had done through history, adopted a second identity as a kind of nom de guerre. Ruholla now signed his private correspondence Mussavi al-Khomeini, "a sayyid descendant of the Imam Mussa from the village of Khomein," and it was as the combination of these two identities that Ruhollah Khomeini would — in the name of Allah, Punisher of Tyrants — eventually lead the fight against Reza's son.

For the next thirty years, Ruhollah Khomeini's sermons in Qom's Faizieh Seminary were marveled over for their erudition and attended to overflowing. He was first recognized as a *mujtahid*, "one who is capable of providing guidance," and then as a *marja'-e-taqleed*, a "source of imitation," at which point he was empowered to issue fatwas. Khomeini reached ayatollah status in 1960. His "grand" appellation was added shortly before his exile in Najaf, more than four years later.

The future imam had transferred his antagonism from Reza Shah to Mohammad Shah in 1941, almost as soon as Khomeini learned that the elder Pahlavi had abdicated in favor of his twenty-one-year-old son. The grand ayatollah to whom Khomeini had attached himself during this period dispatched him to lead a delegation of mullahs to Tehran to beseech the occupying British forces not to recognize the new shah. "We told the British to allow the monarchy to be ended," Khomeini later remembered, "so that our Muslim people could choose a government of their own liking." Unsuccessful, the future imam returned to Qom to concentrate on theology.

Khomeini's path had next crossed the shah's in 1945, at the end of World War II, as the British were preparing to withdraw from Iran, leaving the shah as the head of state in a loosely constitutional government. This occasion marked the first and only time the shah and the imam ever met one-on-one.

Again, Khomeini had gone to Tehran leading a delegation sent by his grand ayatollah. This time they had been instructed to secure an audience with the shah to plead for a pardon in the case of a mullah who had been sentenced to death for participating in an assassination plot against some political opponents. The five-member delegation first met with a court secretary, who asked if they had a written message to deliver. Khomeini answered that no, the message was verbal and would require a face-to-face encounter. In that case, the secretary told them, they were to return to their hotel and await word from the palace. The mullahs waited for ten days, feeling more insulted with each passing day, until finally they were told they could meet with the shah, but only for fifteen minutes, and only one of them could actually be in the room with His Majesty. Khomeini was selected and reported to the shah's palace at the agreed time.

There, he was escorted to His Imperial Majesty's office and greeted by a protocol officer, who explained a few things to the mullah. The shah was not yet here, he said, so Khomeini was to wait for him by himself in the office. He was to wait standing up and he was not to sit until the shah eventually invited him to do so. If the shah made no such invitation, Khomeini was to stand for the entire meeting. Khomeini sat down as soon as the protocol officer left. It had been a tradition between the shahs and the clergy since the sixteenth century that the shahs stood while the mullahs sat, not vice versa, and Khomeini was not about to do otherwise, whatever this court functionary said.

After half an hour, the shah finally arrived. HIM had been immediately nonplussed to find Khomeini seated, but Khomeini paid no attention to his response and stayed in his chair. Finally, after several moments of intense royal embarrassment and unease, the shah just sat down as well. Their conversation lasted only ten of the fifteen allotted minutes, and, though the shah had eventually granted the pardon Khomeini had come to request, the dislike between the forty-five-year-old mullah and the twenty-five-year-old monarch was instantaneous.

Nonetheless, it was another eighteen years before open conflict broke out between Khomeini and the shah, in the spring of 1963, two months after HIM announced the advent of his White Revolution.

Khomeini's anger then focused on the shah's policy of evoking ancient Persia of the fourth century BC — the Zoroastrian empire of Cyrus — as the source of the nation's identity rather than something from the more recent era of Persian Islam. According to the ayatollah, this was yet another insult to the Prophet and his teachings. Khomeini targeted the celebration of the ancient pre-Islamic Persian New Year, Nofruz, in March, to make his point. His instrument was a fatwa declaring that this New Year's Day must be a day of mourning what was being done to Islam, not feasting after the fashion of the Zoroastrians.

Ayatollah or not, Khomeini was still a relatively obscure figure outside of theological circles — where he was thought a radical — and this fatwa was largely ignored. Except in Qom and except by the shah.

In hopes of discrediting the troublemaking ayatollah, the shah staged a

Nofruz day demonstration in the midst of the mourning city of Qom. The shah's organizers were unable to find enough locals to make a crowd, so two thousand employees of the Tehran Water Authority were dispatched from the capital. Each was reportedly paid $3.50 for this day's work. In Qom some of the Water Authority ringers were dressed as mullahs by the costume department of an Iranian film studio. The shah's organizers hoped to make it seem as though even the Qom faithful opposed Khomeini's fatwa. Just in case things didn't go well, the shah's government had also stationed an Army Special Forces unit just outside of town.

The crowd of costumed Water Authority workers first occupied the courtyard of the Shrine of Massoumeh, shouting "Long live the shah." Their hope was to elicit some response from the genuine mullahs, but none was forthcoming, so the mob moved down the block to the Faizieh Seminary and ransacked one of the student dormitories. By the time they were finished trashing the dorm rooms, several of Khomeini's followers had collected a crowd of their own and started fighting back. The mullahs and water workers went at one another out in the street, swinging clubs, staves, knives, and chains. As the shah's mob began to get the worst of it, the Special Forces intervened, firing at the Khomeini supporters, killing two religious students and injuring dozens more.

The ayatollah's chief acolytes met at Khomeini's house afterward, debating and discussing possible responses all night while the ayatollah himself slept. The next morning, Khomeini joined the group and, sitting with them on the floor, announced his conclusions. One of those in attendance wrote down the future imam's statement verbatim, and within hours it was circulating by leaflet throughout the city.

Khomeini looked at the rug in front of him while he spoke. "By creating this catastrophe," he said, "the regime of tyranny has sealed its own doom. It is going to die and we shall be victorious. We have always prayed to Allah that this regime should reveal its true colors, bringing shame on itself. Our prayers have been granted."

The pronouncement was received by his followers as a declaration of war on the shah's regime.

As with all Shiites, the central event in Ruhollah Khomeini's spiritual life had begun on the first day of October, 680 AD, almost thirteen centuries earlier. On the 358-day Islamic calendar, it was the first day of the month of

Muharram, forty-eight years after the death of the Prophet. Then, two armies faced off on the Karbala Plain on the west bank of the Euphrates River south of Baghdad. One army, some four thousand strong, was loyal to Yazid, the caliph in Damascus. The other army, only two hundred strong, was under the command of Husein, grandson of the Prophet, second son of Ali, who claimed the caliphate for himself as the blood heir to Muhammad.

Most of the ten-day battle was spent marching about and negotiating while Husein's forces remained surrounded. Despite his obviously desperate circumstances, Husein refused offers of mercy if he would only acknowledge Yazid's supremacy. On the tenth day, the forces of Yazid waded into Husein's loyalists, and the slaughter lasted all afternoon. Husein, the last to die, charged at his enemies and was swarmed over. His corpse reportedly bore twenty-three spear wounds and thirty-four sword cuts. His head was chopped off and sent to Yazid. After the dust cleared, Husein was anointed the Third Imam, and his martyrdom became a crux of Shiite worship.

That tenth day of Muharram would be recognized by Shiites forever after as Ashura, the most publicly ecstatic holy day of the year. The entire month of Muharram was considered a mourning period. "The mourning ceremonies occur in several forms," one CIA study explained. "Recitations of the story of Husein in the mosque . . . recitations in private homes, dramatic presentations in public, and parades. . . . The intention is to incite the participants into a frenzy of weeping, wailing, flagellations, and [voluntary] beatings. If their tears are mingled with blood, the participants gain even greater merit. . . . In Tehran [for example], as many as 3,000 worshippers, mostly men, may be gathered in a large bazaar mosque. . . . For many blocks [around] crowds are gathered so tightly that movement is barely possible. . . . Several mullahs in succession preach sermons on the Husein theme. As each speaker reaches the climax of the story, weeping and wailing increases. . . . Finally, [with] the main speaker . . . the weeping and groaning [again] increases in volume and many begin to pound their foreheads and beat their chests." Such frenzy ebbed and flowed all month long.

In 1963, when Ashura fell in June, SAVAK expected Khomeini might be planning to agitate the religious frenzy and sent a high-ranking officer to him in Qom. The officer warned the ayatollah that if he didn't keep his mouth shut, SAVAK would "break his bones." The ayatollah, without changing expressions, reminded the SAVAK man that bone breaking played both ways.

That afternoon an enormous crowd gathered outside Khomeini's house in Qom and began calling for the ayatollah to emerge and speak to them. Some were wearing white sheets, indicating their willingness to die for the faith. Others were in mourning frenzy, sometimes whipping themselves or beating their heads against the wall. Finally, after an hour of the crowd forming and writhing and growing, Khomeini walked out into the middle of it, boarded an open-topped car, and led the group down to the Faizieh Seminary. There, he sat humbly on the edge of a platform and gave the most important sermon of his life.

The shah, he told the assembled multitude, was Yazid, a usurper of the throne and tool of Satan himself.

The performance was reportedly electric. People swayed against one another and groaned. Others sobbed and wept. Cries of *"Allah-u akbar"* broke out regularly. This was the first time since the coup against Mossadeq ten years ago that anyone had publicly attacked the shah in such dramatic terms. It would make the ayatollah an almost instant legend.

"Mr. Shah," he railed, "you poor miserable man. I am giving you advice. . . . Stop these acts and change your manners. I do not wish to see the day that . . . you are kicked out [and] people are giving thanks. I don't want you to become like your father. . . . Ponder a bit, have a bit of wisdom, think a little bit about the consequences of your acts. . . . Shall I declare you, Mr. Shah, to be a heathen so that you are chased out of the country? . . . The day there is a commotion and the page is turned, you shall have no friends."

Within twelve hours, a copy of what Khomeini had said was delivered to the shah by the chief of his national police. His Imperial Majesty blew his top.

"Why does no one reply to that miserable goat?" he demanded.

The reply came first thing in the morning on the next day, June 4, Ashura itself. At 3:00 a.m., as part of a national police sweep in which more than two hundred known opponents of the shah were arrested, a company of the Imperial Rangers, an elite army unit, circled the ayatollah's neighborhood in Qom and then kicked in the door of his house. When he surrendered, Khomeini was placed under arrest and driven to the capital. Before leaving, he told his son Mostafa not to worry — the faith needed a second Ashura martyrdom and now it had it.

News of Ruhollah Khomeini's imprisonment touched off three days of rioting in Tehran, Isfahan, and Mashhad as well as in Qom. The demonstrations were eventually quelled when the shah's troops fired into the crowds, killing hundreds of people. Several of the instigators in the Tehran riots were tried in a military court and summarily hanged. Khomeini had hoped this outburst would trigger more demonstrations in an escalating wave, but it didn't.

Ten months passed before Ruhollah Khomeini returned to a becalmed Qom. The first two months had been in prison, the last eight under house arrest in an isolated suburb of Tehran. During this internal exile, he had been surreptitiously acclaimed throughout Iran as the living symbol of opposition to the shah. He had also been publicly recognized by the existing grand ayatollahs as Shiism's newest grand ayatollah, the most elevated of all Shiite ranks. Not surprisingly, the outpouring to welcome him home to Iran's religious capital was joyous and festive, featuring brightly clad dancers, feasting, and merriment. He, ever stern, told people to get back in their black. "We have martyrs," he reminded them, "and our color shall remain black until we have avenged our martyrs."

The new grand ayatollah kept the public peace for six months before raising his voice again. And when he did, he was careful not to make a direct attack on the shah. Instead, Khomeini attacked the shah's ministers and he attacked the shah's favorite ally, the United States.

The issue at hand was legislation just passed by the shah's rubber stamp Majlis as part of a new treaty relationship with the Americans that included a $200 million military aid and development credit for Iran. The new law contained a legal waiver for the American soldiers who would be coming to Iran as part of the shah's military training program, ensuring that the Americans would be tried for any alleged legal transgressions in American, not Iranian, courts. As the new grand ayatollah saw it, this meant that if an American colonel ran over an Iranian's wife, nothing would happen; but if an Iranian ran over the colonel's dog, he would go to prison. Submitting to such terms was an insult to the nation.

Word spread that Khomeini was getting ready to speak again, and Iranians began flocking to Qom. On November 2, 1964, a large group gathered in the courtyard of Khomeini's house and expanded into the surrounding neighborhood and beyond. Loudspeakers to broadcast Khomeini's words were placed throughout Qom's city center. At 8:30 p.m., he began.

"The source of all our troubles," he told the assembled faithful, "is America."

At times in his sermon, the grand ayatollah was intensely moved and struggled to contain his tears. According to one account of his message, "The Ayatollah once again hammered his favorite themes. There was a plot to de-Islamicize Iran in the interests of the United States and Israel. . . . The White

Revolution was nothing but a hoax. . . . All high-ranking officials [in the shah's government] were agents of either the U.S.A. or Israel. The only force capable of standing up to the U.S.A. . . . was the Shiite leadership. That was why the authorities were trying to break up the organization of the mullahs and were still keeping so many mullahs in prison or in internal exile."

According to Khomeini, this new law was obvious evidence that the Americans were now running Iran. "If the country is under American occupation," he challenged, "then tell us. [And] in that case, seize us and throw us out of the country."

Within forty-eight hours, the shah did exactly that.

· 3 ·

———————

THE CROWDS SWARMING IN THE STREETS OF TEH-
ran against Mohammad Reza Pahlavi called him "the American shah," and
they were right on the mark.

Anyone with a map could figure out why the Americans were so attracted
to His Imperial Majesty. His kingdom was situated with the Soviet Union
along its northern border and its southern edge along the Persian Gulf, and
included an oil field so full the crude literally forced its way out of the
ground. Iran offered both a frontline ally in the Cold War and a friendly
spigot for the United States' economy. American listening posts along the
Soviet border were the first priority. American foreign aid, mostly military
hardware and training, began in 1956 and got larger every year thereafter.
Following his reinstatement by the CIA, the shahanshah also took the previous British share of Iran's oil production and allotted half of it to American
companies. From the beginning, the shah left few doubts about with whom
he had thrown his lot.

So, in 1964, even if Khomeini hadn't attacked Mohammad Pahlavi by name, HIM was still not going to stand by and let the Americans be reviled. The shah's prime minister met with the head of SAVAK, who said the government had three options: they could arrange for the ayatollah to have a fatal "accident," they could exile him to some remote location inside Iran, or they could expel him into foreign exile. Worried that the death of a grand ayatollah under suspicious circumstances would cause more trouble than he was worth, the prime minister chose the last option and spent the next day trying to find a country that would accept the future imam as an exile. Pakistan and India both refused, but Turkey agreed.

On November 4, 1964, two days after Khomeini's speech against the Americans, the grand ayatollah and his older son, Mostafa, were arrested in Qom and driven to Tehran. There they were loaded into an Iranian air force transport plane, flown to Ankara, Turkey, and dumped on the tarmac of a Turkish air force base. Khomeini stayed in Turkey for six months and was miserable and isolated through most of it. Then he secured permission from Iraq to emigrate to Najaf to teach.

In the Shiite theology of which Khomeini was a master, there were nine more imams after the martyred Husein. All of them were thought to have supreme spiritual standing as a result of their direct descent from the Prophet. The Seventh Imam, Mussa, Ruhollah Khomeini's ancestor, was notable in that progression for having sired somewhere between 135 and 750 offspring, thus creating the most numerous modern class of sayyid, the Mussavi. The most important imam after Husein and Ali was number twelve, known as the Mahdi. The Twelfth Imam had never died but rather, through occultation, disappeared in 874 AD. All Shiites believed that this final imam would return someday to assume the caliphate of Islam and put everything right in the world.

This promise raised significant theological issues. Islam in Iran had deferred the administration of power in the Mahdi's absence to the shahs. In support of that deference, it was often argued that although the Mahdi would, upon his return, organize human affairs in accordance with the Koran and the teachings of the Prophet, for the clergy to attempt a similar Islamic political organization in the meantime would amount to usurpation of the Mahdi's role and, hence, a sin.

The foremost advocate of the counter theory was the grand ayatollah Khomeini exiled in Najaf. The faithful's willingness to accept the state's enforcement and organization, he argued, all presumed that the state acted in accordance with the laws of Islam. However, the shah, Khomeini insisted, was actively destroying Islam. In that circumstance, to truly defend the faithful as the Prophet required, the experts in Islamic law known as jurists had to lead the people in overthrowing the idolatrous Pahlavi regime. It was a radical theory, initially endorsed by none of the other grand ayatollahs.

It was also just the beginning. The exiled Khomeini obviously chafed at the notion that having righted an injustice, the clergy would then slip once more into the background. "What is the good of us asking for the hand of a thief to be severed," he wrote, "when all we can do is recommend such punishments, having no power to implement them?" The law of the Prophet, he argued, *was* law. It was not a personal code of ethics. The Koran was written to be enforced by people who understood the science of Islam. The blueprint of social organization had been provided by the Prophet, and it was possible, the ayatollah insisted, for the jurists to truly rule without compromising the revelation that the Twelfth Imam would bring when he reappeared. He called this form of government the Rule of the Jurist.

The ayatollah first presented this theory in a somewhat comprehensive way with the 1971 publication of a thin book first titled *The Regency of the Theologian* but soon renamed *Islamic Government*. Much of the book was devoted to proving that it was the intention of the Prophet and of Ali, the First Imam, that their faith actively govern. Islam was meant to be a concrete social structure that protected and extended the interests of Muslims. Khomeini argued that this duty to guard Islam by institutionalizing it in political structures was more important to the faithful than even prayer and fasting. Given the weakness of humans, leaving compliance voluntary was totally insufficient, as was leaving government in the hands of secular forces.

Seminal as it was, *Islamic Government* went through a dozen different editions as well as a rewrite at the hands of the ayatollah's followers during his stay in Najaf. By 1977, hundreds of thousands of copies were in circulation inside Iran. That same year, Khomeini agreed with his followers' suggestion that he name this religious state an "Islamic republic."

In the meantime, the shah's relationship with the Americans escalated to its apex after His Imperial Majesty made common cause with Richard Nixon and his legendary foreign policy architect, Henry Kissinger, shortly after Nixon was elected president in 1968. The shah had known Nixon since the early fifties, when the American had visited Iran as vice president. In Iran it was believed the shah had made a $12 million contribution to the Republican Party's 1960 political slush fund to cement their connection. In any case, Nixon and Kissinger thought the shah was an answer to one of their more pressing foreign policy problems. The British had announced the withdrawal of all their troops from east of Suez, and the Americans, still bogged down in Vietnam, were unable to police the Gulf themselves. The United States needed a surrogate to provide immediate muscle in the region. The "regional superpower" role Kissinger suggested was a dream come true for the shah. Near the end of Nixon's first term, Nixon and Kissinger traveled to Iran for a state visit and negotiated the terms of a new military understanding between the two countries. The deal's principal feature was an unprecedented directive from the president of the United States ordering his government to sell the shah virtually any kind of military hardware he wanted, short of nuclear weapons. No foreign government had ever been given such a shopping spree in the history of American military sales.

When the shah left the final negotiations with Kissinger, one of his ministers asked if they had gone well.

The shah allowed that they had.

"Did you get what you wanted, Majesty?" the minister pressed.

"More than I wanted," His Majesty answered.

Sitting on the flush end of a quadrupling of world energy prices, the shah was an enthusiastic customer. During the first year of this arrangement, his purchases of US hardware rose from $500 million to $2.5 billion. All told, the shah placed some $11 billion in orders during the last four years the Republicans held the White House — and the shah made all of the weapons systems decisions personally. Among the items selected were 240 F-14 and F-15 aircraft, dozens of Hawk missile batteries, more than 100 F-16 aircraft, more than 500 military helicopters, 4 destroyers, and 3 submarines. The arms flow was so heavy that thousands of American civilians were permanently stationed in Iran by American military contractors, servicing their goods. Henceforth, with an army of 500,000, fielding 3,000 battle tanks and the best air force on the Gulf, and backed by the Americans, the shah could claim an acknowledged sphere of influence far larger than his territory.

To announce the advent of this new Iran, His Imperial Majesty threw a spectacular event that drew the entire world's attention — in effect a proclamation of his new superpower status. The occasion was the 2,500th anniversary of the reign of Cyrus the Great, with the shah cast as Cyrus's modern successor. Altogether, the four days of festivities in October 1971 held at the archaeological ruins of the ancient city of Persepolis on Iran's Plain of Morghab cost over $100 million to stage. To prepare the location, the shah's Imperial

Guard had to eradicate millions of poisonous snakes. Then a temporary city of luxury tents was constructed, as well as a luxury hotel. More than four hundred people from seventy countries attended, including some five dozen heads of state. The most visible of the myriad events was an opening ceremony at Cyrus's tomb in Pasargadae, fifty miles away. "The shah was in full military uniform," the New York Times reported, "his chest covered with medals. [The shahbanou] wore a green and white silk ball gown, although it was only eleven o'clock in the morning, and long white gloves. Some of the emeralds in her ten-pound crown were the size of golf balls. Her diamonds were only slightly smaller." Daily entertainments at the Persepolis celebration included endless parades of Iranian military personnel, often wearing period costumes and leading camels. Evenings featured dinner parties where the china was Limoges, the crystal Baccarat, and the food flown in fresh every day from Maxim's restaurant in Paris. The grand banquet on the final night featured partridge with foie gras and truffle stuffing, washed down with vintage Bordeaux. The event sealed His Imperial Majesty's international celebrity.

Unlike the rest of the shah's act, however, SAVAK did not dazzle or even play well in the West. Iran was the subject of numerous human rights complaints from Amnesty International and the International Society of Jurists, which the shah found increasingly embarrassing. As a consequence, over the seventies, the shah made a variety of public defenses of his security apparatus to the western media. First he said that living next to the Soviets, he had no choice but to hunt down communists, but it was only communists he hunted. Next he claimed that no one had brought any complaints about torture to his attention. Then he said that the activities of SAVAK were being enormously exaggerated by those who wanted to make him look bad. Then he claimed that every time he learned of such behavior, he stopped it. Finally, with the advent of a new administration in the United States, the shah announced that SAVAK's actions had simply been part of a stage of development out of which Iran had now passed.

The new administration that His Majesty hoped to convince with this approach belonged to James Earl Carter Jr., thirty-ninth president of the United States, universally known as Jimmy.

In the fall of 1978, Jimmy Carter, fifty-four years old and well into his second year in the White House, seemed to be hitting his presidential stride. Neither he nor anybody else could have predicted what was in store.

That the shah of Iran would be the instrument of his fate was even more unimaginable. All of this, however, had a certain symmetry, at least in retrospect. The odds against Carter's attaining the presidency had been at least 100 to 1 barely a year before he defeated Gerald Ford in 1976.

Jimmy Carter's part of this story is about how a president who ascended out of nowhere to everyone's great surprise was then ambushed and brought down out of nowhere to everyone's great surprise as well.

The particular nowhere from which Carter emerged was Plains, Georgia, population 653 — a hamlet too small to even support a hamburger stand — where the president had been born in 1924 and raised and lived most of his adult life. He still felt more at home there than anyplace else.

Main Street in Plains featured a couple small groceries, a pharmacy, two gas stations, and the tracks of the Seaboard Coastline Railroad. Spreading around it in the red-dirt flat of Sumter County were fields of peanuts, soybeans, cotton, and feed corn. In summer, the air in Plains was thick, and water dripped off the underside of tree limbs. Water moccasins flourished in the brown ponds dotted around the countryside. Half of Plains' population was black, but they tended to stay out of view. This was, after all, the Deep South — 135 miles below Atlanta, almost into Alabama. Americus, the biggest nearby town, hadn't stopped arresting blacks for attempting to register to vote until barely ten years before Jimmy Carter was elected president. The Plains Baptist Church, where Jimmy Carter worshiped and taught Sunday school, had once formally banned admission to "any negroes or other civil rights agitators."

The Carter peanut warehouse, the biggest business in town, had occupied the far end of Main Street since Jimmy came home from the navy in 1953 and had it built. Growing up here, the president spent most of his life barefoot until he started school.

Not surprisingly, when Carter's name first surfaced in the 1976 presidential race, a common response was "Jimmy *who?*"

Nobody asked that question anymore. Now all you had to do was say "Jimmy" and everyone knew who you meant. He had perhaps the most famous teeth in the history of the presidency. Carter smiled reflexively in all situations, and that toothy grin became an instant trademark. Like so much about Carter, the expression was more than it seemed. The shah called it the "coldest" smile he had ever encountered and he was not alone. "Don't pay any attention to that smile," one of the president's fellow Georgians advised. "That don't mean a thing."

More than any president in recent memory, Jimmy Carter had been thrust out of his obscurity by momentous shifts in the political geography around him. Against seemingly impossible odds, he had managed to arrive at two major elbows in the course of American history, one after the other, each at just the right time to enable him to ride those changes out of Plains and into the White House.

The first of those historic turns was called "the New South" in the popular press, and Jimmy Carter was its poster boy. Until Carter, Georgia had been the hard core of the Confederacy. Jimmy's predecessor as governor had been the owner of a fried chicken restaurant who gained fame wielding an ax handle against racial integrationists. This ax handle Old South had separate drinking fountains, lavatories, entrances, schools, theater seating, and lunch counters. Whites were allowed to vote; blacks were not. Blacks got lynched; whites did the lynching. This was the backward South, tied to dying plantations, standing outside the cultural and financial mainstream in order to hold on to the ghost of slavery and lost Civil War glories.

The New South emerged after the Civil Rights Act of 1964 and the Voting Rights Act of 1965 made the Old South illegal. The New South aspired to be modern, industrial, upscale, and integrated, and by 1970 was ready to take on the old-time political machine in Georgia. Its candidate for governor was a peanut farmer and former state senator from Sumter County named Jimmy Carter. A lifetime Democrat — as most of the South was in those days — Carter hadn't been a civil rights advocate but had voted for integration as a school board member, which was no small deed in Sumter, known to be a stronghold of the White Citizens Council, Georgia's leading bigots. Carter had previously run for governor against the ax handle restaurant owner in 1966 and lost. But in 1970 he won, and almost immediately hung a portrait of Martin Luther King Jr. in the Georgia statehouse. *Time* soon had him on its cover, using the tagline "The New Southern Politician." Legitimized as a different kind of southerner from a different kind of South, Carter was now positioned to become the first president elected from the heart of Dixie since Andrew Jackson of South Carolina in 1829.

The force carrying Carter forward from Georgia to Washington DC was the enormous political tidal wave generated by the collapse of Richard Nixon's presidency and his resignation in 1974 under threat of impeachment for using his public office to wage private war against his political enemies and then repeatedly lying about it. The backwash in 1976 revealed an electorate ready — more than it ever had been before — for somebody it hadn't heard of, someone promising all the virtues of small-town America, someone from somewhere a long way from Washington, someone who wasn't a crook. Carter's down-home probity was more appealing than even Carter had expected. Now everybody in America knew where Plains was.

On the eve of enrolling in high school, where he would join the Future Farmers of America and play on the basketball team, Jimmy Carter was already writing notes in his scrapbook about developing "good mental habits": "If you think the right way," he admonished himself, "you will develop: (1) the habit of accomplishing what you attempt, (2) . . . of expecting to like other people, (3) . . . of deciding quickly what you'd like to do and doing it, (4) . . . of sticking to it, [and] (5) . . . of welcoming cheerfully all wholesome ideas and experiences. (6) A person who wants to build good mental habits should avoid the idle daydream; should give up worry and anger; hatred and envy; should neither fear nor be ashamed of anything that is honest and purposeful."

More than forty years later, halfway through his term, Jimmy Carter was still pretty much working off the same list.

He certainly had been a different kind of president so far. He wore cardigan sweaters on national television. For a while, he eliminated the playing of "Hail to the Chief" every time he arrived someplace. He jogged in public. He stayed at the homes of private citizens on several occasions. He acted as his own chief of staff. And two distinguishing characteristics of the Carter presidency had already emerged.

The first was his intelligence. Trained as a nuclear engineer by the United States Navy, Carter digested every intellectual challenge down to the fine print. He had taught himself fluent Spanish. He could converse at length about the virtues of various recordings of Beethoven's Fifth Symphony. He often started his day with two hours of reading and asked for briefing papers that were long and detailed. Katharine Graham, the publisher of the *Washington Post,* called him "by far the most intelligent President in my lifetime." Walter Cronkite, the anchor of the *CBS Evening News,* observed that "his brain power was extraordinary." Tip O'Neill, the Speaker of the House, called Carter "the smartest public official I've ever known. The range and extent of his knowledge were outstanding. He could speak with authority [on] just about any . . . topic that came up."

The second distinguishing characteristic, however, was Jimmy's lack of personal charisma. This was a plain vanilla man who would have great difficulty bringing a crowd out of their seats or even making their palms sweat — almost an anomaly in the age of television. He was stiff on the tube, with the presence of a church deacon, and talked in odd rhythms, invariably putting the emphasis in a sentence at a most unlikely point. His drawl settled over his words like silt on a river bottom. He seemed uncomfortable and passed that feeling along to his audience. Not surprisingly, *tight* was a common description of his performances. "Carter just does not give a lift to occasions," one journalist observed. "He does not seem to know how to. He doesn't evoke very much in people, because he doesn't give very much. He is a withholder. The smile is up front, but he is somewhere back in the weeds."

It was an odd combination of plus and minus, but it still seemed to be working. Though there were some loud doubts about whether he was up to the job, 57 percent of Americans still identified themselves to the Roper Poll as Carter "supporters." Everyone noted how hard he worked. He was about to finish negotiations on a treaty recognizing the People's Republic of China for the first time. He had already negotiated a treaty scheduling the eventual end of American occupation of the Panama Canal Zone and had spent much of the fall of 1978 acting as the honest broker in negotiations between Israel and Egypt that would yield the Camp David Accords. Menachem Begin and Anwar Sadat would receive the Nobel Peace Prize for the Camp David effort, but many thought the prize ought to have included Carter as well.

He and the shah would eventually end up wrapped around each other, tumbling through political free fall, even though the two couldn't have been much less alike. The shah was surrounded by puffery and could not bear to be blamed, Carter was self effacing and quite ready to admit his mistakes, sometimes even before he was sure he had made them; the shah was glamorous, Carter humble; the shah was hand-tailored, Carter was mail order catalogue; the shah was debonair, Carter simply polite. While the shah kicked back at Kish Island, Jimmy played in a local softball league. The shah owned close to a dozen palaces, villas, and houses around the world; Jimmy Carter owned only a fifteen-year-old brick ranch-style house on Woodland Avenue near downtown Plains. While the shah was cavorting with German stewardesses at the Suvretta House, Jimmy Carter's notion of sin was having "lusted in my heart" for women other than his wife, Rosalynn. While the shah looked formidable but was, at his core, insecure and indecisive, Jimmy

Carter came off as soft but was, deep down, in the words of one of his intimates, a "tough son of a bitch."

The only thing the two had in common was the experience of having grown up under a father who left big shoes to fill.

Jimmy's namesake, James Earl Sr., was known to everybody as Earl. Earl had been the big fish in Plains' small pond since before his first son was born, running a farming operation that eventually grew to 5,000 acres and hired more than 250 locals at its peak season. He was something of a Plains legend for being a shrewd businessman who worked harder than anybody in town, taught Baptist Sunday school, loved to take his wife dancing, smoked three packs of cigarettes a day, had a glass of bourbon after dinner, once invented and patented a new design for a plow, served a term in the state legislature, and was known for the generosity of the credit he extended to other farmers, acting as something of an informal local banker. Earl was also known around town for expecting a lot more of Jimmy than most men expected of their sons. "My father was a very firm but understanding director of my life and habits," Carter remembered. "My father loved me [but] he was a stern disciplinarian and punished me severely when I misbehaved."

Earl taught his boy about work, early and often. Jimmy swept the yard, pumped water, cut wood, carried buckets of water to the men in the field, pruned watermelon vines, slopped hogs, and picked cotton. When Jimmy was twelve, just tall enough to see over the car's steering wheel, he drove Earl's vehicle through the neighborhood on Sunday morning picking up kids who needed a ride to his father's Sunday school class. It surprised no one in Plains that Jimmy grew up to be a man compelled to accomplish, who thrived on challenges and filled up all his spare time with efforts to improve himself.

Like the shah's, Jimmy Carter's life would be permanently reordered by his father's end. In 1953 Jimmy was a young naval officer on a rapid rise, already qualified as a submarine commander and selected by the legendary Admiral Hyman Rickover for duty in the new nuclear submarine corps, where only the very brightest officers served. Jimmy and Rosalynn were at their fourth posting, Union College, Schenectady, New York — where the navy had him doing graduate work in nuclear engineering — when his mother sent him word that Earl had pancreatic cancer and would soon be dead.

Jimmy returned to Plains to spend his father's last weeks with him. It was the most human side of Earl that Jimmy had ever seen, and those who knew the future president would depict the experience as a kind of reconciliation between the two. For the first time, the son got to see the dozens of people who had been secret beneficiaries of Earl's back-door generosity as they came by to pay their respects. While Jimmy was in Plains, his mother asked him to leave the navy and come home to run the family business. With Earl dead, there was, she said, no one else to do it. His sisters weren't up to it and his brother, Billy, was too young. Jimmy agreed after some hesitation and was discharged into civilian life in October 1953 at the age of twenty-nine.

Jimmy soon turned Earl's flourishing seed warehouse into an even more flourishing full-service company providing "certified seed peanuts, custom peanut shelling, peanut buying and storage, liquid nitrogen, bulk fertilizer and lime, corn buying, custom grinding and mixing, cotton ginning, and fire and casualty insurance." Rosalynn acted as the enterprise's financial manager. Their four kids were enrolled in Plains' schools. She was den mother for the Cub Scout pack and he was scoutmaster for the Boy Scout troop. He was in the Lions Club, served on the Sumter County Library Board, and in 1961, eight years out of the navy and just fifteen years before he became president of the United States, he was elected chairman of the local school board. Nobody in Plains had been surprised to see Jimmy come home and take up where Earl left off, but no one present for that homecoming, not even his biggest admirers, picked him to go on as far as he did.

Jimmy Carter would eventually describe the crisis generated by his entanglement with the shah's fate as "the most difficult period of my life," without a doubt. The personal elements that would enable him to cope with that difficulty, however, were all deeply embedded long before the fall of 1978.

The first of those was his tenacity. "When I get on to something," Carter allowed, "I am awfully hard to change." That was a considerable understatement. Jimmy Carter was the very definition of doggedness —"one of the most tenacious politicians in memory," according to a Washington political columnist. Among the first campaign meetings Jimmy convened in Iowa was one attended by just a single person, with whom Carter spent the occasion talking and answering questions. Unfazed, he returned to Iowa again and again and again until he finally carried the Democratic Party caucuses. When running for the legislature in Georgia, he had promised to read every bill presented, cover to cover, and when that turned out to be an overwhelming task, he took a speed-reading course and kept his promise. No one had ever seen Jimmy give up on anything to which he had set his mind. "That man is made of steel, determination, and stubbornness," one Georgian remembered. "Carter reminds me of a South Georgia turtle. He doesn't go around a log. He just sticks his head in the middle and pushes and pushes until the log gives way."

Jimmy would also be well served by his religion during the trial that awaited him. The president was not just an occasional Baptist; he was a Baptist seven days a week. He taught Sunday school because he enjoyed it and found the experience fulfilling. He and Rosalynn read to each other from the Bible almost every night, sometimes in Spanish when they wanted to hone their language skills. His religion was indistinguishable from his character by the time he became president. "His religious beliefs," one of his White House staff observed, "were so deep as to be instinctive [and] were not shaped by the Old Testament vision of a wrathful God. He was quintessentially a New Testament man who prized the virtues of personal humility, charity, and forgiveness. . . . He saw the world as an imperfect place but not inherently evil. He believed that adversity could be overcome by hard work, that faith without works is dead. He practiced tolerance as a positive virtue and sought peace through understanding and reconciliation, not confrontation."

The president's religion was also almost indistinguishable from his personality. "He reacted [to events and people] with extraordinary serenity," his national security adviser, Zbigniew Brzezinski, remembered, "and I have wondered at times what is the root of it. . . . I was struck as I got to know him that religion is a genuine part of his makeup and that it is a source of genuine strength."

The final pillar upon which Jimmy would be able to rely during the trouble to come was his first lady, Rosalynn. Theirs had been a textbook case of love at first sight. Rosalynn had been sixteen at the time, Jimmy nineteen. He was home on leave from the Naval Academy during July 1945, the last month of World War II, and she was a close friend of his younger sister, Ruth. Ruth arranged for her friend to come over in the afternoon, Rosalynn and Jimmy hit it off, and they went on a double date to the movies that night. Later, sitting in the rumble seat of his sister's boyfriend's car, Jimmy kissed Rosalynn for the first time. When he got home that night and his mother asked him how he liked Rosalynn, he told her, "That's the woman I'm going to marry."

To symbolize their commitment to each other, Jimmy presented Rosalynn with a silver compact when he came home for Christmas leave, engraved with the letters ILYTG. The abbreviation signified "I love you the goodest," a private Carter family expression of endearment. The two wrote each other almost every day from Jimmy's final return to the academy until he came back to Plains — with a fresh naval officer's commission after having completed a normal four-year course in three — and married her the next July. He was twenty, she seventeen. A new world began opening for Rosalynn right away, starting on their honeymoon in North Carolina. There, for the first time in her life, she saw a white person hire another white person to clean up his lawn.

It was one of the ironies of Jimmy Carter's roots that, redneck as they were, he would be the first president to have a "modern" marriage. He treated Rosalynn as a full partner and presented her to the world as such. She attended his very first cabinet meeting and spent part of it sitting on the arm of her husband's chair. It was widely reported that there hadn't been a first lady like her since Eleanor Roosevelt. Jimmy counted on Rosalynn's judgment and let it be known that he did. "Rosalynn could be as tough as she was charming and gracious," Brzezinski remembered. "On [one] occasion I noted [in my diary] after giving Rosalynn an extensive briefing: 'She is really quite a charmer. She sat there like a demure schoolgirl, taking notes, asking questions, but beneath that innocent air there is a very purposeful and politically shrewd individual. It is good to have her on one's side.' . . . For Carter, she was a tower of strength, a source of serene affection and of good judgment. Whenever an important issue arose, she would quietly sit and listen — and later share with him her views. She had a knack for getting to the guts of a problem."

The president was also still very much in love with her. His face lit up when she was around. Sometimes at the White House she would drop in to his meetings and exchange greetings with him in Spanish. They explained it as language practice, but it seemed to everyone else that it was a way for them to make a private bond in a room full of people. Jimmy still loved to dance with Rosalynn and could still get jealous if another man showed her too much attention. The two of them could sometimes be found sitting all by themselves in the White House movie theater, watching a film and holding hands.

The next most important person in the Carter White House during the fall of 1978 was Hamilton Jordan, thirty-two years old, Jimmy's "aide" and resident political genius. A native of southwest Georgia just like his boss, Jordan had devised the strategy that had vaulted Jimmy out of nowhere, to the governor's mansion and into the White House. The two had an extraordinarily symbiotic relationship, despite the difference in their ages. Ham was the one who always talked straight to the president and brought him bad news even when he knew the president didn't want to hear it. He had been doing that for Jimmy since before he became governor.

The two first met at an Elks Club meeting in Athens, Georgia, in the summer of 1966, when Jordan had just finished his junior year at the University of Georgia. Jimmy Carter, forty-two, candidate for governor in the race he eventually lost, was the guest speaker. "Carter's speech was halting," Jordan remembered, "his voice so soft that I had to strain to hear him. He rambled on with apparent uncertainty for about ten minutes. I was thoroughly unimpressed. But when he started taking questions from the floor and answering them directly and thoughtfully for nearly an hour, I realized that this was a man of considerable intelligence who had a common sense approach to Georgia's problems. He struck me as different . . . and I became intrigued. . . . When I got home, I wrote him a long letter . . . exaggerating my involvement [in a previous gubernatorial campaign] and offering to help him in my home town of Albany." Several days later, Carter phoned and Jordan was off to Atlanta to begin his career as an aide. His first job was driving a car in a July 4th parade with his candidate sitting in back. The next time Carter ran for governor, Jordan was his twenty-four-year-old campaign manager. It was the first big-time race Ham had ever managed. The second was Carter's victory in the 1976 presidential election.

As the administration's most colorful personality as well as second most powerful personage, Ham was quickly reduced by the Washington press corps to the caricature of a hick on the loose in the big city. "In total contrast to the overt Puritanism of his boss," one journalist observed, "he has an undisguised zest for wine, women, and life in general. . . . He gives an impression of the good old Georgia boy — a tad roly-poly, good natured and with a grain of self-deprecating humor." Jordan's first marriage ended before his arrival in Washington and his alleged escapades as a Georgetown bachelor were tracked regularly in the media. His bachelor digs were nicknamed the "Animal House." Most of the stories were idle gossip, but they made print anyway.

The first big explosion was a 1977 report in the *Washington Post* that Jordan had attended a reception thrown by television diva Barbara Walters in honor of the ambassadors of Egypt and Israel. According to the *Post,* Jordan was talking to the wife of the Egyptian ambassador, a noticeably full-bosomed woman, when, in the middle of their conversation, he reached over and pulled the top of her bodice open to better ogle her breasts and said, "I always wanted to see the pyramids."

That was followed by a report that while drinking with some of his bud-
dies in a Georgetown bar, Ham spit a mouthful of amaretto and cream down
the dress of a woman nearby. Both accounts were unsubstantiated, both
were denied by everyone present, but both were very widely circulated, and
the myth of Hamilton Jordan was born.

There would be more. In 1978 there were charges from Jack Anderson,
the foremost investigative columnist in Washington, that Jordan had made a
deal with a fugitive financier to use his influence with the Justice Department on the financier's behalf. Jordan denied the claim absolutely, but it
would take a grand jury investigation before everyone was satisfied that the
charge had been a figment of someone's imagination.

Much was lost in Jordan's public depiction, according to one National Security Council staffer. "Hamilton Jordan's native shrewdness as a political
analyst was unfortunately obscured by the clouds of controversy that settled
about him. In dozens of meetings . . . I was struck most by the seriousness of
purpose he concealed beneath a veneer of sardonic humor. He never stood
on ceremony. In a roomful of inflated egos, he wore the badge of his office
lightly, almost invisibly. Unlike many of his colleagues, he was more likely to
listen than to speak, but when he did speak he cut through the heart of the
issue with common sense. The crude image of Hamilton Jordan portrayed
in the media was worse than caricature — it was a bad joke."

Throughout it all, Ham occupied the corner office on the second floor of
the White House customarily reserved for the chief of staff. Carter, of course,
was his own chief of staff, so Ham's role evolved. He spent the first few
months overseeing the staffing of the new administration, which he found
such "a politically and emotionally debilitating process" he swore he would
never repeat it. After that, he operated as what he called the president's
"short-order cook." Whatever needed immediate attention was Ham's purview.
He dealt with minimum-wage debates, inflation reports, energy programs,
and lots more, always trying to make sure they somehow fit into his boss's
overall scheme. During the negotiations over the Panama Canal treaties, he
even became the principal American contact with Panamanian ruler Omar
Torrijos, who drank beer with Ham, told dirty jokes, and found Jordan a
tremendously simpatico figure.

After the Panamanian experience, Jordan concluded that "foreign policy
is just politics in another country" and felt far less timid about the subject.
By the end of his first year in the White House, he was joining Carter's regu-

lar Friday morning foreign policy breakfasts with the secretaries of state and defense, the vice president, and the national security adviser. Jordan described himself as the resident "amateur" in that company, but everyone else there considered him a valuable asset. Indeed, when Jimmy Carter was eventually blindsided by the fate of the shah and the embassy in Tehran became the center of the American political universe, Hamilton Jordan, Georgia good ol' boy, would come closer than anyone else to finding a way out before it was too late to do his boss any good.

Several days before his inauguration as thirty-ninth president of the United States, Jimmy Carter and his vice president, Walter Mondale, had stood together across the street from the White House, pausing on their way to pay a courtesy call on Gerald Ford, the outgoing president. Mondale, then forty-eight, previously a senator from Minnesota, had been in and around Washington for better than a decade, which was part of why Carter chose him for a running mate. For Mondale, the postcard view his boss paused over was no big deal. Looking across at his future home, the president smiled.

"What's it like inside?" Carter asked his vice president.

At that point, for the first time, Walter Mondale had realized that Carter had never been in the White House before entering it as president-elect — not for a bill signing, not for a dinner, not even on a guided tour. Mondale would later wonder if that had been true of any other modern American chief executive. In the immediate moment, the vice president elect had to work to keep his jaw from dropping.

Jimmy Carter had run for president as the people's champion against the oligarchy of lawyers, press, lobbyists, academics, and public servants who made things in the nation's capital happen, using Plains and its just-folks culture as a positive counterpoint to the cravenness and corruption assumed to flourish inside the Beltway. And Washington's initial response to this contrary candidacy was predictable. When the legendary Democratic power broker Averell Harriman had been asked in early 1976 about this obscure ex-governor from Georgia, he had responded that Jimmy Carter would never be president because "I don't know him and none of my friends know him."

That implicit antagonism was compounded by both the new administration's style and the political circumstances it encountered. The same fragmentation inside the Democratic Party that had allowed Carter to steal a march on the presidency also plagued his attempts to govern now that his party controlled both houses of Congress and the White House. Acting in unison seemed beyond it. Each faction had its own agenda that it was insistent on following. On top of that, the Carterites had gone out of their way upon arrival not to curry anyone's favor or even act like they might, and were quickly labeled as arrogant and unable to manage simple relations with their own Congress.

Carter himself wasn't of much help either. He sought out a relatively small circle for counsel — more often with Georgians involved than not — and never expanded it much. As a consequence, a lot of Washington that was used to feeling in, felt out. Nor was Carter much for the social life that greased the exercise of power around town. In a place where being seen having a word or two informally with the president was precious capital, Jimmy Carter liked being alone or with his family in his spare time and wasn't much for a lot of small dinners or chitchat. He thought he was participating in Washington life by attending the First Baptist Church and enrolling his daughter in a local school. And his relationships outside his inner circle were quite often as stiff as his speeches. Politicians all over town were soon talking about the president's tin political ear. Congressmen began to duck Carter's phone calls because it was apparent when he called that he was reading off a note card.

In truth, Jimmy Carter's unwillingness to tap Washington's supply of experienced policy makers and itinerant public servants was greatly exaggerated, especially by Jordan. "If Cyrus Vance were named Secretary of State and Zbigniew Brzezinski head of [the] National Security [Council] in the Carter Administration," Ham had told one interviewer before the election, "then I would say we failed, and I would quit. But that's not going to happen." In fact, after the election, both those men were asked by Carter to fill both those positions.

Vance was the first to be asked onto the Carter team. He was the only unanimous recommendation Jimmy got from those he sought.

Sixty-one years old in 1978, Cyrus Vance was the epitome of the gentleman lawyer, a New Yorker who had been born in West Virginia, made Scroll and Key at Yale, and was thought by almost everyone in Washington to be the best WASP they'd ever met. Tall with a little stoop, his face pale but his cheeks ruddy, "he had a senior lawyer's take on the world," according to one member of the administration. "His approach was legalistic — you take clashing ideas and find common ground. He was a good man, bright and full of honor. He was also an experienced Washington hand. He disliked violence. He always looked at things in terms of how disputes could be settled. He was very measured, very patrician. He didn't really have the stomach for a big political fight; that wasn't part of his job. He was going to do what he wanted to in an honorable way and make recommendations as he saw them."

Cy had prepped at the exclusive Kent School in Connecticut, and after Yale College he had graduated Yale Law, with honors. He'd served as a gunnery officer on a naval destroyer during World War II before signing on with a distinguished New York law firm as a civil litigation specialist. Vance had first come to Washington in 1958 as an associate counsel on the Senate Armed Forces Preparedness Investigation. During the Kennedy administration he served as general counsel to the Department of Defense, then as secretary of the army. In the Johnson administration, Vance served as deputy secretary of defense, presidential emissary to the crisis in the Dominican Republic, presidential emissary to the handling of the Detroit riots, mediator between Greece and Turkey over Cyprus, presidential emissary to Korea, presidential emissary to the handling of the Washington DC riot, and as a negotiator at the Paris Peace talks over the Vietnam War. Nixon asked Vance to serve as assistant secretary of state, but Vance declined. Back at his New York law firm, he served on the city's Commission to Investigate Alleged Police Corruption and as president of the New York Bar Association.

For much of 1976, Cy had been one of Carter's group of advisers on foreign policy issues. When first asked to help the campaign, Vance remembered, "I talked with . . . old friends who were members of the Carter foreign policy staff — and a few others. What I learned impressed me. Carter was intelligent and hard working. He had a set of values that I found attractive. His thinking reflected a principled approach to foreign affairs, which I believed essential. . . . His views on specific issues . . . were in the centrist mainstream in which I felt comfortable. I concluded that this intense and energetic man had a real chance to become the next President of the United States. . . . As the weeks passed, it became increasingly clear that we agreed philosophically about the main elements of a fresh approach to foreign policy."

While still governor, Carter had tried to enlarge his grasp of foreign policy. He had joined the Trilateral Commission — where he met both Vance and Brzezinski — attending meetings and forums. He now had very definite ideas about what he wanted to do, and Cy shared most of them. On top of that, Vance was not an ideologue but rather a facilitator. He had less ego than any other candidate, a complete contrast to his predecessor, Henry Kissinger, whose ego was the size of Montana. Cy stayed out of the spotlight, would always use ten words where others used a hundred, and didn't need acclaim. The match with Carter seemed natural.

Carter had run for president attacking the Nixon and Kissinger strategy of cutting deals with some of the uglier regimes on the planet, and once in the White House, he and his new secretary of state announced that they would be different. "Human rights," Vance declared, would henceforth be a standard applied to all America's dealings. Cy called it "the harnessing of the basic values of the Founding Fathers to our foreign policy. Historically, our country had been a force for progress in human affairs. A nation that saw itself as a 'beacon on the hill' for the rest of mankind could not content itself with power politics alone. It could not properly ignore the growing demands of individuals around the world for the fulfillment of their rights."

Nonetheless, Carter and Vance did not abandon HIM, despite his authoritarian rule. Whatever criticisms Carter might have had of Iran over its record on human rights, he and his secretary of state went out of their way to publicly declare their support for His Imperial Majesty. It was, they thought, a geopolitical necessity. They needed the shah to watch the Soviets. And they needed the shah to help restrain the price of oil. The relationship was thought important enough that Carter spent much of his first summer in office in a war with Congress over his desire to sell AWACS early-warning radar planes to Iran. On the other hand, Vance was shocked at the unlimited access Nixon and Kissinger had given HIM to American armaments and, with the shah's acquiescence, returned Iran to a more traditional American purchasing process.

Cy would stick by HIM almost to the end, as would Zbigniew Brzezinski, the Carter administration's other leading foreign policy light. Brzezinski, however, had none of Vance's personal quietude and understated affect. Quite the opposite, Zbig, fifty in 1978, possessed a loud voice and a raptor's face — sharp features he set off by combing his hair into a kind of prow that led Ham Jordan to nickname him Woody Woodpecker. (Jordan, however, quickly dropped the nickname when Zbig started calling him Porky Pig in response.) Brzezinski had more self promotion to him than Vance by a factor of at least ten, and more combativeness as well.

Brzezinski was described by those he worked with as "always on the attack." All of his losses were only momentary, and the battle always seemed to energize him. He was an inveterate game player and his goal in every game was to win. At the NSC picnic, he was one of the stars in an intramural soccer game, wearing high-top combat boots and barking whatever shins got in his way. He made no secret of the fact that he liked to dominate whenever possible. At the same time, many of those who dealt with Brzezinski up close found him an agreeable man.

Ham and Zbig quickly became friends and played tennis together regularly on the White House facility nicknamed "the Supreme Court." "He was a good athlete and played a hard, intense game," Jordan remembered, "without subtlety. . . . He would wind up and knock the hell out of the ball. If the ball made it over the net and dropped inside the lines, it was difficult to return, but his game was so erratic that rallies seldom lasted more than several strokes. Either he smashed a winner or, more often, he hit into the net or out of bounds. One day I called to him across the net, 'Zbig, you play tennis like you conduct foreign policy.'

"'You must mean that every shot is well planned, crisply hit, low and hard.'

"'Yes,' I said, 'and usually out.'"

Both men laughed.

Zbig's reputation upon entering the White House was as "the Democratic Kissinger." Brzezinski, a native Pole, and Kissinger, a native German, both spoke accented English; Brzezinski was an academic from Columbia, Kissinger from Harvard; both were acknowledged as "brilliant" by their peers; both were also acknowledged as egotists of the first order. Brzezinski, son of a Polish diplomat, had come to the United States as a refugee from the Nazis and then communism. His wife's uncle had headed the post–Second World War Czechoslovakian government before being assassinated by Stalinists. Zbig would later point out that Poland had often been compared as a culture to the American South. He quickly became one of Jimmy and Rosalynn's friends in the White House.

The president asked Zbig to become national security adviser with a phone call in December 1976. Carter intended to make the position a cabinet level appointment, the first time that had ever been done. Vance had been consulted about the appointment ahead of time and said that although he only knew Brzezinski slightly, Zbig was acceptable as long as he, or whoever else held the post, understood that the secretary of state was the administration's spokesman on foreign policy. Everybody, Brzezinski included, signed on to that understanding.

It didn't last. Turf boundaries in Washington are rarely stable, and in this instance the leverage disproportionately favored Brzezinski. Vance, even as respected as he was, was just a presidential acquaintance who worked across town. Zbig had the office right upstairs from Carter and three scheduled briefings daily. Zbig played tennis with the president on Saturday mornings, was one of only three people who had unlimited access to the Oval Office, and sometimes joined the Carters in the movie theater for old films from the forties and fifties. He and his wife hosted the Carters for informal dinners and snacks. It was no secret Zbig was one of Rosalynn's favorites.

Brzezinski was also, by far, a more public figure than Vance. He enjoyed the press and being covered in it. Ham often encountered reporters coming from or going to Zbig's office. Like Kissinger, Brzezinski had learned to dispense information by the back door and, in his competition with the State Department, was thought by many in the administration to be a regular source of leaks.

He was also far more adept at dispensing information inside the White House. Carter asked Zbig to brief his family on foreign policy; soon he was also briefing the cabinet and other people inside the administration. Vance, busy with all the negotiations over China and the Middle East, accepted the enlargement of Zbig's de facto stature. He soon accepted that Zbig had become the administration's talking foreign policy head on the Sunday morning interview shows as well.

By the fall of 1978, the secretary of state had been reduced from *the* foreign policy spokesman of the United States government to *one of the* foreign policy spokesmen along with Brzezinski. Since Vance and Brzezinski were in agreement nine out of ten times and Carter backed Vance in five out of six disagreements, the tension along their boundary was still minor. But it would get much worse. Eventually many on Cy's staff at State would think of Brzezinski as the devil himself.

Certainly Zbig was already privately critical of Vance's approach. "The basic problem," he complained in his diary that fall, "remains that our foreign policy is being conducted essentially on a contractual-legal basis [by Vance], as if we were negotiating some legal contract. Unless we bring some situations to a head . . . even occasionally through a confrontation . . . we will not resolve the outstanding issues." He thought that Vance's staff at State was dominated by people suffering from "Vietnam syndrome" and hence unable to exercise power in the range that was required.

The fate of the shah would only exacerbate those differences. Brzezinski wanted the shah to stiffen his resolve and use whatever means necessary to ensure the continuation of his rule. If that meant that rights were violated, then so be it; there were other elements more fundamental to the exercise of power than rights, starting with self-preservation. Brzezinski's relationship with the Iranian ambassador was close enough that many also speculated — correctly, it would later be revealed — that he was sending that message directly to the shah without going through State. And HIM took Zbig's informal advice seriously enough to wonder whether it, as opposed to Vance's more high-minded pronouncements, was really what the Americans wanted him to hear. The mixed signals from Washington would not get any clearer.

For his part, Ambassador William Sullivan only managed to amplify Washington's confusion. While Brzezinski was telling the shah to clamp down, Sullivan served as the point man in Tehran for the State Department's vague liberalization policies, seeking at least partial enactment of the democratic reforms that State endorsed but Brzezinski wanted the shah to discard forthwith. State's hope was that the shah, facing unrest, would transform his rule and regain the people's trust.

The shah, however, thought that the ambassador seemed unable to deliver a straight answer from Washington. "Sullivan simply did not do his job properly," one Brzezinski aide later complained. "It turned out he had been sugarcoating things to a considerable degree. He didn't want Washington coming in and micromanaging his shop. He knew that if he started saying that the shah was on his way out that Washington would be in there like a ton of bricks telling him what to do, and this was not what he had in mind at all. So he ended up playing a very complicated double game. On the one hand, he tried to communicate that things were going badly, but on the other hand, did it in a way that would keep Washington out of his kitchen. He was a very slick operator who was used to running things his own way. The end result was that everybody on this end, including the president, eventually came to see him as two-faced and untrustworthy. But, as the fall of 1978 began, we hadn't figured all that out yet."

· 4 ·

————

*I*N RETROSPECT, IT WAS HARD TO BELIEVE THAT the Carter team was actually surprised that their ambassador to Iran had taken policy management into his own hands. When the administration chose William Sullivan in 1977 to replace the shah's old school chum Richard Helms, the New England–born Sullivan was the senior Foreign Service officer still serving in the field and well-known as one of the State Department's "battlewagons," a career player of major standing with a history of running his own show. And two of the words in common usage about him were *egocentric* and *unaccountable*.

A protégé of Averell Harriman, Sullivan, fifty-six, had been one of the State Department architects of the Southeast Asian strategy that became the Vietnam War. He had also served as ambassador to Laos for five years while that war was under way. During that tenure, the ambassador commanded a "secret" front at the direction of the White House — which Congress only learned of four years after it began and which eventually made parts of Laos the most heavily bombed territory in the history of warfare. Sullivan picked targets personally and ordered up air sorties. From Laos he became Henry Kissinger's chief negotiator at the Paris conclaves that eventually ended the war. Then Sullivan moved on to ambassador to the Philippines, where he helped the Marcos dictatorship through a period of insurgency.

William Sullivan looked like an ambassador — tall, straight, silver-haired, and equal parts handsome and imperious. He was also known in the Foreign Service for his cable writing. President Lyndon Johnson had enjoyed his reports from Laos so much he read them personally.

Sullivan was not excited about taking the Iran posting when it was offered. His age pretty much ensured that this would be his last assignment, and Sullivan had been hoping to end his career in his dream job, serving as ambassador in Mexico City. He had never been posted in an Islamic country, nor had he served in that part of the world since a post in Calcutta thirty years earlier. In the end, Sullivan made what he described as a "decidedly restrained acceptance" of his final post. As it turned out, he would be the last United States ambassador to Iran, ever.

The embassy in Tehran was an American flagship, the key link to the United States' most significant ally in the region. Considered a nerve center of the Cold War, it featured an operation almost as large as the one Sullivan left behind in Manila. More than 2,000 American employees and some 3,000 of their dependents were under Sullivan's direct supervision, as well as another 2,000 Iranian nationals — many directly involved in intelligence gathering about the Soviet Union, most of the rest implementing aid and assistance arrangements with the Iranian military or SAVAK. Both the ambassador's residence and the yellow-brick chancery building were located inside the twenty-six-acre walled embassy compound. To go to work, Sullivan had to simply stroll through the wooded grounds. In addition to Sullivan's office, the two-story chancery building featured the latest in high-tech communications gear adjacent to its upstairs code room and an absolutely soundproof and secure chamber for sensitive discussions, hidden in the middle of its second floor. Among the other Tehran embassies, the Americans had a reputation for gathering far more intelligence than anyone else but having little idea how to interpret it.

Jimmy Carter and Ambassador Sullivan met face-to-face for the first and only time in the spring of 1977, when Sullivan was in the nation's capital on his way to his new assignment, the meeting personally arranged by Brzezinski. Carter gave his new ambassador a long rundown of what he wanted from Iranian policy, impressing Sullivan with both his knowledge and his manner. "It had been a most satisfactory meeting from my point of view," Sullivan remembered, "and had filled me with considerable respect for the intellectual abilities, the candor and the grace of our new President." The relationship between them would only go downhill from there.

That Iran was full of political tinder — and that an uprising was possible — had become clear to the imam a few months after Sullivan's arrival, in the days following his son Mostafa's death on October 21, 1977. As news of Khomeini's family tragedy spread inside Iran, it was immediately assumed in the mosques that SAVAK must have had a hand in Mostafa's end. Khomeini himself never made such a claim, and in fact Mostafa had previously been diagnosed with heart disease, but an assassination was assumed and widely resented. In Najaf the grieving imam submerged himself in three days of prayer in his room. Meanwhile, a wave of mourning rituals that became political statements on behalf of Khomeini erupted on the other side of the border, even though the favorable mention of the grand ayatollah's name was still forbidden.

The outbreak opened with a full-page notice taken in *Kayhan,* a mass-circulation Tehran newspaper, by the ayatollah's father-in-law, announcing a memorial service at the Jam'e Mosque, for "the offspring of the Exalted Leader of all the Shi'ites in the World." The notice's publication was an obvious violation of the ban on such favorable mention, but SAVAK did nothing to stop it. Nor did they ban the meeting itself, where, while SAVAK watched, some three thousand people were asked to pray for the "speedy return [of] our one and only leader, the defender of the faith and the great combatant of Islam, Grand Ayatollah Khomeini." The prayer was answered with universal cries of *"Allah-u akbar."*

SAVAK's inaction that October was never officially explained, but most attributed it to His Majesty's desire to convince the Carter administration of his adherence to human rights. Whatever the reason, SAVAK's failure to suppress this outburst opened a window of opportunity that was immediately and spontaneously filled. Soon memorial notices in newspapers — a common custom — began appearing all over, most signed by groups of mullahs, all mourning Mostafa and praising his father. More memorial services for Mostafa spread over the next few weeks as well, many staged by nationalist or labor groups. Even clandestine guerrilla organizations made statements about Mostafa's death "at the hands of SAVAK." The most volatile of the services for Khomeini's elder son was, predictably, in Qom. Afterward, a group of mullahs led several hundred chanting faithful down the street to the Faizieh Seminary, which had been long-since boarded up by SAVAK. Along the way, they fought with local policemen and forced them to retreat. At the seminary, one of the mullahs started to climb the wall and go inside, but before he could, an army detachment arrived and scattered the crowd by firing into it. Several dozen were wounded, but no one was killed.

The outbreak of memorial activity began to die down within a couple weeks, but it had revealed the rough shape and tactics of the movement to come.

Jimmy Carter's personal role in the rising began shortly thereafter, with a visit by the shah to Washington DC over two days in the middle of November 1977, as Jimmy was in the homestretch of his first year in office. The president's initial introduction to his guest came via a briefing paper drawn up by Vance's office. The secret memo advised that the first objective of these meetings was "to establish a close personal relationship and to persuade him of your commitment to a continuation of the special relationship [between Iran and the U.S.]."

On November 15, at 10:00 a.m., His and Her Imperial Majesties had arrived in Washington and been driven to a welcoming ceremony on the south lawn of the White House at 10:30. Anti-shah demonstrators, mostly from the Iranian student population at American universities, were gathered in Lafayette Park across the street. So were the pro-shah demonstrators — some students, some resident Iranians from around the United States flown in by the Iranian embassy. The Park Service police had separated the two screaming sides with a flimsy temporary fence, and, about the time the shah and Jimmy stood on the welcoming platform as the marine band played their two national anthems, the anti-shah forces broke through the fence and started brawling with the pro-shahs. Both sides were wielding sticks, and eventually more than seventy people, including twelve policemen, were injured.

To disperse the melee, tear gas had been fired. Over on the south lawn, wisps of the dispersing gas had drifted across the street and into the welcoming ceremony. The president and HIM were both photographed wielding handkerchiefs to stanch their weeping.

The visit had then moved inside a little ahead of schedule. There — after a receiving line, another photo op, and the presentation of Iran's official

Bicentennial gift to the United States — the shahbanou had departed for Blair House, where the royal party was staying, and the president and the shah had gone off with their respective advisers to do business in the Oval Office.

Over the next two hours, according to Ham Jordan, the shah had shown himself to be "easily the most impressive" of any of the half dozen foreign leaders the president had met so far. The shah had spent the first hour in an articulate monologue about what he perceived to be the grand Soviet strategic design to surround the oil regions in a pincer movement by meddling in Afghanistan and in the horn of Africa. Jordan called it all "a tour de force."

The only time Carter and the shah spent one-on-one was toward the end of the meeting, when Jimmy asked HIM to step into a private office alone for a few minutes. It was there that Carter had decided to raise the human rights issue, so the shah would not be embarrassed in front of his staff.

The president told HIM that he was aware of all the changes the shah had been making and greatly appreciated them, but he also knew "some of the problems." Carter allowed that the shah certainly knew about Carter's statements on human rights and he had to point out that a growing number of Iran's citizens were complaining of His Majesty's violations of those rights. Carter then talked about the opposition inside Iran, a coalition of the religious mullahs, the rising middle class, and students, both in Iran and overseas. Quite frankly, the president claimed, their complaints were damaging Iran's reputation. "Is there anything that can be done to alleviate this problem," he asked, either "by closer consultation with the dissident groups or by easing off on some of the strict police policies?"

The shah took several moments to answer, and when he did, it was in an almost sad voice. "No," he answered, "there is nothing [more] I can do." These laws that his government enforced were made to "combat communism," a problem even more real and dangerous for Iran than for the United States. It was not a subject on which it was prudent for him to take chances. It was possible that at some point, when "this serious menace" had diminished, the law could be changed, but, in any case, that would not be soon. The complaints that the United States referred to were being made by precisely "the troublemakers" from whom the laws were meant to protect his country. But, the shah promised, the United States shouldn't worry. The dissidents of whom the president spoke were, like those ruffians out in the park today, "a tiny minority and have no support among the vast majority of Iranian people."

At that evening's state dinner in the shah's honor, the president had given an extended extemporaneous toast about the importance of the strong bonds between their two countries. It literally moved the shah to tears, something few of even his own entourage had ever seen. HIM later joked about that day as "tears in the morning, tears at night."

The shah and shahbanou had departed on November 16, after a farewell lunch at the White House. The visit was hailed by both sides as a success. The shah "was a likeable man," the president reflected, "erect without being pompous, seemingly calm and self assured . . . and surprisingly modest in demeanor." The shah was relieved at being liked but was, at least initially, wary of the president. "Those frozen blue eyes," he later remarked. "Somehow there are no feelings in them at all."

Nonetheless, Ardeshir Zahedi, His Majesty's ambassador to the United States, was ebullient and told HIM that the Carters had obviously been charmed, especially Rosalynn. Zahedi predicted that relations with Carter would end up being "as warm as with Nixon, if not warmer."

Back in Iran, however, the trip played a little differently. A film of the demonstration and melee in Lafayette Park was circulated among the government's upper echelons to great consternation. When the head of SAVAK saw it, he predicted that the shah was doomed: Carter was obviously preparing to dump HIM — otherwise, the Americans would never have allowed such a demonstration to take place.

The Iranian opposition agreed. As the shah was leaving Washington, Ayatollah Ruhollah Khomeini received an international call at his headquarters in exile in Najaf. On the line was Ebrahim Yazdi, one of the ayatollah's organizers in the United States who had helped assemble the demonstration in Lafayette Park. He too advised Khomeini that Carter was obviously ready to dump the shah, for the same reason. Yazdi suggested to his ayatollah that it was a good time for their movement to increase its pressure inside Iran.

After much prayer, the grand ayatollah responded to the opportunity and issued his December 1977 edict against the shah. The document was titled "A Fatwa from Imam Khomeini"— the first time he had ever used the title "imam" and, according to one historian of the period, "the first time in the history of Iranian . . . Shi'ism that the title [of] Imam was used to describe a theologian." The text officially "deposed" the shah and ordered the faithful not to pay their taxes or obey laws "promulgated by the usurper." If they were in school, they should refuse to attend except for the purpose of demonstrating against the shah. The fatwa was also the first time the imam officially labeled Mohammad Pahlavi as *Taghut*, the Rebel, a satanic identity. The edict required the faithful to express their "hatred of the dethroned *Taghut*" and his rule of "western corruption," and was distributed throughout Iran by Khomeini's network of mosques.

When SAVAK showed a copy to the shah about a week after it was issued, His Imperial Majesty threw a small tantrum and demanded that his minister of the imperial court find out who was responsible for "allowing that vermin to continue to crawl." He then began to vent about what this act by the ayatollah meant. It was, he said, a consequence of Jimmy Carter's election and the triumph of "liberal circles in Washington," though he didn't specify exactly how. The minister of the imperial court tried to dismiss the edict as no more than the ramblings of a senile old mullah, but His Majesty disagreed. On the contrary, HIM insisted that his rule was facing "a major foreign-inspired conspiracy." It would feature the mullahs — what he called the "Black Reaction"— joining hands with the communists — what he called the "Red Reaction"— all in order to thwart his role as regional superpower. Khomeini, he predicted, was out to lead an emerging alliance of "all our enemies." The shah summoned his committee of advisers and demanded they design a strategy for discrediting this "old goat" in Najaf.

In the meantime, Jimmy Carter impulsively decided to repay the shah's visit, as part of his first presidential journey overseas, an ambitious multinational swing scheduled for the Christmas 1977 holiday season. When the itinerary grew unwieldy, the White House decided to break the burgeoning grand tour into two trips, but the resulting logistics left the president's schedule with a vacant forty-eight-hour gap spanning the last day of 1977 and the first day of 1978, between leaving Poland and arriving in Africa. Carter was asked if there was a place he wanted to stop over for New Year's Eve, and the president then asked Rosalynn what she'd like. Rosalynn replied instantly that she wanted a follow-up visit with the shah and shahbanou. The result was Jimmy Carter's second and last face-to-face encounter with Mohammad Reza Pahlavi, a month and a half after the first. It would prove the far more fateful of the two.

For starters, the timing was not fortuitous. In Tehran, where the president and first lady would spend just twenty-four hours on the ground, the first swellings of the wave that would eventually rock the Pahlavi regime to its foundations were just then emerging. "Immediately following the shah's visit to Washington," an internal NSC memo noted at the end of November 1977, "a student demonstration at Tehran University was forcibly broken up by riot police. Since then, riot police have taken up positions on campus and . . . each morning . . . indiscriminately beat up a few students to 'maintain order.' . . . A group of about a thousand [gathered] to hear a (canceled) talk by an opposition figure was attacked by young men who arrived in green buses wielding barrel staves. . . . An open [opposition] meeting . . . outside Tehran . . . was raided by young men who arrived by bus, formed ranks, and waded in with sticks. . . . About a hundred [from the meeting] were seriously hurt. . . . Several student strikes are in progress, at least one university has closed. There are reports of minor demonstrations in other areas. . . . The [US] embassy has been struck by the extraordinary organization displayed by opposition forces. . . . Perhaps the shah is truly running scared. . . . It may have been this [fear] that inspired the violence of [the shah's] counterattack." In fact, the extraordinary political consensus that would topple the shah within a year was already gathering, and the shah knew it.

Carter went to Tehran anyway.

At the time, Jimmy Carter was still viewed in a somewhat hopeful light by those who would eventually corner the shah in his palace. English-language copies of the book Carter had written while governor, *Why Not The Best?*, became "in" reading among the educated classes over the two weeks before his arrival. More than a half dozen open letters to Carter were circulated around Tehran, all of them praising his human rights policy and beseeching him to apply it to Iran. There was still a somewhat frenzied belief that the American would soon bring the shah to heel. Even the exiled Khomeini's response to announcement of the president's visit was mild. The ayatollah had been advised by his American organizer to give this new American government a chance.

None of that optimism would remain after Jimmy Carter left.

In this instance, the president would be undone by his lifelong, typically southern, typically politician's addiction to hyperbole and exaggeration. For Carter, it was not enough to call something "good"— it almost instantly, with a roll of his drawl and a twinkle of his eye, became "great" or "the greatest." Ham Jordan had already warned Carter about reining in that part of his act, but the warning didn't stick. To Jimmy Carter, public exaggeration was just an instinctive oratorical device that humanized the speaker and indirectly expressed affection. Certainly it could be endearing in the right circumstance. In Tehran, however, where every presidential statement was parsed and reparsed, that spontaneous embellishment would only serve to attach the shah to Carter's destiny like an anchor hung from his leg — and at just the wrong time.

For the shah, of course, the visit seemed like a little miracle. He had never expected it and took the date on very short notice, without hesitation. "The shah was thrilled at the prospect [of Carter's visit]," Ambassador Sullivan remembered. "It would . . . show his critics in both the United States and Iran that the great American champion of human rights considered his regime worthy of a personal endorsement." HIM hoped to make the occasion a gala New Year's Eve spectacular, but the White House urged him to tone it down. Still, it was obvious upon Carter's arrival that the shah had brought to bear all his imperial powers to stage-manage the presidential visit.

For an entire day prior to Jimmy Carter's arrival and throughout his stay, the boulevard connecting the airport to Tehran was closed to the public. As the president and the shah motored into town on the empty asphalt, armed soldiers lined the roadway on both sides, one every five yards. Soldiers and police — rounds in chambers and at the ready — manned every overpass and the roofs of most tall buildings nearby. There was time in the president's schedule for a short set of political meetings once in town, at which human rights was one of six major issues Carter was prepared to raise with the shah. There is no record that the mention of the subject had any impact.

The banquet that evening was classic shah. The menu was printed in French and Farsi, neither of which Carter understood. There were some four hundred guests, mostly from the shah's government or his court. The first course was pearls of the Caspian, a kind of caviar reserved only for the shah. The main course, according to one of those present, featured "kebabs, splendidly garnished, a Russian-style pilaf with diced partridge, and salad. Soon the dining room lights dimmed and dozens of waiters marched to the tables with ice cream aflame with cherry sauce. . . . Throughout the dinner, an orchestra serenaded us with compositions by Verdi [and] Chopin."

When the time came for toasts, the shah began by welcoming his distinguished guest. His remarks were short, all to the effect that in Persian tradition, it is believed that the first guest of the New Year is an omen for the year to come.

This was, of course, far truer than anyone there that night dared to imagine.

Then Carter got up and cut loose.

He said he was just going to say "a few words," but the toast ended up longer than that. "Iran," he told the crowd, "because of the great leadership of the Shah, is an island of stability in one of the more troubled areas of the world. This is a great tribute to you, Your Majesty, and to your leadership and to the respect and the admiration and love which your people give to you. . . . As we sat together this afternoon . . . I was profoundly impressed again not only with your wisdom and your judgment and your sensitivity and insight, but also with the close compatibility that we found [between us]."

Carter then ran through a list of topics they had discussed that day and the compatibility they had found on them. The last was human rights. This, the president said, is a "cause . . . shared deeply by our people and by the leaders of our two nations." In total, "our talks have been priceless, our friendship is irreplaceable, and my own gratitude is to the Shah, who in his wisdom and with his experience has been so helpful to me, a new leader.

"And," Jimmy added for emphasis, "there is no leader with whom I have a deeper sense of personal gratitude and personal friendship."

The crowd responded to the toast with a standing ovation, and the shah was the first one on his feet. "I have never heard a foreign statesman speak of me in quite such flattering terms as he used that evening," HIM later remembered. "My favorable impression of the new American President deepened. . . . Carter appeared to be a smart man."

When what Carter had said about the shah at the palace reached the Iranian streets, it stunned some, outraged others. All expectations were dashed. Henceforth, Carter and the shah would be treated as two of a kind.

On the morning of January 1, 1978, Carter and the shah drove back between the ranks of armed troops to the airport. Up the side streets, behind the cordon and out of view, youngsters threw stones at the back of the soldiers and shouted *"Allah-u akbar"* before being chased away.

· 5 ·

———

THE IRANIAN REVOLUTION THAT WAS ABOUT TO emerge in the aftermath of Carter's visit was both remarkably disparate — with more factions than anyone had fingers or toes — and remarkably united — forming a solid front, left to right, Muslims to Marxists, top to bottom, all offering at least momentary deference to Ayatollah Ruhollah Khomeini as their spiritual leader. Two men in particular played central roles in assembling that coalition and managing the imam's connection to the more secular elements of the Revolution. Both, like Khomeini, were exiles and both would soon take to describing themselves as the imam's spiritual "son."

The first of the two was Sadegh Ghotbzadeh (pronounced Hobe-za-day), forty-one, a leading figure among the Iranians in Paris, a longtime organizer with the nationalist Liberation Movement of Iran — a prestigious organization at the heart of the secular opposition — and a player in the shadowy world of Middle Eastern revolutionaries. He now managed the imam's political interests among the exiles in Europe, as well as among the world's Arab leaders, who all knew Ghotbzadeh on a first-name basis. Sadegh carried a Syrian passport — his Iranian one having long since been canceled by the shah — and was tracked by the French security services, the CIA, Mossad, and, of course, SAVAK, who, two years earlier, had dispatched an unsuccessful assassin after him. Unlike most exiles, Sadegh lived well, in a nice apartment in a stylish Paris *arrondissement,* and always seemed to have cash. It was rumored that Ghotbzadeh received a stipend from the Syrians for keeping them informed about his numerous international contacts, particularly with the Lebanese and the Palestinians. In any case, he often wore monogrammed shirts and three-piece suits, spoke colloquial English, and cut a memorable figure on the Left Bank.

"He dominated the room," a Canadian journalist who interviewed him later wrote. "Tall and massive, with black hair and soft eyes, he looked like an elegant bear in a light cashmere coat. He seemed amiable yet somehow dangerous. He was not handsome in any conventional sense, but there was something magnetic about him. The dark eyes seemed to hold secrets, the wide mouth was almost too generous. His physical characteristics so blended with his personality that I imagined his slightly flattened nose had been shaped by his daily confrontations with life. . . . His speech, slightly slurred on some sounds, precise on others, reinforced the impression of an unsharpened knife. . . . Sadegh explained that he had grown up hating the Shah, yet his was not red-faced anger. He had cool contempt for the monarch, as if he were disdaining a worm. I learned later that this elaborate nonchalance was a trademark, and a deceptive trademark at that."

Ghotbzadeh seemed an odd match with the imam on the visuals alone, but his passion for his work with Khomeini was unmistakable, nonchalance or not. Born in Tehran, Ghotbzadeh had indeed grown up hating the shah. His *bazaari* father was a friend of Mossadeq, a supporter of Mossadeq's National Front political party, and a prosperous lumber broker who was revolted by the corruption and influence peddling of Mohammad Pahlavi's rule. Sadegh's mother was deeply Islamic and believed that the shah was God's punishment of Iran for its transgressions against the faith. Sadegh, the second son, was the most religious of her seven children. As a boy, he did some yard work for Mossadeq; he was a teenager when the then prime minister was ousted. By all accounts, Sadegh took the family friend's downfall personally. While auditing classes at the University of Tehran he began attending lectures staged by the precursors of the Liberation Movement of Iran. He was inspired by the speakers' vision of extending Mossadeq's precedent into a full-scale "democratic republic based on progressive Islam." Soon Sadegh was designing and distributing leaflets for them.

SAVAK visited the twenty-year-old Ghotbzadeh shortly thereafter. He was taken to a Tehran police station, shoved around a little, warned about the dangers of communism, and then released. His parents got the message and almost immediately arranged for Sadegh to study abroad, at Georgetown University in Washington DC, where he became a freshman. Sadegh struggled with English at first, studied sparingly and with not a great deal of success, and continued to agitate against the shah, founding the Islamic Iranian Student Association. Though something of a leftist at the time, he figured that the "Islamic" identification would make it more difficult for the shah to act against them. Even so, in 1962 SAVAK requested the cancelation of his student visa, and only the direct intervention of Robert Kennedy, the president's brother and attorney general, kept Sadegh in the United States. Kennedy had met and befriended Sadegh after a protest of the shah's rule during the first days of his brother's administration and became one of Sadegh's heroes after the intervention on his behalf. Two years later, however, with the advent of the Johnson administration, the twenty-six-year-old itinerant Iranian student was denied permission to continue his stay and moved on to several years of shadowy politics in Syria and Paris.

Ghotbzadeh was twenty-nine when he tried to return to America to "finish" his education. By then he was traveling under a Syrian passport and keeping an apartment in Damascus. He had successfully applied for a new student visa, but the Immigration Department revoked it almost as soon as he arrived. At the hearing over his rejection, the immigration officer in charge brandished a five-inch-thick file that he claimed was full of "security information" about this alleged "Syrian" and announced that Sadegh's chances of staying in the United States any longer than a fifteen-day tourist permit would allow were less than zero. Ghotbzadeh then crossed into Canada and enrolled at the University of British Columbia. At age thirty-one, he graduated with a bachelor's in history and returned to Paris, where he resumed his stellar role in the fight against the shah.

The decision to connect with the imam in the early 1970s was taken after lengthy discussion among his exiled cohorts. Sadegh had first been introduced to Khomeini in the mid-sixties, when Ghotbzadeh was reportedly organizing Iranian guerrilla training in Lebanon, and had already come to the conclusion that only religion would give their struggle a genuine connection to the masses. Everyone in the Paris discussion knew of Khomeini's recent tract, *Islamic Government,* though they all agreed that parts of it sounded like a Muslim *Mein Kampf.* Still, Sadegh thought that touch of native fascism could be smoothed out. This was, after all, a holy man in his seventies; he was bound to have rough edges. In any case, Khomeini was the most revered symbol of resistance to the tyrant. Whatever the risk, the alliance was well worth it. "We all thought we knew who Khomeini was then," one of Sadegh's friends remembered. "We expected to use him to get where *we* wanted, not the opposite."

Eventually this Paris caucus of young Liberation Movement organizers delegated Ghotbzadeh to travel to Najaf, make contact, and see if an alliance was possible. The journey would become the pivot point of Sadegh's life.

The grand ayatollah received him on a rug in the courtyard of his tiny house, leaning on a cushion propped against the courtyard wall. Sadegh kissed his hand and addressed him with the honorific "Master." Most of their first meeting was spent with Ghotbzadeh telling him about his group in Paris and what they were doing. Khomeini listened and watched. "His face radiates dignity," Sadegh wrote in his diary afterward. "He is distinguished by his extreme simplicity. And he knows it. This man knows his power. He is analyzing me, too. I've been introduced by three different sources and he knows my work and my name, but that isn't enough for him. He has been looking at me the whole time, making up his mind about me."

Apparently the response was favorable. When Sadegh returned the next morning for a second meeting, Khomeini greeted him with familiarity.

The younger man began this second conversation by saying that the master understood how they were trying to bring down the shah and replace him with a "democratic republic based on progressive Islam." Their organization now needed to go further forward and make common cause with him and his faithful.

After some discussion of the social model provided by Islam, Khomeini asked if Sadegh had read his "lesson," *Islamic Government.*

Ghotbzadeh said he had and then tried to raise his group's objections to the "lesson" as forcefully as he could. *Islamic Government* was, he told the ayatollah, often so vague that it could be interpreted as "too rigid, too orthodox, and too old-fashioned." The "lesson" needed to be clarified if it was to be useful to their movement. Sadegh pointed to the issue of women as an example. If the master insisted on the chador, most women would not support them.

Khomeini interrupted, saying the full-length chador was not mandatory. Only women's hair needed to be covered.

Sadegh moved on to other issues and then suggested that his group in Paris undertake to make some "clarifications" at the same time they translated this "lesson" into Farsi from the Arabic in which the master had written it.

Khomeini readily agreed.

Sadegh also advised the ayatollah to be careful what he said. Religious questions were easy for the master to answer because he had the guide of the Koran, but politics was trickier. He should only speak to the most important questions and then only after identifying the real truth.

Khomeini again agreed and went even further. "My action," he told the younger man, "should be through faith and religion, not politics."

Ghotbzadeh returned to Paris reassured on all fronts, and the alliance was under way.

"He is a real politician," Sadegh confided in his diary. "Sometimes he confirms subjects without mentioning them directly. Sometimes, when he hears something indirectly, he doesn't say anything until the action has been taken . . . and he knows that it cannot be changed; then he rejects the action. . . . By doing that he covers himself, but . . . nobody can blame him for it. If he is surrounded by a group of intelligent and faithful people, he could be a great leader."

More than just politically convinced, Sadegh had returned to Paris from Najaf personally enthralled with the ayatollah as well. The old man touched the younger man's religious passion as nothing had since he acquired it from his mother as a young child, and he felt protective and affectionate toward him. Often when he talked of Khomeini now, it was with a glow, even to the reporters he patiently dogged with news of the imam's pronouncements. Sadegh was soon a dominant figure in the group working with the imam. Many would eventually refer to Ghotbzadeh as Khomeini's "favorite" among all the exiles.

The second of the imam's two exemplary acolytes was Abolhassan Bani Sadr, forty-five, another exiled organizer with the Liberation Movement of Iran and one of the participants in the Paris discussion that dispatched Ghotbzadeh to Najaf. To Bani Sadr eventually went the task of rewriting *Islamic Government*. He was the intellectual, a former graduate student and lecturer in economics at the University of Tehran and the author of some twenty books and pamphlets, all about Islam as a social model, with titles like *Betrayed*

Hope and *Rights of Man*. His fundamental theory was that Islam provided a system of governance that amounted to a third option between capitalism and communism, and offered both economic growth and social justice.

"He was a very peculiar man," a *Le Monde* correspondent who befriended Bani Sadr remembered, "much more an intellectual than a politician, even though he eventually had such political success. He was also an extremely honest man. He always said what he believed and believed what he said. He believed in the truth and he also believed that Abolhassan Bani Sadr embodied it. There was considerable ego there, but he was at heart a kind of naive intellectual. He was a very attractive person but not a politician. He thought you had to write every day to have an impact on events, as though power were an intellectual process. That said, he understood a great deal about how power operated, and, if I had two versions of events — one from Bani Sadr and one from Ghotbzadeh — I would take Bani Sadr's every time. He had a kind of underlying allegiance to accurate information."

The *Le Monde* correspondent met Bani Sadr in the early 1970s when the exile approached him trying to feed his paper information about the situation in Iran, retrieved from an enormous web of contacts throughout his native country. (Abolhassan would later brag that in Paris he knew more about what was happening in Isfahan or Tehran or Mashhad than the people who lived there.) The correspondent took the exile under his wing and the two of them often went down the street to a restaurant near the *Le Monde* offices, where the reporter would buy the Iranian coffee and a sandwich. The food was accepted gratefully. Unlike Ghotbzadeh, Bani Sadr had little money, lived in a shabby flat with his wife, and was often hungry.

One day, while he and the reporter ate and talked about Iran, Bani Sadr relaxed enough to share his own dreams.

"You know," he told the man from *Le Monde*, "I shall be president of the Islamic Republic of Iran someday."

Unable to restrain himself, the correspondent burst out laughing. "He was a young man," the reporter explained much later, "and I never thought the Islamic movement would ever be in power."

With ambitions like that, though, there was already an undercurrent of competition between Bani Sadr and Ghotbzadeh in Paris, even though Sadegh still had far more standing among the exiles. Bani Sadr had first heard of Ghotbzadeh in 1962, when Bani Sadr was the twenty-nine-year-old secretary of the Iranian Student Association and helped stage a demonstration in

Tehran protesting the shah's attempts to have Ghotbzadeh's American visa revoked. The two men actually met face-to-face a year later at a conference of Iranian students held in London. By then Bani Sadr had been arrested in a 1963 National Front demonstration for free elections and, after a brief stay in a SAVAK prison, fled into exile. At the time, both were glad to finally meet. Still, "there was always a certain friction between them," a French lawyer who knew both men recalled. "They were the two most important of the Iranian exiles. Ghotbzadeh was a revolutionary, always wanting to do things, and Bani Sadr was an intellectual, always wanting to talk about things."

Their personal styles were also opposites. Abolhassan had none of the younger man's animal charisma. His presence dominated few rooms. There was nothing at all suave about him. His well-tended mustache seemed to purse his lips and pucker his face like a small rodent's, giving him a strong resemblance to the actor Peter Sellers playing the comic role of Inspector Clouseau. Bani Sadr's mousiness was accented by a pair of black-framed modern glasses with square lenses so large they covered his eyebrows and much of his cheeks.

Poor and often threadbare, he suffered in visual comparison to Ghotbzadeh, but he was by no means intimidated by him. "They made a decidedly odd couple," a woman who knew them both in the fall of 1978 remembered. "Though ostensibly friends . . . Ghotbzadeh railed at Bani Sadr's interminable theorizing, while Bani Sadr fumed at Sadegh's tendency to hold . . . demonstrations without consultation. Each grew suspicious of the other's closest confidants, and Sadegh acted independently rather than trust a secret to Bani Sadr's loose tongue. [In Paris,] the seeds of their future fall were [already] sown."

They did not, however, disagree about making an alliance with the imam. Bani Sadr had been attracted to Khomeini even before Sadegh. He was the one who had first secured a copy of *Islamic Government* and developed a detailed analysis of the ayatollah's "lesson" to present to his fellow Paris organizers. Abolhassan was the second son among the seven children of a respected mullah in Hamadan in northwestern Iran and had first met the future imam while still a child, when Khomeini came by the house to speak with his father. A follower of Mossadeq as a college student, Bani Sadr saw his intellectual role as putting Islam forward as a tool for political and social liberation long before his alliance with Khomeini.

Before undertaking the rewrite Khomeini had agreed to with Sadegh,

Bani Sadr went to Najaf as well. The imam remembered Bani Sadr's father and welcomed the exile as one of the faithful. Abolhassan didn't lack brashness and, having spent a lot of energy developing his own theory of Islamic government, told Khomeini that the ayatollah's take on the proposition was largely unsuccessful. To make his point, Bani Sadr asked the imam if it was his intention in writing his book to make sure the shah never left power.

Khomeini, somewhat taken aback, said of course not.

That would nonetheless be the effect, Bani Sadr argued, since *Islamic Government* was not substantial enough to actually make the imam's thoughts into a system and then show how to make that system work. Such shortcomings would only alienate people.

The ayatollah responded that he hadn't written this "lesson" to be specific or as a blueprint. He had, he told Bani Sadr, written it to give people like Abolhassan the opportunity to develop these ideas into a system. He then gave Bani Sadr express permission to do just that. To make it official, he insisted on writing out a formal invitation to Bani Sadr to undertake this "development."

The result was a revised *Islamic Government* that was as much Bani Sadr as Khomeini. The Paris exile's intellectual vision, one analyst later observed, "assailed Iran's dependence on the West while celebrating the notion of a symbolic or 'generalized' Imamate. The concept called for an Imam whose considerable authority would eventually be diffused to the people, thus turning each individual into an Imam or Leader." The treatise, translated into Farsi, would eventually circulate in more than a million copies and become, in Bani Sadr's words, "the governing document of Iran."

In the process of that rewrite, like Ghotbzadeh, Bani Sadr developed a strong emotional attachment to the imam that far transcended anything political or intellectual. "He seemed to be an extraordinary soul," Bani Sadr later remembered. "He was a living incarnation of things holy. I could see nothing wrong with him in those days. I loved him more than I loved my own father. I only loved the revolution itself more."

The Iranian Revolution broke out barely a week after Jimmy Carter rang in the Gregorian New Year in Tehran. The president's visit seemed to embolden the shah, and afterward he pursued the anti-Khomeini strategy his advisers recommended with uncharacteristic recklessness. His first move was to order his minister of the imperial court to have a newspaper article prepared, presenting the "true" Khomeini. Twice he rejected drafts as too tame. The end product was so defamatory that the newspaper to which it was submitted refused to print it until the minister of information and the prime minister personally intervened and forced the paper to comply. On January 7, 1978, the shah's attack was published under the headline "Iran and the Red and Black Imperialism" and attributed to a fictitious byline. The text, according to one Middle Eastern journalist, "accused the Ayatollah of a catalog of sins, including allegiance to foreign powers, religious ignorance and even homosexuality, and suggested that the mullahs of Iran were conspiring with the Communists to destroy the existing order." Khomeini was described as "a mad Indian," and the mullahs as a whole were described as "a race of parasites, engaged in sodomy, usury and drunk most of the time."

The response in Qom was virtually immediate. Within two hours of the paper's distribution, groups of mullahs were moving through town, burning the publication's sales racks. Within two days, a demonstration had been organized, and on January 9 the Qom bazaar closed in protest against "insults to our religious leadership." A crowd of several thousand mullahs and religious students then gathered at the Shrine of Massoumeh, chanted some anti-shah slogans, marched down the block, and opened the padlocked Faizieh Seminary. After celebrating its "liberation" for a moment, the crowd then began moving through town, armed with rocks, pipes, and staves, assaulting every symbol of the shah's rule it could find. Eventually the mob converged on the central police station and began to attack it. Policemen fired into the crowd, killing seven and wounding many more. As the crowd fled, some holding blood-soaked bandages like talismans, two policemen and a thirteen-year-old boy were trampled to death. Eventually the army came in and restored order with more live fire.

The next day, Khomeini described the events in Qom as the fulfillment of a divine prophecy and hailed his movement's new martyrs. The day after that, the shah delivered a speech in which he described what had happened in Qom as a "minor" occurrence and referred to Khomeini, not by name but simply as "the dog who barks at the moon."

The barking, however, continued. Shiism requires a second mourning period forty days after the first. Mourning for the victims of the shah's repression in Qom began again in February, with police battles that made more martyrs, a vicious circle advancing in forty-day increments, each feeding off the previous, through the spring and summer in an irrepressible tide.

The progression made a quantum leap into full-time uprising early in September, on what would be remembered as Black Friday. On Thursday, September 7, the shah's government declared martial law in Tehran and twenty-three other cities in response to a series of mob attacks on police stations. Troops were dispatched to the city to enforce the new prohibitions, but word was slow to get around. The next day, Friday, September 8, a crowd of twenty thousand people — most apparently ignorant of the ban on such public gatherings — massed at a working-class market area known as Jaleh Square for a public meeting called a week earlier by one of the local mullahs. The army was instantly dispatched to disperse the crowd and seemed to be doing so without disturbance until several motorcycle riders, part of a group known as Motorcyclists for Allah, drove their bikes into the soldiers' formation, shouting *"Allah-u akbar."* The army shot several of the riders, and the crowd attacked the soldiers. The army then started firing at everyone. When the smoke cleared, at least two hundred demonstrators, perhaps many more, were dead. One historian would later conclude that "the incident at Jaleh Square marked the end of the regime." Henceforth, the shah would never know another day of civic peace.

That was not immediately obvious, though. Both Cy Vance and Zbig Brzezinski were with the president at Camp David, participating in the three-cornered negotiations that would eventually yield the agreements returning the Sinai to Egypt and giving Israel its first recognition by an Arab neighbor. Both Cy and Zbig monitored the situation in Tehran regularly, and to them it initially looked like more demonstrations, only larger. On September 9, however, they agreed that the situation was serious enough that the president ought to call the shah to buck him up. Sadat, one of the shah's closest friends, was making such a call that evening.

On Sunday, September 10, at exactly 7:56 a.m., according to White House logs, Jimmy Carter got on the line with the shah. The conversation between the president and the shahanshah lasted six minutes.

"The President said he was calling to express his friendship for the Shah," Zbig remembered, "and his concern about events. He wished the Shah the best in resolving these problems and in being successful in his efforts to implement reforms."

For his part, the shah sounded numb, almost in a state of shock, just putting one verbal foot in front of another. HIM eventually "responded that the planning for the disturbances was 'diabolical,'" according to Brzezinski. "He noted that he had gone far in liberalizing and that was now used against him. Nonetheless, he intended to persist. . . . He then added that it would be good if the President could endorse his efforts as strongly as possible because otherwise his enemies would take advantage of it. The interests of America and Iran were so identified that such an action would be much appreciated.

"The President promised to do just that."

Then the two hung up.

Around the same time, His Imperial Majesty summoned Ambassador Sullivan to the palace and gave him a far more straightforward piece of his mind on the same subject. The shah was withdrawn at first, so terse he seemed almost hostile, slumped in his chair, sulking like a teenager with his feelings hurt, making small talk with no reference at all to Jaleh Square.

Then, like a storm breaking, the shah gushed out a ten-minute diatribe, barely pausing for breath in the rush of words. "This outburst was not delivered in peremptory tones," Sullivan remembered, "but rather in the manner of a man who felt himself unjustly betrayed. The Shah was clearly distraught, his whole manner pleading — almost pathetic. I was frankly astounded."

His Majesty proceeded to list incidents, demonstrations, strikes, bombings, and other attacks on his rule since 1978 began. These reports came from everywhere and among everybody, involving the cooperation of groups who had nothing to do with one another: the leftists in league with the mullahs, the students with the workers, the middle class and the poor — everybody. This was not, he asserted, what happened in Iran. These people didn't make common cause with one another. For this wide a common front to be arrayed against him required the intervention of foreign powers. His Majesty's manner gave those last words an ominous air.

The shah then said he could understand that the Soviets would want to cause him trouble. He even understood that, perverse as they were, the British also had their reasons for wanting to fan this unrest. What he could not grasp was why the Americans would join in as well. At this point, the shah's expression and tone were their most agonized. How could the CIA turn on him like this? he demanded. Only they could pull off an uprising of this scale. The shah seemed almost in tears when he finally paused.

Sullivan was stunned. With his most soothing tone, he tried to walk HIM through it all step-by-step, demonstrating that the CIA wasn't involved. The shah's upset seemed to ease, but his suspicions of the Americans remained.

For his part, Sullivan would later identify this encounter as the moment he became convinced the shah was no longer quite all there.

Not that Sullivan's explanations of what was going on were that much more edifying than the shah's. After the original Qom riots, Sullivan had cabled the State Department that this was the "most serious incident of this sort for years" and made a faltering attempt to interpret the event: "We have amassed enough evidence to date," he reported, "to be reasonably sure that the Islamic movement heads the Iranian revolution both in the person of the symbolic leader, Ayatollah Khomeini, and in the organization, or, perhaps more accurately, interlocking organizations which support him. . . . Our best assessment . . . is that the Shi'a Islamic movement dominated by Ayatollah Khomeini is far better organized, enlightened, and able . . . than its detractors [in the shah's government] would lead us to believe. It is rooted in the Iranian people more than any Western ideology, including Communism. However, its governing procedures are not clear and probably have not been totally worked out."

All well and good, but this generalized embassy assessment hardly expanded in either depth or detail as the uprising burgeoned over its first nine months — an ongoing ignorance abetted by two significant handicaps in the embassy's approach.

The first was its unremitting commitment to the once almost universally accepted assumption among the foreign diplomats in Tehran that the shah's rule was impregnable. Prior to the outbreak in Qom, the only dissent to this surety had come from a French political officer who predicted the shah's downfall in a 1976 memo to his ambassador and was immediately reassigned as mentally unstable. It was late April 1978 before the Israelis reached the same conclusion as the French political officer, and even then, they were alone in doing so. Well into the fall of 1978, Sullivan and the other western diplomats were still insisting that the shah would remain firmly in power for the foreseeable future, making it virtually impossible to distinguish the forest for the trees.

The second handicap involved the embassy's intelligence gathering. From the beginning, one of the terms the shah had insisted upon in his relationship with the Americans was that they not maintain any contact with his opposition. To do so, he insisted, would only undercut His Majesty's rule. If the

Americans wanted to know something about these people, SAVAK would provide the information. The American government had accepted the shah's terms, despite the obvious limitations they placed on its operations, and over the twenty-five years the Americans had played a visible role inside Iran, they developed no relationships with those who resented the shah's rule.

The only reported American attempt to initiate contact with Khomeini came in 1964, after the ayatollah's release from house arrest and before he was exiled. The approach had been made by an apparent CIA operative, working out of the embassy. He asked for a meeting through one of Khomeini's aides and was told the ayatollah didn't want to see him, so he should just leave his message with the aide. The American said he knew the ayatollah was thinking about speaking out against the Americans and warned him to think twice. It was one thing to criticize the shah, he threatened, it was another to attack America. Not surprisingly, when the imam was exiled several weeks later after denouncing the American presence, he blamed much of the outcome on the United States. That botched 1964 intimidation was the last attempt to reach out to him that the United States made.

The Americans also rejected all attempts by the Iranian opposition to initiate even the most elementary contact. There had been two such approaches made in the past year.

The first was in Washington by Sadegh Ghotbzadeh, a couple weeks before the shah's "tears in the morning, tears at night" visit. Ghotbzadeh was in the United States, traveling on a tourist visa, "to make contact with Americans both in and out of the Government." To this end, Sadegh called a man at the State Department he had never met but whose name he was familiar with by virtue of a Senate Foreign Relations Committee report the American had written on military sales to the shah. The State Department man considered the encounter so insignificant that he didn't even bother to write up an account of it until more than a year later.

"Ghotbzadeh called me . . . to request that I have lunch with him," the American's memo eventually explained, "identifying himself as head of an Iranian resistance movement based in Paris. I asked [the State Department's] Country Director for Iran whether he had any information on Ghotbzadeh. [The Country Director] did not know of Ghotbzadeh or his organization. I subsequently had lunch with Ghotbzadeh. [He told me] he and his organization were admirers of the US and the ideals for which it stood. He was particularly pleased with the emphasis being placed on human rights by the Carter Administration, and saw an opportunity to influence . . . the Administration so that it would not repeat the mistakes of previous Administrations, namely — identifying US interests in Iran [with] the views, policies, and indeed the continuing rule of the Shah.

"[He also said] the Shah was universally hated within Iran, and that pressures were building throughout Iranian society against the Shah and his repressive form of government. Despite SAVAK, he and his organization had clandestine contacts with all levels of Iranian society [and] these contacts were reporting that the shah was increasingly unpopular and that a revolution was brewing. [He warned that] the US was identified with the Shah's repression [and] would suffer when the revolution came unless the Carter Administration took steps to avoid identification with the regime. . . . Ghotbzadeh seemed to be a serious fellow who spoke in a moderate, sensible way. He hoped the new Administration would change American policy toward Iran; if so he would welcome it. He did not seem ideologically anti-American."

At the time, the Americans ignored the opening.

Another failed approach would be made to the embassy in Tehran some two weeks after Black Friday. It was precipitated when the Iraqi government dispatched police to surround Ayatollah Khomeini's house in Najaf. The imam was now officially in detention, subject to being expelled from the country. The next day, the US embassy in Tehran was contacted by two unnamed members of the Liberation Movement of Iran.

"At urgent request of LMI representative," the embassy wired Washington, "[an embassy political officer] met with two representatives of Movement Sept. 25. LMI asked for meeting because news had reached Iran Sept. 24 that Iraqi government has placed soldiers around Khomeini house and had only allowed two people, both relatives, through police line. . . . LMI representatives said [their] movement [was] convinced Iraqis would not do this on their own and accused . . . US . . . of 'forcing' Iraq to do this. [The political officer] told LMI pair it was absurd to think US had a hand in such action. . . . LMI seemed mollified and stood down from hostile attitude. . . .

"Senior LMI man present then said [this] meeting with [the political officer] had been requested to arrange 'high level' contact with USG [United States government] to present LMI views. Such [a] meeting could consist of two or three individuals per side and would have as its goal explanation of LMI policies and securing US blessing for transitional arrangements which would culminate in the end of Pahlavi dynasty 'in best interests of both Iran and US.' . . .

"[The political officer] replied [that the] US starts from premise that Shah has [the] key role in future political developments and [the] idea of such a [high level] meeting [with the Liberation Movement of Iran] seemed premature and somewhat grandiose. He promised [a] response later. [Their] request for meeting with 'policy level' US officials, a long term opposition aim, appears [to be an] effort to get USG to help pull LMI chestnuts out of fire."

In retrospect, this overture resembles an opportunity to potentially sidestep a number of the disasters to come, but nothing was ever made of the possibility.

Contrary to the Liberation Movement's assumption during the last week of September, the decision to chase Khomeini out of Iraq was instigated by the shah, not the Americans. His Imperial Majesty's envoy had made the request personally to the new Iraqi strongman, Saddam Hussein. After thinking it over, Saddam sent his brother back to Tehran with his answer. The Iraqi met with the shah at the palace. His brother described Saddam as concerned about the Shiite threat, since Shias made up 60 percent of his own population, and offered that Iraq would be glad to expel this mullah. More than that, Iraq was prepared to arrange a "suitable accident" and eliminate Khomeini altogether if His Majesty wished.

The shah declined. Killing Khomeini, he believed, would just inflame the situation beyond control. Rather, the shah preferred to isolate him. The shah's diplomats had already arranged for all the countries surrounding Iran to refuse admission to the holy man, so the imam would have to flee west, thousands of miles from the flow of religious pilgrims that had given him so much leverage in Najaf. Once removed from immediate proximity, according to the shah, this so-called holy man would quickly lose touch with Iran and become an object of ridicule.

The Iraqi move set off a scramble among the uprising's exile infrastructure. Sadegh Ghotbzadeh flew to Iraq while the LMI was contacting the American embassy in Tehran. Khomeini would obviously have to leave, and Sadegh arrived at the ayatollah's house in Najaf — now surrounded by Iraqi soldiers — with a list of options. Most preferable were places of exile where their movement had enough infrastructure to support an imam. Sadegh's first choice was Syria, where Sadegh was a personal friend of the ruler, Hafiz al-Assad, but, although the Syrians were prepared to allow the imam there as a temporary guest for perhaps a week, they would not allow him to set up shop. Lebanon was full of Shias, but it was also in a state of civil war, and security alone made it impossible. The last two options were Kuwait, on Iraq's southern border, and Paris, where Sadegh and Bani Sadr led a strong exile community.

When Ghotbzadeh discussed the French option with the imam, one of Khomeini's first remarks was to rail that Paris was the capital of the Franks, who had, of course, played a despicable role in the Crusades during the tenth century AD. He also expressed doubts the Franks would allow him to enter.

Sadegh pointed out that the imam could just go to France as a tourist. France and Iran had an arrangement in which you didn't need a visa to enter, just an Iranian passport would do.

Khomeini seemed surprised by that.

Sadegh went on to argue that even though Paris was much farther from Iran than Kuwait, the imam could still distribute tapes from there. He would have access to the international press. He would have a phone system that allowed him to connect to Iran more easily than he could now. Plus, Ghotbzadeh added, the French were "sentimental about revolutions" and he would find a lot of sympathy.

Despite those arguments and the imam's affection for Sadegh, Ghotbzadeh returned to Paris alone. The imam chose Kuwait, apparently heavily influenced by his remaining son, Ahmed, and the followers who had collected around him in Najaf. Once the Iranian embassy in Baghdad issued Khomeini a new passport, however, the Kuwaitis suddenly closed their border to him, apparently at the instigation of the Iranians. Paris or somewhere else in Europe was now the only option. Ahmed called both Ghotbzadeh and Bani Sadr and told them the imam was coming. Without talking to each other, the imam's two self-proclaimed "spiritual sons" began making separate arrangements for Khomeini's arrival, each ignorant of the other's efforts.

The flight carrying Ruhollah and Ahmed Khomeini landed at Paris's Orly South airfield on October 4, 1978, and the two Iranians entered the country as tourists. The French police had no idea that Khomeini was arriving, and no more than a dozen or so exiles and their friends were there to meet their imam, who made a smooth pass through immigration and customs. The only ripples were between Bani Sadr and Ghotbzadeh, both of whom had separately arrived with a car in which to fetch the imam and with a place for the imam to stay — each to the complete surprise of the other. Ahmed sorted the situation out and selected Bani Sadr's arrangements. He explained to Sadegh that Bani Sadr's religious connections and reputation as an "Islamicist" would reassure the faithful back in Iran about what the imam was doing in Paris, a city synonymous with western decadence.

At the terminal curb, Khomeini was quickly bundled into the Mercedes that Bani Sadr had borrowed for the occasion. The imam himself looked a little shriveled and lost, according to Sadegh, "like a fish out of water." Ghotbzadeh declined the offer to ride along with his spiritual father and his rival, and instead traveled behind them in a borrowed Peugeot as they all caravanned through Paris to Bani Sadr's residence in the suburbs.

Back in Tehran, the shah summoned the American ambassador to discuss the imam's move.

"He told . . . me that once the Ayatollah got to Paris," Sullivan remembered, "he would fade from public view and probably never be heard from again."

PART TWO

DOWNFALL

· 6 ·

———————

THANKS TO A BELATED WARNING FROM AMBAS- sador William Sullivan, President Jimmy Carter finally learned on November 2, 1978, that the shah might actually fall.

It was now almost ten months to the day since the Iranian Revolution began, and heretofore, while the cables from Sullivan had detailed the shah's difficulties, they had given no hint that His Imperial Majesty's rule was truly in jeopardy. Indeed, the ambassador had often sounded like a Pahlavi cheerleader, always reassuring those following his cable traffic that the situation was well in hand and required no more than adjustments to His Majesty's customary approach. The past two months of almost constant street fighting and demonstrations had, however, proved impossible to dismiss or even gloss over.

Sullivan's sudden reversal of perspective took Carter and his national security adviser from the blind side, to say the least. "Our intelligence as late as the fall of 1978 was predicting political continuity in Iran," Zbigniew Brzezinski remembered with some bitterness. "So was our Ambassador." As a consequence, there had yet to be any of what Brzezinski called "high-level" meetings on Iran at the White House, the step that effectively anointed any situation a "crisis."

The Thursday, November 2 cable that changed all that was highly classified and circulated only among what one NSC aide called "the inner circle of foreign policy decision makers." It arrived in Washington that morning, and shortly thereafter, Brzezinski took it to the Oval Office to show Jimmy Carter.

The shah was clearly losing heart, Sullivan reported, and his days just might be numbered. In their most recent meeting on Wednesday evening, November 1, His Imperial Majesty had admitted for the very first time that he was thinking about "abdication." HIM also said that at the very least, he was considering replacing his ineffective civilian government, naming an army general prime minister, and supplementing martial law by instituting direct control of all the government's policies and ministries by the military. The situation was critical, and Sullivan asked Washington for "guidance." And he insisted he needed a response to his request within forty-eight hours.

The fuse that would eventually detonate a political bomb under Jimmy Carter's presidency was now lit, and from the beginning, Carter's policy for dealing with it was marked by division and dispute between the two men whose fiefs overlapped the issue.

Brzezinski occupied one pole of that split and sounded the White House alarm as soon as he read Sullivan's secret message. In Brzezinski's judgment, the fate of the shah now officially required "interagency attention under NSC control," so at 6:00 p.m. Zbig convened the Special Coordinating Committee, the administration's primary "crisis management" mechanism, to deal with it.

The SCC occupied the fault line between the State Department's and National Security Council's jurisdictions and, over the next two years of Iranian policy struggles, would become a very familiar venue, with Brzezinski and Cyrus Vance its principal intramural combatants. The creation of the SCC in Brzezinski's initial reorganization of the White House's national security operation not quite two years earlier had been the source of one of the first major conflicts between the two men. At the time, Brzezinski had proposed a committee composed of the secretaries of state and defense, the director of central intelligence, the chairman of the Joint Chiefs, and the vice president, all under his own chairmanship. The membership list and Brzezinski's role as chair were all acceptable to Vance, as was the arrangement for others in the government to attend when the subject required them. What

Cy had objected to was that the reports of SCC meetings and the actual language of directives discussed were transmitted directly to President Carter by Brzezinski, with no prior review by other committee members of what was being reported. That meant Brzezinski was, in effect, acting as an intermediary between the president and the secretary of state, and that was, according to Vance, "unacceptable."

But Cy had accepted it anyway. These were the first days of the administration, and he likely felt it necessary to start with goodwill, so he gave ground. By November 2, 1978, when the future of Iran landed in the committee's lap, he had begun to regret it. "I made a serious mistake in not going to the mat [and] insisting that the draft memoranda be sent to the principals before they went to the President," he remembered. "The summaries [Brzezinski wrote] often did not reflect adequately the complexity of the discussion or the full range of participating views. . . . Sometimes, when the summaries or PDs [Presidential Directives] — with the President's marginal notes, or his initials and signature — arrived . . . at the State Department by White House courier (often marked for my "eyes only"), I found discrepancies, occasionally serious ones, from my recollection of what had been said, agreed, or recommended."

The conflict between Brzezinski and Vance, though never personal, was already out in the open before the issue of Iran even came up. It usually involved the issue of force or dealing with the communists, in Russia, China, or elsewhere, and featured Brzezinski looking to exert pressure and Vance looking for a way to work things out. And, according to one of Vance's assistants, "Brzezinski . . . never accepted a defeat as final or a policy as decided if it did not please him. Like a rat terrier, he would shake himself off after a losing encounter and begin nipping at Vance's ankles, using his press spokesman and chief deputies as well as himself to tell the world that he had won or that only he, Zbigniew Brzezinski, hung tough in the national security game as a foreign policy realist. Vance would refuse to engage and would order his aides not to reply."

The usual currency in this ongoing sniping took the form of leaks to the media. "Brzezinski's office was leaking stuff against Cy every day," one member of the SCC recalled. "I mean every day." And when leaked against in return, Brzezinski was merciless. "Let a refutation of Brzezinski's view appear in the press," Vance's assistant claimed, "and loud, piercing shrieks emanated from the White House. Four, five, and six times a day, Brzezinski would be on the phone to Vance, demanding that he find and fire the leakers, who dared malign the President's adviser; the State Department cabal must be crushed and silenced; an attack on Brzezinski was the same as an attack on the President."

The very first SCC meeting about Iran, like the hundreds to come, was held in the Situation Room — a windowless rectangle in the bowels of the White House, lined with elm paneling, softly lit, and furnished with a single table and ten chairs. To gain a little leverage, Brzezinski had visited the president and articulated his own position before attending the conclave. The national security adviser told his boss that he was prepared to support a military government under the shah because "the situation called for decisive action to restore order and his own authority." Vance could not attend this first meeting in the Situation Room and sent his deputy, Warren Christopher, in his stead. Christopher, a California lawyer who would later serve as secretary of state in the Clinton administration, was cut from much the same cloth as Vance. The State Department's preparation paper for the meeting, of which Zbig had managed to secure an advance copy, called for a series of concessions by the shah instead of handing governance over to the army. Christopher argued that a military government would never be able to address the fundamental problems that were generating the unrest. Brzezinski eventually held sway by leaving the room to speak to the president on the phone, then returning and invoking the president's desire to express unequivocal support for His Imperial Majesty, without getting into the details of just how the shah should act in the immediate moment.

The ensuing "guidance" was sent out to Sullivan the next morning, under Brzezinski's signature. "On the highest authority," it read, "and with Cy Vance's concurrence, you are instructed to tell the Shah as soon as possible":

1. The United States supports him without reservation in the present crisis.
2. We have confidence in the Shah's judgment regarding the specific decisions that may be needed concerning the form and composition of [his] government; we also recognize the need for decisive action and leadership to restore order. . . .
3. That once order and authority have been restored we hope that he will resume prudent efforts to promote liberalization and to eradicate corruption.

To make sure the message got across, Zbig also secured the president's permission to call the shah personally, before he had even talked with Sullivan, and reassure His Imperial Majesty of American support. *Whatever* he wished to do was all right by the United States. One reason Brzezinski made the phone call to the shah was that he had no faith that Ambassador Sullivan would ever accurately communicate a message at odds with his own preferences. And Zbig wasn't alone in that conclusion. After the "inner circle of foreign policy decision makers" considered "guidance" for Sullivan to take to the shah, they also discussed whether or not the thirty-one-year State Department veteran was up to the job he had been given. The ambassador's chief defender was Cy Vance — not because they were close or because Vance had particular confidence in Sullivan, but because Sullivan was one of his, and by this point Vance bridled instinctively whenever Brzezinski attacked anyone at State.

In the discussion about the ambassador, Vice President Walter Mondale asked Vance directly if Sullivan was the right man to have in Tehran.

"He is a good man," Vance answered. "He's been in some hard spots."

Mondale was noted around the administration as a quick wit. He now raised a wry eyebrow at mention of the "spots" Sullivan had been in. The ambassador had left those previous postings with no small amount of political wreckage in his wake.

"He lost all of them, didn't he?" the vice president noted with something of a sarcastic chuckle. No one in the room had to add the punch line that William Sullivan might well be about to "lose" yet one more.

Two days after Brzezinski called the shah with the SCC's advice, spontaneous arson squads, acting under no central direction but professing loyalty to the imam and the Revolution, began laying waste to Tehran. They mostly attacked banks, but also targeted cinemas and liquor stores. In their standard pattern, the mobs began by breaking into the first floor of a building and gathering furniture and other flammables in a central room or foyer while everyone inside was given time to evacuate. Then the pile was doused with gas and the building torched. Soon locations all around the city were in flames. Cars were turned over and set on fire, as were piles of tires. All of this was punctuated with staccato bursts of machine gun fire as groups of soldiers fired warning shots, scattering mobs that then reformed a few blocks away. By noon, the city was shrouded with acrid smoke. It looked as though a battle had taken place.

Sullivan's military attaché was able to call an Iranian army officer he knew and secure an infantry detachment to protect the embassy, so the mobs waving torches and shouting *"Marg bar shah"* never got closer than two blocks away. Just beyond that cordon, however, a twelve-story building burned like a candle all afternoon before finally collapsing across the street in a heap. The Brits weren't so lucky or so well protected. A mob stormed their embassy's gates and, after allowing all the personnel to evacuate the chancery building, lit the structure on fire.

Late in the afternoon, just as the madness seemed to be ebbing somewhat, William Sullivan got a call from the imperial palace. The shah wished to see him immediately. The ambassador promised to get there as soon as he could.

Sullivan next consulted a network of demonstration watchers the embassy had established around the city. They reported that the way to the palace was somewhat clear, so, a half hour after the shah's call, Sullivan boarded his armor-plated Chrysler limo, from which the diplomatic plates had been stripped as a security precaution, and ventured out into the darkening city. Signs of battle were everywhere, but the ambassador's driver knew his way and steered around possible confrontations, encountering no mobs on the journey. As usual, the palace was surrounded by a line of huge Chieftain battle tanks and Imperial Guard troops in strong points protected by machine guns and antiaircraft weapons. The ambassador, a familiar figure who visited the shah at least every two or three days, was waved into the palace driveway.

The palace itself was eerily deserted. Usually the shah's front door was manned by a doorman, but the doorman was nowhere to be seen, so Sullivan tried the latch and, finding it unlocked, entered the lobby. Usually an aide-de-camp was stationed here, but the aide too was nowhere to be seen. The same was true in the main drawing room. While Sullivan was trying to puzzle out what to do next, the shahbanou walked in and was startled to find him there. When he explained that the shah had summoned him, Farah went off and found an aide. The aide brought the ambassador up to His Imperial Majesty's study.

There, Sullivan found the shah "strangely calm." He had been for a helicopter ride over the city from which he'd only just returned, somewhat stunned at the sight of Tehran aflame. He told Sullivan that "destruction was everywhere."

Then the shah got right to the point. He now had no choice, he told the ambassador. He had to establish a military government. This was just too much.

Despite Brzezinski's previous declarations over the phone, the shah still "asked whether I could quickly ascertain whether Washington would support him in this move," Sullivan recalled. "I told him that I had already anticipated this request and had received Washington's assurance that he would be supported in this action by the President and the United States government."

The shah seemed "enormously relieved" and called for his aide to fetch the ambassador a glass of scotch.

As they relaxed, the shah said he had summoned the British ambassador as well. Sullivan allowed that the Brit's tardiness would be understandable given what had happened to the British chancery building.

Assuming a quizzical expression, the shah asked what had happened to the chancery and was surprised to learn from Sullivan that it had been torched.

That, the shah responded, would explain why the British ambassador had requested an escort of armored personnel carriers to pick him up at the French embassy, where he was apparently stuck.

While they waited for the Brit, the shah and Ambassador Sullivan made small talk, much of it devoted to how annoyed the shah was at the BBC for what its Farsi-language broadcasts were saying about HIM. This was, the shah observed, part of the Brits' long-standing grudge left over from 1953.

The shah also spoke twice on the phone while Sullivan remained in the room. The first call was with the shahbanou. "I could make out that he was telling her of his intention to install a military government," Sullivan remembered, "and answering some of the reservations she was expressing about such a decision. It was a gentle, patient sort of conversation with nothing peremptory in its tone. He informed her at the end that the United States government had agreed with the wisdom of this course of action."

After hanging up with Farah, His Imperial Majesty called the army's chief of staff and summoned him to the palace immediately. Though the chief of staff didn't yet know it, he was about to be named prime minister.

In the meantime, the British ambassador finally arrived with his armored personnel carrier escort. The shah informed him of the coming military government and apologized profusely for what had happened to the chancery. Then Sullivan and his Brit counterpart left the palace together. On their way down the front steps, they passed the chief of staff going the other way. As Sullivan remembered it, the general looked "anything but power hungry."

The next day, November 6, having informed the Americans and the British of his decision, the shah went on national television to inform everyone else. It had been several months since his last such public appearance, and this speech would end up being the last time Mohammad Reza Pahlavi ever addressed Iran as its reigning monarch. One NSC staffer described the effort as "almost pathetic."

While the occasion was the announcement of a "stern" new approach that was designed to scare the crowds out of the streets and reestablish "order," the shah was instead overwhelmed by his need to be loved by his subjects and decided to reach out to "his" people and play his self-appointed role as the fount of the Iranian national identity. The resulting apologetic tone, often couched in the royal "we," made him come off like a jilted lover begging to be taken back.

"In the climate of Liberalization which began gradually two years ago," the shah told his audience from the palace, looking into the camera as he had been coached, "you arose against oppression and corruption. . . . The waves of strikes, most of which were quite justified, have lately changed in their nature and direction, causing the country's economy and the people's daily lives to be paralyzed. . . . We exerted all our efforts to establish the rule of law and order and peace by trying to form [a civilian government] but we [now] had to appoint a caretaker government. . . .

"I am aware of the possibility that past mistakes and oppressions will be repeated. . . . But I promise that [they] won't be repeated. . . . I guarantee that after the military government, freedom and the Constitution will be freely reimplemented. . . . I commit myself to make up for past mistakes, to fight corruption and injustices and to form a national government to carry out free elections. . . . The revolution of the Iranian nation cannot but be endorsed by me both as the Monarch and an individual Iranian. . . . In this revolution of the Iranian nation against colonialism, tyranny and corruption, I am at your side. . . . I am the guardian of the constitutional monarchy, which is a God-given gift, a gift entrusted to the shah by the people."

Iran's reaction to his address was quickly apparent. "Yesterday's fires [still] smolder," the embassy reported to Washington in the first hours after the shah's speech, "and a few new fires may have been started. . . . Shooting, including tank, machine gun fire — mainly in the air it seems — is reported in the southern end of the city." And that was just in Tehran. "Tabriz reports situation heating up, with large crowds gathering again," the telex resumed within twenty-four hours of the inception of military government. "Telephone report from . . . near Dezful indicates armed farmers are attacking some bridges in area. . . . Large [pro-shah] demonstration in Zanjan, accompanied by soldiers, which competed with [anti-shah] demonstration. Large [anti-shah] demonstrations also occurred in Mashad. . . . Only reported disturbance today was group who tried this morning to change name of Shahyad monument to Khomeini monument. They were dispersed by troops. . . . Projected confrontation between students and military at Tehran University appears likely. . . . Disturbances are reported in several provincial cities, including one death in Kashan. . . . Students at Tehran University tore down statue of Shah which stood at entrance to campus. . . . American-owned automobile was firebombed in Isfahan. . . . Serious clash in Mashad yesterday afternoon . . . reportedly left number of dead (though official admission is only two or three)."

The military government's failure to subdue the situation was largely on the shah's account. The first promise the military government made was that anyone violating the martial law prohibition on demonstrations would be shot, and the government had to live up to this promise if it was to stand a chance of making any headway. When His Majesty's troops confronted these mobs out in the street, they needed to be able to fire into the crowds and make it clear they weren't talking through their hats.

The shah, however, insisted that they operate on a self-defense-only footing and continue to fire into the air if at all possible. He was the shah, the troops were "his" troops, and these were "his" people. Firing would only be permitted in situations of extreme danger. One of his commanders even threw himself at his sovereign's feet and, weeping, begged to be allowed to do more, but the shah still refused. "The instructions I gave were always the same," HIM later remembered. "Do the impossible [in order] to avoid bloodshed." He expressed the belief that only "tyrants" killed their subjects and he was no tyrant — conveniently ignoring the thousands who had already died at the hands of his agents.

The day after the shah named his army chief of staff as prime minister, Ambassador Sullivan went by the prime minister's office at the new occupant's request. When he arrived, Sullivan was ushered into a small side room off the regular office, dark except for the light of a dim bulb.

The new prime minister was in there, lying on a bed, having suffered a mild heart attack during his first twenty-four hours in office. The prime minister motioned for the ambassador to come closer. A loud whisper was all he could muster in the current moment. Sullivan bent his ear over the bed.

"The shah will not permit me to use military force," the prime minister told Sullivan, "and if I cannot use military force, this country cannot survive. You'd better tell that to your government."

Ambassador Sullivan did so in a cable dispatched on November 9. It marked the first time anyone among the upper reaches of the American chain of command broached the question of what to do if the shah actually fell. "This military government . . . represented the shah's last chance for survival," the ambassador explained. "If it failed to restore law and order . . . the success of the revolution, I felt, was inevitable and we should face the consequences of that."

The November 9 message was headlined "Thinking the Unthinkable." Sullivan described it as an examination of "some options that we have never before considered relevant."

According to Sullivan, the two principal political forces that had to be accounted for in the situation were the "military" and the "religious." Though they were currently in conflict, the ambassador expected the two would eventually have to "reach an accommodation" that would no doubt include the shah's abdication "in favor of an Islamic Republic." Sullivan's cable constructed a possible scenario for maintaining American interests in such an eventuality. The scenario began with the imam's return to Iran, as part of his accommodation with the military. There, it was expected he would assume a "Gandhi-like" position of spiritual elevation. "While it is difficult to predict the sort of government that might emerge . . . there would be reasons to hope that it would maintain Iran's general international orientation. . . . It would probably be a Kuwait writ large. . . . Although US involvement would be less intimate than with the shah, it could be . . . essentially satisfactory . . . particularly if the military preserves both its integrity and its status as one of the pillars of the nation."

But, Sullivan cautioned, "all of this rather Pollyannish scenario could come about only if every step along the way turned out well. Any single misstep anywhere could destroy it and lead to unpredictable consequences. Therefore, [this cable] should not, repeat, *not* be interpreted as this Embassy's prediction of future events."

Nor, according to the ambassador, was this cable a proposed change in strategy. He reiterated that "our current posture of trusting that the Shah, together with the military, will be able to face down the Khomeini threat is obviously the only safe course to pursue at this juncture."

When Sullivan's cable reached Jimmy Carter, the president scribbled off longhand notes to both Vance and Brzezinski, as well as Harold Brown, the secretary of defense, and Stansfield Turner, director of Central Intelligence, chastising the failure of American intelligence and demanding to know why he hadn't been told before that things were this bad with the shah.

For his part, Brzezinski agreed with Sullivan that the ambassador's cable was indeed a "Pollyanna prospect" and would mock Sullivan's characterization of Khomeini's projected "Gandhi-like" role for months to come. The national security adviser would also spend much of that time denying that the situation was as irretrievable as Sullivan and Vance's "Vietnam syndrome" crew over at the State Department thought.

William Sullivan himself, however, never received any response at all from Washington to his November 9 cable. The deafening silence on the other end of the line convinced the ambassador that the situation was slipping away. The president and his advisers, he concluded, had their heads in the sand. To the ambassador's way of thinking, that left but one option. Sullivan, chain of command or not, would have to save the American interest in Iran on his own.

· 7 ·

———

$\mathcal{F}$OR AYATOLLAH RUHOLLAH KHOMEINI, ONLY one more short exile remained before realizing the central dream of his adult life.

Nevertheless, France was an enormous adjustment for a seventy-seven-year-old who had never before been farther from Iran than Istanbul. Khomeini took refuge in a moment of denial riding in from the airport that first night — slumped far enough down in the seat so he couldn't look out the windows and see where he was. Suffering from jet lag and culture shock, the leader of the Iranian Revolution then spent his first few days in Paris holed up in Abolhassan Bani Sadr's small apartment, still unwilling to venture out and wishing he had been able to flee to a place much closer to Mecca.

But more appropriate housing was found quickly, in Neauphle-le-Château, a leafy village out among the spreading chestnuts and luxuriant flowers in the countryside on the west edge of Paris. And there, the imam began to adjust. Khomeini's rented compound was often described as a small "villa" and consisted of two nondescript white stucco buildings with chocolate-colored shutters at the bottom of a hill, facing each other across a road. To accommodate the imam, the toilet in his living quarters had to be changed to a Turkish style — he wouldn't use a European model — and the large reception space had to be partitioned so Batul and the other women would have their own room in which to retreat from male company. A large blue-and-white-striped tent was also erected on the property to serve as a makeshift mosque at which the Grand Ayatollah Khomeini could conduct prayers. It, like the reception room, was bare save for several worn carpets underfoot. At times, the imam also sat on a rug spread beneath an apple tree in the yard.

Before settling in, however, Khomeini had to deal with the French police, who were very embarrassed and very angry. They had been caught totally unawares by the imam's arrival and only learned of it when they read the newspaper accounts of a press conference by Ahmed the day after his father's entry, announcing that the grand ayatollah was in town to visit "the renowned Islamicist" Abolhassan Bani Sadr. Those responsible for the police's intelligence breakdown immediately questioned the legality of Khomeini's entry. Christian Bourguet, a prominent French human rights attorney as well as next-door neighbor and close friend of Sadegh Ghotbzadeh, handled the negotiations with the immigration ministry. Bourguet and his wife had been involved with the Iranian exiles since his inspection of the shah's legal system for an international lawyers committee in the early 1970s. He had also helped Sadegh translate the imam's speeches into French.

"Someone from the ministry got in touch with me," the attorney remembered, "and he played it really hard-ass. At first, they were insisting Khomeini leave immediately. They were caught with their pants down and had no idea he was coming and they didn't even know he was here until he was already walking around in Paris. So the police wrote a false report, claiming Khomeini had been smuggled into France in the trunk of a car from Belgium. I straightened it out, but we were eventually warned that Khomeini couldn't spread any inflammatory messages while he was in France and he couldn't stay longer than three and a half months."

As it turned out, that was almost all the time the imam would need.

The stucco houses in Neauphle-le-Château were beehives of activity within a few weeks of the imam's taking up residence. From inside the building set aside for a headquarters, according to one journalist's account, the ayatollah "bombarded Iran with his taped messages as his aides kept the telephone and telex lines to Tehran constantly busy." A nearby audiotape production

facility agreed to put aside all its other contracts and manufacture a huge order of the imam's sermons for shipment to Iran. To provide security, a squad
of fifty Iranians had been flown in and, with French permission, were armed
with light weapons when on duty. The security detail's only serious concern
for the duration of Khomeini's stay was an ice cream van spotted cruising
the neighborhood on a number of occasions. The imam's guards concluded
it was a CIA listening post.

Seemingly oblivious to much of that, the imam rose at his customary 2:00
a.m. and began his day with four hours of prayer. Then he napped briefly, ate
his goat cheese breakfast, and spent the morning in audiences. One of those
meetings was always with Bani Sadr, who briefed the imam each day on
what was going on back in Iran and elsewhere in the world. The imam often
met with Ghotbzadeh as well. In the middle of the day, he broke for a lunch
of bread and gravy. He led prayers in the afternoon and also, breaking with
his previous policy, he now talked personally on the phone, usually at length
with his chief lieutenants in Qom and Tehran. Often he also addressed his
followers, usually around sunset from under the apple tree out in the yard.
Then he had a dinner consisting of two slices of toast, yogurt, raisins, and
nuts. The imam was usually off to bed at 11:30 p.m.

By November, Neauphle-le-Château was a frequent dateline in the international press, and upwards of a hundred reporters and cameramen regularly
waited for the grand ayatollah to appear. "Noffal," as the Iranians named the
village, also became an instant destination for Shiite pilgrims. Altogether,
over his three and a half months in France, the ayatollah would give 132 interviews and greet more than a hundred thousand Iranians who would leave
behind over $35 million in donations for his cause.

In retrospect, perhaps the most remarkable aspect of the imam's Paris
performance was just how "on message" he remained throughout it all. That
consistency and discipline allowed the old mullah to defy all His Imperial
Majesty's predictions and flourish in the sudden glare of international attention, projecting a largely benign presence to all concerned. In practice,
Sadegh Ghotbzadeh, Abolhassan Bani Sadr, and a couple other exile organizers were as much responsible for this as the imam himself. They formed
the committee that played ventriloquist to Khomeini's dummy from the
moment his plane landed in Orly.

"He was scripted," Bani Sadr remembered. "Just like Ronald Reagan. We
told him what to say and he memorized it and recited it verbatim. . . . He
was unsure of himself, which is why he repeated whatever he was told. . . .

Khomeini was like an exiled chieftain, a pope barred from the Vatican. . . . In Paris [at first] he did not think it possible to overthrow the Shah. Two or three times a week I reassured him by telling him that the Shah was going to relinquish power. . . . We [also] had to formulate an ideology [for him] worthy of a revolution. . . . Our work was meticulous and the answers we prepared [for Khomeini to tell reporters] were carefully thought out. We chose as our reference that period of the Prophet's life when the basic values were founded on the principle of equality among men, which presupposes democratic process and participation . . . under a republican system. . . . [Khomeini] promised to respect . . . an Islam that teaches . . . independence, democracy, tolerance, and progress."

For most of the imam's 132 interviews and a myriad of other press events, the media's questions were submitted in advance and the exiles' task force constructed their answers, which Khomeini would then commit to memory. Recalled Bani Sadr, "We . . . prepared a nineteen-point political platform and I carefully explained to Khomeini that he had to adhere to it if he wanted to preserve his credibility. Elaborating on it or digressing from it could cost him his reputation and his future. He understood this and his political life began. . . . He owed everything to the revolutionary program and those who developed it. Imagine him left to his fate in Paris; in no time, he would have been saying anything that came into his head. [And] the revolution might have continued without him."

The carefully crafted image played well with both the western press and the Revolution back home. "To the liberals," one historian would later note, "he was a man fighting a dictatorship and calling for the people's right to choose the government. The Left loved him for his demands for 'justice and equity' and 'an end to exploitation.' The conservatives saw in him a champion of tradition against the hasty and harmful innovations of the Pahlavis. Since everyone assumed that Khomeini and the other mullahs would return to their mosques once the Shah was overthrown, Iran's future was depicted by almost every faction as one of democratic development and pluralistic politics."

Indeed, Khomeini was so good at staying with his script that it worried Bani Sadr and eventually prompted him to confront the imam about his sincerity.

Are you just going to say this here and then repudiate it when we are back in Iran? Bani Sadr asked straight out. Are you just deceiving the rest of us?

No, no, Khomeini insisted. He would always honor anything he said. He was a man of his word. He kept his commitments.

Abolhassan Bani Sadr, Sadegh Ghotbzadeh, and the rest of the committee believed him.

In the meantime, back in Tehran, the paramount secret continued to be the one being held by His Imperial Majesty.

The shah's French doctors still commuted regularly from Paris to monitor his condition, and thus far the purpose of their visits had remained undiscovered. There were, however, several close calls. On one occasion, one of the shah's ministers almost stumbled over the truth. He had to see the shah over some pressing business and was ushered into an office anteroom, where he found His Imperial Majesty in bed, weak, pale, and, the minister was told, suffering from a bout of "the flu." Their business was quickly done, and on the way out, the minister almost bumped into some strangers, talking to each other in French and hauling some equipment into the shah's office. He assumed they were TV technicians setting up for an interview, though it did strike him as odd that the shah would be talking to the press while sick in bed.

The diagnosis reached on that camouflaged visit, like all the others his French physicians undertook that fall, was that the shah's condition was "stable." The chlorambucil, which the shah now took religiously, was containing his lymphoma.

Just as important, his secret had also not spread. The Americans were, according to Ambassador Sullivan, "aware that [the shah] took constant medication," but the medication they knew about was the Valium HIM nibbled on throughout the day, and neither Sullivan nor his government yet had even a hint that His Imperial Majesty was also being treated with mild chemotherapy. Even the shah's twin sister, Ashraf, didn't know, and when His Majesty's own eighty-seven-year-old mother was diagnosed earlier in the year with the same disease as he and her doctor asked if there was any other history of lymphoma in the family, the shah said nothing.

The only person actually in on the secret besides his doctors was, of course, Farah, his wife. But even with her, the shah confided little of his feelings about his disease. "We talked a great deal about His Majesty's illness," she remembered. "But he played the game as if I didn't know [that his illness was actually cancer], while I pretended not to know what was wrong. It was a strange game: sweet and sour, tender and painful at the same time."

While the shah struggled, Farah did her best to bolster him. She praised her husband's inclination not to use the army to attempt to simply stamp out the opposition. She too ignored his previous history and declared that such behavior was beneath a monarch. She also tried to help him craft a political response to his troubles, conducting her imperial duties and making widely publicized pilgrimages to the birthplaces of the imams Ali and Husein in an attempt to defuse the religious frenzy in advance of Muharram. She put the shah in contact with a circle of intellectuals she had cultivated, hoping they might provide him the guidance he needed, even though he had always scorned such men as the dregs of public policy. She even offered to stay behind in Iran to try to save the dynasty while the shah fled, but he would hear none of it.

His wife's nurturing often buoyed His Imperial Majesty's spirits, but nothing she did could alter his appearance, and that almost gave his secret away despite all his other efforts at concealment. By November the shah had lost a full quarter of his former body weight, and his clothes hung off him in loose bunches while his neck swam inside his previously snug shirt collars. His trademark tan was faded, and his skin looked like paste.

Secretary of the treasury Michael Blumenthal, who had last visited His Majesty during 1977, returned to Tehran in November 1978 and found the contrast with the shah's previous visage of majesty and self-assurance stunning. The secretary described the current HIM as a "ghost" of his former self. The shah's voice was shaky, and he spent much of their conversation in long silences during which he stared glassy-eyed at the floor. As he often did with international visitors, he repeated that he "didn't know what to do" and had no idea "what they want me to do." Otherwise, he had little cogent to say.

When Blumenthal returned to Washington, he immediately went by Zbigniew Brzezinski's office.

"You've got a zombie out there," he warned the national security adviser.

Nonetheless, in the middle of November, the shah shook off his paralysis and took his first steps toward living up to his televised promise to "correct the mistakes" of his regime.

The shahanshah's initial move was to announce that his new military government was launching an investigation into the royal family's own business dealings. The avarice of Mohammad Reza Pahlavi's relatives was, by this time, legendary. One of his sisters, Princess Fatimah, had amassed a fortune of some $500 million, much of it in the form of "commissions" extracted from military contractors by her husband, the commanding general of Iran's air force. Another sister, Shams, and his twin, Ashraf, were both linked to huge fortunes as well, some of which were reportedly amassed in the opium trade and the rest accumulated, again, through "commissions." It had been a standard operating procedure for anyone seeking to complete a business deal in Iran to recruit a Pahlavi to assist them, paying for that privilege with either stock or outright cash, and the Pahlavis were extraordinarily rich as a consequence. Eventually the Iranian government would accuse the royals of making off with over $70 billion.

The largest single visible repository of that royal fortune was the "charitable" Pahlavi Foundation, which controlled billions of dollars' worth of assets, including cement factories, hotels, sugar mills, the largest Iranian insurance company, 15 percent of the Iranian banking industry, and a full quarter of Iran's arable land. One of the shah's trusted financial intermediaries later testified in a British court that "the shah set up the Pahlavi fund to receive bribes." The foundation was widely used as a funding source by the hundreds of royal family members, though by law its proceeds were supposed to be spent on the poor. When the military government announced its investigation, the shah pledged that the Pahlavi Foundation's books would be opened to public scrutiny, let the chips fall where they might. "This suggests," Ambassador William Sullivan observed in a cable to Washington, "a sensitivity bordering on panic in his effort to placate critics." And, though the ambassador didn't say so, it also suggested a ruler trying desperately to shift the blame and save himself in the process.

The investigation's most immediate effect was to send the Pahlavis who remained in the country dashing for the exits. Within days of the announcement, sixty-four members of the royal family — including the shah's brothers, his sisters, and his in-laws — fled. By the middle of November, the only Pahlavis left in Iran were the shah, the shahbanou, and some of their children.

Next, His Imperial Majesty struck at the corruption practiced by his court and cronies — a phenomenon even more legendary than that of the royals. One of the courtiers who had pimped for the shah had a monopoly on helicopter purchases and reportedly skimmed close to $100 million off the government's $500 million deal for several hundred surplus American helicopters. Another crony who helped the shah develop Kish Island was allowed to take tens of millions out in consulting contracts. A health minister made huge sums reselling opium seized by the government from lesser smugglers, as well as embezzling hospital construction funds. The general who was in charge of Iranian preparations to host the 1974 Asian Games skimmed millions out of the effort, including putting his son on salary at $500,000 a year. The practice was of epidemic proportions. "In one deal I know of," a foreign banker remembered, "eight people received bribes [each] involving sums which I would not make in several years." Most analysts believed that the shah used such corruption as a means of buying loyalty.

In any case, that practice was officially ended with a wave of November arrests by the new military government, followed by a second wave and then another. Several of those targeted fled the country before they were seized and at least one escaped by committing suicide. In the end, eighteen former ministers and an equal number of former civil service officers were arrested and either thrown into prison or placed under detention in their own homes. At the top of the list was a man who had served as the shah's prime minister and then court minister for some thirteen years, almost right up to the time of his arrest. Also arrested was a former head of SAVAK, who had been handpicked for his job by the shah and had held it for fifteen years. Almost all of those the shah ordered arrested had once been among His Majesty's closest associates.

The shah pointed to these arrests as proof of his revolutionary intentions, but few Iranians accepted it as such. "Iranians have become so cynical about . . . corruption," the *Washington Post* noted, "that only public executions for the guilty seem likely to persuade them that Shah Mohammad Reza Pahlavi is serious about his promised crackdown on wrongdoers." In the meantime, the move only served to convince those loyalists of the shah who still remained that the situation was now "every man for himself."

The shah's obvious desperation also convinced Ambassador Sullivan to stop waiting for Washington to see the writing on the wall.

Without instructions, the ambassador began actively pursuing contact with the Liberation Movement of Iran and its Islamic allies, whose overture he had ignored two months earlier. This was a clear violation of the long-standing deal between His Imperial Majesty and the United States, but Sullivan unilaterally jettisoned that understanding with few second thoughts. The Islamic organizers were now reluctant to talk, but by late November, the American ambassador had met with at least one high-ranking mullah in the imam's organization. The outcome was only a conversation, but even that was unprecedented, as was the fact that Sullivan failed to inform the shah of what he'd done.

The ambassador was convinced that the United States would soon need to arrange a reconciliation between the religious uprising and the army, as he had already proposed to the White House's deaf ears. This, he hoped, would salvage the American position in Iran, allowing the United States to survive the coming transition with a relationship intact, preserve the American interest, and put a suitable crown on the end of his own diplomatic career.

Though unaware of Sullivan's secret contacts, Brzezinski was already quite open with his feelings that he and America's representative to the Peacock Throne were at cross-purposes. "Instead of strengthening the Shah's morale," Brzezinski complained, "our Ambassador . . . contributed to his indecision by diluting our urgings that the Shah act."

In response, the national security adviser had begun sidestepping Sullivan's bottleneck by dispatching his own emissaries to Tehran to provide the NSC with independent reporting, as well as a direct back channel to the shah.

The first of those emissaries was an American businessman who had once been the CIA's Tehran station chief and whose company was now seeking a very lucrative contract from the shah's teetering government. The businessman met with His Imperial Majesty on November 14. The shah began by again expressing his appreciation of the national security adviser's previous phone call but still seemed suspicious of what the Americans were up to. He noted that Hamilton Jordan, the president's right-hand man, had commented on a television talk show recently that the United States had to consider "all possible contingencies" in Iran. The shah wondered out loud whether that meant the Americans were preparing to "adopt" his opposition. When His Majesty went on to assess how the situation had become so dire, the emissary reported to Brzezinski that the shah found recent events "baffling, incomprehensible, and almost overwhelming," and voiced suspicions that the Brits and the CIA might well be behind the crisis.

Sullivan had been informed of the businessman's mission ahead of time and provided the emissary with the full services of the embassy, but sent off a complaint to Brzezinski afterward, questioning the propriety of using someone seeking a large contract from the shah to deliver messages from the White House. At this point, according to Sullivan, Washington's antagonism toward him emerged into the open. "Brzezinski," he remembered, "sent back a sharp, tart report suggesting that what the Administration chose to do was none of my business. I was aware from the tenor of this reply that my views were no longer held in much regard. [Henceforth,] I began to discover that any sensitive message I sent, no matter how highly classified, that digressed from the views of the National Security Council staff would appear, almost verbatim, in *The New York Times* [in an attempt to undercut my position]. I therefore had to use the secure telephone exclusively to communicate with the Department of State."

The emissaries from the White House also continued. The secretary of the treasury arrived next. He was followed by the number-three man at the CIA and then the Senate majority leader, all instructed by Brzezinski "to convey to the shah the strongest assurances of our support and to encourage him to take the action necessary to defend his throne." The treasury secretary's experience was typical. He reported to Brzezinski that the White House had better find some other option than the shah, because the shah did not seem capable of saving himself. Nonetheless, the national security adviser pressed forward with his attempts to buttress His Imperial Majesty and prod him to crush his opposition before it was too late.

The most direct vehicle for that agenda was Zbig's close relationship with Ardeshir Zahedi, the Iranian ambassador to Washington. Zahedi was the son of the general who had led the troops who ousted Mossadeq and reestablished the shah in 1953. Brzezinski wanted Zahedi to return to Tehran to push the shah toward military action. The ambassador agreed and spent much of November and December back in his homeland, speaking with the shah on a daily basis, zealously attempting to bolster the shah's resolve to repress the Revolution, and, according to Sullivan, reporting the results of those conversations to Brzezinski in the White House over an open phone line.

Sullivan visited Ambassador Zahedi at his palatial home in Tehran's northern suburbs that November, and his host opened their conversation by describing the situation in Washington in a loud conspiratorial whisper.

"Brzezinski has taken over Iran policy," Zahedi announced.

Then, according to the American ambassador, the Iranian "described how he had been summoned to the White House by Brzezinski and been told that the situation in Iran had alarmed the President, and the Shah needed to be stiffened in his resolve. . . . Brzezinski had then encouraged him to return to Tehran to inspire the Shah to take stronger measures to protect his regime. . . . When he had protested that he could not leave his embassy in Washington, Brzezinski had ushered him in to see the President, who told him that he, President Carter, would be the Iranian ambassador in Washington and that [Zahedi] should feel it was his primary duty to return to Tehran and stiffen the Shah's spine as he confronted these sharp political challenges."

While Zahedi was in Tehran, his house became the rallying point for an

Iranian faction that agreed with the American national security adviser. They were seeking the immediate arrest of perhaps as many as ten thousand "troublemakers," and in preparation for such a move, the Iranian ambassador to Washington had held long consultations with the Chilean ambassador to Washington about how Chile's dictator, General Augusto Pinochet, had succeeded with such maneuvers in his 1973 coup. Back in Tehran, some of the ambassador's allies even went so far as to draw up plans for turning various stadiums and other locations into detention camps for as many as one hundred thousand.

While most of this was going on, Secretary of State Cyrus Vance had much more on his plate than Iran — including the Strategic Arms Limitation Talks with the Russians and diplomatic recognition treaties with the Chinese, as well as the Camp David Agreements and a host of lesser demands. As a result, the secretary had largely left the management of the Iran "crisis" to his deputies. All of them were increasingly convinced that the only issue left to resolve was how to make the shah's eventual exit as graceful as possible. They also considered Brzezinski their foremost antagonist at his best, and an evil influence at his worst.

The impetus for Cy's intervention in Brzezinski's back channel came from a former assistant secretary of state who, as Vance explained it, "had come to Washington at our request to conduct a special review of the situation in Iran." From him, Vance "learned . . . that Brzezinski had opened his own direct channels to Tehran and had carried on discussions with Zahedi without the knowledge of anyone at the State Department [and thus] contributed to the Shah's confusion about where he stood."

Vance immediately went to the White House to confront the national security adviser face-to-face. "I told him," Vance remembered, "that I had heard from an impeccable source that he was communicating directly with the Iranians and that this was intolerable. He denied the accusation. I told him that I believed otherwise and that I wished him to come with me to see the President. The President met with us and I told him what I had learned. He asked Zbig if this was true. Zbig denied it. The President then asked that he be supplied with copies of all communications between the White House and Tehran. This was the last I heard of the matter, but the back-channel communications stopped."

Between Cyrus Vance and Zbigniew Brzezinski, however, the truce was only temporary.

· 8 ·

———

UNDER THE STRIPED TENT IN HIS BACKYARD OUT-
side Paris at Neauphle-le-Château, during the last week of November, the
imam issued an *elamieh,* a set of instructions for the movement in Iran to
follow during the approaching month of religious holidays.

"The holy month of Muharram," Khomeini announced, "is being anticipated with heroism, bravery, and sacrifice. [This is] the month blood will triumph over the sword, the month of the strength of the right, the month the
oppressors will be judged and the Satanic government abolished. This month
will be famous throughout history: the month that the powerful will be broken
by the word of the right, the month that the Imam of the Muslims will show
us the path of strength against the oppressors, the month the freedom fighters
and patriots will clench their fists and win against tanks and machine guns.
The Imam of the Muslims has taught us to overthrow tyrants. You should
unite, arise, and sacrifice your blood. . . . The government has been put in the
hands of anti-Muslim officials to benefit the Satanic ruler and his parasitic
henchmen and, thus, ruined the country. . . . During the month of Muharram,

when the sword is in the hands of the soldiers of Islam, the high clergy will lead the Shiites and this tree of oppression and treason will be cut down. . . . The people demand that all their forces be exerted to depose the Shah."

Among other things, the *elamieh* asked for volunteers who were prepared to martyr themselves as had the followers of Husein on the Karbala Plain thirteen centuries before. More than fifteen hundred volunteers came forward in Tehran during the message's first twenty-four hours in circulation. More than seven thousand volunteered in Qom. As a symbol of their willingness, they would all wear white burial shrouds when Muharram began with the rise of the new moon on December 1.

That evening, after the 9:00 p.m. curfew set by the shah's military government, a host of zealous Iranians took to the avenues where the shah's forces were waiting. In Tehran, the 20,000-man Imperial Guards, the 1,600-man Special Forces Brigade, a 2,200-man Artillery Group, and part of an Armored Division were all deployed against the revolt. They, like the 15,000 soldiers assigned the maintenance of domestic order and internal security in the rest of the country, could call on the Airborne Brigade and two other infantry divisions for emergency support from among the remainder of the shah's 600,000-man military assigned to external security. The domestic-order deployment seemed a huge and formidable force, though a pre-Muharram CIA analysis worried that since "junior officers and enlisted men are drawn largely from the same disadvantaged lower and lower middle class groups as are most non-student demonstrators . . . there is no certainty that they [will] obey orders to fire on demonstrators solely to protect the shah."

But, at least on the first evening of Muharram, the troops hardly hesitated.

"Thousands of Iranians poured into the streets," one western reporter recounted. "They were wrapped in symbolic white shrouds [and] surged back and forth, a sea of ghostly white bodies, like resurrected forms of the long dead. . . . Terrified, the shah's soldiers fired. White bodies crumpled and fell to the ground. Red blood covered their white shrouds." The death toll on that first night was less than a hundred according to the government, and more than a thousand according to the demonstrators.

In any case, that evening was simply prelude. The full force of the movement began being felt the next day, when crowds of protesters gathered throughout Tehran. At their base, these huge assemblages were organized in small groups, neighborhood by neighborhood, mosque by mosque. As they proceeded toward the main line of march, they flowed together in tributaries, stopping and starting, singing and chanting according to the instructions of leaders carrying bullhorns or riding in minibuses equipped with loudspeakers.

"The processions themselves were without chains and flagellation," one American embassy employee remembered, "for the emphasis was elsewhere. This was underlined when a military helicopter flew overhead and almost every fist spontaneously went into the air against it while anti-regime cadences rang out. Above all, the discipline and coordination were impressive. Food [for the marchers] was distributed from trucks, ambulances waited for emergencies and coins were handed out for people to invite their friends by telephone to join the crowds. . . . Even the chanting of 'Death to the Puppet Shah' was orchestrated and seemed matched to the obscene references to President Carter scrawled in paint over walls."

Organized or otherwise, outbursts cropped up everywhere, touching everyone, day after day as Muharram progressed. "Violent confrontations with heavy firing in at least five sections of [Tehran]," the embassy reported.

> Govt announced 7 killed, 26 wounded, over 100 arrested. Source in position to know says figure may be substantially higher. . . . Heavy firing from . . . beginning of curfew. . . . Armor also heard moving in northeastern Tehran. . . . Crowds had broken out of most sizable mosques in south Tehran and were engaged in confrontation with military. . . . Large peaceful march took place in Mashad. . . . Tabriz reports quiet with all shops closed. . . .
>
> Rumors abound regarding huge numbers of dead and wounded. . . . Isfahan reports considerable violence . . . with shooting in at least eight locations. Loudspeakers on one building called for holy war against the regime. People on roof threw projectiles on soldiers. . . . In apparent ambush, one crowd pursued by troops ran into mosque, whereupon men stationed on roof threw down heavy concrete blocks onto soldiers. . . . A number of bodies were brought to hospitals. . . . Firebombs were thrown yesterday into office of Ford [Motor Company] subsidiary. . . .
>
> We believe present lull is merely brief resting period and that massive disturbances will take place as Ashura draws near.

On the latter, everyone was agreed. Ashura, the tenth and holiest day of Muharram, would be the Revolution's biggest moment yet.

*   *   *

During the first six days of the month, Jimmy Carter played little direct role in the instigation of events in Iran, though he was, of course, an omnipresent symbol among the parades and mob actions. Whenever the shah was chanted about, chants about Carter were used as accompaniment, proclaiming the American president as the shah's puppet master or his pimp or his sodomite partner, depending on the day and the crowd.

On December 7, however, with Ashura less than seventy-two hours away, Carter inadvertently provided the Iranian crowds with a tangible sign that they were winning. The source of the encouragement was an extemporaneous remark made by the president at a question and answer session during an 8:50 a.m. breakfast with the White House Correspondents Association.

It was an eventuality that Ambassador Sullivan had warned against earlier in the week. "We recommend utmost reticence by officials in Washington in making public statements about Iran," the ambassador cautioned in a cable on the eve of Muharram. "No matter how carefully they are crafted and what nuances are introduced, they are spread [here] in distorted form. . . . We realize the problems of restraint . . . especially when Iran once again becomes a major focus of attention in the days ahead, but we wish to emphasize the sensitivity of the problem here."

As usual, however, Sullivan's view was ignored by the White House — and it might well have been even if the ambassador had been in better graces than he was. Jimmy Carter was not an easy man to restrain from speaking his mind. It was, in part, the downside of his intelligence and obvious mastery of the details of government. He felt well prepared to answer any question about any subject, whatever the circumstance. Carter also felt he had won the presidency on the promise of opening the government up to public inspection and did not want to assume the posture of concealment. All questions should, if possible, be answered with openness and honesty. Finally Carter was on a foreign policy roll at that moment, still flush with his triumph at Camp David with the Israelis and the Egyptians, so he felt little intimidation at the prospect of maneuvering between hypersensitive issues at a breakfast with the White House press corps.

Iran was the first subject raised. The president responded with his trademark smile and then launched into a summary of Iran's strategic importance to the United States, as a military bulwark against the Soviets and as an influence on the ever escalating price of petroleum in America's floundering economy. Of course Iranian instability was worrisome.

The inevitable follow-up question raised the issue of whether the shah would survive his current troubles. As usual, the president tried to make his response intellectually sound and emotionally forthright.

"I don't know," Jimmy answered in his usual plain-speaking manner. "I hope so. This is something that is in the hands of Iran. We have never had any intention and don't have any intention [now] of trying to intercede in the internal affairs of Iran. We primarily want an absence of violence and bloodshed, and [we want] stability. We personally prefer that the shah maintain a major role in the government, but that is a decision for the Iranian people to make."

The White House press corps treated the presidential response as just one more item in a morning full of presidential statements, but in Iran, with the shah teetering on his throne and Ashura on its way, the statement warranted banner headlines. Though undoubtedly an honest reflection of Carter's thinking, it was nonetheless, as one of Brzezinski's aides later observed, "the wrong signal for the President to send at that critical moment." Indeed, in Iran December 7 would often be identified as the day when Carter first decided to "dump" the shah, even though that had not been Carter's intention and no such decision had, in fact, been taken. Nonetheless, as Sullivan had warned, the president's unscripted remarks were soon being repeated everywhere as evidence the Americans were running away from their puppet.

For his part, the shah's reading of the statement was that the president had supported opening the future of the Pahlavi monarchy to a popular referendum, a move His Imperial Majesty had consistently said he would refuse to comply with under any circumstance. HIM fell almost immediately into one of his deepest depressions yet.

The State Department attempted to rectify the president's blunder by issuing an immediate "clarification" denying any change in American policy. To further make the point, Brzezinski called Zahedi, told him the same thing, and urged him to let His Majesty know. A few days later, at another press opportunity, Carter corrected himself and stated again, as he had been saying all fall, that the United States' support for the shah was unequivocal.

By then, of course, no one in Iran believed him.

The heaviest immediate impact of Jimmy Carter's December "misspeak" was on the preparations by the shah's military government to deal with the upcoming Ashura demonstrations. Facing the possibility of the most enormous confrontation yet, saddled with a dispirited shah, and now harboring large doubts about their American backing, the military government blinked and cut a deal with the representatives of the demonstrators. The final terms revealed just how shaky the military's hold on events actually was: The opposition agreed to maintain order on these holy days — refraining from attacks on the army or police and from organized arson or other destruction — and the army agreed to suspend the martial law ban on demonstrations for the next forty-eight hours, withdraw its forces from the southern half of Tehran, and temporarily abandon most of the city to the followers of the imam for the rest of their "religious celebration."

When the traditional two days of frantic mourning began on December 10, virtually all the Tehran units of the shah's army pulled back behind a barricaded east-west line that required a special set of identification papers to cross. This northern portion of the city under military control included the royal palaces, military headquarters, foreign embassies, and the city's richest neighborhoods. Inside the army's barricades, it was impossible to drive for more than a minute or two in any direction without encountering a roadblock manned by well-armed troops.

In the southern end of the nation's capital, however, it was difficult to find any evidence of the army or the shah's authority. At 9:00 a.m., demonstrators assembled at mosques and then the marching began, slowly, in groups of a thousand or two at first, flowing into tributaries and shouting *"Marg bar shah"* or "Khomeini is our imam" or "the Pahlavis must go." The groups eventually converged on Shah Reza Avenue and followed it as it turned into Eisenhower Avenue and ran west out toward the airport and the enormous Shahyad Monument, where the crowd would gather to hear speeches.

At two in the afternoon, the line down Shah Reza Avenue stretched for almost four miles. Both that day's crowd in Tehran and the next day's were estimated by the American embassy at "several hundred thousand," though other estimates were well over a million. Altogether, throughout the country on those two days, the aggregate marching crowds were estimated as large as eight million. Iran had never seen anything like it before. They seemed an endless mass, punctuated everywhere by the black slashes of chadors and occasional portraits of Khomeini held overhead. There were rumors that the shah planned to attack the line of march with helicopter gunships, but the marchers came anyway. There were rumors that the shah would use poison gas on them, but they were undeterred and some even brought their entire families. Most of them believed the shah had killed more than sixty thousand demonstrators since the first martyrs in Qom last January, but they fell into line anyway. "Laborers, teachers, shopkeepers, bazaar merchants, women in western dress and women enclosed in the black folds of the *chador,* children and clerics in green, black, and white turbans," one western correspondent observed, "all shouting in unison." They chanted that His Imperial Majesty's twin sister was a whore, that he and his father were bastards, that Islam would never be free until the shah was run out of the country on a rail, but they attacked no one and nothing — an "extraordinary" demonstration of discipline, according to the CIA. When they reached the towering, four-footed, fluted columns of the Shahyad Monument — built by the shah to commemorate 2,500 years of the Persian monarchy — the crowd spread into the open spaces around it. Then all one million together chanted "Death to the American cur" and "With Allah's help we will kill the impious traitor."

Out at Mehrabad Airport during Muharram, it was obvious which way the wind was blowing. There, according to one observer, "an endless stream of dignitaries, princes and princesses, former premiers and ministers, governors-general, high court judges, wealthy tycoons, leading film stars and middle-class families" were lined up, awaiting flights to the West. Their luggage, according to another account, included "suitcases and crates crammed with carpets, pictures, furniture, diamonds, strings of pearls, ruby rings, emerald earrings, tiaras, [and] silver services." By the end of Muharram, eighteen days after Ashura, $2.6 billion in cash had been transferred out of Iran to western banks, a load of currency traffic that overwhelmed Iranian banks' capacity to complete the necessary paperwork. Eventually, bank employees went on strike simply to stop the flow of currency reserves out of the country. It was later estimated that at least one hundred thousand Iranians flew into exile during the last three months of 1978.

Nor was the flow just of Iranians. The exodus included significant numbers of Americans as well. The day after Jimmy Carter's press breakfast, the Grumman Aerospace Corporation, one of the shah's major military contractors, chartered airliners to begin ferrying out its employees and their dependents. So did Westinghouse Electric and several other American corporations. Three-quarters of the American military dependents in the country had already fled very quietly during November, as had some ten thousand corporate employees. By the end of Muharram, some twenty-five thousand more had left as well. Those whose companies didn't provide private transport joined the crush at Mehrabad.

Back in the United States, however, the shah's roster of American backers remained steadfast, and influential. Close to the top of that list were the brothers Rockefeller. David, chairman of Chase Manhattan Bank, was His Imperial Majesty's banker, and Nelson, former governor of New York and vice president during the Ford interregnum, was one of the shah's friends. Nelson had visited Iran on a number of occasions and consulted with HIM on the phone regularly, commiserating over his troubles and sometimes game-planning in a conversational way. Nelson told his aides that he admired the shah and what HIM had done in Iran, and he wanted to be of whatever help he could.

As it turned out, Nelson's most lasting contribution to his friend was the services of one of the former governor's former aides, Robert Armao. Not yet thirty in the fall of 1978, Armao, the son of a Portuguese doctor who immigrated to New York, was often called Bobby because he was thought so young. He had been trained as a labor lawyer and had acted as Nelson Rockefeller's labor counsel during his brief vice presidency. Bobby was devoted to "the governor," as he always called his former boss, and he was a young man looking to make his way up the ladder as quickly as possible.

During the last weeks before Muharram, Armao walked into Nelson's Rockefeller Center office while the governor was on the phone with the shah, and Rockefeller silently motioned him to sit while he continued the conversation. With Armao listening, Nelson commiserated with the shah and wondered out loud how the situation in Iran had gotten so bad so fast. After he'd hung up, Rockefeller told Armao — who had recently founded a lobbying and public relations firm — that there ought to be something Bobby could do to help his old friend. Nelson said he was going to put his former aide in touch with the shah's sister, Princess Ashraf.

Armao was then contacted by Ashraf directly. She asked him to come by her town house on Beekman Place to talk about what was happening to her brother. Once Armao was there, the notorious princess spoke at great length about how the people of Iran had failed to understand what the shah had done for the country. She had been talking to a number of New York PR firms about this lack and the need for someone to assist the shah with what was widely described as "image building." Armao, who had met the shah previously in the company of the governor, tried to slide away from the task. He only knew what he read in the papers, he offered, but it looked as though things in Iran might be past the image building stage. Still, Ashraf wanted him to think about what he might be able to do.

Soon after the meeting with Ashraf, Nelson Rockefeller asked his former aide outright if he wouldn't just go to Iran to evaluate the situation. At that point, Armao agreed and packed his bags.

He landed in Iran as the uprising there was escalating to its fiercest high points in the aftermath of Ashura. "I could see right away that the situation was hopeless," Armao remembered. "Things were in very bad shape as far as image building went. There was nothing for me to do."

Though Armao's December visit was of no consequence, the intervention of the Rockefellers was far from over. Nelson's brother David would eventually become one of the exiled shah's foremost lobbyists with the Carter administration, and Bobby Armao would become His Majesty's combination prime minister and majordomo as his exile played out.

After Ashura, that looming exile had become an item of regular discussion between the shah and the American ambassador. According to Sullivan, the shah's acceptance of this fate "took place in a curious set of stages. One day he would talk to me in terms of going to Bandar Abbas, down on the Persian Gulf, and living in a navy compound where he would be out of public communication but where he would not physically be absent from the country. A few days later he amended this to a willingness to go out to the island of Kish . . . where he had a winter home. Subsequently, he talked in terms of going out on the imperial yacht and staying within the Persian Gulf. Finally, he was prepared to have the yacht moved out to international waters and be literally absent from Iranian territory. It was only in the last part of December, when his desperation became acute, that he was willing to talk in terms of leaving the country for an extended period and naming a regency council to rule in his absence."

· 9 ·

AS HIS IMPERIAL MAJESTY'S EXILE LOOMED, THE imam's exile was approaching its end, though there was still only speculation about exactly when that end would arrive.

In the meantime, Khomeini met with the press at his impromptu shrine in Noffal and described his nemesis as "a wounded snake" who needed to be "finished off," lest he revive himself and bite again. The military government was "a plot that would not work," and the shah was "committing more and more crimes because he is on the verge of downfall." In the government that would replace HIM, he proclaimed, "the ulema themselves will not hold power in the government [but instead] exercise supervision over those who govern and give them guidance."

All of those sound bites and hundreds more like them were couched in a generalized posture that made the hard and angry old mullah seem benign in western eyes. "He put himself forward as a moderate man," one historian observed, "who only asked for an end to tyranny and corruption, and went out of his way to reassure the Iranian middle class that the fall of the Shah would not change the country's social and economic system and that every 'rightful privilege' would be retained. He also allayed the West's fears that an Islamic government might threaten the flow of oil and trade in the Persian Gulf. . . . He spoke of 'liberty' and 'morality.' His was a 'moral and spiritual revolution.' He was in his late seventies and could not have ambitions of his own. All he wanted was to rid Iran of dictatorship and then allow the Iranian people to choose their form of government and the men they wished to put in charge of the country."

In response to more pointed probing, the imam simply became increasingly vague. An interview given that December with a correspondent from *Le Monde* was a typical performance. "I had just returned from Iran," the correspondent remembered, "and this was to be the official *Le Monde* interview. In it, I told him that at this moment it was evident that he was going to win. His victory was some weeks away but he was winning. So, I wanted to know, what will be the status of women in the new Iran?

"He answered that our women were fighting like lions and deserved all our admiration and in the future Islamic state they would have the place to which they are entitled. I tried to get him to expand, but that was all he would say."

In this ongoing dance with the world media, any identifiable doubts about Khomeini were soothed personally by Ghotbzadeh and Bani Sadr, circulating among the reporters like salesmen working the showroom. The imam, they assured everyone, was "the Gandhi of Islam."

Despite the public relations success quickly crafted by the imam's Paris brain trust, the French Ministry of the Interior remained uneasy about the Iranians' presence. Most of their suspicion focused on Sadegh Ghotbzadeh. French police agents had been keeping Ghotbzadeh under surveillance for years and tracking his dealings throughout the Middle East. The file they had amassed on him included information about his very close ties to the PLO — even running the Palestinians' Paris office for a while — the suspicion that he was a Libyan agent, and an Israeli allegation that he had opened a Swiss bank account with a $5 million deposit from the president of Syria. That December, the ministry decided to act on the dossier by ordering Ghotbzadeh out of France.

French political realism, however, won out. Sadegh appealed to the Foreign Ministry, and the foreign minister, thinking that perhaps Ghotbzadeh would be part of an Iranian government in a matter of months, forced Interior to rescind its deportation.

Shortly after that, Sadegh repaid the favor when the Foreign Ministry called and asked him to stop by for a conversation. The men he met with explained that French president Valéry Giscard d'Estaing would be meeting with Jimmy Carter, as well as the chancellor of Germany and the prime minister of Great Britain, at a summit on the island of Guadaloupe shortly after New Year's. The meeting was largely concerned with policy toward the Soviets, but the French were considering raising the issue of Iran and wanted to be briefed confidentially about just what the imam and the rest of Sadegh's crew planned to do when the shah fell.

Ghotbzadeh must have licked his chops at the request. One of his goals had long been to convince the French to advocate the Revolution's position to the Americans. According to one French journalist, Sadegh's three-hour tour de force of the coming Islamic republic, all following the script already designed by the committee out in Noffal, was "brilliant." After his meeting at the Foreign Ministry, Sadegh informed the imam that the French were finally going to make the Revolution's case to the Americans.

At the same time, the imam's other self-proclaimed "son," Abolhassan Bani Sadr, was being contacted by the Central Intelligence Agency. The secret approach was filed at the agency under the code name SD LURE/1. The idea was to infiltrate someone into close contact with the unwitting exile, for some unspecified future use.

The agent involved used the name Guy Rutherford. His previous name had been William Foster and there was another name he used before that. After a failed operation in Syria in the late fifties, he'd become station chief in Amman, Jordan, then gone into "deep cover." According to the CIA records, on this occasion he represented himself as a "European based U.S. businessman with high level contacts in both the U.S. business and official worlds" and eventually met with Bani Sadr twice. Though, according to one CIA memo, "the meetings were complicated by the presence of students, journalists, and other hangers-on, Rutherford seems to have managed to lay the groundwork for a confidential relationship between the two of them. [Bani Sadr] was apparently sufficiently interested in Rutherford to agree to [the] latter's request to meet him privately if/when he traveled via Iran on a future business trip to the Far East. Rutherford mentioned that he expected this travel to take place in early Spring 1979."

These first meetings in Paris were no doubt little more than a flash in passing for Abolhassan, but they and the other seemingly inconsequential encounters that followed would eventually surface and haunt him, despite his own innocence about Guy Rutherford's true mission.

*   *   *

Back in Iran, the imam's forces had been catching their breath since Ashura, but as Christmas approached, they began flexing their muscles again.

"Confrontation yesterday outside Reza Shah Hospital," the US embassy reported, "in which troops first threatened to disperse crowd but then granted permission for large funeral procession from hospital to cemetery. . . . Opening of high schools in Tehran this morning predictably brought instant anti-Shah rallies at many of them. . . . Bands of shouting young people have marched in various parts of the city. One such group passed [the] Embassy this morning shouting 'Yankee Go Home.' . . . Large crowds of high school and college students massed outside University this morning. Troops sealed off Shah Reza Avenue and campus. . . . In Tabriz . . . a mutiny occurred among troops called upon to quell demonstration. . . . Between 200 [and] 400 troops have surrounded Tehran University and [are] preventing traffic from entering area."

Throughout, the shah remained ambivalent about just how to respond when the imam's army next rose in force. The visiting head of the French Secret Service, who was one of His Majesty's most fervent backers inside the French government, discussed the issue with him that December. The French spy and the shah met in a darkened room off the royal office. Throughout their conversation, the monarch wore an oversize pair of tinted glasses, removing them only once — long enough, however, for the Frenchman to note that the shahanshah looked absolutely "ravaged."

The French intelligence director urged the shah to ask France to deport Khomeini before it was too late, but HIM allowed that this crazy old man would be more of a threat if he moved back to the region. France, he said, was the best place for him.

"You understand that I can never fire on my own people," the shah then declared without being asked.

The Frenchman's expression drooped, and, after a long pause, he finally responded.

"In that case, Your Majesty," he said, "you are lost."

Back in Paris the following day, the French Secret Service chief met with the French president. In their conversation, France's chief spy described the Iranian monarch as Louis XVI, approaching his end.

At least one significant player in the US State Department had reached much the same conclusion.

During the third week of December, Henry Precht, the head of State's Iran desk, floated a memorandum up the chain of command that, taking

Sullivan's "Thinking the Unthinkable" cable a step further, proposed that the shah was done for and ought to be dropped. It was a risky bureaucratic move. "The overwhelming reluctance of officials at all levels to be perceived as backing away from support of the shah . . . was so deeply ingrained in the minds and policies of everyone responsible," one member of the Carter administration's foreign policy apparatus explained, "that even a carefully reasoned expression of doubt was regarded as a heresy that could destroy a career." Precht took the risk anyway.

The six-page memo dismantled the major arguments for continuing to back the shah and also dismissed the military as any kind of immediate option. "Under its present leadership," he pointed out, "the military is damned for its association with the Shah and for its harsh methods. It will not constitute a viable choice for Iranian stability until its top ranks are purged."

Instead, the answer was to reach out toward the imam and his uprising. Precht proposed that the United States "enlarge our contacts with the opposition and independent Iranians with the object of assuring them that the U.S. is interested in Iran and downplaying our interests in the future of the Shah. . . . We should extend these contacts in a direct way to the Khomeini factions. . . . We should move vigorously to promote with the Shah and the opposition a [transition] scheme . . . that will preserve a minimal role for the Shah as constitutional monarch. We should be prepared to fall back fairly quickly from this position: acquiescing in the departure of the Shah if we cannot obtain him a 'King of Sweden' role. [And] we should be prepared in advance for a surprise abdication."

Precht did not lose his job over his suggestions, but, like Sullivan's earlier proposal, this memorandum was simply ignored by the White House.

Nonetheless, two days later an NSC memo warned that "unless an effective government [is] established in Iran by the first week of January, the Shah and his dynasty are going to be swept away." Though they disagreed about almost everything else, all of Jimmy Carter's advisers now at least recognized that one way or another, the shah's endgame was upon him.

And Mohammad Reza Pahlavi would spend much of that endgame trying to convince someone to form a government in his name. It proved an almost impossible task. His Majesty's former army chief of staff, debilitated by his heart condition and demoralized by the shah's accelerating political slide, could not continue as prime minister any longer, and the only military figures who were willing to replace him insisted that any government they formed be given the freedom to use an iron fist. Finally, at the very end of December, after having been refused by a host of possible candidates, the shah offered the job to a National Front member who had served as a junior minister in Mossadeq's government and spent two years as a political prisoner. The choice took the Americans a little by surprise, and the former junior minister agreed only after some hesitation. The shah then promptly flew his helicopter to an Iranian ski resort for a couple days spent recovering from the strain of his search and thinking hard about his immediate future. He and William Sullivan were still in almost constant dialogue, and by the end of the month, their discussion had reached a point where Sullivan had declared that His Majesty would most likely have to leave very soon, for the good of Iran if nothing else.

The statement hung in the air, but the shah made no move to dispute it. He was not fond of the American ambassador, but their contact over the last months had built a bond and a kind of intimacy. They had seen each other through a lot. This time, with what Sullivan described as a "beseeching" expression and a toss of his hands, the shah simply asked where the Americans thought he could go.

Sullivan as yet had no instructions on the subject, so he first tried to deflect the inquiry by asking about the shah's house in Switzerland. Couldn't HIM go there?

No, no, the shah responded, the security in Switzerland would be impossible. What about His Majesty's home in England?

England was so cold, he pointed out. His Imperial Majesty didn't need to add that he was also so suspicious of the English he would never be comfortable settling there.

Having thus rejected all the preexisting exile options, according to Sullivan, the shahanshah fell silent and looked expectantly at the American ambassador.

Sullivan got the hint.

Would His Majesty like him to "seek an invitation" to go to the United States? the ambassador asked.

The shah's preference was obvious. "Would you?" the Light of the Aryans answered eagerly. "Would you really?"

William Sullivan promised that he would, he really would. And, with that exchange, the issue that would define the rest of the shah's life and dominate the remainder of Jimmy Carter's presidency was placed squarely on the table for the very first time.

Also foreshadowing the disaster to come that December, the American embassy now became a primary target of Iranian outrage.

Twenty-six wooded acres in the middle of Tehran, the American compound's main defense was the eight-foot masonry wall surrounding the entire property, topped with wire and other obstacles. Of the compound's two principal buildings — the chancery, where its administrative offices and communications centers were located, and the ambassador's residence, where Sullivan lived and entertained — the chancery was the more vulnerable. It sat immediately behind the embassy's main gate. The residence sat behind a separate gate off a side street. Among the embassy's other buildings were a large warehouse, housing for various personnel, a separate consular section, separate space for several top-secret radio scanners, and a motor pool. Some three thousand people came in and out on a typical day, sometimes far more. The external perimeter of that huge compound was defended by a platoon of Iranian soldiers stationed outside the residence gate. The embassy's defense from inside the walls was assigned to a thirteen-man guard of United States Marines, largely concentrated at the chancery.

As Christmas approached, tension was again building throughout the country. A Tehran funeral procession for a young university professor — killed when the army fired on a sit-in at the Ministry of Science and Higher Education — was itself fired upon by a detachment of Iranian Army Rangers, killing "a substantial number" among the seven thousand mourners. Students were roaming the city in spontaneous marches, despite government orders to return to school. Several of these bands had passed the embassy early in the day on Christmas Eve, shouting "Yankee go home" but doing nothing more. Shortly after noon, however, the embassy learned of a demonstration nearby at the headquarters of the shah's National Oil Company. When the Americans inquired with Iranian authorities about the demonstration, they were told not to worry, the gathering was peaceful and would soon disperse.

It did indeed disperse, but the largest fragment of the remaining demonstrators marched in the direction of the embassy. Once the Americans were notified that a crowd was on its way, the embassy entrances were locked down as part of standard security procedures. The marine guards chained the compound gates, and the radio communication center notified all the embassy vehicles outside the perimeter that the compound was being buttoned up and instructed them to stay away until given the all clear. One of the Americans' cars, driven by an Iranian employee, nonetheless attempted to dash inside through the main gate before the crowd arrived, setting the stage for trouble to come.

Upon reaching the gate, the driver found it locked, but instead of speeding off, he got out to argue with the guards, hoping to convince them to open up. As he stood there yelling at the marines, the crowd from the National Oil Company demonstration appeared down the block and, spotting the scene the driver was making, charged along the avenue and swarmed around the car and in front of the gate. Then someone threw a Molotov cocktail into the vehicle's backseat. The car erupted in a ball of flame, and the driver fled. With that, the demonstrators began screaming and throwing anything handy — rocks, chunks of concrete, pieces of bricks — at the gate and the marines inside. At several places, Iranians mounted the wall as though they were about to breach the perimeter.

When Sullivan was notified, he raced down from his second-floor office in the chancery to the first-floor security center, where the situation could be tracked on security camera monitors. His first step was to dispatch a messenger to the residence gate to try and convince the Iranian platoon there to come down to the main gate and disperse the crowd, but the officer in charge had panicked and refused to move. Without waiting for the Iranians, the ambassador took command of the security center's radio microphone and issued orders to his marines. All of them were now deployed with shotguns and tear gas canisters. Sullivan told the marines they were not to fire unless they received a direct command from him and only him. Then he ordered them to launch tear gas into the crowd. At the time, the enraged demonstrators were doing their best to tear the padlocked main gate off its hinges.

"[The] crowd threatened to come over the wall," Sullivan reported to Washington at the end of the day, "but never actually penetrated the compound. Marine guards fired tear gas, reducing crowd pressure, but [the] mob remained in threatening posture for nearly another hour, still throwing rocks and burning objects over the walls." Eventually the army platoon at the residence gate mustered its courage and sent four soldiers, firing automatic weapons into the air, to clear away the crowd that remained.

By the time light began to fade, Sullivan accounted the situation "back to normal." The charred automobile in front of the main gate had been dragged away and the gate reopened, Iranian army reinforcements had erected a cordon designed to shield the embassy from any further disturbances, and the marines had been ordered to stand down. Throughout the surrounding business district, occasional rounds of automatic weapons fire sounded as the army warned marauding demonstrators to stay away.

· 10 ·

———

Sullivan's plan was to maximize the con-
nections the embassy had been able to make with the Liberation Movement
of Iran. The LMI had a lot of status, but little popular base and hence little
practical leverage on any post-shah struggle for power. Sullivan hoped to
match them with the army and by the last week of December, without seeking any explicit clearance, the ambassador had framed the basic outlines of
a deal between the two. The LMI had pledged the Revolution to nonrecrim-
ination against the military after the shah left, and the military had been
given a list of some one hundred officers who would be expected to resign
and depart with His Imperial Majesty.

Sullivan also pushed the notion of making contact with Khomeini. This
time he included Secretary of State Cyrus Vance in his effort. Jimmy Carter
as yet had no idea what the two of them were doing.

"I recommended that the United States . . . send a senior emissary to Paris
to discuss this matter directly with the Ayatollah," Sullivan remembered. "I

ruled myself out for such an undertaking because of my accreditation to the shah and because it seemed an unwise time to leave Tehran." After several back and forth exchanges, State named a veteran foreign service ambassador to act as an emissary whenever the plan went forward.

In the meantime, Brzezinski had reached the end of his patience with the shah's inability to form a government. On the morning of December 28, shortly before the president left to take the rest of the holidays at Camp David, Zbig met with Carter and declared that the United States was "failing to provide the shah with the needed guidance." Carter agreed, and the national security adviser summoned the secretary of defense, the director of central intelligence, and the secretary of state to a meeting on the subject shortly after the presidential helicopter took off. The goal of the meeting was to come up with a set of explicit instructions for Sullivan to relay to the shah.

Vance presented a draft cable that stated the United States would not accept any iron fist option and wanted HIM to form a new civilian government. He also wanted to officially authorize Sullivan to make the contacts he had already secretly begun to make with "responsible political elements in the government, the opposition, and the military" in order to "urge establishment of a civilian government with firm military support that would restore order and guide Iran from autocracy to whatever new regime the Iranian people themselves decided upon."

Vance, however, found virtually no support among the others for his position and by the end of the morning had no choice but to sign off on an alternative cable that would go out under his name to Sullivan as soon as the president cleared it:

"We wish you to convey the following message to the Shah," it began:

1. Continued uncertainty is destructive of Army morale and of political confidence.
2. If a civilian government is possible soon that is moderate and can work with the United States and with the Shah and maintain order, then obviously it is the preferred alternative.
3. But if there is uncertainty . . . about . . . such a government or its capacity to govern or if the Army is in danger of becoming more fragmented, then a firm military government under the Shah may be unavoidable.

4. You should tell the Shah the above, clearly stating that the U.S. support is steady and that it is essential, repeat, *essential* to terminate the continued uncertainty.

For his part, Brzezinski described the instructions as "the clearest and most direct effort [yet] to get the shah to do what needed to be done." Vance, however, had an appointment with Carter that afternoon and helicoptered out to Camp David intent on at least "clarifying" some of the cable's language.

The Jimmy Carter he visited there was, as always, a few degrees less constrained than he was at the White House. The president was wearing a windbreaker and had something of a reflective air when Cy arrived in his lawyer's suit, white shirt, and nondescript tie.

After Vance brought up the cable, he later recounted, the president "acknowledged the dangers of the Shah's continuing flirtation with the iron fist and the probability that his presence in Iran would prevent any understanding between the moderate opposition and the military leaders." Carter and his secretary of state then spent several minutes rewriting the end of paragraph 3, after "if the Army is in danger of being fragmented." When they were done, the paragraph closed with "then the Shah should choose without delay a firm military government which would end the disorder, violence, and bloodshed. If in his judgment the Shah believes these alternatives to be infeasible, then a regency council supervising the military government might be considered by him."

Vance, now convinced that the shah could not "fail to see . . . that we would support the military government only to end bloodshed, but not to apply the iron fist to retain his throne," sent off the edited cable to Sullivan as soon as he returned to Washington.

Shortly after that, Sullivan raised the stakes again. On January 3, 1979, in an "eyes only" cable to Vance, the ambassador said the "moment of truth" was upon them and it was time to tell the shah he had to leave — and the only way the shah would accept such a decision was if it came from the president himself, along with an invitation to enter the United States. The move was required, the ambassador argued, if the new government headed by the once junior minister to Mossadeq was to stand a chance of stabilizing the country. All the government moderates were saying the shah had to leave immediately so the new prime minister could bond with the military. There were military officers still lobbying the shah to switch to the iron fist. There was also talk inside the army about a coup.

The National Security Council convened at noon that same day to discuss jettisoning the Light of the Aryans. Vance took the affirmative right away. The resistance Cy encountered was, aside from Brzezinski's, mostly inertia. "There was no disagreement among those present that the Shah was irreparably wounded," an NSC aide remembered. "However, there was a deep reluctance, even repugnance, to force him to step aside." The NSC made no attempt to reach a decision during their discussion; that would be done when they met the president himself for lunch, where they would be joined by Walter Mondale and Hamilton Jordan.

All business, Carter — scheduled to depart for the allied summit meeting on the island of Guadaloupe the next day — framed the discussion right away. Did they think he should ask the shah to step aside?

Brzezinski jumped right in. "I immediately said that in my view," Zbig noted in his diary that night, "if the question is whether we should ask him to step aside and not whether it is desirable that he should step aside, the answer is clearly no. . . . I was differentiating between the desirability of stepping down, which might in fact be desirable . . . and the desirability of the U.S. asking him. [The latter] could be damaging to us in the future."

Next, Stansfield Turner, the director of central intelligence, argued that the shah had to go. He had no political viability left.

Vance then pointed out that the president would only be shoving the shah a little in the direction he himself was obviously heading. And if his new prime minister was to stand any chance, he would have to be freed of the yoke of His Imperial Majesty. The departure would be presented as simply a "vacation" for the shah, but in all likelihood the new prime minister's government would be the transition out of autocracy.

Carter still felt a personal loyalty to the shah and wondered if there wasn't a way to frame this so that the United States was just approving the shah's own decision to leave.

Brzezinski countered that such deniability would amount to kidding themselves. The Iranians would read whatever the Americans did along these lines as a recommendation that the shah leave. He reminded everyone that direct military rule was still an option for maintaining order after the shah's exit.

Vance objected that in fact, the military was no option. They could not and should not govern.

Walter Mondale allowed that the United States might just encourage the shah to leave without appearing to have forced him to.

Carter then reminded his advisers that the question was whether or not the shah's departure was good for the United States. And on that front, Vance was now carrying the day. At one point, well into the lunch, the secretary sensed as much and left briefly to call State and arrange an invitation for the shah's use of the Palm Springs estate of wealthy American publisher Walter Annenberg when His Majesty arrived in the United States on his "vacation."

Back in the meeting, Zbig was lecturing the group on the need to protect the Iranian military at all costs. They needed to be told explicitly that the United States "supports them completely no matter what trends in the circumstances may arise."

Finally the NSC approved a cable from the president to the shah saying that the United States supported his decision to leave Iran once his new civilian government had formally taken office. It also invited him to proceed to the United States when that time came.

Brzezinski, always comfortable pronouncing the last word, ended the lunch meeting by telling the president that the message of disengagement he was sending would cost the United States in the region and eventually cost the president himself domestically. Many present may have accounted this final hyperbole little more than Zbig's predictable unwillingness to concede a lost debate, but the warning would later resonate in ways that Brzezinski himself could not have imagined.

The next day, in his beach bungalow on Guadaloupe, the president was hanging around in his bathing suit talking with Ham Jordan when the operator rang to announce a conference call from Cy Vance and Walter Mondale, who were holding down the fort back in Washington. Brzezinski had traveled to Guadaloupe with the president and was immediately summoned straight from poolside in just a suit and a towel. He found Carter, shirtless, sitting atop a small refrigerator off the bungalow's sitting room with the telephone receiver pressed to his ear. Ham, also in his bathing suit and shirtless, was sprawled on a couch. Cy was on the other end of the line, "in a state of considerable agitation."

Vance had worrisome news out of Iran. Sullivan had been unable to see

the shah to deliver their most recent message and felt he was being inten-
tionally kept at a distance. It would be sometime tomorrow before they
would meet. In the meantime, however, the ambassador had been visited by
several leaders of the military who told him outright that they would not allow the shah to leave Iran. They planned to keep him on the throne and seize
power in his name in order to "clean up Iran and eliminate violence," a
process they admitted would be extremely repressive. In the immediate moment, they were going to allow the new prime minister to form a government, but they were poised to move if that didn't work.

Mondale's assessment was that the shah knew all about this coup, a fact
later confirmed by the shah himself. In any case, Vance insisted, this move
had to be stopped.

Brzezinski leaped to challenge Vance. He would later describe himself as
"dismayed that anyone . . . would actually wish to prevent what was clearly
in the collective interest of the West." This, he insisted, was the moment they
had been waiting for, when the shah and the army were finally prepared to
do what they needed to do. Blocking that would mean assuming an enormous historical responsibility.

The argument went back and forth for half an hour, with Vance and
Mondale on the line and Brzezinski stationed next to the president feeding
him a steady stream of written notes.

Finally Carter issued instructions to Vance. He wanted his secretary of
state to "stick with the shah and the military." He also wanted Sullivan to delay giving the good-bye cable to the shah. Rather, when they met he should
simply ascertain what the shah's attitude was toward this coup.

Brzezinski thought these new instructions a clear indication that with the
shah's blessing, Carter was prepared to rescind his previous decision and
back a military crackdown. He later described the president's approach that
day in the bungalow as "hard-line."

If so, it didn't stay that way. The next day, the president's conversations with
the allied nations took a very different tack. As Ghotbzadeh had been promised, France's president — one of Carter's favorites among world leaders —
raised the issue of Iran. Neither the French nor the Germans had anything
good to say about His Imperial Majesty. (Ironically, only the British even
bothered to praise his previous contributions to the West.) "I found little
support for the Shah," Carter later remembered. Possible coups were apparently never discussed.

That afternoon Sullivan reported his conversation with the shah. According to the ambassador, the coup had in fact been His Majesty's suggestion. The army would only take over should his new prime minster falter, but in the meantime the military pledged to support the shah's choice of government. In further conversations, the ambassador had learned that the army had now decided that it would not block the shah's departure. Indeed, his leaving "in a Constitutional manner" in order to help the new government was part of the plan being discussed.

That was apparently enough for Carter. With the possibility of a coup off the front burner, the president sent word from Guadaloupe that Sullivan should deliver the original cable.

Back in Tehran, the ambassador returned to the palace and finally communicated the president's message. His Imperial Majesty took the news more calmly than might have been expected. It was only a "vacation," the ambassador pointed out, probably a couple months or so, and the shah had the president's personal invitation to spend it in the United States. The arrangements had already begun.

The shah made no objection. He looked tired. He didn't believe the "two months" estimate and didn't think Sullivan did either, but he accepted the fiction and was prepared to operate under it. Fate had spoken.

Afterward, in the palace, with the snow on the Alborz visible out his window, the King of Kings seemed stunned and passive. The only remark of his that has survived in subsequent lore was reportedly made to one of his aides.

"The Americans have told me I have to leave," His Imperial Majesty said.

The other Iranian question that followed the president to Guadaloupe was Sullivan's proposal to reach out to the imam. Waiting so late in the process to get the president's blessing was a risky strategy but one Vance felt had been dictated by the circumstance. When Carter bounced the question off Zbig, however, Brzezinski was taken aback and tried to buy time by insisting that they run it by the shah before going any further. State then dispatched Sullivan to the palace. He reported that the shah was amenable to the contact and asked to be kept informed about the discussions. The president then let Cy know that the subject was too serious to sort out over the phone and a meeting was scheduled for Carter's first day back at the White House, January 10.

One of Brzezinski's aides later described this gathering in the Oval Office as "rancorous." Besides Carter, Vance, and Brzezinski, Mondale and the secretary of defense were also present.

Vance revealed that State had tentatively scheduled a contact in Paris and pled with Carter to endorse a secret meeting with Khomeini's organization. The shah was done, and now the United States needed to prevent a showdown between the military and the religious forces. Vance argued that Khomeini "could be persuaded . . . to remain in Paris long enough to give [the new government] some breathing room." The point wasn't to negotiate with the imam and his revolutionaries, but simply to buy time for the new prime minister to establish a viable government.

Brzezinski countered that news of this "secret" approach would leak — thereby embarrassing the United States at just the wrong time by making it seem as if the shah was being dumped. He added that this seventy-eight-year-old religious fanatic was not going to be won over by one conversation with an emissary anyway and that it would only undermine confidence in the new prime minister's regime rather than raise it. Not to mention how it would demoralize the army for the Americans to be talking with its enemies.

After much back and forth, Carter concluded that the United States should put its full weight behind the new prime minister. He was the shah's choice, and as far as the president was concerned, that was sufficient to establish his legitimacy. The military should be encouraged to back the government. The planned meeting in Paris with Khomeini's representative was to be cancelled on the president's orders. Instead, Carter was going to ask the French to contact the imam's people and forward a request that they give this new government a chance to restore order.

Ambassador William Sullivan was notified about the president's decision in the middle of the night Tehran time and thought the entire approach idiocy. Without America's securing Khomeini's agreement through direct discussions, the deal he'd struck between the LMI and the army would be null and void, and LMI was his only link to the Islamic forces.

"As far as I could see," Sullivan remembered, "the United States government was [now] facing the situation in Iran with no policy whatsoever. . . . Unless some understandings were reached for an accommodation between the armed forces and the Islamic forces, I felt that an explosion would occur. . . . These wishful thoughts [of the president's] were pure moonshine. . . . We should instead be preparing ourselves for the fact that the revolution was going to succeed and that we needed to accommodate ourselves to it in the most effective way in order to protect United States national interests."

Unable to restrain himself, Sullivan dashed off an "eyes only" cable to Vance in the middle of the night. The resulting document was only eighteen lines long — perhaps the shortest of Sullivan's tenure — but it would lodge in Washington's craw.

"You should know," the ambassador advised Vance, "that [the] President has made [a] gross and perhaps irretrievable mistake by failing to send [an] emissary to Paris to see Khomeini. . . . I can not, repeat, [can] *not* understand the rationale for this unfortunate decision. . . . In view of urgent appeals from [the] Iranian military that we arrange [a] relationship between them and Khomeini, I urge you immediately [to endorse a] plea [to the president] for sanity. . . . Failure [to reverse this decision] could permanently frustrate U.S. national interests in Iran."

After dispatching his cable, William Sullivan went back to bed, though he hardly slept all night. That the ambassador had crossed over a line with his outburst was confirmed in the morning, when Washington responded to his midnight message. Sullivan later described this return cable as "most unpleasant and abrasive," including "an unacceptable aspersion upon my loyalty."

This treatment, he later admitted, "proved to be too much for my tolerance. I was, after all, the senior United States Foreign Service officer on active duty and I felt that my reports and assessments deserved some fair consideration. . . . When I was told by telephone from the State Department that the insulting message had originated at the White House, I thought that I no longer had a useful function to perform on behalf of the President [and] I therefore made up my mind to resign [as soon as the pace of events allowed] and to leave this totally unsatisfactory situation behind."

In the meantime, however, Sullivan was under orders to notify the shah of the decision to cancel the meetings with Khomeini and, at 11:30 a.m., he did so. The shahanshah, Sullivan remembered, was "more drawn and tense than usual. It appeared that he had not slept very much and that events were crowding in on him. He was nevertheless his usual urbane self . . . as we sat down to drink our ritual small cup of tea. When I told him of the instructions . . . from Washington, he became agitated. He asked . . . how we expected to influence [Khomeini's] people if we would not even talk to them. He threw up his hands in despair and asked what we intended to do now. I had no answer."

And with the lack of such an answer, the shah's expression fell.

"Until this point," Sullivan explained, "[I think] he felt we had some grand national design that was intended to save his country and perhaps, somehow or other, his dynasty. In the light of that assumption, he was prepared to make personal sacrifices for the larger goal. It now suddenly became clear to him, as it had to me, that [the United States] had no design whatsoever and that our government's actions were being guided by some inexplicable whim."

Back in Washington, Jimmy Carter was every bit as furious as Sullivan. The president later described the eighteen-line cable from Tehran, in which "Sullivan apparently lost control of himself," as "bordering on insolence." He called Vance almost as soon as Sullivan's midnight outburst reached him and told Vance in no uncertain terms that such language was insulting and intolerable. Carter wanted Sullivan recalled from Tehran immediately.

Vance told his boss that replacing the ambassador at this juncture, with governments changing and the Revolution advancing out of the wings, would be a logistical nightmare and begged for him to wait a few weeks. Carter eventually agreed not to fire Sullivan on the spot, but only with great reluctance.

In any case, the ambassador's diplomatic career was, for all intents and purposes, over as soon as his cable was delivered. William Sullivan, the final American representative to the Peacock Throne, would last barely two months longer at his post than the shah would at his.

On January 11, 1979, Cyrus Vance formally announced from the State Department in Washington that the shah would be leaving Iran for a "vacation" on January 16, as soon as his new prime minister was approved by the Parliament and a regency council was in place.

Shortly thereafter, the shah's palace confirmed the reports out of the United States of his upcoming "vacation." His Imperial Majesty would spend his remaining five days finalizing his itinerary. In addition to his American invitation, his friend Anwar Sadat of Egypt had invited the shah to stop by, as had the king of Morocco. The shah eventually decided to take those two up on their offers of hospitality before traveling on to Palm Springs. He wanted to hang around in the region in case something new developed and he didn't want to be seen as running straight to the Americans. Accordingly the palace announced that the shah's first stop would be Cairo.

On January 16, 1979, the day the shah left Iran for good, a frigid wind swept down off the Alborz and stampeded through the streets of the capital.

The gusts dispersed the rising smoke and scattered papers and candy wrappers along the sidewalks. At the palace, the trees swayed and rustled. The shah paid a last visit to his office late in the morning, pausing for a long time in front of the bust of his father in the anteroom. When he emerged, the steps outside were lined with servants and Imperial Guardsmen — some in tears, others reaching out to touch him as he walked by.

Farah was waiting at the helicopter for the ride to the airport. An entire airliner full of clothes and the like had already been shipped ahead to the United States for their eventual arrival. Now, two Boeing 707s were waiting on the tarmac at Mehrabad to fly them, their dogs, and a small entourage to Egypt. Farah, wearing a dark dress without significant jewelry, looked to be in misery. His Imperial Majesty was wearing one of his best charcoal gray suits with a bright striped tie and a charcoal overcoat. He was pale and had barely slept a few hours in the last week. He had been dreading this moment his entire life and it was all he could do not to show it. Before boarding the chopper, he mustered a wan smile for his servants.

One last official ceremony was scheduled for the Imperial Pavilion at the airport. It was here that the shah had once greeted visiting heads of state, including Jimmy Carter himself the year before. Now the new prime minister was here to meet HIM and say good-bye. Upon entering the Imperial Pavilion he bowed deeply to the last of the Pahlavis. Their exchange was brief and followed immediately by the shah's walk out to his waiting planes.

"Now you have everything in your hands," the shah told his new prime minister. "I hope you will succeed. I entrust Iran to you and to God."

When this exit ceremony was broadcast to Iran, pandemonium broke out. People danced in the streets for hours, some brandishing Iranian currency from which the shah's picture had been cut. Traffic was often frozen in place, and people mounted the roofs of their cars to call out the joyous news. Portraits of the shah were collected and burned at most intersections. Statues of HIM and his father were assaulted and toppled. Reza the Great's tomb was opened and then reduced to rubble. All the street signs with the Pahlavi name on them were torn from their poles. Some army enlisted men broke ranks and joined in the spontaneous celebration. Instant newspaper editions were distributed with mammoth headlines declaring "The Shah Has Gone."

And yet he hadn't, at least not yet. Out on the tarmac, the wind cut HIM to the bone, sweeping through the loading bays where most of the planes were parked, grounded for days by striking pilots and mechanics. He would later remember above all else that freezing blast and the ghostly quiet of the airport. At the boarding ramp, His Majesty stopped for a few last farewells with his generals and others. Everyone was in tears except the shah, whose eyes had welled full but didn't leak. One of his generals threw himself at the shah's feet; another broke out of the crowd to kiss his hand.

A photo of the latter would be flashed around the globe, appearing on most front pages the next day. In it, the general was bent over at the waist, grasping the shahanshah's hand in both of his own and forcing his lips against it. Half embarrassed and half distraught, the shah looked off at the pavement. He tried to smile, but that simply spread a grim line across the width of his face, flattening his affect as though he were pushed up against a window. Mohammed Pahlavi looked like a man caught in a moment he could only endure.

Then it was over; the lead 707, with the shah himself at the controls, taxied away and — at 1:15 p.m. Tehran time — took off. His Majesty didn't relinquish the pilot's seat until the plane left Iranian airspace. Once finally out of the cockpit, the last of the Pahlavi dynasty reportedly broke down in tears, the pain more than he could bear.

PART THREE

REVOLUTION

· 11 ·

————

W_{ITH} THE SHAH GONE, ANTICIPATION OF THE
imam's triumphal return to Iran dominated the last two weeks of January.
Martial law was in effect, public demonstrations were banned, and squads of
chomaq-be-dast, government-sponsored "stick wielders," roamed the streets
after curfew, smashing the windshields of cars with Khomeini signs on
them, but the approach had little success at intimidating the uprising. The
new prime minister closed the airports, mostly to prevent a quick return by
Khomeini, and in response, one hundred thousand of the imam's supporters
demonstrated in Tehran. The troops fired into the crowd, killing forty and
wounding hundreds. Two days after that, another huge demonstration took
to the streets just west of the University of Tehran. The crowd threw stones
and shouted slogans, screaming that the prime minister's government was
just the shah wearing a new dress. In response, the army opened fire and kept
it up for a full five hours until night fell. At least thirty-five died and hundreds more were wounded. The following day, January 29, a police general
was pulled from his car and pummeled by a mob while troops killed at least

seven more demonstrators. Some military officers suggested letting Khomeini fly back and then shooting his plane down as soon as it entered Iranian airspace, but the idea was abandoned when the shah, now in Egypt, refused to endorse the assassination. Finally, late that evening, following secret negotiations between six of the imam's mullahs and two army generals, the holdover prime minister's government announced that Iranian airports would be opened the next morning.

That move left Sadegh Ghotbzadeh and the imam's nerve center at Neauphle-le-Château scrambling to find a jetliner in which to make the five-and-a-half-hour flight. No scheduled airlines were still operating into Tehran. The most obvious carrier for Ghotbzadeh to approach for a charter was Air France, but the company was worried about Iranian instability and refused to take payment at its Tehran office in Iranian currency, with which the uprising's coffers were flush. To ease the airline's worries, Ghotbzadeh approached the French Foreign Ministry, which agreed to guarantee the entire payment of some $500,000 in French currency the airline was demanding. Air France, however, did not consider such a guarantee sufficient and demanded an immediate $100,000 deposit at their Paris headquarters as well. With a sly grin and no explanation, Sadegh returned a few hours later with a shopping bag full of cash. The charter was booked.

During their last days at Neauphle-le-Château, Bani Sadr attempted to prepare Khomeini for what the Revolution's victory would mean, much as he had prepared the imam for each of the day's events during his French exile. Bani Sadr felt that his role as "devoted son" required that he act as the holy man's designated conscience. Years later, one conversation in particular would stick in his memory.

"You are no longer Khomeini now," the acolyte began. "Now you are Power. Iran will be at your feet." Bani Sadr cautioned that this power, like all power, corrupted, and asked his spiritual father for a promise that he would not allow himself to be sucked in by that dynamic. It would be a challenge, Bani Sadr explained, and just in case the imam slipped in his vigilance, Bani Sadr would take it upon himself to make sure he kept his promise. He also demanded that the imam promise that if Bani Sadr ever came to him and said that he was being corrupted, the imam would desist and change his ways.

Khomeini laughed. He might sin, he allowed, but begged his spiritual son not to stop talking to him over it.

The imam then observed that in this regard Bani Sadr was just like his actual father, a mullah all the others had considered blunt to the point of rude, and that Bani Sadr should feel free to say whatever he liked to him, just as his father always had.

Bani Sadr felt reassured.

The imam, Ayatollah Ruhollah Khomeini, finally packed up and left the land of the Franks on the morning of February 1, 1979, in an Air France 747. Some one hundred others came along, including a large contingent of international press. The Iranians were jubilant and the press eager, but none of them could imagine the scope of what awaited them in Tehran. The greeting given Ruhollah Khomeini there was beyond anything ever before witnessed by anybody anywhere.

A correspondent from *Le Monde* estimated the crowd at ten million people — a demonstration the size of the populations of Greater Chicago and Los Angeles combined — all of them gathered to see and adore the imam. Other sources estimated the multitude at upwards of four or five million. In any case, most speculated that the imam's welcome might well have been the largest assemblage in one place ever for a single event in the history not just of Iran, but of the entire planet.

The day itself was unseasonably warm, the air dry and dusty. In the bazaar, it was said that the chill wind at the time of the shah's departure had left with him, and now that Khomeini was coming home, the sun had arrived. The airport was now in the hands of his armed followers, and, as part of the deal cut between the army and the mullahs two days earlier, the southern mass of the city was now turned over to the uprising as troops withdrew. When the imam's 747 landed, he would motorcade through this liberated territory to the Shahyad Monument and then on to a cemetery where "martyrs of the Revolution" were buried. There, he would give his first public speech, in honor of the revolutionary dead.

A journey from the airport would have normally lasted for perhaps a half hour, but Khomeini's took most of the day because the crowd was so thick the imam's limo could only inch forward. Iranians were wedging in solidly for as far as the eye could see and all of them were chanting that Khomeini was their imam. Movement on the ground finally had to be abandoned and the imam ferried to the graveyard in a helicopter.

Now that he was home after fourteen years away, the difference in Khomeini was obvious. In France, the imam had been a prisoner of the situation, ignorant in the ways of the West, and the wisest course had been to allow the exiles who knew the turf to script him. But on the ground in Tehran, the exiles who had managed the stay in France were no longer in charge. As the Noffal brain trust had mapped it out on the eve of their return, Khomeini was to have set up headquarters in an empty school in south Tehran. But when his helicopter lifted him away from the cemetery at the end of his triumphal February 1 procession, he was taken instead to a different school, this one arranged by the imam's domestic network of clerics. At the same time, the imam's office was taken over by eleven mullahs under the direction of his son, Ahmed.

"From the very beginning," one of the Noffal brain trust remembered, "there was a struggle over controlling access to Khomeini. The religious faction wanted more leverage over the vision of the revolution and they got it. At first, it wasn't possible to cut off the rest of us. But as things went along, that was increasingly the case."

Nonetheless, Abolhassan Bani Sadr and Sadegh Ghotbzadeh continued as acolytes. Both also raised objections with Khomeini over the new arrangements during their first days back.

Predictably, Ghotbzadeh's objection was the most demonstrative. It erupted when he went to the school to visit the imam and found him in conference with an ayatollah notorious for his friendship with the shah and for his fierce opposition to Mossadeq back in 1953. Sadegh convulsed in fury at the sight. Pointing at the imam's guest, Ghotbzadeh shouted that people like that would be the end of the Revolution. The leader, he exclaimed, had no call to embrace the likes of this bootlicker of the Pahlavis. Then Ghotbzadeh stomped out of the room, swearing he was through with this herd of holy men and going to return to Paris.

That afternoon, Khomeini sent word for Sadegh to come back.

The imam wanted to know what was troubling him.

Ghotbzadeh answered that the imam's sitting down with that parasite was what troubled him. How could Khomeini do such a thing?

The imam described it as necessary "to bring all the brothers together," even the misguided ones who must now mend their ways. "Have you lost faith in me?" he asked.

Sadegh responded that he had never lost faith in his "master," but he had no faith in the rest; they disgusted him. Though he didn't elaborate with the imam, Ghotbzadeh privately referred to the great mass of mullahs as cretins and half-wits.

"You need only have faith in me," Khomeini replied.

Sadegh affirmed that he still had faith in his imam above all others.

Good, Khomeini said. He needed Ghotbzadeh and did not want him to go back to the land of the Franks. There was too much to be done here. He wanted Sadegh to take over the national radio and television network that was already in the hands of the Revolution. Ghotbzadeh tried to refuse, but the imam insisted. He left the headquarters that day with a media network to run.

Though Ghotbzadeh had been the top dog in Paris, Abolhassan Bani Sadr returned to Iran the more famous of the two — recognized for his leadership of a student uprising before his exile, his numerous books, and his role as the imam's host in Paris. Both men were stunned by the enormous force that greeted Khomeini's return, and, like Sadegh, Bani Sadr noticed the shift in the imam immediately, starting with his speech at the cemetery. Bani Sadr had been writing the imam's speeches back in Paris, but he didn't write this one. "I was surprised by it," Bani Sadr remembered. "It was the speech of a politician more than the speech of a religious leader. It was all about setting up a government. I hadn't expected that at all."

Somewhat troubled by the speech and all the deification of Khomeini, Bani Sadr was in no hurry to visit the imam at his new headquarters. After a day or two, Khomeini finally sent for him.

The imam wanted to know why Abolhassan had not been by before.

Bani Sadr explained that it was different here than in Paris. In Paris Khomeini had been his guest. Here Bani Sadr was his master's guest. Plus he did not know if he was welcome. He wasn't sure if Khomeini had forgotten that he wasn't here to replace the shah. The imam was not a political leader. He was a religious leader. He should not forget what he'd said in Paris.

Khomeini allowed that what was said in Paris was fine for Paris. Tehran was different.

Bani Sadr was quick to disagree. The imam would not change things by becoming the shah himself, he snapped. If he tried, he would be lost. There would be a lot of people who would anoint him shah and become his lackeys, but Bani Sadr wasn't among them. The imam was acting like a different man than the one he'd known in France.

Khomeini denied it. He wasn't trying to become shah, he said. Abolhassan had misunderstood. "I am not a man of government," he declared. And he still needed Bani Sadr's help.

Whatever Bani Sadr's misgivings, that invitation was more persuasive than his doubts. Having registered his complaint, he reaffirmed his allegiance to Khomeini and plunged into the political vacuum at his imam's side.

The first week and a half of Khomeini's return would later be remembered in Iran as the "Ten Days of Dawn." At the time, Ghotbzadeh described them simply as "anarchy." The army was unwilling to risk reasserting its control of south Tehran and often huddled together in defensive positions. Desertions were burgeoning, and the soldiers who remained on post all looked frightened. Order was now mostly a block-by-block proposition, enforced by whoever happened to be armed or aggressive. At the universities, classes had been canceled in favor of slide shows featuring authentic photos of the mutilated bodies of the Revolution's martyrs or instruction in bomb making and the care of machine guns. Vigilante justice was being administered spontaneously out in the neighborhoods to settle old scores. SAVAK assassins were on the loose as well. "The tension in the city grew increasingly electric," William Sullivan remembered. "Clashes between military units and the Ayatollah's followers were endemic and the nightly fusillade of stray automatic weapons fire became a regularly accepted phenomenon."

Against this backdrop, the Revolution proceeded with the strategy designed before the imam left Noffal.

Its first thrust was the continuing attack on the legitimacy of the shah's leftovers. The shah's last prime minister attempted to make contact with Khomeini upon his return, but Khomeini would have none of it. The shah might be gone, the imam pointed out, but his government remained, as did the foreigners' control of the army. All of them had to go before the Revolution would be safe. He was back, Khomeini told his followers, "to kick them in the teeth."

The imam announced at his first Tehran press conference the day after he arrived that he was backing the formation of a provisional government. The intention was for it to simply take over governmental functions from the existing bureaucracy, which all good Muslims would henceforth boycott. According to the imam, this provisional government was to run the country while a constitution was written and approved and a new government selected. Within a week of the imam's announcement, half of the government ministries had simply switched sides.

To form this transition arrangement, the imam called upon Mehdi Bazargan, an icon of the National Front and the Liberation Movement of Iran, a seventy-year-old engineer and dean of the University of Tehran's engineering faculty. Bazargan had implemented the nationalization of the oil industry under Mossadeq and had suffered three years in solitary confinement for his role in the 1963 rising that had forced the imam into exile. He had been an inspiration to Ghotbzadeh at the time of Sadegh's own exile. Short and impeccably dressed, fluent in English and French as well as Farsi, Bazargan was described in a CIA assessment as "a particularly devout Shi'a Muslim [who] has written extensively on religious matters. Although he is narrow minded almost to the point of fanaticism regarding Islam and its precepts, he is otherwise an intelligent man who can be receptive to the ideas of others. . . . His name [is] known and respected in opposition circles." His role as provisional prime minister in this story would only amount to a cameo, but a critical one nonetheless.

As would also be the case with the provisional government's designated foreign minister. Ebrahim Yazdi was a forty-eight-year-old medical researcher who had been living in exile in Waco, Texas, until the imam moved to Paris. Yazdi had been the imam's American organizer who, having watched the tear gas drift through the shah's first visit to Jimmy Carter, advised Khomeini to increase the pressure inside Iran. As provisional foreign minister, he had already visited several Islamic nations on behalf of the coming government even before returning to Iran on February 1. Bearded and looking younger than he was, "he maneuvered deftly," one American embassy hand later remembered, "switched from hot to cold . . . and always demonstrated what a good revolutionary he was. . . . But at least he worked . . . according to diplomatic norms."

This provisional government managed the social machinery, but policy continued to be made by the Revolution. To steer that process, the imam also created the Revolutionary Council, in which the provisional prime minister was just one member among eighteen, including several leading clerics as well as Ghotbzadeh and Bani Sadr. The Imam instructed the council to work by consensus if at all possible. When the Revolutionary Council had made a decision, they would bring it to him for final approval. The council met three times a week in someone's home in the early weeks, then three hours a day in an office. The very first meeting was convened at the imam's new headquarters on the night of February 1. Khomeini met with them on this occasion but, after an hour, fell asleep.

Eventually these structures, designed during the imam's French exile, would create an approximate order to the country's transition, but during those first ten days, they were little more than lists of names on a piece of paper. Before order could be established, something more primal had to be worked out. William Sullivan had warned Washington that a showdown between the army and the Revolution was inevitable unless the Americans reconciled the two, and now, with them still unreconciled, that showdown loomed in the night outside, thick with random small-arms fire.

Outright battle commenced on the evening of February 9, at an air base outside of Tehran. The catalyst was a television documentary about events surrounding the imam's return, broadcast by Ghotbzadeh's network. After watching the nation's joyous welcome replayed, a unit of *homofars*, the technicians who serviced planes, decided to demonstrate in support of the Revolution. They were joined by a group of air force cadets and junior officers, and when they refused to return to their barracks, the demonstration grew into a full-scale mutiny. A detachment of the elite Imperial Guard responded by attacking the rebels, and when that wasn't sufficient, Imperial Guard reinforcements were dispatched, including tanks. In the meantime, the *homofars* seized the base armory and distributed weapons to all comers. The initial firefight lasted all night inside the base perimeter.

Word of what was going on spread throughout Tehran, and a huge crowd — eventually upwards of one hundred thousand angry civilians — surrounded the base, erecting barricades of overturned cars, furniture, and even transit buses. The vanguard was made up of fighters from Marxist guerrilla organizations and several nationalist factions, but other combatants kept appearing out of nowhere, seemingly led by no one. Weapons were passed out from the armory stash, and by the morning of February 10, a steady rain of small-arms fire was falling on the Imperial Guard units inside the fence. The shooting only increased as mobs rampaged throughout town, attacking other armories in order to further arm the assault at the air base. Before noon, the base had fallen, much of the Imperial Guard detachment had mutinied, and the captured tanks led the huge mob across town to assault the Imperial Guard's barracks. The fuel depot there was set on fire, spreading a thick black cloud over everything, and two trucks were crashed through the perimeter fence, followed by an armed horde. Before 2:00 p.m., the guard base had been taken, and the crowd, following the tanks, turned its attention to the military headquarters complex just two blocks from the American embassy.

"A vicious battle ensued," William Sullivan remembered. "Stray rounds from the fighting fell into our compound all afternoon and evening. As darkness came, I watched some of the action from the rooftop of my Residence, but the increasing number of spent bullets ricocheting off the walls of the house made it an unsafe vantage point."

Meanwhile, Sullivan was frantically trying to pick up the pieces. Several American military assistance officers were missing somewhere out in the chaos, and at one point he had been worried enough about the embassy's safety that his staff had begun burning sensitive files. The smoke from that desperate destruction was sufficient that the nearby Swiss embassy, seeing something burning in the American compound, called to make sure everything was all right. By the end of February 10, Sullivan was reporting to Washington that the Iranian military was collapsing as a political force.

The Iranian army's chief of staff confirmed as much the next morning at a hasty press conference. Henceforth, he declared, the army would be nonpartisan. There would be no more military governments. All troops were to be withdrawn from the streets and returned to their barracks. In the space of two days, the Revolution had won its only fight, and it had done so without anyone ever having ordered it into battle. The imam didn't even endorse the fighting until it was almost over, but the men breaking through the military perimeter and laying down carpets of automatic weapons fire were nonetheless chanting that God was great and Khomeini was their leader. Shortly after the army gave in, a small remnant of the crowd went by the imam's headquarters and brought him five captured generals. While Ghotbzadeh's television cameras filmed the spectacle, the generals were summarily executed on the building's roof. By then, the shah's holdover prime minister, having spent only three weeks in his post, had disappeared into hiding. He would next be heard from in Europe. The provisional government was now all the government Iran had.

Shortly after the army announced it was surrendering the field, while Sullivan was in the middle of phone negotiations to retrieve twenty-six American military advisers who were still trapped behind the insurgents' lines in the nearby Iranian military headquarters, the ambassador received a phone call from an NSC aide in the White House Situation Room. Sullivan was forced to halt his negotiations in order to take it. The call from Washington came in over a clear, unsecured international line — a lax procedure that pissed Sullivan off even more than he already was — but he struggled to maintain his composure.

The messenger told Sullivan that Brzezinski wanted him to assess the possibility of the army staging a coup to succeed the dying holdover government.

Had the ambassador not been as stressed as he was, he might have laughed out loud at the absurdity of the notion. A coup? The generals would be lucky just to stay alive, much less seize power. At this very moment, the entire Iranian general staff and the American military personnel who were America's liaisons to the general staff were holed up in a bunker in the middle of a firefight that included captured tanks. The situation was hopeless. He'd been telling Washington as much for more than a day and had told them again over the phone barely a half hour earlier. Didn't this asshole at the NSC listen to anybody but himself? The fighting of the last two days was exactly what Sullivan had been warning about for months.

Tell Brzezinski to "get hosed," Sullivan snapped.

The aide, taken aback, stuttered a few times before suggesting that such remarks weren't very helpful.

Sullivan responded by offering to translate his epithet into Polish, just in case the national security adviser didn't understand. Then he hung up in a rage.

Some seventy-two hours later, on Valentine's Day, February 14, 1979, the United States officially recognized the imam's provisional government as the rulers of Iran.

Following instructions that had arrived from Washington overnight, Sullivan dispatched a note to the provisional foreign minister making the recognition official. Actually delivering the communication to Yazdi — who was not at his ministry or at his house — took a while, and Sullivan was on the phone several times with the minister's deputy making sure the delivery took place.

The ambassador then turned from that chore to other phone calls and paper shuffling. The embassy staff had been winnowed in December and January, and there was much to do. The ambassador worked efficiently, no doubt looking out his second-floor window during stray moments.

Then, around 10:30 a.m., the window was blown in — suddenly, without warning, exploded into shards by a string of .30-caliber bullets stitching along the embassy wall. The fire was coming from heavy machine guns set up on the surrounding rooftops looking down on the embassy compound. Sullivan dove to the floor, slithered out of sight, and took cover in the hallway as the fusillade continued. The gunners assaulted the building itself, blowing chunks out of door frames and window casements in methodical sweeps. After instructing two staff members to call the emergency phone numbers they had been given by the provisional government, Sullivan used a walkie-talkie to confer with his marine detachments outside in the compound — the embassy's only defenders since the Iranian army had withdrawn its guard detail several days earlier. From the marines he learned that a group of seventy-five well-armed guerrillas were over the wall and making for the residence. Sullivan ordered the marines at his home to withdraw to the chancery if possible and leave the guerrillas alone. They were to use their sidearms only in extreme cases of self-defense. Sullivan also notified Washington.

The chancery remained pinned down by automatic weapons fire while the guerrillas ransacked the residence for more than an hour. Sullivan used that time to move everyone in the chancery upstairs and eventually into the second-floor communications vault — except for the marines, who gathered in defensive positions in the lobby. By then all the building's steel outside doors, though bolted shut, were riddled with bullet holes, and large pits and chinks had been blown into the building's brick facing. The vault was the safest place to hide from stray bullets, and a crew in one of its rooms was frantically shredding documents and code books, and sabotaging communication links. When the guerrillas finally staged an attack on the chancery itself, Sullivan ordered the marines to lay down a protective layer of tear gas and then join the rest of the Americans in the vault. As the marines retreated, Iranians were breaking in the chancery's front door.

One of the first guerrillas inside thought to make a show of his entrance by blasting the glass front of the embassy's central security station to smithereens. He, like all of the assault team, was carrying a new G-3 infantry rifle of German design, liberated from an armory earlier in the week. He hadn't anticipated, however, that the security station window he targeted was bulletproof, and one of his own ricocheting G-3 rounds hit him in the middle of the forehead, dropping him in his tracks. After finding the ground floor otherwise empty, the rest of the assaulting guerrillas charged up the stairs.

Just as they did so, however, the huddling Americans in the vault heard a new round of firing open up, from different directions, and quickly realized the Iranians must be fighting one another. Apparently, Sullivan's Mayday call to the provisional foreign minister had worked. The imam's new chief diplomat had personally led a force of fighters to the rescue, and they were quickly surrounding the assault.

When Sullivan finally opened the vault door, admitting waves of tear gas, all the Americans had already been disarmed at his orders, to avoid any irreparable incident. A stack of sensitive documents had been successfully shredded and the cipher and communications machinery disabled. Two competing groups of Iranians were waiting outside in the corridor and escorted them outside.

"The scene in the courtyard was considerably disorganized," Sullivan remembered. "The Embassy employees . . . were now standing in a group along the wall of the parking lot. In the parking lot itself, reaching out towards the main gate, a group of Iranians milled about, some armed, some obviously spectators. A line of armed men in various pieces of military uniform had their rifles lowered and were pressing toward another group clustered in front of the gate. That group, which apparently had been the nucleus of the attacking force, was making a slow retreat toward the gate. Many of its members wore the familiar checkered scarf of the Fedayeen [leftist guerrillas]. . . . A large bearded ayatollah seemed to be positioned between the two military forces, attempting to urge the Fedayeen group to leave in quiet good order."

Also present was Ebrahim Yazdi, the provisional foreign minister, standing on the hood of a car with a bullhorn, urging the milling crowd to leave. When Sullivan approached him, Yazdi dismounted and shook his hand. The Iranian apologized profusely for the attack, pointing out that these attackers were not representative of the Revolution. The imam himself sent apologies as well. The situation was now, however, under control.

When the compound was completely cleared of attackers, the ambassador and the provisional foreign minister sat down in the residence for a longer discussion. Yazdi proposed that the Americans evacuate the compound altogether in the interests of keeping a low profile, but Sullivan refused that option. So, to ensure the embassy's safety, the foreign minister proposed leaving behind a force of forty fighters to guard the outside of the walls and another forty to be stationed inside the compound. Sullivan thought the latter arrangement highly irregular but accepted it anyway.

As soon as the chancery's communications links were back up, the ambassador updated Washington on the situation. The episode had lasted a little more than two hours. None of the staff from the chancery had been injured in the attack, and all of them had been accounted for except a marine sergeant who had last been seen trying to surrender to the guerrillas after being cornered in the cafeteria building. The compound itself was now back in American hands, and the embassy, at least for the moment, was secure.

$\mathcal{T}$HE EVENTUAL NOVEMBER 4, 1979, CAPTURE OF the American embassy and its occupants would be labeled "unthinkable" when it happened, but, actually, that possibility was central to the US government's thinking about Iran from February 14 on. For the next eight months, the subject came up every time the embassy was mentioned at the White House or the State Department.

In the immediate aftermath, of course, there was the marine sergeant still missing from the Valentine's Day assault to be dealt with. The provisional government had no knowledge of the prisoner but finally discovered that the fedayeen faction that had led the assault was holding him. He was wounded but not severely. After a week of negotiations between the imam's people and the fedayeen, the sergeant was returned and his liberation announced at the White House.

At the same time he was seeking his missing marine, Sullivan was also evacuating Americans who had remained in the country. The United States government flew three flights a day in and out of Tehran for a week, starting on February 17, with seats for any American nationals who wanted to leave. Exactly 3,636 availed themselves of the offer, and some 3,000 others decided to stay despite the embassy's declaration that it could not be responsible for their safety. Part of this migration stateside was a result of Sullivan's clearing the embassy's decks as well. The permanent American staff, once close to 1,500, was reduced by the end of the month to 60. All the sensitive documents that hadn't been destroyed were shipped stateside, and operations were reduced to a skeletal level. There was some discussion among the Americans, both in Tehran and in Washington, about closing the embassy altogether, but it was decided that a direct connection with Iran was too important to forfeit.

Not surprisingly, security was the paramount issue for the remaining operations inside the Americans' Tehran compound. At first, it was virtually impossible to resume work at the chancery because of the tear gas embedded in everything. Even after all the carpeting and drapes were replaced, the building smelled like the Valentine's Day assault for months. The refurbished building was also "hardened." The new doors were of much heavier steel, and remote-control tear gas devices were installed, as were more security cameras, bulletproof glass, and hardened steel grilles on all the first-floor windows.

The rest of the embassy's new security, aside from the marines, was supplied by the eighty fighters assigned by the provisional foreign minister. They were apparently a rogue band affiliated with a mullah and led, Sullivan remembered, by "a huge, hairy butcher . . . who was armed to the teeth and who occasionally administered discipline to his unit through a sharp cuff to a young man's head. . . . When I went out . . . they accompanied me in 'chase cars' just like the Iranian police bodyguards used to do. [I always] arrived accompanied by two carloads of these bearded, thuggish-looking characters armed with G-3 rifles and strung with bandoliers." This security detail also occasionally tortured captured Iranians in their guard shack, and pilfered goods and liquor out of the compound warehouse, but, as Sullivan pointed out, they were the best the Americans could do for the moment.

The other big change in the embassy was the looming departure of William Sullivan. The ambassador's time had run out. By the end of March, before the work on the chancery was complete, Sullivan would say his good-byes to the remaining staff and fly back to the United States to begin his retirement. His exit would be on a high note, with his February 14 performance described by *Newsweek* as "shrewd, stylish, and incredibly cool." The president officially accepted the senior diplomat's resignation "with special gratitude for [his] dedication, purpose and personal courage." It was assumed that a new ambassador to Iran would be named and accredited shortly.

In fact, that would never happen. Although no one yet knew it, William Sullivan was the last of his kind.

So too, of course, was the shah. Unlike the American ambassador, however, Mohammad Pahlavi was anything but out of the picture. The Valentine's Day assault on the embassy would have more immediate impact on HIM than anyone, exile or not.

Pahlavi had continued to dither over what to do next ever since leaving Iran. Anwar Sadat gave him a full state reception at the airport in Cairo, complete with Iranian flags, huge posters of his portrait, and a military review. Overwhelmed, the shah was in tears by the time the two old friends were in the limo together. His Imperial Majesty confessed to the Egyptian ruler that he felt guilty about having left his country, but said that the American pressure had been difficult to resist and that he had wanted to save Iran from a civil war or worse. He said he felt his life as a monarch was over, but he also said that events might yet turn his way, as they had in 1953 — oscillating between expectancy and despair and back again, sometimes within the same sentence.

All the while, he continued to behave like a visiting monarch. His Imperial Majesty and the shahbanou stayed at the Oberoi, a luxury hotel built on an island in the Nile that was theirs for their stay, and were photographed touring mosques with Sadat. They also received a few visitors and many phone calls. Most of the visitors were Iranians, almost all of them with plots of one sort or another to bring to His Majesty's ear. Sadat spent hours talking with the shah, and the Egyptian ruler's frustration with the Iranian's inability to make up his mind was noted in a January intelligence report forwarded to the NSC. "Welcome to the club," an NSC specialist scribbled in the report's margin.

The subsequent welcome in Morocco was far more subdued. King Hassan had labeled this a "private visit," so Mohammad Pahlavi arrived without pomp, and the international press was prevented from even watching his car drive by on its way from the airport to the king's palace outside Marrakech. Several days later, at his first press opportunity, the shah was made available for photos on a palace terrace, wearing a very expensive checked sport coat, slacks, an open-collared shirt, shoes polished to a mirror finish, and his usual oversized rectangular glasses. He still seemed dapper, but his spectacles now looked almost like goggles on the physically shrunken former shahanshah. He gave a few individual interviews while in Morocco as well, with several among the international press he trusted most. To a British reporter, he claimed that the mullahs weren't the real power. The communists were the ones behind his downfall, he said, but none of them would be able to run his country. He predicted that as that became apparent, the monarchy would be appreciated for what it had done. To American television personality Barbara Walters, he said he had never abdicated and never would. He had no specific answers about how long he intended to stay in Marrakech or where he would go next.

The shah continued to maintain his ambivalence about traveling on to the United States as late as February 11, when he met with a CIA emissary in Marrakech. This visiting "senior U.S. Intelligence officer," disguised with dark glasses and a heavy mustache, spent two hours with the shah at the king's palace. "He found the shah to be virtually a broken man," an NSC aide remembered, "traumatized by events and lacking any plans for the future."

Finally, on February 22, eight days after the embassy in Tehran had been overrun and one day after Sullivan retrieved his missing marine, the shah finally concluded that there was no point to hanging around in the vicinity of "his" country anymore and sent a note to the American ambassador to Morocco. His Imperial Majesty was at last ready to go to California, he informed the American representative. His plan was to move there a week hence.

The ambassador said he would inform Washington and get right back to HIM about the travel details.

As far as Washington was concerned, however, the timing of the request could not have been worse. The Valentine's Day assault was still fresh, and at that very moment Sullivan was in negotiations to free several captured American military personnel who had been operating listening posts in Iran along the Soviet border. When consulted about the shah's proposed entry, Sullivan responded immediately that it "would confirm the worst suspicions of those Iranian revolutionaries who assumed that the U.S. was plotting to restore the Shah to power." It would also sabotage any hopes of relations with the new Iran. Even Brzezinski's own staff concluded that the likelihood of American hostages being taken in response to such a move was high.

Nonetheless, Brzezinski remembered, "my position never wavered. . . . At stake were our traditional commitment to asylum and our loyalty to a friend. To compromise those principles would be to pay an extraordinarily high price . . . in terms of our self-esteem [and] in our standing among our allies, and [all] for very uncertain benefits. I was aware that Sadat [and] the Saudi rulers, and others were watching our actions carefully."

The national security adviser's argument swayed no one, including Jimmy Carter himself. The Special Coordinating Committee instead decided to send an emissary to His Imperial Majesty to let him know that developments in Iran made the situation at the moment very dicey and that although the invitation was still open, it would be better for everyone if he didn't take the United States up on it just yet.

Ironically, it fell to Brzezinski to pass on the first hint of the new American policy, before any emissary had been chosen. Shortly after the SCC meeting, he received a phone call from his friend, now former ambassador Ardeshir Zahedi. Zahedi was at his home in Switzerland. His Majesty wanted to travel to the United States within a few days, he pointed out, but Washington hadn't yet responded. Was there some problem?

As a matter of fact, Zbig admitted, there was. He then launched into a long list of the difficulties the shah might encounter were he to come. The government couldn't guarantee he wouldn't be sued by the new Iranian government or a disgruntled Iranian citizen. Nor could it ensure that he would not be made the object of congressional action. On top of that, what had been going on in Tehran made this a very difficult moment, and all the pro-Khomeini Iranians inside the United States might pose a significant security threat. It would have been far better if he had come in January, when the invitation was first made. Washington would be sending someone out to the shah to discuss it soon.

Zahedi said he understood, but Brzezinski found the role he'd had to play over the phone disgusting. The following day, Zbig raised the issue again with the president. This decision had to be reversed, he insisted, before it was too late.

Brzezinski's proclivity for reopening closed issues could be irritating under any circumstance, but in this case it was particularly so. The president had been deeply shaken by the Valentine's Day attack and the brief capture of the marine sergeant, and, though he found Brzezinski's argument compelling, it paled for him next to his feelings of responsibility for the safety of the Americans in the embassy. That they might end up hostages was an all too real possibility, and he did not want the shah in Palm Springs playing tennis while they were in captivity. Nor did he want his national security adviser constantly jabbing the open wound the dilemma left him with. Period. End of subject.

The message still had to be passed on, however, and an emissary selected. While the shah waited for the promised conversation, the NSC and the State

Department scrambled to find the right person to tell him. In desperation, State even approached the shah's two biggest American supporters, David Rockefeller and Henry Kissinger, in hopes one of them would act as the bearer of bad news. Rockefeller, point man for the family's connection to the shah since his brother Nelson's death a month earlier, was outraged at the decision and at the request and refused indignantly. Kissinger did as well, bridling particularly at the suggestion that he convey a position he wholeheartedly opposed. In the end, the task fell to State's man in Morocco, who had been the only prominent voice in the department arguing to admit the shah rather than shove him away.

The two finally spoke on March 17, in the library at the king of Morocco's palace. The shah was wearing a sport coat and seemed at ease. The more formally dressed ambassador was anxious and got straight to the point.

His Majesty was always welcome in the United States, he told him, but now would be a very "inconvenient" time. The ambassador then elaborated on all the issues of harassment and security that would be raised inside the United States, including the possibility of huge demonstrations against HIM. It would be in the shah's best interest, he argued, to avoid such a tinderbox situation and refrain from taking the United States up on its invitation.

The shah swallowed the news without flinching and did not have to be told twice. He made no recriminations, just indicated that he understood.

The ambassador went on to say that he was aware that His Imperial Majesty's host, the king, needed the shah to move on. The United States, knowing that His Majesty was without the resources of a diplomatic network, was canvassing nations for invitations. Thus far, however, the only two nations that had indicated a willingness to accept him were South Africa and Paraguay.

Though bitterly disappointed, the shah addressed these options without revealing his feelings. Rather, it was as if he were talking to his travel agent. He said that South Africa was where Reza, his father, had died and had very bad associations for him. He could never live there. As for Paraguay, it might as well have been New Guinea. It was simply too far out in the boondocks for HIM. If he couldn't come to the United States, he would prefer Mexico, close enough to where his mother was living in Beverly Hills that she could visit him easily. The ambassador to Morocco said that the Mexicans hadn't yet responded to the American inquiries, but the United States would continue to push the issue.

The first person to fly to the shah's side at this turning point was his twin sister, Princess Ashraf. "The Black Panther" had been in New York and this was the first time she had seen her brother face-to-face since she left Iran the previous fall. Her devotion to HIM was still complete. Just her presence was bolstering to the shah, but she was also quick to grasp the need to reorganize her brother's support system. So far, handling the logistics of his traveling household had been a patchwork arrangement, as he waited to see how things worked out. Now he needed someone to pilot his stateless ship and keep it functioning.

For this, Ashraf turned to Bobby Armao, the now thirty-year-old New York public relations man she and Nelson Rockefeller had sent to Iran during the last weeks of Pahlavi rule. His job was part majordomo to the transient Pahlavi household, part personal secretary to His Imperial Majesty, part prime minister of the Kingdom in Exile. Without him over the coming months, the shah would have been largely helpless. Armao would later say that if he had been paid for his work by the hour he would have emerged a multimillionaire.

Having hired Armao, Ashraf turned to rallying her brother's American supporters. Two of them, David Rockefeller and Henry Kissinger, would become His Majesty's principal lobbyists with the Carter administration.

As part of the shah's Moroccan reorganization, David Rockefeller assigned a Chase vice president to handle the shah's finances and, when the occasion called for it, act as His Majesty's direct liaison to the American government. Rockefeller was also prepared to use his considerable personal leverage on His Imperial Majesty's behalf, but almost entirely in private. Henry Kissinger handled most of the public statements for the shah's lobbying campaign, as well as all the overt attacks on Carter's handling of the situation. Though now out of office, the former secretary of state was still a man with considerable influence on public debate, with whom Carter did not want to be drawn into conflict if he could help it. That reluctance gave Kissinger additional leverage, and he was prepared to use all of it to bring the shah to the United States. One administration foreign policy hand would later describe Henry Kissinger's efforts as "obnoxious." Carter himself would eventually describe Kissinger as "a liar and also irresponsible."

Ashraf assembled her brother's new team while he was still in Marrakech, worrying about where he could go next. The list of refusals was daunting. Switzerland, where he owned a house, would not admit him. Nor would Britain, where he owned another house. France didn't want him, nor did any other European nations. He could have returned to Egypt, but everyone agreed that would have put his friend Sadat in a difficult political position.

And Bobby Armao had been told by His Imperial Majesty's Moroccan hosts that the shah's presence was becoming an issue there and the king needed his guest to move on very soon, even if that meant taking South Africa up on its offer. This prospect put the shah's new team into overdrive.

It was Ashraf who first suggested the Bahamas as an alternative possibility. Subsequently Kissinger flew there to meet with the prime minister, and when those conversations were positive, Ashraf called Armao and dispatched him to the Caribbean nation to formally negotiate. The discussions were long and very detailed. Although the country consisted of some 700 islands and 2,400 cays, the government would grant the shah a visa to stay only at Paradise Island, where a new resort had just been opened that the government was trying to hype. His quarters there would be a beach house, in full view of the hotel and absolutely tiny by His Majesty's standards. Armao objected that the arrangement was totally unsuitable and a security nightmare, but the offer was take it or leave it. A deal with the Bahamians was cut just hours before the shah was scheduled to fly to South Africa.

Since His Imperial Majesty had long since sent his own plane back to Iran — saying it belonged to the nation, not to him — transportation for the move across the Atlantic Ocean was provided by the king of Morocco, who loaned HIM his personal Boeing 747. On the morning of March 30, 1979, the shah and shahbanou traveled west in it with half a dozen retainers, their dogs, and 368 pieces of luggage.

The next four months would be remembered in Iran as *Bahar Azadi,* "the Spring of Freedom." "There was a layer of chaos," a French diplomat remembered, "but part of that chaos was a lovely chaos. I never saw so much freedom of speech. There was an eruption of newspapers, hundreds of different papers. People were hungry for it. For centuries they had never had this in their life. I hadn't been in Iran since 1975, when the shah had everyone looking over their shoulder, and when I visited in 1979, freedom of speech was everywhere. You could just say anything that came to your mind. There were booksellers on the sidewalks and you could find anything: Che Guevara, Lenin, anything. I went to meetings where people criticized Khomeini and the Revolution, I went to meetings where people criticized everyone who criticized Khomeini. There were often 100,000 people showing up for these events. These were very heady times, when politics of every sort was on everyone's lips. That's what gave the chaos its loveliness."

The spring's paramount political issue remained the question of exactly what would come next. When the imam and all others were still back in Noffal, they had endorsed the vague notion of creating an "Islamic republic" to replace the shah, but few had any specific ideas of just what that meant. The closest model was assumed to be the sixth-century caliphate of the First Imam, Ali, before his martyrdom, although what was known about the governance of that era bore little resemblance to a modern republic. To gain some definition, a group of lawyers in Paris had been assigned the task of drafting a possible constitution and they continued their work after Khomeini's return to Iran. Rather than wait for that document, however, the imam wanted to seek the people's endorsement of an Islamic model as soon as possible, and, at his insistence, the Revolutionary Council decreed a referendum that the provisional government would conduct. The question would be simple: Should the nation drop the monarchy and reformulate itself as an "Islamic republic"— to be defined later in a new constitution — yes or no? All Iranians over the age of sixteen would be allowed to vote, both men and women.

Announced in the first week of March, the referendum was conducted on the last two days of the month. The ensuing three-week campaign was one-sided. The imam weighed in for voting "yes," noting that doing so was in obedience to "the orders of God." The only prominent personage to criticize that notion was Bazargan, the provisional prime minister, who asserted that there was no theoretical basis in either Islam or politics for such a form of government — then voted for it anyway. He was joined by 98 percent of 17 million voters, most of the adult national population.

By now, Khomeini had tired of his life in Tehran, where he couldn't move about on the streets without a hundred armed men to protect him and had to employ a taster to screen all his food for poison. So at the end of February, the imam moved back to his old home in Qom, a two-hour drive away. Here, he said, he could participate in the revival of his long-shuttered seminary and resume his life as a theologian. The seeming renunciation was an illusion. Greeted by a huge crowd when he arrived in Qom, he sounded anything but retiring. Instead, the ayatollah vowed to "devote the remaining one or two years of my life" to reshaping Iran "in the image of Mohammad. . . . All the corrupt practices of the West must be eliminated. The West has debased us and destroyed our spiritual life. . . . We will amend the newspapers. We will amend the radio, the television, the cinemas. All of these should follow an Islamic pattern. What the nation wants is an Islamic republic. . . . We do not want our judicial system to be Western. We do not want our laws to be Western. We have divine laws."

The administration of justice was one of the first powers the imam sought to wrest from the informal *komitehs* that now controlled Iran on a neighborhood level. For the first month and a half after Khomeini returned, it had been a catch-as-catch-can enterprise, with "trials" occurring instantly, lasting perhaps ten minutes, often conducted right in the street where the arrest took place. The first set of executions, after the fall of the air base and the Imperial Guard barracks, was typical. Among the captives was the former head of SAVAK. His rank and affiliation were enough to seal his fate without any further hearing, so he was taken directly to the roof of the imam's headquarters and displayed to a crowd below, most of whom had brought knives and meat cleavers. They were screaming to be allowed to do the job themselves. The SAVAK general cowered above them, in the words of one western journalist, "like a beaten rabbit." Then one of the imam's men fired a pistol into the base of his brain and threw him down onto the street, firing a couple more rounds into the falling corpse.

No count was kept of the executions during that first month and a half, but the range was wide and the offenses for which people were shot observed no statute of limitation. One shah official was shot for things he said about the imam in 1963. The now doddering commander of the troops that had fired into the Mashhad mosque in 1935 was executed as well. Generals were fair game for everyone, and the executed also included a half dozen or more members of the shah's rubber stamp Majlis.

In March, apparently at the insistence of the provisional prime minister, the imam announced that "all trials from now on must take place under the direct supervision of the Revolutionary Council and the Revolutionary Government." While this reined in the process somewhat, Khomeini's pronouncement did not change the end product much. Justice, as reformulated, was now administered by revolutionary tribunals run by Islamic jurists, outside of the administration of the provisional government, under the jurisdiction of mullahs. Over the next sixth months, according to the US State Department, these tribunals were responsible for "more than 600 executions by firing squads . . . of political and military figures identified with the previous regime." The trials preceding these deaths lasted on average less than three hours.

In the meantime, the lawyers who had begun working in France on a possible constitution had completed their draft and circulated it among the revolutionary inner circle. It included 175 articles, many of which were based on similar provisions in the constitution of France's Fifth Republic or in Iran's short-lived 1906 version. Among other things, free speech was to be absolute except in time of war, and the establishment of any foreign military base on Iranian soil was forbidden. The official head of state would be an elected president who would then appoint a prime minister. The president was also designated military commander in chief. An elected Majlis would make laws. To ensure that both did not violate the constitution or Islam, a Council of Guardians was envisioned, composed of five "religious leaders who are aware of the requirements of contemporary times" and six "experts in judicial matters"— three of whom must be professors from Iran's law schools, along with three judges from the country's Supreme Court selected by the Majlis.

At first, the draft was warmly received. The Revolutionary Council found it sufficient basis upon which to proceed and sent it to the imam to review. Khomeini's initial response was to suggest only a few minor changes, even though there was no mention in this draft of the Rule of the Jurist that had been at the heart of his theory of Islamic government.

The difficulties began when the Revolution tried to decide what to do next, now that it had a draft text.

There were two competing proposals. The provisional prime minister and his secular allies wanted the next step to be the election of a constituent assembly that would then review and revise the draft constitution before approving it. That approach was opposed by a large faction of mullahs who had recently founded the Islamic Republican Party to pursue an Islamic political agenda. The IRP insisted that the constitution be approved by a public referendum after an Assembly of Experts, all appointed by the imam, had reviewed it for Islamic content and prepared a final draft for the vote, projected for some point late in the year.

The disagreement between the two factions came to a head late in the spring, when the imam summoned the contending parties to Qom to thrash the question out in front of him. Two dozen people were at the meeting, and the debate was fractious, with the sides breaking down largely along religious versus secular lines.

The last word belonged to the imam, and he endorsed the mullahs' position wholeheartedly. The secular losers in that argument would later identify it as a decisive moment in the history of the Islamic Republic of Iran.

· 13 ·

Mohammad reza pahlavi and his wife, the shahbanou, stayed in the Bahamas for ten weeks and hated it.

For starters, the house was the size of a bandbox, in full view of a public beach. There was only room for the shah and Farah and one servant to sleep there. To gain privacy from the public gawkers, the royal family had to retreat to the cottage's inner courtyard, lined with rows of their suitcases. To have a meal alone together, they had to sit inside while everyone else stepped out onto the beach. Security was a nightmare, so Bobby Armao hired fifty rent-a-cops from Wackenhut to supplement the shah's half dozen bodyguards. Iran's most notorious "hanging judge" among the revolutionary tribunals had already sentenced the shah and his entire family to death in absentia, there was a reward of $70,000 on His Imperial Majesty's head, and one Qom newspaper offered an all-expenses-paid trip to Mecca to anyone who managed to kill him. When the shah walked the public beach — where he was besieged by rich Americans on vacation who wanted to tell him how much they admired him — so did his bodyguards, with their submachine guns hidden in the briefcases they incongruously carried along the edge of the surf. Altogether, the scene was claustrophobic to the extreme.

His Imperial Majesty sent Armao to the Bahamians to request that they be allowed to move to some other location, but the Bahamians would hear nothing of it. It was there or nowhere. And the price was dear: Every week the local officials presented the shah with a bill for $120,000 and demanded immediate payment. On top of that, he was expressly forbidden from making any public statement about his treatment or about the situation back in Iran. HIM was also cited at one point for letting his Great Dane run loose on the beach.

Even Farah, who had often shouldered the responsibility for lifting her husband's melancholy, felt suffocated and deeply depressed. She chain-smoked and hid from the press. Mostly she was photographed with telephoto lenses, looking, according to one western journalist, "like a fawn at bay." She granted one interview, to a woman from *Paris Match* she had known for a long time. She recalled to this reporter an incident in the preparations for the opulent celebration at Persepolis, the shah's coming-out party as the inheritor of Cyrus the Great. A famous French pastry chef had created an enormous cake for the event, topped with an actual golden crown, but while he was moving it, the confection had collapsed in a heap. "He was devastated," the shahbanou pointed out. "All his work, his art, in crumbs. That's a bit how I feel today. Everything we tried to create, all our work, in crumbs."

For his part, the shah took refuge in routine. At 6:00 a.m., he rose, unrolled a prayer rug, bowed toward Mecca, and prayed. When finished, he began reading newspapers: the *New York Times,* the *London Daily News,* the *Wall Street Journal,* the *Nassau Guardian,* and anything else reasonably recent from Paris or London that could be found. He had a cable connection to CBS Television and spent hours scanning BBC and other radio broadcasts for news of his country. He also started working on his memoirs with a French ghostwriter. They would eventually be published under the title *Answer to History.* The Bahamians limited the number of visitors who could see him, and the daily quota was usually filled, mostly with diplomats. He spent a lot of time on the phone, often with other royals or heads of state, but took a break in the midafternoon for a swim in the ocean and usually played an hour of tennis as the sun was going down. Otherwise, he watched videos of first-run American movies when there was nothing else to do.

Perhaps the shahanshah's favorite time on the island was spent with his twenty-year-old son, Crown Prince Reza, who flew in on a break from school in the United States. The two played tennis together and walked on the beach. Young Reza had already completed flight training with the American air force and was now studying political science at the University of Southern California. The shah had refused to abdicate his throne in order to keep his heir's right to succeed him intact, and it was now his hope that even if his own time was done, someday his boy might reclaim the dynasty. During his son's visit, His Majesty tried to pass on his accumulated lessons in kingship. The ritual gave him a deep sense of meaning.

All in all, however, Mohammad Reza Pahlavi was miserable. The humidity wore him down, his Valium dosage could not keep his anxiety entirely at bay, and, as his ghostwriter would put it for him, his "Bahamian vacation was anything but a holiday."

Perhaps the worst moment of the shah's stay in the Bahamas came just a week after he arrived, with that day's news from Iran. The former prime minister the shah had desperately imprisoned for corruption and then left incarcerated when he fled had finally come up for judgment at a revolutionary tribunal. There were seventeen charges, starting with "corrupting the earth." The defendant had obviously been seriously beaten during his time in prison, according to court observers, and his face was disfigured. The trial lasted through several three-hour sessions, which local reporters were allowed to observe. In the end, the verdict was guilty and the sentence was death. The judge personally garroted the former prime minister until he was half dead, then assigned a machine gunner to finish the job with a fusillade of bullets.

The shah's depression was compounded by his ongoing chemotherapy. His French doctor came and went, his mission hidden behind a cover story identifying the physician as a gynecologist treating the queen. During his examinations, the doctor discovered that the shah's lymphoma was becoming more aggressive and insisted that it was time His Majesty checked into a hospital for a more comprehensive exam. That would, of course, entail revealing his secret, and the shah refused.

While the shah suffered through his Caribbean exile, the team his twin sister had set in motion made sure the issue of his fate was not allowed to die along the Potomac. Henry Kissinger made contact with Zbigniew Brzezinski a week after the shah landed in Nassau. Without wasting much of his legendary charm, the former secretary of state castigated Brzezinski for what the administration was doing to HIM. His anger was not only strong, but apparently dismissive and condescending as well. Brzezinski later summed it up as a "rather sharp" diatribe. The national security adviser told Kissinger he was talking to the wrong guy; Brzezinski agreed with him. He advised Henry to call the president and said he would arrange it.

Kissinger and Carter spoke later that day. Kissinger made his argument far more politely than he had with Zbig, but the point was the same. He told the president he knew that David Rockefeller was scheduled to see him a couple days hence and went on record ahead of time that he also backed whatever Rockefeller said.

According to Hamilton Jordan, who was in the room with Carter when he took the Kissinger call, the president responded, "As long as there is a country where the shah can live safely and comfortably, it makes no sense to bring him here and destroy whatever slim chance we have of rebuilding a relationship with Iran. It boils down to a choice of the shah's preferences as to where he lives and the interests of our country."

Rockefeller's turn came in the course of a visit to the White House during the second week of April. "I told him of my concern," Rockefeller remembered, "that a friend of the United States should be treated in such a way and said I felt he should be admitted and we should take whatever steps were necessary to deal with threats [to the Embassy]. I didn't tell him how to deal with it, but I said it seemed to me that a great power such as ours could not submit to blackmail. . . . I got the impression the president didn't want to hear about it."

Carter noted in his diary afterward that "David Rockefeller . . . came in to spend some time with me. The main purpose of this visit apparently is to try to induce me to let the shah into our country. Rockefeller, Kissinger, and Brzezinski seem to be adopting this as a joint project."

And they were by no means yet done.

Short of entering the United States, the shah still hoped to move on to Mexico, but, as the end of May approached and the Mexicans still hadn't been heard from, Armao filed a notice with the Bahamian government that His Majesty and the shahbanou were applying to extend their visas, due to expire in the middle of June. The shah waited and waited, without any official Bahamian response to the request until the visas had only ten days left. Then, according to the shah, with "no explanation, no expression of regrets, and no further discussions with Bahamian officials," their application to extend their stay was declined and His Imperial Majesty was given until his visa expired to leave.

As far as the shah was concerned, this sudden eviction smelled of British intervention. "British influence in this former territory remained strong," he explained, and "I have a long-standing suspicion of British intent and British policy which I have never found reason to alter." It would, he thought, be just like the Brits to kick him when he was already down.

Kissinger then came to the rescue. The former secretary of state made a personal call to the president of Mexico to plead for HIM's sanctuary, and, two days before being booted out of the Bahamas, the shah was issued a six-month tourist visa by Mexico, effective immediately. Bobby Armao was dispatched there to finalize arrangements and advance the move.

Armao's most pressing task in Mexico was to find a place for the shah to live. Mexico City was a possibility, but it was perhaps too much of a mega metropolis for good security. Acapulco, where the shah's sister Princess Shams had a home, also had potential, but as a tourist town on the beach, it had many of the same security disadvantages as the Bahamas. Frustrated, Bobby lamented his search's initial lack of success in a phone call to a New York friend. She suggested Cuernavaca. Just thirty-seven miles south of Mexico City, high in the Sierra Madre del Sur, the climate was pleasant and the air still good, and the town included a very wealthy international colony in which Armao's friend owned a house. She told him to go up there and use her place as a base while he scouted around for a property to lease. Indeed, one of her friends knew of an estate that was vacant and ready to occupy.

The Villa of Roses, as the vacant house was known, had been empty since its owner's death four years earlier. Nonetheless, Bobby rented it at first sight, signing a three-and-a-half-month lease. The gardens, covering the hillside in terraced flower beds, were a little overgrown, but that could be tended to. The house was more than ample enough for the shah's retinue and lifestyle, though it had no furniture. At the end of a cul-de-sac, backing up on bluffs over a watercourse and surrounded by a continuous stone wall, it would be relatively easy to establish very tight security.

The royal couple, their servants, their dogs, and their baggage arrived at Mexico City International Airport by private jet from the Bahamas on June 10. Before taking a car caravan to Cuernavaca, replete with an escort of Mexican Federales, His Imperial Majesty met with the press at the airport.

Would the shah be using Mexico as a stepping-stone for moving on to the United States? one of the reporters asked.

That, the shah replied, "would depend on whether we were welcomed."

For the rest of the summer, His Majesty's children were at the Villa of Roses, on vacation from their American schools. His mother visited, and so did Ashraf, on several different occasions. And when his twin wasn't in Cuernavaca, she talked to her brother every day on the phone. Otherwise, the shah lost himself in the daily routine he had adopted in the Bahamas. He read the papers and followed the news. He worked on his memoirs and would be almost through the first draft by the end of summer. A good portion of his day was also spent with visitors.

The two most distinguished of those were Americans. Henry Kissinger was the first to arrive. He stayed for two days, meeting with His Majesty for hours to discuss world politics and the stuff of superpowers. It was bolstering for the shah to have a momentary whiff of the upper echelons where he had once held sway.

The second visit was from Kissinger's onetime boss, the disgraced former president, Richard Nixon. Nixon and the shah went way back to the Eisenhower years, and the former president had a special fondness for His Majesty. When Nixon had been at one of his own political nadirs, having lost the 1962 election for governor in California, the shah had invited him to Tehran and given him a full-blown state reception, including military review and parade through adoring crowds mustered by the palace for the occasion. It had curbed Nixon's depression and turned him back to politics renewed. When the Watergate scandal drove him from office twelve years later, once again the shah had welcomed him. Nixon never forgot and felt honor bound to stand by His Majesty.

As placid as that summer in Mexico seemed for the shah and his family — taking the sun among the gardens in the Sierra Madre, at poolside, and on the tennis court — there was still a threat lingering just offstage.

The hanging judge's sentence had been reiterated back in Iran, and his revolutionary tribunal claimed to have dispatched assassins to carry out the will of the court. The judge announced that these executioners had been on Pahlavi's trail in the Bahamas, but the shah had left before they could kill him. The judge told reporters in Tehran that the same assassins were now on their way to Mexico, under instructions to kill the shahbanou as well as the shah, though he offered her clemency if she would kill her husband. On top of that, Yasir Arafat, chairman of the Palestine Liberation Organization, had publicly offered some of his group's shooters to do the job as well. Arrayed against this threat were the shah's half dozen bodyguards and an equal number of Mexican plainclothes police.

Understandably, everyone was a little jumpy.

That much was made plain in an incident that had started out as just a little Pahlavi family fun. The crown prince was already a qualified pilot at the age of twenty and one day, thinking to surprise and impress his parents, he arranged to rent a helicopter and take it out on a joyride. His idea was to come darting up the river canyon and buzz the Villa of Roses. When the Mexican guards saw the chopper, however, they thought it was a Khomeini-inspired assault and began blasting away at it with their submachine guns. Fortunately for the crown prince, they didn't hit a thing. Afterward, the shahbanou ran down to where the guards were standing with shell casings scattered around their feet and extravagantly praised them all for being such bad shots.

· 14 ·

———————

$\mathcal{H}$AMILTON JORDAN HAD BEEN WORKING ON CAR-
ter's reelection effort for six months by the time the shah landed in Mexico
and already had strong organizations in the field in Iowa, New Hampshire,
and Florida, the first three places where votes would be cast in the 1980 primary campaign. Jordan wrote his boss regular memos about the political
situation and was not shy about forecasting rough waters ahead. He told
Jimmy to expect that someone would challenge him from inside the Democratic Party and that the most likely challenger would be Edward Kennedy,
senator from Massachusetts, liberal icon, and scion of the nation's preeminent political family. Jordan expected to win, but he knew full well it would
not be easy.

Simply put, the country's economy was a mess and the principal culprit,
the price of oil, was far beyond Carter's control. The Organization of Petroleum Exporting Countries, OPEC, had discovered its potential as a cartel
and had been steadily reducing its members' production levels and tighten-
ing supply at the same time that Iran, formerly the second largest producer

on the planet, had almost disappeared from the market altogether in the disorder of the Revolution. The result shattered the ceiling on the price of gas at the pumps, throwing the United States into a tailspin. Lines began appearing at gas stations as shortages developed, home mortgage interest rates were soon at 13 percent, and inflation ballooned into double digits. Already car sales, the traditional engine of the economy, were down 25 percent. And as was always the case in American politics, the nation held the president responsible.

Needless to say, that left the campaign Jordan was about to run with a serious handicap. In an ABC News poll at the end of March, almost the middle of his term, only 31 percent responded positively when asked how good a job Jimmy Carter was doing, down from over 70 percent early the year before. While respondents had no doubt about Carter's probity and gave his foreign policy very positive reviews, his reputation for "leadership" was taking a severe beating. His White House was thought to be in disarray, often at cross-purposes with itself, and his inability to get along with the Congress dominated by his own party was held against him. "No one seems to be in charge," the president's media strategist complained. "We still seem at times to have two or more foreign policies. Cabinet members contradict one another on major policy and it is never made clear who is speaking for the Administration. People get reprimanded from time to time but *no one ever gets fired.*"

How to govern better, however, was not an easy question to answer. More than a few at the White House, including the president himself, thought Jordan was the answer. On three different occasions over their first two years in the White House, Carter had asked Hamilton to act as his chief of staff and bring internal order to the management of his presidency, but Hamilton had always found a way to reject the request. Though, he admitted, "there was a need for less democracy and more organization in the White House," he had refused because of his own ambivalence about the job. To do it right, he would need supreme authority in a lot of operations, and the internal politics of that would be a lot to take on, especially if he tried to mind the president's political campaign as well.

The urgency felt inside Carter's reelection effort as the summer began was rooted in a trend pointed out by the president's pollster in the course of some background polling on the mood of the public at the end of 1978. When a sample was asked to give a numerical rating to their perceptions of five years ago, now, and five years hence, the numbers generated by the responses headed straight downhill by the largest margins the pollster had ever seen.

"America is a nation deep in crisis," he reported. "Psychological more than material, it is a crisis of confidence marked by dwindling faith in the future. . . . It can be read in the polls which monitor the vital signs of the body politic, it can be heard in the growing real despair of elites and ordinary citizens alike as they struggle to articulate . . . the malaise which they themselves feel. This crisis is not your fault as President. It is the natural result of historical forces and events which have been in motion for twenty years. [Nonetheless] this crisis . . . has the potential to consume your Presidency politically. . . . It [also] has the potential to elevate your Presidency, historically, to the first magnitude."

The president's smartest option, according to the pollster, was to treat this dire situation as an opportunity. "Jimmy Carter can become a trans-forming leader," the report argued, "evolving into a great President who leaves an imprint as great as Washington's, Lincoln's, Wilson's, Kennedy's, or Roosevelt's. . . .

"I am surer that this assumption is valid," the pollster declared, "than I have been of any previous judgment in my life, including the possibility of your [1976] election."

Jimmy Carter decided to follow his pollster's advice and on July 15, in a nationally televised prime-time appearance preempting regularly scheduled programming, sought to reach out to this national emotional undercurrent. Carter had spent the previous ten days on a widely publicized retreat at Camp David to reassess his presidency, including interviewing a number of promi-nent Americans about what they thought the country needed from him. The speech that ended that episode of self-examination would be remembered as "the malaise speech," though the president never mentioned the word *malaise* in the text. He came on television from the Oval Office at 10:00 p.m. eastern daylight time, on a Sunday night, exactly three years to the day since he had first received the Democratic Party's nomination for president.

"I want to talk to you right now about a fundamental threat to American democracy," he declared. "The threat is nearly invisible. . . . It is a crisis of confidence . . . that strikes at the very heart and soul and spirit of our na-tional will. We can see this crisis in the growing doubt about the meaning of our own lives and in the loss of unity of purpose for our nation [that] is threatening to destroy the social and the political fabric of America. . . .

"We are at a turning point in our history. There are two paths to choose. One is . . . the path that leads to fragmentation and self-interest. Down that road lies a mistaken idea of freedom, the right to grasp for ourselves some advantage over others. . . . It is a certain route to failure.

"All the traditions of our past point to another path, the path of common purpose and the restoration of American values. That path leads to true freedom. . . . We can take the first steps down that path as we begin to solve our energy problem. Energy will be the immediate test of our ability to unite this Nation, and it can also be the standard around which we rally."

Carter followed this setup with a six-point energy policy, replete with a rousing call to action. None of the points was new — they were mostly recycled from previous proposals — but the larger point he was making gave them a bit of a new twist. He also promised to reframe and refocus his presidency in keeping with his own call for national renewal.

Twelve hours later, Carter followed up this address with a speech in Kansas City on the same subject and then gave another later in the day in Detroit. And the message seemed to go over well: In the polls taken that Monday and Tuesday, the president's approval rating jumped up eleven points.

Two days after the speech, the president was back in Washington, having been greeted with great cheers as he got down to his shirtsleeves and rode his Sunday night wave through Kansas City and Detroit. Immediately, Carter set about reframing his administration as he had promised. Jordan was passing out evaluation sheets on all the White House staff, and the cabinet was summoned to the Oval Office and told that they too were being reexamined. Carter already knew he was going to make some changes, most likely over the next two or three days, and promised to do it in a way that didn't embarrass anyone. Although he didn't say so at his meeting with the cabinet, Carter had already identified the three of them he wanted to replace: the only question was how and when.

Cy Vance suggested to the meeting that the whole cabinet, the entire executive board of the American government, submit their resignations. Then the president would be in the position of accepting some resignations and rejecting others. It would be as if he were starting the government all over again. His suggestion was greeted with unanimous acclamation by the rest of the cabinet.

Carter had heard the suggestion before, during the Camp David retreat, and it seemed a reasonable idea. Both Carter and Jordan knew the outcome, whichever approach was taken, so, without looking up at the onrushing bungle, both approved this approach with a kind of "Sure, why not?" attitude.

When word of the mass resignations spread, the press and politicians —

until then in a state of suspended disbelief on the president's promised new self — were stunned. Foreign governments made anxious inquiries about American political stability, and the public was dumbfounded at what was going on. It was the same old Carter government out of control, and the whole message Carter had carried through Kansas City and Detroit was almost instantaneously tuned out.

Within two weeks of the bungle, the entire eleven points Jimmy Carter had added to his ratings with the July 15 speech had dissipated, and he was back where he had started. A month or so after that, his approval rating had fallen to 19 percent, lower than Richard Nixon's was on the verge of his resignation.

While Jimmy Carter was thrashing his way downward in the polls, Iran's Spring of Freedom had ended. At the imam's urging, the provisional government promulgated a new press law that summer that tightened controls over the outpouring of free speech and closed a number of newspapers, sparking an open political firefight. A protest march by ten thousand leftist students at the University of Tehran chanting "Death to the fascist government" was attacked by a crowd of a thousand Islamic militants, flinging stones dumped in the street by hired trucks, then charging forward to shouts of "Death to the communists." At close quarters, the two groups used staves and clubs on each other. Islamic mobs attacked leftist targets for the next two days, setting off street battles that included gunfire. Along the way, someone discharged several rifle grenades into the American embassy compound. One leftist group deployed tanks to defend its headquarters. When the fighting died down, the Islamic forces staged a march of close to a million people who cheered at oaths to crush "leftist troublemakers." In his subsequent radio address, the imam warned his leftist critics that the Islamic masses could "throw them into the dustbin" anytime they wanted.

All summer long, the provisional government maneuvered in the middle of this loud standoff, trying to restore order. According to a report generated by the CIA's Tehran station up on the second floor of the chancery, "The country's basic political problem remains the failure to reinstitute governmental authority over the activities of the revolutionary committees, which remain largely unchecked and only sometimes obey orders from Khomeini himself. [The Provisional] Prime Minister . . . has complained bitterly to Khomeini about committee interference with his government and on at least two occasions threatened to quit. Bazargan now seems resigned to

Khomeini's assertion that the committees are necessary until a regular military force can be built. Bazargan is now trying to coopt some members of Khomeini's Revolutionary Council into his cabinet. He hopes thus to bring more government functions under his control, but the more likely result is an additional power for the Revolutionary Council at the government's expense."

To meet the objections of his secular allies, the imam had agreed that the Assembly of Experts — which would finalize the new constitution before it was put to the people — would be elected, rather than appointed, so now a vote had to be held for the assembly's seventy-four seats. The imam issued a statement "discouraging" leftist and secular critics of the provisional government from running, and only candidates from the Islamic Republican Party were allowed radio and television time by Ghotbzadeh's media ministry. Seventeen political parties boycotted the election in protest of the imam's pressure tactics, and one of the country's five grand ayatollahs urged his followers to stay away from the polls. Not surprisingly, when the dust cleared, a majority of the new Assembly of Experts were mullahs allied with Khomeini.

Among these Experts, Abolhassan Bani Sadr was a leading voice in the rearguard action to save as much of the first draft of the new constitution as possible. The second largest vote getter in the Tehran region, he was by now the provisional government's finance minister as well as a member of the Revolutionary Council. Most members of the assembly expected him to run for president whenever the constitution was finalized. Since his return, he and his family had been living with three of his married sisters who occupied three adjoining apartments in south Tehran. Bani Sadr was accompanied by bodyguards wherever he went, one of the conditions of membership in the Revolutionary Council. At the daily sessions of the assembly, he made spirited, carefully researched speeches in defense of individual liberties.

Bani Sadr also served on the seven-man committee of Experts that considered the most hotly disputed subject of the entire deliberations: *Velayat-e Faqih,* the Rule of the Jurist. Under the Rule of the Jurist, the ultimate authority of the new republic would be a guide who excelled at Islamic law or, in the absence of someone of that stature, a committee of religious jurists to steer the state. Bani Sadr, though still an acolyte of the imam, refused to endorse the concept. He thought allowing the mullahs to control the state was a distortion of Islam and a threat to freedom.

"At issue was the question of whether spiritual matters took precedence over temporal matters," Bani Sadr later explained. He "therefore decided to resist by publishing articles warning the public about this law, which would lead straight to religious fascism, and by waging a public attack based on historical research. We showed that 90 percent of the foremost Shiite religious leaders were opposed to the sovereignty of the Islamic jurist. Even Khomeini opposed it in Paris. . . . We did everything we could to stop the passage of this article of law. . . . Our task was to determine whether national interest or the law should prevail. . . . How can a religious jurist understand the economic, political, and military interests of the country? The mullahs could not answer these questions and therefore refused an open, public debate on this subject, preferring instead to insist without explanation that national interest and the law are identical."

Bani Sadr's resistance, though persistent, was insufficient to stop the Assembly of Experts' stampede in the imam's direction. At the end of the summer, the US embassy would report to Washington that "the Assembly of Experts . . . examining the new Iranian constitution approved . . . by a vote of 63–9, [an] article [that] establishes the *Velayat-e Faqih*. . . . In the short term, the adoption of this article appears to clear the way for Ayatollah Khomeini to take charge openly of all secular and religious authority."

Despite his defeat on that issue, Bani Sadr's stature as a commanding political figure piqued American curiosity, and during the Assembly of Experts' deliberations, the CIA reactivated the connection made during the imam's last weeks in Paris, when the former chief of the agency's Amman station, using the name Guy Rutherford, had twice made contact with Bani Sadr. Rutherford had previously told the Iranian leader that he would be in touch in the spring of 1979, but it wasn't until summer that he actually phoned. He told Abolhassan he was going to be traveling back to Europe from India later in the summer and was going to stop in Tehran on the way, as part of a prospective business venture. He asked Bani Sadr if he could see him when he was in town. Bani Sadr agreed, and Rutherford promised to call as soon as his arrival date firmed up.

That arrival turned out to be in the third week of August. When Rutherford reached Tehran, he had a complete cover story and carried bona fide credentials identifying him as a consultant to Carver Associates, a legitimate company that sold rural electrification and agricultural equipment, as well as sewing machines, to the developing world. (Carver's owner had performed similar favors for the agency before.) Rutherford would spend 60 percent of his time in Iran on actual business development for the company but would be supported by one of the resident CIA agents on the second floor of the chancery. The plan was for Rutherford to form a commercial relationship with Bani Sadr that involved economic and political consultation, then attempt to turn that enterprise into a more direct connection to American intelligence sometime down the road. Eventually Rutherford hoped to hand Bani Sadr over to the second floor of the chancery to be managed as an "asset in place." The Tehran station accounted his cover "fully back-staffed" and provided the agent with a twenty-four-hour phone number to use in emergencies.

Rutherford made contact by phone in the last week of August and arranged to drop by Bani Sadr's home for a quick meeting at 8:00 p.m., just to renew their connection and schedule a second contact. That second contact was set for September 2 at Bani Sadr's apartment. Rutherford showed up on time, but Abolhassan wasn't there. Finally Bani Sadr called, apologized, and said he'd been held up at a meeting of the Revolutionary Council and couldn't get away. Could they meet tomorrow?

True to his promise, the following day Bani Sadr left a session of the Assembly of Experts to spend two hours with the man from Carver Associates. Bani Sadr still had no idea Rutherford worked for the CIA. After catching up on some of Abolhassan's personal information, like the status of his Paris apartment and his children who had stayed in France to go to school, the subject got around to what was happening in Iran. Bani Sadr said the chief loci of power were the Revolutionary Council, the chief prosecutor at the revolutionary tribunals, and the *komitehs*. The last usually confined themselves to local matters but could still be a pain in the ass. Bani Sadr was frankly frustrated at the unwieldy character of the provisional government, but optimistic. Other subjects included the future of the provisional prime minister, the status of the provisional foreign minister, possible nationalization of the banks, and the revolt among the Kurds along the northwestern borders with Iraq and Turkey. When they met again for another hour and a half two days later, the subjects also included potential future arms purchases by the provisional government and prospective changes in foreign exchange regulations.

Having now seen Bani Sadr face-to-face three times within a week, Rutherford forwarded an assessment to Washington through the Tehran station. "It would appear that [Bani Sadr] predictably has changed since accepting positions of responsibility in the newly established government," he noted. "Although he continues to refer to himself as a revolutionary and seems to enjoy the publicity that accompanies his position in the movement and the trappings of power . . . he, in reality, appears to be more of a bureaucrat than a revolutionary. Although always a soft-spoken intellectual, he nevertheless seems to be mellowing now that he is [back] in Tehran. He has developed a bit of a paunch, wears carefully fitted tailored suits and exhibits an expensive appearing new gold wristwatch."

Rutherford would get as far as negotiating a retainer of $1,000 a month between Bani Sadr and Carver Associates, for consulting about economics and politics. That was a critical step in the CIA strategy, but, before any money could actually change hands, events at the embassy would put Guy Rutherford and SD LURE/1 out of business for good.

Throughout that last summer and fall, America's diplomatic outpost in Tehran remained not only shorthanded, but also without an ambassador. The Americans had nominated a replacement, foreign service officer Walter L. Cutler, shortly after Sullivan departed for good at the end of March. In May, however, the United States Senate had passed a resolution condemning revolutionary Iran for its human rights violations. This "slander to Iranian sovereignty" led the Revolutionary Council to instruct the provisional government to refuse the American nominee's credentials, leaving the two countries at loggerheads over the ambassador's post. To cover things while State tried to sort this out, foreign service officer Bruce Laingen, fifty-six, was asked to fill in as the embassy's new chargé d'affaires. Laingen had been scheduled to inspect South American embassies but was sent to Tehran instead. He was told he would be there only four to six weeks. Laingen had previously served in Tehran for two years immediately after the CIA reinstatement of the shah. He returned as chargé in June 1979.

At the end of July, Cy Vance had cabled him with what was becoming a regular request. The department was continuing to field pressure "through various channels" for the shah to be admitted into the United States, Vance explained. He wanted the chargé's "personal and private" estimate of the impact in Iran of such a move, specifically on the safety of the embassy. After a couple days considering the subject, Laingen wired Vance back. Any such move by the shah would be "seriously prejudicial" to the embassy and its occupants, he explained.

On an informal level, opinions were also sought on this subject among the other embassy staff. One press officer responded that if they let the shah in, they should promise to give embassy personnel twenty-four hours prior notice so they could all flee town first.

———

THE "VARIOUS CHANNELS" APPLYING THE PRESSURE
cited by Cy Vance in his cable to the chargé all led back to the same source.
Henry Kissinger and David Rockefeller's campaign was still going full bore.
Indeed, Vance's inquiry had been the direct outcome of their latest success.

In the last week of July, Kissinger, with a lot of help from Brzezinski, had
finally persuaded Vice President Mondale to back His Majesty's admission.
Mondale wrote the president a memo saying as much, and then, at a Friday
morning foreign policy breakfast on July 27, he and Brzezinski double-
teamed Carter on the issue of the shahanshah and urged him to relent.

Carter growled as soon as the issue was raised. He complained that Kissinger
and Rockefeller had been waging a constant campaign on this and that Zbig
bugged him about it every day. That he was fed up was more than apparent
as the discussion proceeded. After hearing Brzezinski run on about the national honor, et cetera, Carter exploded.

"Fuck the shah," Jimmy Carter snapped at his national security adviser.
The shah had a safe place to stay for the moment; let him stay there.

Vance was also at the breakfast and was adamantly opposed to any change in the United States' posture. The discussion finally ended with the issue being tabled while Vance wired Tehran for a new assessment of the potential risks to the embassy. When Tehran cabled back over the weekend, Carter reaffirmed his refusal to budge.

He reaffirmed it again several days later when Kissinger sent word that he would be unable to give the administration any public support on its controversial strategic arms treaties with the Soviets as long as the shah was denied entry. Another week and a half after that, Carter reaffirmed his refusal yet again when Princess Ashraf sent a personal letter to the president on her brother's behalf. Carter sent the letter on to Brzezinski with instructions to prepare a polite and noncommittal reply.

By the end of September, however, the issue was back yet again. Now the exiled monarch's physical distress was obvious, even to those who didn't know him well. He had lost thirty pounds over the summer, was jaundiced, and often suffered from severe stomach pain and nausea. His Mexican doctors, having no idea of the shah's cancer, were treating him for what they thought was malaria, and, not surprisingly, he wasn't responding. His French doctor was still commuting from Paris to surreptitiously administer chemotherapy, but His Imperial Majesty continued to refuse to check into a hospital or inform anyone else of his disease. He had convinced himself that revealing his illness would only undercut those who continued to champion his rule and demonstrate to his enemies just how weak he had become.

The shah's concealment began unraveling when Bobby Armao, back in New York for a little time off, got a call from the assistant he had left behind to monitor things in Cuernavaca. The assistant said the shah looked even more seriously ill than the last time Bobby had seen him, with malaria or whatever it was, and didn't seem to be getting better. Some new medical initiative was required.

Armao took the problem to the vice president at Chase whom David Rockefeller had assigned the task of managing the shah's finances. In this instance, the Chase VP took two steps immediately. The first was to recommend a New York tropical disease specialist whom Armao knew and who had treated both Princess Ashraf and David Rockefeller. Armao agreed, and the American doctor was dispatched to Cuernavaca immediately to consult about what was ailing the shah.

The Chase vice president's second step was to call an undersecretary at the State Department who was his designated contact there. Since the administration wanted no official contact with His Majesty, the Chase vice president also served as the principal unofficial contact between the two. The shah, he informed the undersecretary, was seriously ill and at some point in the near future might have to come to the United States for treatment. The undersecretary, wary and suspicious from months of being muscled by the Rockefeller and Kissinger campaign, replied that the State Department would require "very strong justification" to even consider that possibility — proof not only that the shah was ill but also that the United States was the only place he could receive the appropriate treatment. The Chase vice president said he'd keep the undersecretary posted.

On October 1, Vance informed the president during his evening briefing that something was up. The shah was ill, he told Carter, and David Rockefeller had sent his personal physician down to examine him. Vance reported that Rockefeller's people were saying the shah might have to come to the United States for treatment. Vance had already checked with the embassy in Tehran, and it looked even more dangerous there now than it had during the summer. Vance promised to monitor the situation.

The shah, however, continued to keep his secret and made no mention of his cancer treatment when Rockefeller's doctor arrived in Mexico to examine him during the first week of October. The shah's French doctor came to Cuernavaca shortly after the American left, however, and found the shah's disease rampant. Obviously the chemotherapy had been overwhelmed and could no longer hold the lymphoma in check. The lymph nodes on the back of his neck were badly swollen, and his jaundice was pronounced. The latter was probably the result of gallstones or the cancer, but there was no way to find out exactly what was going on and continue to keep the secret. The French doctor demanded that His Majesty check into a hospital for the full examination that had been put off for more than five years. And this time, the shah agreed. His only condition was that the hospital not be in America. After the way they had treated him, he told his French doctor, he wouldn't go there "even if they begged me on their knees."

That vow was a telling expression of His Imperial Majesty's bitterness at how the American government had treated him, but little more. Once he decided to be hospitalized, he never really considered going anyplace else.

Before the French doctor could do anything about the shah's decision to be hospitalized, Bobby Armao returned to Cuernavaca to see things for himself and was stunned. His Majesty looked as though he might die any minute. His skin was so dark it was almost black, and he seemed shrunken.

When Armao asked what was going on, the shah introduced him to his French doctor, and the thirty-year-old majordomo of the shahanshah's exile learned of His Majesty's five years' worth of cancer treatment.

Armao took it all in and then called the Chase vice president. It was a new ball game, Bobby said. The shah had been holding out on them, but now the secret was on the table.

The Rockefeller apparatus responded with alacrity. Armao wanted Rockefeller's doctor to return to do a second evaluation, so the doctor was dispatched on the next plane. Rockefeller's vice president also reserved rooms at Manhattan's New York Hospital for the shah's arrival, even though His Majesty hadn't yet even requested entry to the United States. Then he called his contact at State and informed him that the shah's situation had deteriorated further and that Rockefeller's physician had been dispatched for a second evaluation. There were some indications that it might be cancer. In all likelihood, HIM would soon formally request entry to seek medical treatment. The undersecretary gave Rockefeller's vice president the name of the department's chief medical officer, who would have to be included in the loop.

"The medical information changed everything," Ham Jordan remembered. "Now the President was faced with the prospect of letting a sick man die on his doorstep."

Still, there was a verification process to be gone through, and State pursued it. The department's chief medical officer was immediately dispatched to Mexico to meet up with Rockefeller's doctor, who had now consulted with the shah's French cancer specialist.

"There is no question but that he has a malignant lymphoma which is 'escaping' standard chemotherapy," the State Department doctor reported. "The situation is urgent and becoming increasingly so. Each day of worsening jaundice and physiological deterioration lessens the chances of recovery."

With that conclusion, the first of State's two necessary proofs had been met. Vance was completely satisfied that the shah was indeed very seriously ill and never bothered to ask for another opinion.

The second required proof was that it be shown that the United States was indeed the only place he could receive appropriate treatment. This issue was fuzzier — though not to the shah's advocates. "We checked it out," Armao argued, "and medical arrangements down there in Mexico were a nightmare. Nobody spoke English, the hospitals were mediocre, the equipment we would have needed was spread out between a half dozen hospitals. People would later say that it was possible for him to be treated in Mexico, but this just wasn't doable. All the Mexicans we asked said anybody who could afford it went to the United States for health care, always. Wasn't the shah entitled to at least the same rights to the best available treatment as a rich Mexican?"

Still, the case that Mexico couldn't provide what the shah required was less substantial than the proof of his illness. The evaluation and surgery the shah was about to undergo were hardly cutting-edge and were done in Mexican hospitals. Diagnostic equipment there was older and less available, but again arguably sufficient to the level required. One of the key allegedly unavailable machines was a CAT scanner, of which, it later turned out, there were thirteen in Mexico, most of the same vintage as those in the United States. In retrospect, glossing over this issue would make the due diligence taken by the State Department seem less than complete and the process, hurried. This was evidence, perhaps, of the obviously growing momentum for His Majesty's entry, being pushed forward by the now daily urging of Kissinger and Rockefeller's lobbying effort. Or perhaps it was just evidence of medical urgency.

In any case, on this last outstanding issue, State's chief medical officer's report — filed after consultation with Rockefeller's doctor — tipped the scales. "Highly technical studies are needed to completely diagnose this lymphoma," he wrote, "to grade it, determine its involvement in the process which has produced the jaundice and decide on further treatment. . . . These studies cannot be carried out in any of the medical facilities in Mexico."

The medical officer would explain that the latter conclusion was based on his consultation with the doctor employed by the Mexico City embassy, but that same Mexican doctor would later claim that, contrary to what had been reported, he had told State's doctor that such things were done in Mexico all the time.

Vance, however, was completely convinced and switched sides on the question at the president's October 19 Friday foreign policy breakfast. The secretary of state's defection left Jimmy Carter the only remaining member of his administration who still did not want to let the shah into the United States.

According to Jordan, the president's frustration at being isolated on the issue grew steadily as the breakfast progressed. Finally he told Vance to double-check the medical information. He also instructed Vance to inform the provisional government that the United States was admitting the shah for medical treatment and ascertain their reaction. Then he would make the final decision.

With the issue dealt with for the moment, Jimmy Carter looked around the table at his advisers. He hadn't liked being ganged up on, and it showed in his sardonic flash of teeth.

"What are you guys going to advise me to do if they overrun our embassy and take our people hostage?" Carter asked.

No one in the room made a response.

After noting the silence, Jimmy Carter spoke up again. "On that day," he predicted, "we will all sit here with long drawn white faces and realize we've been had."

Vance cabled the embassy on Saturday night with a copy of the State Department's draft press release about the shah's medical condition. Attached to it were orders to notify the provisional government at first opportunity that the United States was going to admit the former monarch on humanitarian grounds. He told chargé d'affaires Bruce Laingen that "we are planning for [the] Shah's arrival here as soon as possible but will await your notification of delivery of message and [the provisional government's] reaction prior to making final decision." Fortuitously the head of State's Iran desk was in Tehran on a fact-finding trip and he and the chargé had an appointment with one of the ministers in the provisional government at 10:00 a.m. the next day. When they met with the minister as scheduled, they would drop in on provisional prime minister Mehdi Bazargan with their urgent news.

When the chargé and the head of the Iran desk surprised Bazargan with their Sunday morning visit, he was not pleased. They were soon joined by the provisional foreign minister, Ebrahim Yazdi, who was even less so. For whatever it was worth, both the Americans indicated they did not think much of the decision State had forwarded them either. The head of the Iran desk, according to Yazdi, "was bitterly against this. He openly blamed it on Kissinger and Rockefeller."

The men from the provisional government were stunned at the news the Americans delivered. Iran was a place where thousands of political rumors were in circulation at once, and neither the prime minister nor the foreign minister had ever heard one about the shah's having cancer. Incredulous, they indicated they had their doubts about this medical diagnosis. Several times they asked for Iranian doctors to examine the shah to verify these claims. Otherwise, the provisional foreign minister pointed out, most Iranians would see this as a ruse, preparatory to the shah's reinstallation.

Laingen tried to defend American intentions, but it was an uphill struggle. The Americans made it clear that admitting the shah was being done solely on humanitarian grounds. The United States accepted the change in Iran and had recognized the provisional government accordingly. They were not trying to reinstate the shah. The chargé indicated that he understood this might provoke passions in Iran and wanted the provisional government's assurances that it would continue to protect the embassy.

Yazdi was quick to say that the provisional government would not shirk its responsibility to protect the embassy but was far less than sanguine about the public reaction. "You are playing with fire," he warned the Americans. Anything could happen and probably would.

At the end of the discussion, the provisional foreign minister summarized the Iranian position. If it was indeed necessary for the shah to find treatment outside of Mexico, the provisional government requested that it be done anywhere but the United States. American involvement would only inflame the Iranian street. Yazdi had been an oncology researcher during his exile in Texas and knew full well that this proposed procedure could be done all over Western Europe. If the United States insisted on bringing the shah to America, any city other than New York would be "marginally" better in terms of moderating the Iranian public's response. New York, the foreign minister pointed out, was thought of as "a center of Rockefeller and Zionist influence." The Iranians also reiterated their desire to have Iranian doctors verify the shah's illness and pressed for an answer to how long the shah would be in the United States, but the visiting Americans could not provide it. Yazdi also wanted a guarantee that the shah would engage in no political activity to advance his cause while in the United States. To this, the Americans promised to "emphasize to the shah our desire that he avoid any political activity, either with the press or otherwise."

In parting, the provisional foreign minister warned the Americans once again. "You are opening Pandora's box," he said. "Who knows what will pop out?"

Afterward, Laingen assessed the provisional government's response as "mixed, but generally subdued" in the cable he flashed to Vance. The provisional government didn't like what the United States was doing, but the Iranians would continue to guarantee the embassy's safety.

That assessment was sent to the president at Camp David. And, on the basis of it and the full formal medical officer's report that had just reached him, Jimmy Carter called Brzezinski on Sunday morning and told him to notify the shah that he was welcome to fly to New York and check into the hospital.

* * *

The next evening, October 22, 1979, the Light of the Aryans loaded the shahbanou, Armao, and several of his dogs onto a chartered Gulfstream executive jet and left Mexico for the United States. The shah could barely shuffle from his limo to the airplane. His departure was meant to be a secret, but somehow a press photographer made it to the airport and snapped several photos on the runway before the Gulfstream lifted off.

When he reached New York Hospital on Manhattan's East Side early the next morning, Mohammad Reza Pahlavi had already been registered under an assumed name and was taken straight up to the seventeenth floor. There, he was installed in a two-room suite on the corner at the end of a hall, behind a set of French doors. The entire hallway leading to that suite had been blocked off and several more rooms given over to the shah's security details. Police patrols outside had been increased, and armed guards watched the elevator and manned stations at the head of the corridor.

To the shah, it felt just a tiny bit like coming home. He had spent two days in exactly the same room thirty years earlier, when, still in his first decade as King of Kings, he'd come to the United States to visit President Harry S. Truman. Then, however, Mohammad Reza Pahlavi had registered under his own name and had only been scheduled for a checkup.

Within hours of his arrival on October 23, the shah was given a battery of tests. His French doctors were nowhere to be seen, and his case was now being managed by Rockefeller's doctor, who had brought in a team of American specialists. By that afternoon, they had determined that he had gallstones, at least one of which was blocking his bile duct and causing his jaundice. His spleen was also swollen to three times its normal size. His bile duct needed to be cleared, and his gallbladder removed, as well as his spleen, but the extent of the proposed surgery posed a dilemma. The patient still had fever and chills, and such a comprehensive operation would leave him with two enormous holes in his abdominal cavity in which infection could lodge. On top of that, he might not be strong enough in his current state to recover from so much surgery. The Rockefeller doctor's final call was to play it safe: The surgeon would extract the gall bladder and its stones, pull a lymph node for analysis, and leave it at that. They would have to go back later for the spleen.

On October 24, two days before his sixtieth birthday, Mohammad Reza Pahlavi went under the knife. His gallbladder and a lymph node were removed, and in the process his liver was observed to be "extraordinarily abnormal," perhaps tumorous, and his spleen appeared as ugly as they had expected. The ensuing biopsy of the lymph node also revealed a large cell lymphoma of an aggressive type. Rockefeller's doctor made the odds of His Imperial Majesty's living another eighteen months as fifty-fifty at best.

That night, before bed, Jimmy Carter was given his usual stack of "Presidential Reading Items," brief one- or two-paragraph summaries of particular events or circumstances he wanted to track. Included was an item on the shah's operation. After describing what the surgeon had found, the two paragraphs noted that "the Rockefeller people will keep us informed as the medical evaluation develops." It also noted that "thus far, the reaction to the shah's travel here by the Iranian Government and public has been mild and the situation in Tehran is calm."

As promised, the provisional government had immediately reinforced the Revolutionary Guard contingent at the embassy. Then Provisional Foreign Minister Yazdi met again with the American chargé and the visiting head of State's Iran desk and again expressed skepticism about the illness and formally requested that Iranian doctors be allowed to examine the evidence. The United States denied his request. Provisional Prime Minister Bazargan then wrote a personal letter to the shah, asking him to abdicate his throne in the interests of the country. The Americans refused to deliver it to him. The provisional government then filed a formal protest, but there was nothing else for them to do, since Iran had no extradition treaty with the United States.

In the meantime, public response in Iran was slow to build. Even the Iranian press, normally somewhat hysterical, at first seemed subdued by the news — simply running wire service accounts with relatively passive headlines, as though in shock. There were the usual daily demonstrations in Tehran, sometimes with crowds in the hundreds of thousands, but none of them targeted the United States directly. Only a couple of the marches paraded down Taleghani Avenue, past the embassy's front gate and the chancery, shouting *"Marg bar Amrika"* as they did. None of the crowds stopped. The marines slept in the chancery lobby one night when the turmoil in Tehran was particularly intense, but otherwise the Americans seemed to be getting off lightly and were tempted to exhale and declare that they had managed to avoid the explosion they had so feared.

The imam's initial response was simply to note that he had heard that the shah had been received by the United States because he was supposedly afflicted with terminal cancer. The imam only hoped that the report of his illness was true and that the Pahlavi scoundrel would soon die a terrible death.

PART FOUR

CRISIS

· 16 ·

————

*T*HE IDEA THAT WAS SOON TO BECOME THE IRAN Hostage Crisis was first advanced by Ibrahim Asgarzadeh, a twenty-two-year-old engineering student at Tehran's Aryamehr University of Technology, in a late-October conversation with two other students. They rendezvoused in the village of Shemran on the north edge of Tehran, where the city ends and the wild expanse of the Alborz begins. Shemran's long street of tea shops and eateries, flanking a stream of cascading snowmelt, was frequented by young people on their way to hike the numerous mountain trails. During the months of protest against the shah, when Asgarzadeh, a native of Khaash in Balouchestan Province, had first affiliated himself with the politics of the imam, students had used the wilderness refuge next to Shemran to congregate out of the reach of SAVAK's eyes and ears. Asgarzadeh, tall and handsome, was widely respected among them for his "keen analytical mind." He and his two close friends — one studying engineering at Tehran's Polytechnic University and the other at the University of Tehran — were all active in the

Union of Islamic Students, a leading force in campus politics representing what Ibrahim called "the religious faithful who supported the Revolution."

Asgarzadeh announced to the other two that it was time for a dramatic act that would seize the political initiative. By way of explanation, he pulled out a handwritten manuscript he had finished composing the night before and read it to them in a voice just loud enough to be heard but not over-heard. All of this, he warned, had to be discussed with the utmost secrecy. The basic point of his draft was that the Revolution was still incredibly vul-nerable. The people seemed to be losing their focus on the machinations of the United States — just when, with Pahlavi in New York, it was likely some reprise of his 1953 reinstatement was being hatched. Ibrahim proposed to rectify this void with direct action by the student faithful.

He told them he wanted to seize the American embassy.

His two friends sucked breath, almost in unison.

This would not be like the assault of last February, Asgarzadeh cautioned. That had been a leftist enterprise out to inflict harm. Theirs, on the other hand, would not resemble a "terrorist act or military action" in any way. In-stead, it would be pursued with the same spirit of peaceful defiance and civil disobedience as had been used against the shah. They would seize the em-bassy for forty-eight or perhaps seventy-two hours — unless the provisional government evicted them earlier — and while they held it, they would use the accompanying spotlight to articulate their grievances against the United States. The object of their action was not revenge but illumination.

The two others signed on with little argument and, after the friends sealed their intentions over a pot of tea in one of Shemran's outdoor cafés, they set about organizing among the Union of Islamic Students' branches at each of Tehran's four universities, spreading word of a secret meeting to be held at Polytechnic University on November 2. In the meantime, the situation only intensified.

On November 1, Iran's provisional prime minister Bazargan and provi-sional foreign minister Yazdi were both in Algeria for a ceremony marking the anniversary of that country's independence. So was National Security Adviser Zbigniew Brzezinski. At the Iranians' suggestion, they met in private to discuss "matters of mutual interest," including the status of the shah. Yazdi again raised his doubts that the shah was really ill, and Brzezinski reacted with indignation to the suggestion. Otherwise, the national security adviser came away with a positive impression. Neither side, however, gave enough heed to the potential explosiveness with which their contact would be received in Iran.

That was left to the Iranian media. News of the meeting with Brzezinski — complete with a photograph of the American shaking hands with Bazargan and Yazdi — was spread over the Tehran front pages on November 2, when the students met at Polytechnic to begin organizing themselves. Few Iranians were talking about much else that day. Most of the public speculation was that the provisional government was preparing to align itself with the United States, and, as far as the students meeting at Polytechnic were concerned, that was an abomination. "The Americans were obviously looking to make history repeat itself," Ibrahim Asgarzadeh said, "and we had to deliver a blow to make them come to their senses."

The several dozen students he convened in one of Polytechnic's classrooms were all respected members of the Islamic movement, invited by word of mouth and sworn to secrecy. They were told only that the meeting would discuss organizing a "significant action" to be taken very soon. Two students watched the door to make sure no uninvited came through it. One of Asgarzadeh's friends from the Shemran discussion, a renowned orator, addressed the room.

"In the name of Allah," he began, "the merciful and compassionate."

"In the name of Allah," the group answered.

He got right to the point. By allowing the shah to enter the United States, he said, the Americans had started a whole new conspiracy against the Revolution that had to be answered. If there was no answer, Iran would end up back on America's leash, just as it had been before. "Now," he declared, "is our chance to do something about it."

The room fell silent with anticipation. Participants would later describe the moment as pregnant.

"What we are proposing," the speaker continued, "is a peaceful occupation of the American embassy."

Jaws dropped around the room, and after half a minute of dead air while they digested what had just been said, everyone seemed to start talking at once. The ensuing discussion lasted several hours before agreement was reached to proceed and the group broke down into working committees to take charge of the preparations.

One of those preparatory tasks was finding a name for their ad hoc group. Though all of those present were members of the Union of Islamic Students, they couldn't commit the larger organization to their enterprise and did not want to break secrecy by seeking its endorsement. The name they eventually settled on was Muslim Students Following the Line of the Imam.

Under that identity, this room of heretofore anonymous young men and women were about to become Iranian legends.

In addition to their perspective on the intentions of the United States, the other fundamental agreement shared by all of the Muslim Students Following the Line of the Imam was their devotion to Ayatollah Ruhollah Khomeini. "We knew the Imam very well," one student remembered. "He had consistently . . . led the resistance to the shah from exile. [His] decisions would not be influenced by personal aspirations or tainted by selfishness, of that we were certain. . . . The Imam had defined religion, God, love, life, and death in such clear and understandable terms that he seemed not only to be speaking a profound truth, but pointing the way toward salvation. . . . To the extent of our own limited understanding and capacity, we had chosen the Imam's road."

And they were by no means alone. The day the provisional government met with Brzezinski, more than two million Iranians marched through Tehran shouting *"Marg bar Amrika."* The next demonstration was scheduled for November 4, honoring the first anniversary of a massacre of students by the shah's troops during the Revolution. In a message released in advance of this event, Khomeini noted that "it is incumbent on students . . . to expand their attacks on America [to force it] to return the criminal deposed Shah."

That statement struck a responsive chord among them, but the Students Following the Line of the Imam — who were planning to piggyback their own smaller, still secret action onto that November 4 memorial demonstration — nonetheless wanted the imam's specific blessing for their venture as well. They sent a request to him through a mullah who was acting as their spiritual adviser, but they received no direct response. They assumed the imam's silence meant "yes" and went on with their planning.

In the meantime, their target, the American embassy, was still blinded by a growing sense of functional security. Staffing had almost doubled over the last six months, from Sullivan's final "bare bones" level of forty to close to eighty. Many of the "nonessential" documents that had been shipped out under Sullivan had now made their way back into the country, and the embassy's files were again bulging. The ragtag guard detail of armed militia assigned to the compound's protection last February had been replaced at the end of the summer by a far more disciplined detachment of Revolutionary Guards, which had then been additionally reinforced by a squad of regular police. There were still bullets from the February attack embedded in the chancery lobby, and some sections of the carpet still yielded tear gas when scuffed, but the new doors and window grilles made the yellow-brick building feel like a bastion. The marine guards now called it "Fort Apache."

Even the rising Iranian outrage at the shah's taking refuge in the United States didn't break the spell. The huge anti-American demonstration on November 1 had been treated as a security test case by the embassy and the State Department, and as far as they were concerned, the provisional government had passed with flying colors. Iranian police forces had diverted all but a few demonstrators away from the embassy, avoiding any incidents.

Meanwhile, however, members of the Muslim Students Following the Line of the Imam had already begun their reconnaissance of the American stronghold. Some visited the consular section or found an excuse to enter the chancery itself. Others circulated in the surrounding neighborhood, tracking the routine of the guards outside the wall and the marines inside it. Others talked their way past the doormen of several nearby buildings and mapped the compound's layout from their roofs. By the time the Muslim Students' final organizing meeting was called to order by Ibrahim Asgarzadeh, the students had developed several crude maps of the compound and its buildings, as well as a reasonably detailed schedule of the comings and goings of the security forces.

All of that material had been drawn up on three portable blackboards that were turned toward the wall when the crowd filed in. By now, the Muslim Students had recruited the full complement of three hundred they estimated would be sufficient to accomplish their occupation, but this was the first exposure of most of them to the exact nature of the act about to be undertaken. All the crucial details had heretofore been kept secret. When the blackboards were reversed so the assembled volunteers could see them, the sketches were quickly identified as of the American embassy, before any announcement was made.

Again, there was a moment of shocked recognition generated by the audacity of the secret that had been revealed.

Asgarzadeh warned the group that the enterprise could be dangerous — there might be martyrs — but only a few availed themselves of the opportunity to pull out.

* * *

Sunday, November 4, 1979, opened with a gray drizzle, Tehran's first rain of the season. After a brief staff meeting, the embassy's chargé and two of his ranking staff left for a 9:30 a.m. meeting at the Iranian Foreign Ministry. Their diplomatic limo skirted the memorial demonstration marching to the University of Tehran, but the Americans were not particularly worried by it, and the demonstrators paid little attention to them. As Laingen had pointed out to the morning meeting, this march wasn't aimed at the United States, and he expected that any trouble it might pose would be in the afternoon, after it broke up, when the participants filtered into the surrounding city.

About the time the embassy's senior leadership reached the Foreign Ministry, the Muslim Students Following the Line of the Imam finished mustering at Polytechnic, some twenty minutes by foot from the embassy. All of the men were bearded and many had tied on headbands proclaiming *Allah-u Akbar.* The women wore black chadors looking like shrouds, with pictures of Imam Khomeini pinned to their chests. Each of the four universities was represented by a contingent, each assigned a set of tasks in the approaching invasion. Overall direction was in the hands of a central committee made up of Asgarzadeh and four others. The student troops had been instructed to come unarmed and to take Americans captive but not to abuse them. The plan was to breach the embassy's front gate at 10:00 a.m., and they were right on schedule.

First, a cluster of black-clad women marched up Taleghani Avenue, as though they were just a little demonstration, shouting "God is great" and "Death to America." Then, just as they passed the embassy's main gate, they reversed themselves and congregated in front of it. A few words were exchanged with the obviously sympathetic Iranian policemen on guard, and the policemen got out of the way. Then the rest of the students, some three hundred of them, swarmed from hiding places on the side streets. The most nimble men among them climbed over the gate and snapped the lock and chain with a pair of bolt cutters; soon everyone was inside. As specified in their advance plan, the students closed the gate after themselves to keep anyone else out and stationed students to guard it. Then preassigned groups headed for the embassy's four principal buildings. One of the women who advanced on the chancery carried a hand-lettered sign in misspelled English saying "Don't be afraid. We just want to set in."

The marines almost immediately triggered an alarm that security had been breached. Then, following standard, well-drilled procedures, the chancery was sealed behind the new iron doors that would require at least a bazooka to force open. Outside, the students' chancery detail flowed around the building looking for a way in. Since all the windows were now grilled, the invaders were momentarily stymied. The same was true across the compound at the consulate building. In both cases, however, the operative word was *momentarily.* The chancery was the first one to be pierced. Two of the basement windows had grilles that, unlike the rest, could be unlocked and opened as a fire safety precaution. When the students discovered this, they brought up their lock cutters and were quickly into the basement. A marine detachment held them at bay there with leveled shotguns but, as more crushed in, had no choice but to slowly retreat while the embassy attempted to reach the chargé d'affairs for instructions about using live fire.

Laingen was first notified about what was going on by radio phone as he was leaving the Foreign Ministry. He was told that the Iranian security detail had been worthless and the head of the Revolutionary Guard unit had been seen hugging one of the people who came over the gate. Laingen went right back inside and demanded to see the provisional foreign minister. He, however, had just returned from Algiers that morning and was still on his way to the office. In the meantime, the chargé ordered the marines not to create any violent incident. A barrage of tear gas was laid down as the marines were overrun. Those who could extricate themselves retreated up the stairs to where the staff was waiting on the second floor. Another bazooka-proof iron door there was sealed behind them. Just to be sure, furniture and appliances were also piled up against it.

The Muslim Students Following the Line of the Imam now found themselves in a momentary stalemate. "From the second floor I looked out the windows," one marine remembered. "The Iranians had the whole building surrounded. They were all excited and ran around like little kids in an amusement park or something. They were flipping us off, and I was standing there flipping them in return and saying, 'Get out of here, you raspberries!'" The Iranians lit a little fire in front of the second-floor door, but that didn't get it open either. Inside, the ten men on the document-destroying detail had retreated into the top-secret communications vault. Some shredded paper and pulverized microfiche. Others dismantled the teletype and the classified-communications machines. Most of the Americans, however, were still hopeful that this would prove a repeat of Valentine's Day and rescue would soon be on its way.

Back at the Iranian Foreign Ministry, the chargé had finally sat down with the provisional foreign minister, but things did not look good on the rescue front. From the start it appeared that Yazdi, having just returned to a public uproar over the photograph of him and Brzezinski on the front pages, was very likely powerless to deliver on any promise, as was his boss, Provisional Prime Minister Bazargan. Laingen demanded rescue, and the foreign minister attempted to muster a government response over the phone but was entirely unsuccessful. Laingen then insisted that Yazdi lead a military detachment over to the embassy personally, as he had in February. The provisional foreign minister excused himself from doing so by offering that in February the Americans' lives had been threatened. And, he insisted, that wasn't the current case.

At the embassy, however, the people on the second floor of the chancery weren't quite so sure. Several marines had not made it up from the basement and were already captive. The barricaded Americans made contact with the besiegers on one of the marines' captured radios, and John Limbert, an embassy political officer fluent in Farsi, went outside to try to negotiate. He was confronted by a group of Iranians who were holding a pistol to the head of one of their captives. They said they'd blow the marine's brains out if the second floor wasn't surrendered. Limbert asked if there was someone from the Iranian government present, and the student told him they didn't care about the government. When he asked the same thing about the Revolutionary Council, the response was the same.

"While this type of discussion was going on," Limbert remembered, "they were arguing among themselves a lot. . . . They kept referring to a five-man council that they had agreed would make all the decisions. . . . One would say, 'Let's go in now.' Another would say, 'No, we've got to let the council make this decision.' Another would say, 'Let's knock down the door.' . . . Finally, [a] fellow with [an] Isfahani accent said to me, 'Tell them if they don't come out we are going to kill . . . both of you.' Then they put a blindfold on me and hollered through the door, 'We'll give you ten minutes. If you guys don't come out in ten minutes we're going to shoot both of these guys.'"

When he learned of the threat, Laingen ordered the second floor to surrender. The now captive Americans filed out one by one and were frisked and blindfolded, their hands bound. Then they were led out of the chancery. Similar collections were being made from the consulate and the American-occupied buildings in the surrounding neighborhood at around the same time.

The last holdout was the top-secret vault, whose door had been sealed when the second floor's was opened. Ten men inside continued to shred and disable for another hour and a half before finally giving in. The students' patience was worn by then and they slapped most of these last Americans around when they surrendered. The vault crew then joined the others and, with the exception of six staffers who had been outside the compound and found refuge at the Canadian embassy, all of the American diplomats in Tehran were captives, including the chargé's party, who would remain as long-term guests, confined in a room at the Iranian Foreign Ministry "for their own protection." None of them had suffered any serious injury.

It was barely 2:00 p.m. Tehran time, and the twenty-six-acre American embassy compound and its sixty-three occupants were in the hands of the Muslim Students Following the Line of the Imam.

The Crisis had begun.

Cyrus Vance was the first among the upper echelon of the Carter administration to learn what was happening. The secretary of state had been awakened at his Washington home by a phone call from the State Department's Operations Center shortly after 3:00 a.m., Washington time. The plane returning him from a mission to Korea had landed only six hours earlier, but he shook off his drowsiness. The department reported that a mob, perhaps three thousand strong, had stormed the embassy gates and was inside the compound, though not yet in the chancery. Vance dressed immediately and, an hour later, was in State's brightly lit seventh-floor Operations Center. The crew there now had open lines with the chancery and with the chargé at Iran's Foreign Ministry. Both were patched through on speakers at either end of a long table, and the news was not comforting. The invaders were now inside the chancery and the second floor was nearing the end of its holdout. Vance's first response was to demand that the provisional government live up to its promises to protect the embassy, but that approach was already looking fruitless.

Around 4:30 a.m., the secretary called the president at Camp David to let him know, only to find that Brzezinski had beaten him to the punch. The national security adviser had been awakened by the ringing of the phone next to his bed twenty minutes earlier and been informed of Tehran developments by the White House Situation Room. His subsequent call to Carter was short but electrifying. The president, almost instantly awake, was visited by a nightmare fantasy as soon as Brzezinski hung up.

"I could picture the revolutionaries keeping the . . . hostages," he remembered, "and assassinating one of them every morning at sunrise until the Shah was returned to Iran or until we agreed to some other act in response to their blackmail."

The image would haunt him for months to come.

When Carter fielded Vance's call shortly after Brzezinski's, the two discussed the provisional government's response and then arranged to meet later in the day with the whole collection of the president's foreign policy brain trust, after Carter returned from Camp David.

Hamilton Jordan was awakened by the White House Situation Room about the same time as the president spoke with the secretary of state. As part of the administration's promised renewal, Jordan was now the official White House chief of staff as well as Carter's foremost campaign operative. He was in Maryland for the weekend, at a friend's house, and it took a dozen rings before he found the phone and stuck it against his ear. He thanked the operator for the news and fell back into his bed in the dark, his eyes wide open. Until that moment, Jordan had expected this day to be triumphant. CBS's *60 Minutes* was scheduled to run a filmed interview that evening with Massachusetts senator Ted Kennedy, Jimmy's likely challenger in the Democratic primaries, and by all accounts Kennedy's performance was a political pratfall of the first order, described as embarrassingly inept in the advance reviews.

Jordan was considered something of an embarrassment himself these days. In August the White House chief of staff had received a late-night visit from the FBI. Ham knew something heavy-duty was up when the agents opened the conversation by reciting his Miranda rights.

The FBI wanted to know if he had, during the spring of 1978, visited a New York discotheque, Studio 54?

Jordan said that he had been there for a half hour while in town on business, just to get a look at New York's hottest nightspot.

Did he use cocaine there?

Jordan bridled. Absolutely not, he answered. He then demanded to know who said he had.

The agents admitted that the two owners of the nightclub were the source. Both men were up on federal tax evasion charges and had offered to expose Jordan as part of a plea bargain. The Ethics in Government Act required that the New York federal attorney investigate their claims.

The papers had grabbed the story the next day —"FBI Investigating Alleged Cocaine Use by Jordan"— and would return to it in regular spurts well into 1980. Jordan would win complete vindication on this charge, but only after nine months of brutal headlines.

Now, lying in the Sunday morning dark, exactly a year before Election Day, Ham asked himself two questions about the news from Iran. The first was, Does this mean war? The second was, What will this mean for the campaign?

At 4:57 a.m., while Jordan was on the phone with a White House staffer, confidently predicting that the incident would be over in a few hours, the chancery in Tehran announced it was surrendering and its occupants were entering captivity. With that, the open line to Washington went dead.

By that afternoon, when Carter and most of his advisers were huddled at the White House, nothing had changed. Although this was the moment he had predicted two weeks earlier, when this same group had unanimously advised him to allow the shah into the country, there was no I-told-you-so in the president's manner. He was crisp and businesslike but obviously troubled.

Vance reported that Iran's provisional prime minister had stayed in his ministry office until well past midnight Tehran time, consulting with the American chargé, but no rescue had materialized. Khomeini had apparently refused all requests to intervene. The occupiers — who claimed to be students but, according to the State Department's wildly inaccurate guess, were probably a communist cadre — had issued a communiqué from the embassy denouncing America for "granting asylum and employing the criminal Shah while it has its hands in the blood of tens of thousands of women and men in this country." That was all they currently knew about who these people were and what they wanted.

Everyone in the room was angry and revolted, but options available to deal with the situation were virtually nonexistent. Even Brzezinski seemed stumped. The Joint Chiefs of Staff had come up with a quick estimate of the military's capacity to rescue the embassy staff but ruled out any such action in the immediate moment because, according to Vance, "there was no way to get a rescue team into the middle of the city, with thousands of demonstrators milling about, without getting the hostages killed in the process." Brzezinski and the secretary of defense briefly discussed diverting an aircraft carrier battle group to within striking distance but, again, rejected the idea "for fear of giving the kidnappers an excuse to kill their hostages." Aside from initiating a massive effort to find someone in Iran with whom to talk, the meeting generated little in the way of response other than the blind hope that somehow this incident might still end the way the one in February had.

The NSC's overnight analysis delivered the next morning was, however, quite unsettling. Brzezinski's Iranian specialist argued that the seizure's continuation for more than twenty-four hours was a sign of the growing rift between "the religious authorities on the one hand, acting through the *komiteh* and revolutionary guards, and the secular forces of Bazargan and his associates on the other." Indeed, the provisional prime minister's government might very well fold, leaving only Khomeini to be dealt with, and the NSC predicted that Khomeini would "use the hostages for his own political purposes" for as long as it suited him. The NSC's analyst thought the best shot they had at extricating their diplomats was for the United States to "make every effort to convince [Khomeini] that this was a losing game by mobilizing all the resources and pressure at our command."

That was far easier said than done. At the moment, the United States didn't even have a way to contact the imam, much less influence him.

From November 5 on, the bureaucratic mechanisms for grappling with this circumstance were divided into operational and policy spheres. The former was handled by the Iran Working Group, quickly established in the State Department's Operations Center, and on call twenty-four hours a day. Composed of lower-ranking executives and specialists from a number of departments, its purview, according to one of those involved, included developing "channels of communication, sources of information, instruments of influence and pressure . . . working-level coordination in Washington . . . responding to the press, conducting relations with other governments, [and] briefing and consulting Congress." The Working Group's tactical activities were guided by the Special Coordinating Committee, assigned the task of constructing a strategic overview with which the Crisis might be managed. The SCC met to discuss the hostages for the first time on the morning of November 5 and would meet almost every day around 8:30 a.m. for the next six months.

That first SCC meeting, on day two of the Crisis, was convened in the White House Situation Room, like almost all of those to follow. Brzezinski was in the chair. Vance was present, as well as the vice president, the secretaries of defense and treasury, and the director of central intelligence. The discussion opened with a query to Stansfield Turner about just what his agency knew, and he admitted that the CIA knew virtually nothing. They weren't even sure who had seized the embassy or just what connection, if any, they had to Khomeini. Even though the threat of such a takeover had been an active part of American decision making for more than eight months, neither the CIA nor any other part of the administration had made contingency plans for this worst-case scenario.

After the CIA presentation, Brzezinski and Vance both pushed the discussion toward what the national security adviser called "the diplomatic initiatives the United States needed to take." Brzezinski had spoken with the president before the meeting and suggested to him that the best course would be to send an emissary to Khomeini immediately. The president, he reported, had "crinkled up his nose and was visibly reluctant . . . but did not veto the idea." Vance chimed in that he too had spoken with Carter and been told that an emissary should be sent "to ensure that the [Iranians] understood we had no demands other than the release of the Americans and the return of the Embassy." Much of the meeting was then spent discussing possible emissaries and eventually a delegation of two was chosen: former Attorney General Ramsey Clark and William Miller, a staff member of the Senate Intelligence Committee. After that, the SCC discussed the possible effects of the Crisis on oil supplies, how to deal with the thousands of Iranian students in the United States, how to cut off military supplies and other exports to Iran, the status of Iranian diplomats in the United States, how this would affect the international financial markets, and the best ways to monitor any unusual transfer of Iranian assets out of American banks.

The other item on the agenda was the discussion of military options. Everyone agreed that there were none in the immediate moment that made any sense, but a small subcommittee headed by Brzezinski was assigned to examine possible future actions. These, according to one of Brzezinski's aides, were primarily focused on "planning for a possible rescue mission, on punitive steps that could be taken in retaliation for [possible] Iranian actions, and on preserving the integrity of the oil fields in southwestern Iran." Otherwise, all they could do was wait.

At the end of day three, with still no change in the situation, Ham Jordan summoned a White House limo to take him home. By now Jordan had abandoned his initial faith that this episode would end up a replay of the Valentine's Day incident. This was clearly something far more complex, far less tractable, and far more explosive than the chief of staff had first imagined.

Just how charged the situation already was became apparent when Jordan's

White House driver turned onto Massachusetts Avenue and traffic slowed. Up ahead, a spontaneous demonstration had broken out in front of the Iranian embassy. Several hundred Americans were chanting "Let my people go," and when an Iranian diplomat came outside to confer with the District of Columbia police protecting the building, the crowd jeered.

Jordan had his car pull over while he watched. "I felt the anger of that crowd," he remembered, "and I saw it etched on every face. Their rage, their very presence seemed to be saying, We've had enough! . . . This is the last straw — Americans held hostage by a bunch of terrorists. We won't stand for it anymore!"

And it wasn't just in Washington DC. In Newark, New Jersey, two city employees burned Iranian flags in front of city hall. In Los Angeles and Houston, when pro-Khomeini Iranian students demonstrated, they ended up in fistfights with American students. All of this upset was played on the evening news, along with film clips of Iranians mobbing outside the Tehran embassy, chanting *"Marg bar Amrika"* and burning an American flag. When the wife of one of the hostages tied a yellow ribbon to the tree in front of her house as a sign of waiting for her husband to come home, it seemed as if the whole country began flying yellow ribbons as soon as television passed along the image. Hundreds of thousands of Americans sent cards and letters addressed to the embassy in Tehran in hopes of bolstering the captives there. The fate of the embassy was already the lead news story on virtually every media outlet in the United States and would be until the hostages were returned. Soon ABC would field a daily program to track Iranian events, and CBS, the most watched evening newscast in the country, would begin closing each of its news broadcasts with a recitation of how many days the hostages had been kept. From day 1 to day 444, the Crisis dominated America's collective attention as it seemed nothing else ever had. By the end of November, 98 percent of Americans would indicate to pollsters that they were aware of the Crisis and 81 percent would describe themselves as personally angry about it.

On November 6, Hamilton Jordan could already see the approaching storm. He finally had his driver pull away from the crowd as he slouched in the back to avoid being seen. "I was glad the people cared," he remembered, "but [I was already] bothered that they cared so much. . . . I thought to myself [that] an ugly mood will develop in this country if the hostages aren't out soon. . . . The American people won't be satisfied for long with meetings at the White House."

· 17 ·

———

FROM THE VERY BEGINNING, JIMMY CARTER, LIKE
much of the rest of America, took the Crisis personally.

That was perhaps most evident in the tangible bond he felt with the captive diplomats. As president, he declared that any solution to the Crisis had
to preserve national honor and save the lives of the hostages, but many in the
administration thought that, in truth, his order of priority was the reverse.
He was a man for whom the personal connection was central, be it with his
God or his body politic, and his feeling of connectedness with those who had
been taken prisoner on his watch was almost instantaneous, even though he
had known none of them before their captivity. When the families of the
hostages first gathered in Washington, he had himself driven across town to
the State Department to meet with them personally, though no one had expected he would and everyone was genuinely surprised at his appearance.
Others, most notably Brzezinski, avoided such encounters for fear the experience would impair their judgment. Not Carter. When presidential decisions were required, his first question was always how any action would

affect the hostages' safety, and he made it very clear that he wasn't going to have the death of these innocents on his conscience if he could avoid it. Emotionally he assumed the role of father of the victim as well as that of chief negotiator over the kidnap ransom.

In keeping with this bent, the Crisis instantly became the first item on Carter's agenda. One of Brzezinski's aides described this obsession as "the central, dominant feature of the Carter Administration from the day [the seizure] happened [until] the day that Jimmy Carter quit being President. It was the one thing that drove everything else in the White House." No detail concerning it was too small for the president's attention, and often the government's initiatives reflected his personal touch.

Back on the afternoon of day three, Hamilton Jordan had found the president in his study, off of the Oval Office. The room was his most intimate work space, where he retreated for many of what Jordan remembered as the "most rewarding and difficult moments" of his presidency. Jordan, who often barged into the Oval Office unannounced, always made a point of knocking before entering the study. This time, the president was inside writing a note to Ayatollah Ruhollah Khomeini on the pale green stationery he reserved for "personal communications of the highest order." He told Jordan to come back later.

When Ham did, the president explained his missive. "I told him that the Americans being held were not spies," he said, "that it was inhumane for them to be held as hostages, and, for the sake of both nations, there should be a quick and honorable solution." Carter described the tone as "firm, but not antagonistic or threatening." He wanted the emissaries being dispatched that day to deliver it.

They never got the chance. When the two Americans reached Istanbul to await permission to enter Iran, the imam sent word that the emissaries were not welcome and should turn around and go back where they came from.

The priority the Crisis would receive in Jimmy Carter's White House was set in stone on November 8, day five. The move was initiated by Hamilton Jordan in response to the president's previously scheduled visit to Canada, planned for the following day. The chief of staff was worried about the implications of undertaking such travel at this moment. On the evening of day four, CBS had devoted 55 percent of its news broadcast to the Iranian situation, and that morning NBC's *Today* program had spent twenty of its first thirty minutes talking about the hostages. In light of that focus, the Canadian trip "didn't feel right to me," Ham remembered.

He broached the idea of postponing or canceling the trip with Carter after their regular 10:00 a.m. White House staff meeting but received a peremptory "no" before he had gotten much of his argument out of his mouth. Carter pointed out that it had been ten years since an American president had visited Canada and he could stay in easy touch with the White House from there.

Not content with that response, Jordan went back to his corner office and drafted a memo. He had long since learned that if you wanted to change Carter's mind, it was best to write something on paper. "If I went into his office to argue with him," Jordan explained, "armed with five reasons to do something, I would rarely get beyond point one before he was aggressively countering it. . . . He couldn't argue with a piece of paper."

"Mr. President," Jordan wrote, "this crisis is a crisis in every sense. It is a crisis for your Presidency, for the hostages, and for our country's image around the world. I can see no good or valid reason for you to leave the country — even for 24 hours — while this is going on. . . . It would have to be made clear that you are staying merely to give this situation your complete and undivided attention [but] I don't see how you can justify your trip under these circumstances." To make sure his memo came to the president's immediate attention, Ham carried it into the Oval Office when Carter was absent and placed it on top of the president's in-box.

An hour later, Carter summoned Jordan. Without mentioning the memo, the president simply announced that the trip to Canada was canceled.

Jordan left the Oval Office quite proud of himself for having fended off potential political difficulties. Without knowing it, however, he had also locked the president into a posture from which he would find it almost impossible to extricate himself. Several days later, a trip to Pittsburgh would also be canceled — adding domestic travel to the restriction — and several more journeys after that. All the cancelations were made under the same logic Jordan had advanced on day five: Nothing was to be treated as more important than the Crisis, and the only place for the president while it was going on was at the helm of the government. Having set this stationary benchmark as proof of his presidency's relevancy, the president was then committed to staying at the White House or up at Camp David until the Crisis was resolved. By this logic, doing otherwise would be an admission that he was playing hooky on the nation's most important business. The press eventually dubbed this new Washington-bound presidency as "the Rose

Garden strategy," but whatever it was called, Jimmy Carter had for all intents
and purposes made himself a hostage by the time the Crisis was six days old.

Word of what had happened at the Americans' gold-brick building on
Taleghani Avenue was every bit as electrifying to the Iranians as it was to the
Americans. "It was as if we had been asleep," Ibrahim Asgarzadeh remembered.
"Here we were praying for rain and then there were floods." Crowds began
congregating around the captured embassy almost instantly. By the time the
students issued their first communiqué, several hours after their takeover was
complete, hundreds of ordinary citizens had already flooded the streets outside
the compound wall. By day two, the crowd's numbers had grown to thousands,
by day three to tens of thousands. People from the countryside started making
pilgrimages there, often walking long distances. Muharram would soon begin,
and many who came to surround the embassy were in a religious frenzy when
they arrived. Those who couldn't come sent letters to the students. "Someone
had to stand up in the face of those who have imposed so much suffering upon
us," a farmers' cooperative from the province of Khorasan wrote. "You have
made our hopes come true." Employees at a steel mill in Isfahan declared, "We
stand behind you firmly. Our dignity is in your hands." Trade unionists from
near the Persian Gulf told the students, "You have spoken our words. You have
humiliated our enemy and . . . lifted the burden of decades of . . . enslavement
from our backs." No one in Iran seemed untouched by the takeover and almost
all of them identified with it.

"That chanting went on all afternoon and on into the night," one of the
captive marines remembered. "It sounded like hundreds of thousands of
people in the street — and they weren't that far away, either. They were just
on the other side of the wall. Those people could really make some noise.
Over and over again, '*Marg bar Amrika! Marg bar Amrika!*' It was so loud the
sound . . . would just kind of throb through me. I was worried that things
might get out of hand and those people would come over the wall. I couldn't
understand Farsi, and I didn't know what the speakers on the other side of
the wall were telling those people. Finally, I asked one of the [student]
guards, 'Hey, what is this *marg bar* shit?'"

At first the Muslim Students Following the Line of the Imam were
shocked at the enormity of the public's response. "When the crowd began
collecting," Asgarzadeh remembered, "we kind of panicked at what we had
set off. What if this angry crowd decided to storm the place? What would we

do then? But we calmed after a while." By day two, it was obvious that in the space of twenty-four hours, their little "set in" had become Iran's political epicenter. Leading figures from all factions started calling, hoping to affiliate themselves with the takeover. The students' action had welded an instant national consensus. The heretofore frequent armed clashes in the streets between leftists and Islamicists eased, as both groups endorsed the seizure and the students' paramount demand that the shah be returned to Iran for trial. "Everyone in the country supported them," a *Le Monde* correspondent observed. "It was almost unanimous."

The Muslim Students Following the Line of the Imam were inspired by their sudden acquisition of enormous power and dropped all notion of leaving after seventy-two hours as they had originally planned. The students agreed in their meetings and side conversations that the seizure was now a sacred trust to be carried out to its end and began to reorganize for the long haul. They saw themselves and their occupation as the Prophet's instrument for saving the Revolution from American control and returning the criminal shahanshah to face the nation he had abused.

Over the first three days of the Crisis, the captors installed their organizational chart.

The students' five-member Central Committee, composed largely of the takeover's initial organizers, had the final word on overall policies. Underneath this committee was a larger council of fifteen students assigned the task of translating the Central Committee's policies into operational procedures. There would also be parallel weekly caucuses of each university contingent at which issues were raised and discussed.

To carry out operations, this command structure oversaw six subcommittees. The subcommittee concerning security organized the students into guard shifts of two hours each during which they would watch the hostages and patrol the inside of the compound equipped with G-3 infantry rifles supplied by the Revolutionary Guards, who had supported the students from the first and still watched the compound from outside the walls. There was also a services subcommittee to handle logistics, including the huge quantity of foodstuffs discovered in the embassy's internal supermarket — enough, according to the students, to feed a small village for several years. There was also a large stash of captured American cash, which was used to fund the operation on a daily basis. Just how much cash was involved would never be disclosed. The information subcommittee focused on developing intelligence, while the public relations subcommittee handled press interviews and contact with other Iranian political forces.

The final two subcommittees had the most impact on the ongoing Crisis. The first of those concerned itself with documents. Despite the frantic activity in the second-floor vault aimed at destroying the embassy's secret paperwork, the chancery yielded an enormous harvest of undamaged memos, letters, cables, and reports. All of these would be painstakingly sorted, translated into Farsi, and referred to higher committees for exposure or publication. The documents subcommittee also refused to accept as final the document destruction that transpired in the vault before it was captured. Upon entering it, they found an enormous pile of shredded paper. Soon, the documents subcommittee had volunteers slowly piecing together the shreds.

The last subcommittee was devoted to hostage affairs and handled everything concerned with the welfare of the captives the students insisted on officially referring to as their "involuntary guests." Initially all the hostages were kept with their hands bound and their eyes blindfolded and were forcibly prevented from communicating with one another. They were spread among the compound's various buildings, including the ambassador's residence, the consulate, staff housing, and one of the warehouses, as well as the chancery. Many were tied to chairs or tethered to walls for extended periods. At least a half dozen were briefly moved out of the embassy altogether and held in a north Tehran mansion that had once belonged to a member of the royal family. To feed the Americans, the students retained the embassy's Pakistani cook, who knew how to fix what they liked to eat, including fried chicken, meat loaf, mashed potatoes, spaghetti, and french fries. None of the hostages were allowed newspapers or current news, though they sometimes were able to overhear the students listening to their transistor radios. When they needed to use the bathroom, they were escorted to and from by their captors. Each was also subjected to an interrogation, and the results were filed in an individual dossier kept by the students, assessing the captive's role in what was now almost exclusively referred to as the Den of Spies.

Soon the captors developed a daily routine. The students began preparing the prisoners' breakfast at 6:00 a.m., the security shift changed at 7:00 a.m., and the document sorters began work at 8:00. Everyone stopped for noon prayers, and the entire congregation of students prayed together on Fridays, out in the embassy courtyard, in front of the gate, or on the compound's sports field. Throughout the day, guards supervised the prisoners' sporadic moments of outdoor exercise. The students also used their afternoons to hear religious sermons or participate in classes that had been started up inside the embassy. They ate together in the cafeteria — consuming a far simpler diet than the Americans, using food bought in Tehran and appropriate for Muslims, with the men sitting separately from the women. Twice a month, all students had to serve on a housekeeping detail, and everyone did a regular shift washing dishes. Most refused to use the western-style toilets, so they lined up to use the embassy's few native facilities. In the early days, a number of the students were involved in ransacking the residence, and by peeking beneath loose blindfolds, several hostages were able to watch young Iranians making off with pieces of furniture and Persian rugs. The diplomats' private apartments were looted as well.

By day four, a new English banner had been erected over the front gate. "No Negotiations," it read, "Just Delivering Shah."

The principal uncertainty facing the Muslim Students Following the Line of the Imam during their initial three days inside the embassy was whether they were indeed following the imam's line. The first overt hint that they might be was provided by Khomeini's son, Ahmed, who visited the Den of Spies on day two. Wearing a gray floor-length mullah's tunic and his black sayyid's turban, he was escorted by two men carrying submachine guns. The imam's son was given a quick tour inside the chancery and then taken out to the compound wall, where he was hoisted up to make a brief speech. "This is not an occupation," Ahmed proclaimed. "We have thrown out the occupiers." The crowd roared.

Still, the imam himself hadn't yet spoken, and there were at least two significant efforts to keep him from making an endorsement. The first of those was made by Abolhassan Bani Sadr. Bani Sadr had been outraged by the takeover as soon as he heard of it. He found fault with the strategy even more than the hostage taking per se. "This was just a new form of dependence," he explained. "True independence means you don't have to exercise your internal politics externally, converting domestic policy to foreign policy. We had waged a revolution to get the United States out of Iran and now, by taking hostages, we were letting the United States back in."

Bani Sadr immediately took his worries to Khomeini out in Qom but discovered they were not reciprocated. The imam described the students' move as divine justice. "They are not diplomats," he said of the hostages. "They are spies." At that point Khomeini seemed to be thinking that they would be held a few days and released.

The other effort to derail Khomeini's approval was made by the provisional prime minister, Mehdi Bazargan. He called Khomeini in Qom but could never get him on the phone personally. Instead, he spoke with Ahmed, who was blunt. "It is better if the government does nothing," the imam's son told him. "The Revolutionary Council will handle the matter."

The next day, Bazargan raised the issue at the Revolutionary Council meeting. He was furious and insisted that action be taken. This was an international crime. The government was obliged to protect foreign diplomats, and he had given his personal assurances to the Americans that Iran would provide such protection. If Khomeini didn't order the students out, there was no use having a government.

Much to the prime minister's dismay, the mullahs on the council were unwilling to turn against the groundswell of sentiment that was steadily filling Taleghani Avenue. During a break in the council's deliberations, Sadegh Ghotbzadeh took Bazargan aside and advised him not to buck the trend either. Ghotbzadeh told him he thought the takeover was stupid and self-defeating but was unwilling to risk open opposition to it. The best policy would be to take the occupation over and control it for other purposes. The public was overwhelmingly behind it and, Sadegh warned, so was Khomeini. The only option was to yield.

The argument carried no weight with the provisional prime minister. That evening he and Provisional Foreign Minister Ebrahim Yazdi sent letters of resignation to the imam. This was not the first time they had done so, but always before Khomeini had refused to accept the resignations. This time no such refusal was forthcoming. At 1:30 p.m. on November 6, the fall of the provisional government was announced.

Shortly after the announcement, the imam went on the radio for a live broadcast from the holy city of Qom. He dubbed the United States "the Great Satan" and the embassy the "Den of Spies," and he endorsed the students' takeover. The students were, he said, helping make a "second revolution" even more important than the first. Now the Great Satan had no choice but to keep his distance and return "the criminal" who had once been shah.

At the embassy, the students learned of the imam's blessing over their transistor radios. Groups of them scattered at various locations around the compound had paused in their duties and were clustered around the tiny receivers, concentrating on the imam's every word. "They'd turn the [volume] all the way up and seven or eight . . . would all get around this one little radio and stick their ears right to it," one of the hostages remembered. "They looked like a bunch of mice around a piece of cheese." Their reaction to Khomeini's announcement was sheer joy. All of them broke into spontaneous cheers, several ran around the room they were in screaming in ecstasy, and one even did a celebratory backflip. "The imam has blessed us," one student breathlessly exclaimed to his captives.

"We had been anointed," Ibrahim Asgarzadeh remembered. "We had been given a mission which we could not in good conscience refuse even had we wanted to. Now there was no turning back."

Shortly after settling in for the long haul, the students added fasting to their regular agenda on Mondays and Thursdays. This ritual, one of them explained, "was an act of worship and a form of spiritual and physical discipline. We believed that by controlling our powerful physical drives, we could educate ourselves to behave as our logic and wisdom guided us, and not be the slaves of our desires. When we fasted, it was as if we were departing from selfishness and moving toward perfection and toward God. It gave us a feeling of lightness, of spiritual buoyancy."

The Muslim Students Following the Line of the Imam never, however, lost their political grounding. Asgarzadeh, for one, thought of their activity as an offshoot of student movements like the French one that controlled the streets of Paris for weeks in 1968. They discussed world events among themselves and spent hours developing analyses of larger currents in the politics of the Third World versus the Superpowers. They were also very careful not to let other Iranian political agendas grab a piece of theirs and were especially wary of the leftist "guerrillas." The organization kept strict control over the number of students involved and tracked every coming and going into the buildings under their control. They also watched over one another's discipline. There would be a constant minor flow of people in and out of the group, but over time, they would count on intramural familiarity to limit access to only the faithful.

In his message about the Great Satan's Den of Spies, the imam had instructed the students to treat the Americans as "guests," so they set out to do their best to treat their bound and blindfolded charges accordingly.

"There were three sources of danger for these hostages," one of the students later explained. "First, there was the students themselves. Several had suffered as victims of . . . persecution, repression and intimidation [by] the Shah. . . . Feelings ran deep. . . . There were some among us who would have liked to take personal revenge. . . . Our next source of concern . . . was the people themselves, our strongest allies. . . . Sometimes the physical pressure on the front gates on Taleghani Avenue was more than the locks and chains were meant to bear. . . . Our [final and] greatest worry [for the hostages' safety] was . . . the incompetence of the Carter Administration."

Whatever the students' claims for their custodial approach, there were some obvious egregious breaches in their professed discipline. One of the first of those took place out at the gate on day three. Don Hohman, an army medic who had been at the embassy on a temporary duty assignment, was being held in a unit of staff housing in the compound, just sitting in a chair with his hands bound but without a blindfold. Then the door was opened, and several students pulled him to his feet and wrapped a blindfold around his head. "We go," his captors said. After walking a while, Hohman could tell they were approaching the front gate and Taleghani Avenue. The ground was shaking from the roar of the crowd. *Marg bar Amrika. Marg bar Amrika. Marg bar Amrika.* The student escort halted him three or four feet from the gate, then whipped off his blindfold. The first thing the American saw in the midst of this thunder was a wall of screaming Iranians pressing at the gate until it seemed sure to break, howling, trying to claw him with their hands but unable to reach far enough. The medic had never seen a demonstration as large as this one, and their chants made his ears numb. He thought for sure his guards were about to hand him over to the masses to be torn to bits on the spot.

After two minutes trembling there, his hands bound, Hohman was blindfolded and taken from the scene. When Asgarzadeh learned what had happened, he was furious. The student responsible was judged "a traitor from the guerrillas" and expelled from the embassy within hours of the incident.

Hohman was still shaking when his captors returned him to his quarters.

Much of the students' approach to handling their captives seemed to indicate a history of direct experience with SAVAK or at least having at some point read a manual on interrogation. The Americans were grilled in good cop–bad cop teams, sometimes rousted in the middle of the night to answer questions, and moved often, to keep them from becoming too comfortable in their circumstances. According to one hostage, the whole routine had "a feeling of a technique half mastered."

Perhaps the worst stop on the rotation of confinement locations was the warehouse in the middle of the compound, soon nicknamed "the Mushroom Inn." Windowless, stifling, and often dank, it was a much better place for growing fungi than keeping "guests." Most of those who were sent there had apparently been judged antagonistic by their captors.

Robert Ode was one of those. At sixty-six, he was the oldest of the hostages — having been called out of retirement to do temporary duty in the consular section. He was part of the group originally captured in the surrender of the consulate and was anything but submissive. He later described the students as "like a bunch of children who had cornered an animal of some sort. They didn't know what to do, except either to plague us, or do a small kindness of some sort." When Ode was being held, bound and blindfolded, in one of the residence's bedrooms on day one, a student tried to feed him a date by pressing it against his lips, but he refused to eat anything he couldn't see and kept his lips shut as tight as a suitcase lid. Later, another guard took Ode's embassy identification card out of his pocket, and Ode objected as loudly as he could.

"I am a diplomat," he insisted. "You are not even permitted to touch me! You keep your hands off me!"

His captor ignored him and kept the ID card for inclusion in Ode's dossier.

Ode was then taken downstairs to the residence living room, along with a number of other bound hostages, and fed sandwiches. None of them were allowed to talk to one another, and Ode spent the night tied up and stretched out on the floor. The next day, he and another dozen captives were taken into the dining room and tied to chairs around a table. That night, his hands were rebound and he was allowed to sleep on the floor under the table, covered with a piece of drapery. On the morning of day three, when Ode was tied to a chair at the dining room table again, the students came through and seized everyone's personal items for "security reasons." Ode tried to hide his by sitting on them, but they were taken anyway. He lost his gold wedding band, a cameo ring that had been given to him by his parents on his twenty-first birthday, a ballpoint pen, a pocket comb in a leather case, a wristwatch, and a small leather-bound notebook.

That night, Robert Ode was awakened, brought out from under the table, handcuffed to another hostage, and, with a blanket over his head, transported in an embassy car from the residence to the Mushroom Inn.

Barry Rosen joined him there. Rosen, thirty-three, was a press officer, fluent in Farsi, who had arrived in Tehran in November 1978 and been decorated with the State Department's Award for Valor for his role in the Valentine's Day takeover. When captured this time, he had engaged in a short debate with one of his captors in the kitchen help quarters where he was first taken.

The student demanded to know if the Americans had any idea of the enormity of the crimes that the shah had committed.

Rosen allowed that he might even agree with them about the shah, but the shah wasn't the issue at the moment. "I can't answer for his mistakes," the press officer snapped. "Are you going to answer for the [mistake] you're making today?" In an interrogation that followed, Rosen insulted the woman interrogator by suggesting that the two of them have a drink from a bottle of whiskey found in the room where he was being kept. The next day, still blindfolded, Rosen was moved to a reception area at the residence, with what he guessed, from the sounds he could hear, were some twenty others. He was kept there, tied to a chair and blindfolded, for two more days before being awoken in the middle of the night and driven to the Mushroom Inn.

The room into which he was taken had once housed radio equipment used to monitor the Soviet Union. There were about twenty others in there, bound and blindfolded. "It was a very weird place to be," Rosen recounted. "The atmosphere down there was disgusting. The thing I remember the most is the abominable heat and the darkness of the place. It was intolerable. . . . The huge ventilating units [in the warehouse] made a deafening noise but added to the heat rather than providing a fresh breath. . . . Many people were not able to sleep. No matter how you moved, the floor was hard [and] it was hot and uncomfortable. . . . You'd lie there and think, 'When am I going to get out of here? How am I going to get out of here?' And I'd wonder about whether or not I was really there. It was very strange. At times it seemed as if it was just a very, very bad movie. . . . But what could I do?"

The following afternoon, day four, the students brought in an Iranian camera crew to film the Mushroom Inn hostages. The lights the crew used made the place even hotter.

When the filmmakers approached Rosen, they asked if he had anything he'd like to say to his relatives, and he made a terse statement advising his wife not to worry.

When they reached Ode, he said nothing and just flipped them the bird.

· 18 ·

O<small>NE OF THE NAMES THE HOSTAGES OVERHEARD</small> on the snippets of transistor radio news consumed by their captors was Abolhassan Bani Sadr. From day three on, he played an increasingly central role in the struggle that had already begun inside Iran's dominant circles over the hostages' fate.

Bani Sadr was still widely considered the second most powerful figure in the country after only the imam himself. The final draft of the incipient Islamic Republic's constitution was due to be released within the next few weeks, and Bani Sadr, appropriately, took much of the credit for having preserved the elements of the first draft that remained. Bazargan, the now resigned provisional prime minister, had publicly attacked the projected document, but Bani Sadr had decided to settle for half a loaf and keep his relationship with Khomeini intact, waging no last-ditch public effort to block it.

On day four, the imam turned to Bani Sadr and asked him to form a government without a prime minister, to handle things until the constitution could be approved and a permanent government elected. Bani Sadr would take over the Foreign Ministry in addition to serving as finance minister. That the imam made this request at this critical moment despite Abolhassan's objections to the embassy takeover speaks to just how strong their bond remained.

Bani Sadr visited the Den of Spies himself shortly after taking over the Foreign Ministry and met briefly with the Central Committee. The two parties started the encounter suspicious of each other and only got more so once Bani Sadr opened his mouth.

"You think that you have taken America hostage," he lectured them. "What a delusion! In fact, you have made Iran the hostage of the Americans." In case they missed his point, Bani Sadr openly criticized the students' refusal to listen to other viewpoints the following day in an article in the newspaper he controlled.

At the same time, he took the reins at the Foreign Ministry. Bani Sadr had accepted the job after receiving assurances from the imam that he would not meddle, and he behaved like a man with power and the latitude to exercise it. His initial instinct was to assume that the ministry diplomats were incompetent because they were holdovers from the shah, so he recruited Ahmed Salmatian, one of his old Paris comrades, to help him sort the place out. After an intense day talking with the Iranian diplomats, however, Salmatian found what he later described as "some pretty good people" with whom to work. Bani Sadr and his assistant then put their ministry through a marathon twenty-four-hour review of the history of Iran's relations with the United States and the international law on hostage taking. They had hoped to find at least some kind of legal basis for the embassy takeover, but along the way, according to Salmatian, they concluded that "we were totally wrong. Hostage taking in this circumstance was totally out of bounds." Absent a loophole, Bani Sadr, his assistant, and the rest of the ministry decided "the quicker out of this thing, the better."

Bani Sadr's next step was to devise a strategy that would allow him to extricate Iran from this situation and still score some kind of victory for the Revolution — and, of course, for Bani Sadr. The resulting approach featured two thrusts. The first would be to change what was said. They would stop using *hostages* to refer to these captives and instead define them as people who were being prevented from working. The second thrust would be to find what Salmatian called "a way of getting rid of the people from the Embassy without appearing to be losing something." In a direct meeting with the Americans to resolve this, it would be virtually impossible not to lose at least some face, so there had to be a third party to act through. The UN was the obvious vehicle, since the Americans had already gone to the international body to formally complain of the violation of the rules of diplomacy. Bani Sadr and his assistant finally concluded that the solution to Iran's problem could be for the UN to draft a resolution calling on Iran to release the people being prevented from working. This would allow Iran to exchange the hostages for official language absolving Iran of the international onus on hostage taking. A resolution could also require the United States to help Iran retrieve the money stolen from it by the shah and his cohorts, giving Bani Sadr a prize to hold up to the crowds on Taleghani Avenue. He was also considering insisting on some kind of international tribunal to examine the crimes of the shah, another potential Iranian coup.

At the end of the first week of the Crisis, Bani Sadr summoned all the foreign diplomats in Tehran, save the captive Americans. He requested that they "consider the circumstances" and pressure the United States to resolve this crisis by making three commitments. The first was to "admit that the property and fortune of the shah were stolen." The second was to "refrain from further intervention in Iranian affairs." The third was to "extradite the shah so he can be judged by a court with all international guarantees."

When asked, Bani Sadr also, according to an Iran Working Group report, "responded positively to a Western ambassador's testing of the idea that [the] U.N. Secretary General . . . assist in resolving the crisis. Bani Sadr said he would consult the Revolutionary Council." He also made it clear that Iran wished to continue relations with the United States.

One of Bani Sadr's principal internal adversaries in his campaign for a quick exit from this Crisis would be Sadegh Ghotbzadeh — despite the two old Paris comrades' having supposedly "reconciled" and the fact that both wanted the same outcome.

Sadegh had come a long way since Paris. His old friend and attorney, the Frenchman Christian Bourguet, had been shocked by just how much he had changed. The two saw each other in September, more than a month before the Crisis erupted, for the first time since Sadegh had returned to Iran with the imam. Bourguet was in Tehran with an international jurist group investigating human rights violations by the revolutionaries' new justice system.

The Sadegh he saw bore little visual similarity to the Paris bon vivant. Always a natty western dresser, now Sadegh was wearing what Bourguet remembered as some kind of "Islamic Mao suit"— black, shapeless, and drab. He was also at the height of his "spiritual son" of the imam stage. At the Radio and Television bureau, his only programming, as Bani Sadr derided it, was "Imam, this and Imam, that and Imam, there."

When Bourguet and another French attorney arrived at Sadegh's office for their reunion, the two old friends collided right away, after Bourguet raised the question of the Iranian tribunals.

"You can't shoot these men without a trial, Sadegh," he pleaded. "Everybody deserves a trial."

Sadegh disagreed. These people were too bad for that, he insisted. It would be a waste of time.

Bourguet said he sounded like the shah.

The two went at it for an hour until Sadegh finally backed down to the position that Iran needed a better justice system, but it needed so much else as well that doing something about it was just out of reach. He said he had a roomful of letters next door favoring the executions and no time to try to put a stop to them. Bourguet said he'd better make time; the old Sadegh he knew would have never taken that approach.

At that moment, as near as Bourguet could tell, Sadegh had an epiphany. The Iranian suddenly broke into tears — long sobs that shook his body. "It was as if he'd looked in a mirror," the Frenchman remembered, "and saw that the man he had become wasn't who he wanted to be. He cried for a long time and, after he stopped crying, he reverted to the man he had been in Paris. It was quite remarkable. He changed completely what he was saying and I never saw that Mao suit again."

Sadegh learned what had happened at the embassy on day one, when the students' mullah came to him to request the Radio and Television bureau's backing. Ghotbzadeh was furious at the United States for having admitted the shah, which he considered a calculated insult to the Iranian nation. The mullah told him the occupation would last no more than five days, so Sadegh signed on, sending broadcasters to Taleghani Avenue and running constant bulletins. The filming done in the Mushroom Inn was by cameramen from his bureau. As it became clear that the occupation wasn't going to end in five days, however, Sadegh started seeing the hostages as a tremendous weight on Iran that would distort the country.

The result was a double game by Ghotbzadeh, playing both sides of the fence.

While taking no formal position on the takeover, Sadegh used the state media to help the students beat their public drum. For him, the seizure of the embassy and, with it, the world's attention was an instrument to be used for the Revolution's purposes. Despite a certain ambivalence, he had been glad to see the provisional government fall, because he had worried they would hand the country back to the interests of the Americans. Yet he also privately viewed the hostage holding with great contempt.

The difficulty between him and Bani Sadr was that they both had their eyes on the same prize. As Sadegh saw it, if Bani Sadr went to the UN and resolved this, he would be an overwhelming favorite in the presidential elections to be held sometime in the next few months, once the new constitution that was about to be submitted by the Assembly of Experts had cleared a referendum. If, however, Bani Sadr failed, perhaps Sadegh would be the Islamic Republic's first president instead. And Ghotbzadeh had long since decided he was going to run for the office whenever the election was held.

For his part, Bani Sadr moved forward despite the forces lining up against him and instructed Salmatian to prepare to travel to New York. He was going to be named Iran's special envoy and sent to the United Nations to lay a base for Bani Sadr's plan.

To the Revolutionary Council, the new foreign minister avoided revealing the outcome for which he was hoping. Instead, he pointed out that the issue of the hostages was being taken to the international body by the United States, and Iran needed someone there who could respond to the situation. As it currently stood, Iran's UN delegation amounted to a few shah holdovers who could be counted on to perform perfunctorily and little more. This new envoy would ensure that Iran's posture there was in keeping with the new Foreign Ministry's approach. On that basis, the Revolutionary Council — including Ghotbzadeh — gave the dispatch of the envoy their unanimous approval.

Three days later, Bani Sadr and Salmatian went out to Qom to meet with Khomeini and secure his approval as well. The imam's son, Ahmed, also sat in on the session. After listening to Bani Sadr's reasoning, Khomeini too agreed.

Then, however, Ahmed jumped into the conversation. He suggested to the imam that this trip to New York should only be permitted under the condition that the envoy not speak directly with the Americans when he was there.

Khomeini nodded enthusiastically.

Salmatian explained that it was never their intention to negotiate directly with the Americans, but simply to use this UN forum for Iran's purposes. Still, it would be better not to have to do so in such a straitjacket.

Ahmed, however, having seen his father's nod, was now adamant. That was the imam's condition, he insisted, and the trip would not be allowed unless it was met.

Bani Sadr and his envoy accepted this unanticipated limitation, but Salmatian, at least, was left with trepidations about what the imam might next pull out of his hat. Bani Sadr told him not to worry.

Two days later, halfway through November, the Iranians' new United Nations envoy landed at New York's Kennedy Airport and was driven under police escort into Manhattan. Both sides of the road were lined with Americans, screaming at his limo and chanting "Bomb Iran. Bomb Iran."

A dozen blocks away from the UN, the shah still occupied his prime suite of rooms on the seventeenth floor at New York Hospital, overlooking Sixty-eighth Street and York Avenue. His October operation had missed at least one gallstone, which still caused him discomfort. He also suffered from intense night sweats, making his doctors wonder if this was the onset of pneumonia. In the meantime, the radiation treatments planned for his spleen and the knot on his neck had to be postponed until his episodic fever was under control. He still looked dreadfully ill. "I hardly recognized him," one old acquaintance remembered. "His features were the only thing that preserved his identity; he had wasted away to a gaunt shell."

What had surprised His Imperial Majesty about the events of November 4 was just how weak the mullahs must have thought the Carter administration was. The shah admitted to having underestimated that level of disrespect by a wide margin. He explained to Armao that his people were childlike: If you let them steal one piece of candy without a scolding, they'd end up taking the whole bowl. These crazies now attempting to run his country thought they could push the Americans around, and they were right.

Mohammad Reza Pahlavi's bitterness was now closer to the surface. He watched a lot of television coverage — shots of the mob on Taleghani Avenue burning American flags, intercut with talking American heads saying things about Carter's government that shocked the deposed shah. He could not imagine how any society interested in order could permit such things to be said. In all the coverage, he also heard himself depicted as a despot and a torturer. The pickets outside the hospital entrance even called for his return to Iran for trial.

This was an option that Jimmy Carter had categorically rejected from the very beginning, but over the Crisis's second week, the lesser possibility of pressuring the shah to move on to some other country was raised at the SCC on at least two occasions by Secretary of State Cyrus Vance. He argued that doing so might very well deprive the embassy occupiers of their rallying point. Vance's most vocal ally in making a case that the shah should be asked to leave was Vice President Mondale, and their principal opponent was Brzezinski. Brzezinski thought any such pressure on His Majesty would compromise America's national honor and amount to "giving in to a student mob in Tehran." The two factions went at it back and forth, but Brzezinski mustered little support. Finally it was agreed to kick the question upstairs.

Jimmy Carter considered the issue at a smaller meeting in the Oval Office, at which just Vance, Brzezinski, Jordan, and a couple of cabinet members were present. Again, each side made its case. Vance argued that the shah had received the medical treatment he had come for, so there was no reason for him to stay longer. Brzezinski again invoked the national honor and wondered out loud why it was he, a naturalized citizen, who had to do so.

The deliberations were interrupted at one point by one of Carter's aides. He informed the president that his wife, Rosalynn, was on the phone from Thailand, where she was visiting refugees, and Carter briefly left the room to take the call. Rosalynn had already acquired an internal reputation as the administration's "superhawk," always seemingly ready to come down harder than almost anyone, Brzezinski included. Ham Jordan took the interruption occasioned by her phone call and the president's absence as an opportunity to lighten things up with a joke. "When he comes back," Jordan quipped, "he'll probably declare war on Iran."

Carter didn't, but he did side with Brzezinski in the dispute over how to handle the shah. The meeting ended with the president's flat declaration that he would not force HIM out of the United States "as long as Americans were being held prisoner."

Vance, however, kept pushing. On November 14, when Brzezinski arrived at the Oval Office for his standard 7:00 a.m. briefing, he was surprised to find the president closeted there alone with the secretary of state. "Such a one-on-one meeting was quite unusual," the national security adviser noted. Apparently Vance had put it to good use. Cy felt an overriding sense of responsibility for the hostages and played on those same feelings in his boss. That the shah would have to return to Mexico was a small price to pay, Vance insisted, if his doing so made it more possible to retrieve the captive diplomats. Before giving way to Brzezinski's briefing, Vance secured Carter's agreement to "an exploratory approach" to Rockefeller's people on the subject.

David Rockefeller called the president the next day. The banker told him that the shah recognized the difficulties his presence had brought to the United States and felt bad about it. Fortunately his health was improving. The radiation treatments had begun, and His Majesty was responding well to them. Rockefeller thought the shah might be fit enough to travel in "a few days." In the meantime, he was able to sit up and receive visitors. He was hoping that the president would send Vance to visit him to help figure out what to do next.

Carter pointed out that any such visit, as visible as it would inevitably be, was the last thing the administration wanted. That would surely be read as America giving in to Iranian pressure, a conclusion the president did not feel he could afford to have in circulation.

Rockefeller sympathized but pointed out that sooner or later the administration was going to have to bite that bullet and assume responsibility for the shah's movement. Rockefeller himself, he reminded Carter, couldn't keep performing that role much longer.

While nothing formal changed in response to Rockefeller's phone call, Carter did move on an informal level. Shortly afterward, the president designated his vice president to act as behind-the-scenes point man in the effort to get the shah out of the United States as soon as possible.

Everyone hoped that would help, but no one in Washington possessed much surety about any of their possible options. The State Department's Bureau of Intelligence and Research had already developed a top secret report on the prospects ahead, and according to one of those who read it, State's analysts had concluded that "diplomatic action had almost no prospect of being successful in liberating the hostages and that no economic or other U.S. pressure on the Iranian regime, including military action, was likely to be any more successful in securing their safe release."

The analysts' best estimate was that this Crisis would last for months to come.

Indeed, at this point, the Carter administration was still struggling to find any information it could about what was going on at the captured embassy. Almost everything they knew came from foreign ambassadors who had been given tours. Those diplomats included one from Sweden, one from Belgium, and one from Syria. When the papal ambassador took his tour, the hostages were served meat loaf in his honor. All those who saw the captives reported to Washington that, other than bondage and blindfolding, there seemed to be no signs of any significant abuse.

Meanwhile, unbeknownst to the White House or almost anyone else, the students' subcommittee on hostage affairs continued its program of location shuffling.

Barry Rosen left the Mushroom Inn about the same time Cyrus Vance was convincing Jimmy Carter to explore the idea of sending the shah on his way. Rosen was taken out in the middle of the night, blindfolded and by himself. For the first five minutes, while he was being led through the warehouse corridors and then out into a very cold night, he thought he was being taken to be shot. He changed his mind when they wedged him into a van with a number of other hostages he could hear but not see. Packed full, the van left the compound, straining on grades, and traveled north through Tehran, higher into the mountains. For a while Rosen speculated that they might be taking a roundabout path to the airport, but that didn't jibe with their constant uphill passage. Finally the hostages were unloaded in front of a massive mansion and herded inside through a cold drizzle. The ostentatious house felt as though it had been abandoned in a hurry. Rosen and two others ended up at the top of a huge staircase in what seemed to have once been a woman's bedroom.

Shortly after arriving there, Rosen was told to fill out a mimeographed form developed by the students, asking his name, address, and embassy duties. When he refused, he was blindfolded, taken downstairs, and shoved into a chair. When his blindfold was removed, he found himself looking across a desk at a young man he guessed was about eighteen years old. He was seated, his feet hardly hitting the floor beneath his chair. When Rosen again cited diplomatic privilege for refusing to fill out the form, the eighteen-year-old motioned for the guard to put the barrel of his G-3 rifle against Rosen's temple. He told the American he was going to count down from ten and if he didn't start filling out the form before he reached zero, the student with the rifle was going to blow Rosen's brains out. When the count reached one, Rosen picked up the form and did as he was required. For days afterward, Barry Rosen flinched when he thought he heard the sounds of guards coming to fetch him.

Robert Ode was rotated out of the Mushroom Inn around the same time as Barry Rosen. He was taken only as far as the embassy residence, where he was confined in what had once been the ambassador's bedroom. Somewhere along the line, he managed to secure a pencil and paper and began keeping a diary. "I again slept on the floor," he noted, "with student guards in the room, lights burning all night, always much talking, whispering, and coming and going by the student guards. During the day the drapes were closed and we were required to sit on chairs facing the wall. There were approximately five other hostages in this room but we were not permitted to converse with each other. Our hands were kept tied day and night." Ode too was told to fill out a mimeographed form and did so under protest. After the second week, Robert Ode stopped waiting for rescue and started taking off his shoes when it came time to sleep.

Perhaps the most intense student activity during those first weeks following the capture centered on their documents subcommittee. The Muslim Students Following the Line of the Imam were somewhat stunned at all the paper they had seized. "We didn't start out looking for anything in particular," Asgarzadeh remembered, "but just the sheer volume of what fell into our hands convinced us we had captured something of significance." The Americans' shredding crew in the vault had managed to purge most of the top secret documents, but in the hurried retreat to the second floor, many safes and file drawers had just been slammed shut with their contents intact, including second and third copies of some of the secrets that had been shredded in the vault. One source at the NSC later described the captured trove as a "huge archive" whose size "came as a stunning surprise" to the Americans once State was able to assess just how much had been seized. The students left all of the documents in the locations in which they were found until a policy for dealing with them was set by the Central Committee.

In the meantime, the rank-and-file students marveled at what a Den of Spies the embassy seemed to be. They were awed by the safe room in the heart of the chancery, where an absolutely soundproof chamber had been constructed to allow the Americans to conduct conversations without any risk of being overheard. None of the Muslim Students had even imagined such things existed. Many arranged to come over from other parts of the compound to get a look at it. They could only fantasize about what kinds of dark subjects had to be spoken of in such secrecy.

Among the students' other initial discoveries were a collection of forged entry stamps and visa seals for countries around the world, including more than a thousand counterfeit passports from the Republic of Ghana. There were also several other forged passports with some of their hostages' photos under false names and nationalities. They even found a document providing a detailed description of the imam's house in Qom, including the location of all doors and windows. That such information had been collected with malice in mind was taken for granted among them.

One of the documents subcommittee's first initiatives was simply to retrieve all the available embassy paperwork from wherever the Americans had hidden it. After the file drawers and offices had been searched, the students were left with seven locked safes for which they had no combinations. They brought in a locksmith who, by listening to the locks' internal tumblers, was eventually able to open three of them. The students then tried to open the other four themselves, using the same technique, with volunteers lining up to give it a try, but those efforts went for naught, so they brought in a high-powered drill, a welding machine, and a saw that would cut through steel. The last safes yielded to brute force within days.

The Central Committee set its policy for handling the captured American secrets before the first week was over, devising a detailed organizational chart for document processing. First, each document was to be given a quick read and a summary translation prepared. On the basis of this, the document was classified according to a system the students designed and assigned a priority for more precise translation by the students most fluent in English. Every afternoon, the translators, working a four-to-six-hour shift, would produce Farsi versions of the day's documents, which were then funneled to an ad hoc committee charged with deciding whether to release the document for public exposure, refer it to the judicial system, or just hold on to it for posterity. This ad hoc committee was made up of what one of its members described as "people who actually handled the documents, more politically mature students with a capacity for analysis, as well as some members of the Central Committee itself." It met daily.

"We simply wanted to expose the names of those [Iranians] involved in the betrayal of their country," one of the students remembered. "It was certainly not our intention to strip people of their dignity and reputation. . . . In those emotion charged days, to release a person's name in connection with the United States, especially with the 'traitor' label attached, could mean for that person imprisonment or worse. Revolutionary justice was swift and cared little for . . . due process. . . . But we were single-minded and intent; those considerations weighed lightly indeed."

The format the students developed to announce their public exposés was a regular weekly session broadcast live by Ghotbzadeh's television bureau. Two students were delegated to read from the texts and were under instructions not to embellish or make comments but just to let the documents speak for themselves. This weekly exposé quickly became one of the most watched programs in Iran. If the documents subcommittee came across something they thought deserved even more immediate public scrutiny, the students released it as one of their daily communiqués, read out loud at the front gate to the Iranian and international press who now clustered there twenty-four hours a day, looking for news.

To American audiences, the most visible Muslim Student Following the Line of the Imam soon became a nineteen-year-old Polytechnic sophomore in chemical engineering known as Sister Mary. Her real name was Massoumeh Ebtekar, and she had adopted the pseudonym Mary, or the Iranian synonym Maryam, because Massoumeh was a difficult name for westerners to get their mouths around. She invariably held center stage at the front gate whenever the students needed to make a statement to the press in English, always in a long shapeless coat with a large scarf covering her hair and tied securely under her chin. One Canadian reporter eventually described her as "a dour young woman with a horsey face that looked out from under a homely scarf [with a] miserable rabbit-like demeanor." She was, however, fluent in colloquial American English. The hostages nicknamed her Mary the Terrorist and Sister Philadelphia.

The latter was a reference to one of the sources of her fluency in English. As a child, she had attended elementary school in Pennsylvania while her father was studying for a doctorate in mechanical engineering at Penn. After her family returned to Iran and her father took up a post on the faculty at Polytechnic, she had been educated in one of Tehran's international schools, making her even more fluent. Her father, something of a religious intellectual, had been arrested on numerous occasions under the shah but was never imprisoned for any significant length of time. Massoumeh joined the Revolution during her freshman year at Polytechnic, as the shah was falling. After the imam's return, she joined a "reconstruction" campaign in which she was a literacy tutor to a class of some thirty factory workers. She had several friends who had been among the original group that stormed the embassy gates on day one but had not been one of those initially invited to join them.

Her invitation came on day three, delivered by one of "the brothers" from the Union of Islamic Students. He had just come from the Den of Spies, he told her, and now that they had the imam's endorsement, it looked as though the occupation would be lasting a lot longer than they had planned. The group was going to need help with English translation and public relations. Would she be willing to volunteer?

The next day, Massoumeh Ebtekar reported to the front gate on Taleghani Avenue and assumed her identity as Sister Mary. "I realized that my own moment of decision had come," she remembered.

Sister Mary's first direct contact with a hostage came when she was taken on a tour of the Mushroom Inn. The warehouse had been divided into makeshift rooms by the erection of partitions, and as she stuck her head into one of the partitioned areas, one of the Americans demanded to know if she spoke English.

She admitted that she did.

He then asked her if the Soviets were paying them to do this.

Sister Mary laughed and answered that they weren't communists, they were "religious-minded people." She told him that the Americans always used this Soviet business as an excuse to suppress any movement for change.

The American scoffed at the notion that any religious person could do "such a thing" as taking hostages.

"Maybe that's because you have a different idea of what a religious person is," Sister Mary retorted. "We have new definitions for old terms."

With that, the conversation was over.

Later she would admit to feelings of ambivalence about the Americans and the role she was playing with them. From her childhood, she remembered Americans as simple, religious people, with strong values. This, however, was in sharp contrast to the American foreign policy she encountered in Iran, and it was the foreign policy, not the people, that had moved her to join the Students Following the Line of the Imam.

Soon, Massoumeh Ebtekar became one of the few students who had any direct contact with the American government, though the encounter was extraordinarily brief. Almost every evening, one of the chancery phones rang with a call from the United States. The head of the State Department's Iran desk was on the other end of the line. He invariably attempted to strike up a conversation with anyone who answered, hoping to make a connection that he might somehow be able to enlarge. As part of her public relations duties, Sister Mary often used the phone room to speak with sympathizers around the world who reported regularly about the response to what the students were doing. On one of those occasions, she took his call. He had no business calling here, Ebtekar told the head of the Iran desk, and he should stop. No one was going to talk to him, and he was wasting his time.

Concerned that some of the phone room regulars might be engaging in conversations with this American, Ebtekar took the question to the Central Committee. "Any display of willingness to talk with the Americans could have grave consequences for our movement," she explained. "We must act in harmony, speak with one voice, remain determined and unwilling to succumb."

The Central Committee later transferred two of the student supervisors of the phone room when it was learned that at least one of those on their shift had gotten bored and chatted with the head of the Iran desk at length.

Like all of her comrades, Sister Mary was involved in ongoing discussions about their American captives and the policy they had adopted toward them. One day, she ended up in a long conversation with one of the brothers who felt they were being far too nice to these "spies." People were starving in Iran, the brother complained, in no small part because of American policies. These people they had captured were part of those policies, yet they were being fed steaks and the like while the students themselves got by on rice and lamb scraps. The Americans slept on beds while the students slept on the floor.

Mary responded by pointing out the example of Ali, the First Imam, who, while on his deathbed, had forgiven his assassin and forbade his mistreatment. "We have not come here to eat well," she told him, "or sleep comfortably or take personal revenge. We're here for a superior goal."

Just to make sure their discipline wasn't broken, Mary also raised with the Central Committee the potential threat these kinds of feelings posed for their mission. The five leaders of the Muslim Students Following the Line of the Imam agreed with her that vigilance was necessary and eventually expelled six of their group who were thought to be too bitter for their mission's good.

The first hint of possible resolution of the "hostage issue" came at the end of the second week, when Bani Sadr went to the imam directly with an idea to break the impasse by releasing the black and female hostages. During a visit to Qom, he framed it to Khomeini as a statement to America's oppressed that the imam sympathized with their plight. The approach appealed to Khomeini's sense of righteousness. Bani Sadr also told him that the move would generate a sympathetic response among the American people. Bani Sadr did not tell him that he also thought the American government would read the move as a signal, which he then hoped to pursue.

A momentarily supportive Ghotbzadeh followed Bani Sadr's visit to the imam with one of his own. He told his adopted spiritual father that such a move would display the imam as the protector of the oppressed and demonstrate Islam's special respect for womanhood. He also suggested ways the imam could make such a release and still not look as though he were cutting the Americans any slack.

That apparently persuaded Khomeini. On November 17 he issued a public instruction to the Muslim Students Following the Line of the Imam that they should release all the women and blacks who "were not spies" and let them go back to America.

The students, as usual, took every one of the imam's words to heart. Such strict attention, however, ended up slowing the process. Before doing anything, they first discussed among themselves at length just what the order meant. The students were particularly concerned that the imam wanted them to certify that all the blacks and women they released had not been engaged in espionage. That was a challenge to their still rudimentary intelligence gathering system. On the evening of November 18, a select group of students, including Sister Mary, met to consider the files they had collected on six women and ten black men. They concluded right away that it was highly unlikely that a half dozen of the blacks — all marines with minimal security clearances — were involved in spying. The students then prepared those six marines for release by showing them films about the Iranian Revolution, as well as lecturing the group on Iranian history under the shah. The other blacks and all the women were subjected to another round of interviews, with no explanation of why.

Meanwhile, Cyrus Vance brought the Americans' first "informal" information about an impending hostage release to the president's Friday morning foreign policy breakfast on November 16. This was the only positive the group had to talk about in what was otherwise a daily procession of dead ends. Over the last week, the president had begun expelling Iranian students studying in the United States, declared an American boycott of Iranian oil, and frozen $12 billion in Iranian assets that were still on deposit in US banks. Those actions, while satisfying, seemed to have had no discernible impact on the status of the hostages until, perhaps, now. To many of the Friday breakfast's participants, this new development sounded like the breakthrough for which they had all been waiting.

Jimmy Carter was nonetheless hesitant to acclaim it. He told Vance that he would believe in the release when he saw it. And if this information did turn out to be accurate and some of the hostages were returned, the president insisted that Vance "not appear to be thanking Khomeini" for the gesture. The

Iranians, he noted, "don't deserve anything but condemnation," and he did not want anyone to create the impression that somehow a partial release would reduce Iran's responsibility for "every single American" being held hostage.

On November 19 the student committee cleared two more blacks and five women. The students had their doubts about the remaining two blacks and one woman, so they would remain in captivity. The thirteen suitable for release were freed in two groups over the next two days. The Swiss embassy, having accepted the role of looking out for American interests in Tehran, made all the necessary travel arrangements.

Sister Mary and the public relations subcommittee staged press conferences for each set of departures in front of a painted banner saying "The United States Government Is Our Common Enemy." She read two communiqués from the Central Committee. The pronouncements were aimed at American blacks and American women, urging them to ally themselves with the Iranian Revolution.

The students' appeal went over in *Amrika* like a lead balloon. "I realize how naive we must have seemed," Ebtekar would later remember. "I guess in a sense we were. Our intention was to convince the Americans that because of the wrongs Iran had suffered at the hands of the United States government, we were justified in taking hostage . . . American diplomats. . . . The [release] was intended as proof that we had nothing against the American people."

The thirteen freed hostages were flown to Washington after a stop for medical processing in Germany. None of the other fifty-three Americans who remained in custody knew of the release.

The aftermath did not quite lead where Bani Sadr had hoped, however, largely because Ayatollah Khomeini granted an interview shortly after the impending hostage releases had been announced in which he declared that the remaining hostages would all be tried as spies unless the shah was returned for trial. Ghotbzadeh was translating Khomeini when the imam made the statement, and when Bani Sadr later chastised Sadegh over Khomeini's remark, Ghotbzadeh claimed he had been taken totally by surprise. Nonetheless, Ghotbzadeh himself followed Khomeini's interview with several of his own in which he declared that the hostages would definitely be tried. The imam also repeated the threat in other venues, and the students added it to their own statements upon the release of the thirteen hostages.

Carter was already angry and looking for some way to strike back even before he heard the talk of trials. "We were dealing not only with a government that had flouted the law of nations," one White House hand remembered, "but with a regime that was historically illegitimate, unfit, [and] despicable. I suspect that all of us . . . experienced a sense of physical revulsion [toward the ayatollah and his henchmen] at one time or another." The president also felt that a certain amount of fury was required of him if he were to have any hope of managing the situation. "I've got to give expression to the anger of the American people," he told Ham. "I guarantee that if I asked the people of Plains what I should do, every last one of them would say 'Bomb Iran!' I've got to keep a lid on their emotions. If they can perceive me as firm and tough in voicing their rage, maybe we'll be able to control this thing."

But Ayatollah Khomeini was not through.

On Tuesday, November 20, in a speech in Qom, he noted that Carter had condemned Iran for having taken the diplomats from the Den of Spies captive and had also denounced the idea of putting them on trial. "At times," the imam railed, "Carter intimidates us with military threats and at times with economic threats, but he himself knows he is beating an empty drum. Carter does not have the guts to engage in a military operation."

Carter, incensed, called Cy Vance from Camp David as soon as he heard the remarks. He told him to convene the SCC immediately to craft a response.

That afternoon, Vance, Brzezinski, Mondale, the secretary of defense, the director of central intelligence, the chairman of the Joint Chiefs of Staff, the president's press secretary, and Jordan gathered in the Situation Room. The atmosphere, Jordan remembered, was "ominous."

Mondale chaired the meeting and called on Vance to start things off. The secretary of state was wearing his trademark half glasses, slid slightly forward on his nose. "As always," according to Jordan, "Cy's voice was calm and rational . . . [and he was] looking slowly around the room at each person to reinforce his point." He said that it was important to remember that Khomeini had not said he was going to try the hostages, only that he might. He thought the ayatollah was just baiting the Americans. His own revolution wasn't working so he was using this anti-Americanism to keep people distracted. He would like nothing better than for the United States to "do something rash."

Brzezinski began speaking as soon as Vance stopped. They might very well be baiting us, he stormed, but they were also "humiliating our country and our President." We looked like a helpless giant to the whole planet.

The discussion went around the table like that, bouncing back and forth between those two poles, for another half hour before Vance called Carter at Camp David with a progress report.

Carter, obviously out of patience, told Vance to have the group wait right where it was. He was coming in to sort it out himself.

Less than an hour later, the president's helicopter landed on the South Lawn of the White House. "The President," Jordan remembered, "walked quickly toward the West Wing. He always walked erect, but today there seemed to be a special determination in the way he moved. He held his head high in an exaggerated, almost defiant way, as he marched toward the Cabinet Room. *He must have read what Khomeini said about him,* I thought. Jimmy Carter was a proud man, and the last thing in the world he would ever want would be to appear unsure of himself or afraid of Iran."

"Did you see what he said about our country and about me?" Carter demanded. "We have to begin to spell out for Iran the serious consequences of harming a single one of our people or putting them on trial. I will not sit here quietly as President and see our people tried."

Carter pulled out a notepad on which he had been writing at Camp David. He had made a long list of actions the United States could undertake at this juncture, including breaking diplomatic relations, punitive strikes against Iran's oil fields, and blockading Iranian harbors. Carter wanted an evaluation of these larger options on the day after Thanksgiving, three days hence, when the SCC would come out to Camp David to meet with him again. Just to make sure Khomeini got the point, Carter also dispatched a carrier battle group from the Philippines to the Indian Ocean within striking distance of Iran, bringing the total number of such battle groups on station there to two. This was the largest naval armada to sail the Indian Ocean since World War II.

When all that had been arranged, the president, with no trace of a smile, told the SCC he would see them on the day after Thanksgiving, walked out the French doors and through the Rose Garden to the South Lawn, and boarded his helicopter for the trip back to Camp David.

· 19 ·

———————

At 7:30 A.M. ON NOVEMBER 23, THE DAY AFTER
Thanksgiving, the presidential helicopter left the South Lawn for Camp
David with most of the SCC on board. The stated purpose of the gathering
was "a policy review" focused on the list of options the president had presented to the group three days earlier. Most of those present had been chew-
ing over the president's list for the last two days.

First on the agenda was Carter's desire to break diplomatic relations with
Iran immediately and expel all the Iranian diplomats in the United States.
Vance responded that though this might provide a momentary relief to the
president's frustration, it was not likely to get them any closer to a solution.
They had a hard enough time communicating with Iran as it was. To eliminate one of the few avenues of approach available would only make the situation more intractable. Vance obviously felt strongly, so after the SCC had
chewed it over for a while, Carter agreed to momentarily table the idea.

Next, the president raised the military options. His favorite was the idea
of mining Iran's harbors. He was convinced that the combination of the

economic embargo already in place with such a mining would "bring Iran to its knees." Maps were brought out and examined for military specifics. Possible punitive air strikes, targeting Iran's oil refineries, were also discussed and traced on the map. The principal target would be the huge oil center at Abadan. The president proposed a series of escalating steps, which he listed as "condemn, threaten, break relations, mine harbors, bomb Abadan, total blockade." Carter also made it clear that even if the hostages were all released tomorrow, things had already gone far enough that a retaliatory strike of some sort was required.

The ensuing discussion around the table was sometimes heated and, despite wide variations in each individual position, was almost unanimously against taking such steps in the immediate moment. Once again, Jimmy Carter and his advisers were on entirely different pages. Even Brzezinski only pushed military action as a future possibility, not an immediate option. The director of central intelligence warned that the Iranians might be able to last out a blockade for far longer than the president imagined. The secretary of defense weighed in against it as well, but the dominant voice of opposition was Vance's. He argued with great passion that all such acts of belligerency ought to be ruled out — except if the hostages were actually harmed. After a while, CIA Director Stansfield Turner remembered, "since no one was enthusiastic about the use of military force, not even the mining, the whole discussion of the subject just died."

That left the immediate issue of possible hostage trials occupying the meeting's center stage. Khomeini, Ghotbzadeh, and the students had repeated their previous statements about trials several times since the SCC's last meeting. On top of that, the students had also declared they would execute the hostages if any American military action was taken against Iran.

The president made it very clear that he wanted to put the Iranians on notice about just who and what they were fooling with. He wanted to send a message, directly describing the specific penalties that would be visited upon them for specific acts they might take. If they put a hostage on trial, he was going to mine their harbors. If they harmed a hostage, he was going to call for a military attack.

Vance recommended against making specific threats, and Mondale worried that doing so might interfere with the diplomatic irons State had in the fire — one of which, at the UN, was looking promising. At the very least, Mondale, Vance, and the secretary of defense argued, it should be a private warning, to avoid further polarization. Jordan, on the other hand, pointed out that there was no possibility of Carter's ever getting reelected if he did not act firmly. Carter agreed to send the message secretly.

The note that was then drafted was addressed to Bani Sadr and Khomeini and would be delivered by the Swiss embassy in Tehran. It made four points. The first was that the United States preferred a peaceful solution, which it would "pursue through channels available to it." The second was that any trial of the hostage American diplomats would result in "the interruption of Iranian commerce." The third was that "any harm to any hostage" would lead to "direct retaliatory action." The fourth and final point was that the United States was sending this message through a "highly secure channel" so that there would be "no misunderstanding about the seriousness of the message."

No Iranian official ever acknowledged receiving Carter's warning, but public threats to try the hostages diminished as soon as the Swiss delivered the American note.

The other pressing issue at that moment was, of course, the disposition of the shah. Lying in his New York Hospital bed out of public view, His Imperial Majesty wondered to one visitor "if there was any coherence to Western policy toward Iran beyond a successful effort to destroy me." To others, he talked of the Brits and the Americans as having plotted against him and having controlled him when they were allies. He often suspected his room was bugged and communicated with some visitors by writing on a pad. To one he passed a note saying, "If something happens, know that there was a plot."

In fact, Mondale had already asked the CIA to tap the shah's phone at the hospital and had been put off by Turner. Before the Camp David SCC meeting, President Carter had also made it clear through Brzezinski that he wanted the tap. The CIA director, however, continued to act the bottleneck. Turner told Mondale and Brzezinski that putting that tap in would be a violation of the Foreign Intelligence Surveillance Act of 1978, passed in response to the Nixon-era domestic spying scandals. The director's objections led to a prolonged bureaucratic jousting match before the tap was finally approved.

Even without listening to his phone conversations, it was obvious the shah had two options if he left the United States — excluding South Africa and Paraguay, which were still anathemas to him. One was, of course, Mexico, where his household in Cuernavaca was still intact. The other was Egypt. His friend Anwar Sadat had called him in New York and opened the door to the shah's return. This option, however, was an anathema to both State and the president. Sadat was already under tremendous pressure for the Camp David Agreements and adding the stigma of accepting the shah might well be more than he could bear politically. Word had already been sent to the shah through Rockefeller's vice president and Armao that Washington did not want him to accept Sadat's offer.

In any case, the shah himself found it humiliating to have to stay someplace where he was clearly unwelcome. He told Bobby Armao that he didn't want his children to have to "live with remorse" because Americans thought that their father was responsible for the fate of the hostages. He was insulted at being depicted as clinging to the United States in a desperate attempt to save his own skin. He wanted no part of it, he told his majordomo. He wanted "out of here as fast as possible."

The shah made his choice on November 27, when his last remaining gallstone was extracted with a nonsurgical procedure and Rockefeller's doctor pronounced him ready to be released from the hospital in five days. Since His Majesty and the American government still had no official contact, Rockefeller's vice president gave the United States notice of the shah's intentions through his contact at State. His Imperial Majesty would be heading back to Mexico immediately after his discharge from the hospital.

That departure couldn't happen soon enough as far as Jimmy Carter was concerned, but on this too he would be denied a simple solution.

On the last day of November, Bobby Armao received a phone call at New York Hospital, where he was often on duty in the room the shah's people had transformed into an office from which to manage His Majesty's protection. Mexico's New York consul general was on the line. The Mexican said he needed to talk immediately, so the two met at 3:00 p.m., down on Fifty-seventh Street, in a restaurant. The consul blurted the news out as soon as they sat down.

The shah could not return to Mexico to stay, he said. Although the shah's current Mexican visa still had a few days to run and would be honored, no new visa would be forthcoming.

Armao was stunned into momentary silence. Then he sputtered that this was impossible, the president of Mexico himself had promised the shah. Indeed, Armao had talked to the Mexican president's office just that morning and had been told everything was "a go."

The consul suggested Armao call the Mexican ambassador in Washington if he wanted confirmation.

Armao and the consul then went out to the Mexican's car and used his car phone to talk to the Mexican embassy. The ambassador there told Bobby that he had received a cable that morning from Mexico City. "The shah is not welcome in Mexico," he said. It was nothing personal. In light of what had happened to the American embassy, the situation was too volatile. "His presence is becoming a threat to our national interest."

Bobby Armao caught a cab back to New York Hospital in a state of depression. For almost an hour after his return there, he sat in the headquarters room, unable to bring himself to go next door and tell his boss what had happened. One of the shah's guards broke him out of his paralysis. He poked his head in and said there had been a breaking TV bulletin about what Mexico had done. His Majesty's television set was on a different channel, but it was only a matter of minutes before the news would spread to the channel he was watching.

Armao immediately went next door and told the shah that the Mexicans were not going to allow him to return.

His Imperial Majesty just shook his head in disbelief, over and over again.

The Mexicans' move took everyone else by surprise as well.

Jimmy Carter learned about it at 6:30 p.m., when Cy Vance called him with what Carter dubbed "the unbelievable news." The president blew his stack. As his anger gathered, he denounced the Mexican president to Vance as "a liar" and accused him of having "just double-crossed us" for no reason but "to cause problems." He told the secretary of state that the Mexican president was "currying favor with the Third World by mistreating the shah."

In any case, Armao framed the issue for the administration almost immediately. Faced with an unsolvable dilemma, Bobby bypassed using Rockefeller's vice president as a cutout, called the contact at State directly, and went ballistic. They didn't want the shah to go to Egypt, he pointed out at the top of his voice, and they wouldn't let him go to his sister's town house on Beekman Place, and he had no diplomatic status to negotiate directly with other countries to find some other location. Armao pointed out that David Rockefeller had warned them that this moment would eventually come, when the shah required the government's direct intervention. Over the entire last eleven months, the shah had never made a formal request for assistance from the United States government, but, Armao announced, that was changing right now. His Majesty was officially throwing himself on the administration's mercy. They had to accept their obligation to find him a safe haven. Otherwise, the shah would move to Beekman Place and defy the White House to stop him.

Carter was now faced with the necessity of official United States intervention in arranging the shah's fate, exactly what he had heretofore sought to avoid at all costs.

On November 23, the same day Carter convened the SCC out at Camp David, the Assembly of Experts in Tehran had submitted the Islamic Republic's proposed constitution to the imam. The document, composed of almost two hundred articles specifying all the intricacies of Iran's future government, "based on Islamic principles and standards," was immediately scheduled to be put to a vote in a yes-or-no public referendum on December 2 and 3.

The proposed constitution envisioned a government that ran on two parallel tracks. On the one hand, it was a representative democracy in which a chief executive, the president, was elected by popular vote, and, among other functions, empowered to designate a prime minister to form a government with the backing of the popularly elected parliament. This Majlis was described as a legislative body in which all legislation was to be "based on the Koran." On the other hand, this constitution also established a theocracy at whose apex sat the leader, or guide, an Islamic jurist whose justice and piety were acclaimed by a "decisive majority" of the faithful. This leader had ultimate veto power over anything done by the elected government and controlled the judicial system through a council of clerics. Clerical primacy, the proposed constitution declared, "is under all conditions to be the leadership recognized by the people." Otherwise, the constitution had little to say about the mechanics of how the two tracks were to relate to each other, leaving those issues to be sorted out after the system was in place.

Khomeini, recognizing that he still needed the secular politicians, like Bani Sadr, to hold the situation together, touted the half-and-half compromise. Still, there was opposition. An Iranian judicial association attacked the document as violating rule by the people, minority rights, and judicial independence. A number of Iran's several hundred political parties, including those representing ethnic Kurds and Baluchis, several leftist organizations, and the one associated with the former provisional prime minister, denounced the compromise as well.

Though Bani Sadr was uncomfortable with the document and its clerical primacy, he had made his fight against it in the Assembly of Experts and voiced no open opposition in the referendum campaign. Like everyone else, he accepted that Khomeini would be Iran's first guide and had faith that the imam's special attributes would ameliorate his persistent worries about the mullahs' taste for power. Instead, Bani Sadr focused on the Foreign Ministry, where he already had his hands full trying to extricate Iran before the Crisis went much further.

By now, at least the broad outlines of Bani Sadr's UN gambit were known throughout Tehran. His envoy, Ahmed Salmatian, had been working hard at not only "proximity talks" with the Americans — in which each took turns communicating through UN Secretary General Kurt Waldheim — but also a lobbying campaign among the members of the Security Council. The secretary general had offered the Iranians an international tribunal to hear their grievances against the shah and a Security Council session devoted to their issue — but only if the hostages were freed first. The Iranians rejected his overture, partially because Salmatian thought he had enough Security Council support to call a session without the secretary general's backing.

Back in Iran, developments in New York were watched closely by the Revolutionary Council. It was known the Americans were pushing very hard to make contact with Bani Sadr's envoy and that Vance's right-hand man, Warren Christopher, was now in New York looking to open direct negotiations. These were, of course, forbidden by the imam's directive, and almost as soon as Christopher started camping out in hopes of dealing with the Iranians face-to-face, the possibility of such forbidden contact was used by the enemies of Bani Sadr's gambit. Sadegh Ghotbzadeh and others raised the issue with Khomeini, and on several occasions Salmatian was forced to explicitly deny his intention to engage in any such contact.

Ghotbzadeh's other criticism of Bani Sadr's strategy was largely about the UN itself and whether it was a place where the Islamic Republic could hope to get justice. This was an American venue, Ghotbzadeh argued, not an Iranian one; Iran would only be embarrassed and humiliated in that context.

Pushing ahead despite the criticism, Bani Sadr sent an open letter to the secretary general on November 24, pointing out that the Americans could resolve the Crisis almost instantly by simply returning the shah to Iran, along with the money he had absconded with. In the immediate moment, the best thing the UN could do was "grant the Iranian people the right . . . to speak up for the truth." Iran wanted to go before the Security Council to describe the shah's "treason, crimes and corruption," to demand his extradition, to reveal "the circumstances of the U.S. Government's rule over Iran, and to explain how the former U.S. Embassy had been transformed into the real center for ruling Iran." The Americans were described by Bani Sadr as "world devourers," and Carter in particular was accused of "satanic provocations," such as the fleet he had assembled in the Indian Ocean.

According to Bani Sadr's envoy, at this point, Waldheim realized that Iran had the necessary votes to convene the Security Council on its own, so he decided to leap into the breach. Utilizing a rarely used section of the UN Charter, he personally summoned a Security Council meeting for an "urgent" debate of "the Iranian situation"— which he described as "the most serious threat to peace since the Cuban missile crisis." The meeting, called at the secretary general's request instead of Iran's, would be convened sometime in the next seventy-two hours.

The news was all over the Iranian headlines the next morning. It was also widely reported that Foreign Minister Abolhassan Bani Sadr was going to fly to New York to speak for the Islamic Republic in what promised to be its first international showdown with the Great Satan since the Muslim Students Following the Line of the Imam had seized the Den of Spies.

Bani Sadr blamed Ghotbzadeh for what happened next. The state electronic media monopoly Ghotbzadeh oversaw had immediately described the scheduling of a Security Council debate as an American victory, citing articles in the American press to the same effect, and repeated its allegations over and over. Now, Ghotbzadeh contended, the United States would be able to denounce Iran's foreign minister to his face and humiliate Iran in the process. Ghotbzadeh was the first to inform Khomeini that the Americans had a veto over whatever the Security Council did. The imam was astonished at this arrangement and then furious at the prospect of an American-controlled debate on the issue.

The imam then called Bani Sadr from Qom. The foreign minister's plane was scheduled to leave for New York in two hours, but the imam told his acolyte that he needn't worry. Bani Sadr was not going anywhere.

Bani Sadr demanded to know what Khomeini meant.

Just what he had said, the imam answered. This UN session was an American trap, and if Bani Sadr left for New York, the imam was going to announce that Iran had no foreign minister as soon as his plane took off.

Bani Sadr argued that this move at the UN was in Iran's vital interests, but he made no headway.

"Khomeini had a lot of information," Bani Sadr remembered, "and much of it was false. That was all coming from Sadegh. I knew it. Sadegh was pushing Khomeini in the wrong direction, just making for a bigger disaster."

In case Bani Sadr hadn't got the imam's message, Ghotbzadeh broadcast it to the entire country an hour later. "In the name of God, the compassionate, the merciful," Khomeini announced, "our nation does not agree to this made-to-order Security Council session. . . . Our nation knows that the verdict of any council or court that sits under the direct influence of the United States has been dictated by the United States from the start. . . . The appraisal of the case of the deposed Shah and that of the spies in the Den of Spies is only possible in Iran."

Unwilling to leave it at that, Bani Sadr called New York and instructed Salmatian to seek a postponement of the Security Council session, then called around Tehran to the members of the Revolutionary Council and convinced them to accompany him to Qom to discuss this with the imam directly. They flew there in an army helicopter on the day before Ashura. The country was in a raw state only accentuated by the upsurge in religious ecstasy.

According to Bani Sadr, the imam "received us in a severe, distant manner." Still, the foreign minister pushed ahead. He told Khomeini that his decision was going "to make Iran look ridiculous in the eyes of the whole world." Bani Sadr was the one who had requested a Security Council session — with the imam's permission —"for the purpose of obtaining extradition of the shah, the return of his assets, and the formation of a committee to investigate the Americans' dealings in Iran."

Ghotbzadeh and the other "moderates" on the Revolutionary Council responded by accusing Bani Sadr of being soft on the Americans and leading Iran toward "a major defeat."

Bani Sadr answered that the Americans "had done everything they could to prevent this UN meeting." It was only diligent lobbying among the Security Council members that had allowed Iran to outflank them. Outside of America, the world's media almost all considered this "a diplomatic coup and a virtual slap in the face of the United States."

Khomeini interjected that he could not accept the idea of Iran being condemned in Bani Sadr's presence.

So what? Bani Sadr exclaimed. The UN condemned countries every day. Iran would still gain its objective of "beginning negotiations on the double basis of the hostages and the shah." His ministry had already gathered documents from its files that incriminated the shah, his family, and their American protectors — including a secret list of payoffs that contained the names of several American journalists and politicians. It was Bani Sadr's intention to make a tour of the United States, presenting Iran's position and the information behind it.

Khomeini was unmoved by the argument, but Bani Sadr took no steps to cut his losses. Instead, he next denounced the embassy seizure as unworthy of any organized state, against international law, and against Islamic hospitality. It was isolating Iran in the world. It was also a "gift" to Jimmy Carter that allowed him organize the world against Iran and "to smother" Iran economically. And, on top of everything else, it was a threat to the Revolution. This mobilization of the people around a single narrow issue was keeping them from addressing the country's other major problems. "The longer the hostage problem continues," he insisted, "the greater the danger of a collapse of the Islamic Republic when it is resolved."

The imam remained unmoved, and the meeting adjourned with Bani Sadr's UN gambit reduced to wreckage. Bani Sadr called it "yet another failure for Iran."

Back in Tehran, the Muslim Students Following the Line of the Imam were stringing barbed wire along Taleghani Avenue, in front of the embassy wall. The students also announced that land mines had been laid inside the Den of Spies to thwart any American rescue attempt.

Bani Sadr and Ghotbzadeh flew back from Qom together in a military helicopter and by the time it landed in Tehran, Bani Sadr was no longer able to contain his anger at the collapse of his UN mission. He lit into Ghotbzadeh while the two of them stood on the helicopter landing pad, shouting over the whine and whirr of the rotors and blades.

Bani Sadr called his old Paris comrade a bastard and a backstabber. He had sabotaged it all. He was the one who had fed the imam endless disinformation and turned his head about the UN. Everyone had told Bani Sadr that Ghotbzadeh was out to destroy his efforts and destroy him. Well, he wasn't going to succeed at the latter. Bani Sadr swore he was now getting out while the getting was good.

"You wanted it," he screamed over the helicopter noise, "so you've got it. You can be foreign minister now. I quit."

Sadegh tried to conciliate his old friend. Yes, he had campaigned against this UN venture, he admitted. But that was to save Bani Sadr, not destroy him. Going to the UN would have been the end of him. He would have been so humiliated that he would never have been able to get the hostages freed.

Bani Sadr dismissed that argument as so much bullshit.

Ghotbzadeh also insisted he didn't want to be foreign minister.

That was too bad, Bani Sadr answered, because he was going to be it, like it or not. Bani Sadr wanted nothing more to do with the post.

And he meant it. The Revolutionary Council met later that evening in Tehran and confirmed the switch. Though he continued to hold on to the finance ministry and his functional role as head of the government, Bani Sadr was now out at the foreign ministry and Ghotbzadeh was in.

Jimmy Carter learned of the reshuffling twelve hours later, when evening reached Washington and the Swiss embassy passed the word along.

"We were notified that . . . a guy named Ghotbzadeh was made Foreign Minister," the president commented in his diary that night. It seemed like "every time one of the Iranian government officials shows any sign of rationality, he is immediately incompatible with Khomeini and is replaced."

The last day of November brought the final act in Abolhassan Bani Sadr's turn at the foreign ministry. While the shah was being rejected by Mexico and becoming an official American responsibility, Salmatian closed up shop in New York and returned to Tehran. The proximity talks and the Security Council strategy were now both dead, as were all prospects of a speedy end to the Crisis.

Bani Sadr's envoy completed his mission with the submission of a seventeen-page written report and an oral summary to the Revolutionary Council. He told them that the situation was the same in New York as in Tehran. Both places were now captured by political instability. Carter, he said, couldn't control public opinion and, as a consequence, could no longer make diplomacy over politics. Everywhere, the Street was in control.

The day after Salmatian left the UN, Jimmy Carter dispatched White House counsel Lloyd Cutler to visit His Majesty at New York Hospital.

The counsel got right down to business. He began by reading the shah a long list of the countries that would not allow him to enter. Then he told him the three who would — South Africa, Paraguay, and, of course, Egypt. The United States government continued to object to Egypt, and the shah continued to object to the first two. Until they could work out a solution to this impasse, the counsel explained, His Majesty was obviously welcome in the United States, but staying at Princess Ashraf's on Beekman Place was out of the question. Instead, the government wanted to transport His Majesty and the shahbanou to Lackland Air Force Base outside of San Antonio, Texas, in hopes of escaping the New York spotlight at least. The shah was familiar with the facility. Hundreds of pilots from his Imperial Air Force had trained there. The counsel said Lackland had an excellent medical center. They wanted to move him there that evening.

The shah's aide, Bobby Armao, objected strenuously. "Some fool must have come up with the idea of Lackland," he remembered. "The security was a nightmare. Lackland was one of the few bases that wasn't closed, with a perimeter that could be protected. It was like a college campus. The security was absolutely ridiculous."

The shah, however, overruled him. Lackland it was.

At midnight, the transfer began. The object was to escape detection by the twenty-four-hour anti-shah demonstration outside the hospital and the pool of reporters watching the hospital exits for telltale signs of his movement. Bundled in a wheelchair and surrounded by FBI agents, all carrying serious weaponry, His Majesty was taken from the hospital basement through an underground tunnel to the Sloan-Kettering Institute across Sixty-eighth Street and through that building to an unwatched exit onto First Avenue.

The shah was then loaded into an unmarked van and sped to LaGuardia Airport in a caravan bristling with armed agents. Dozens more were waiting at LaGuardia, as was a US Air Force DC-9 passenger jet, its engines running. As soon as the shah, Farah, two enormous dogs, one of Armao's staff, and half a dozen retainers were loaded, the airliner taxied away and was instantly cleared for takeoff.

At first light, the last of the Pahlavi dynasty landed at Lackland Air Force Base. He and the shahbanou were helped from the DC-9 and into an ambulance, which drove them to the base hospital. Here, they were to be housed in the psychiatric wing. It was, they were told, the most secure location on the base.

The shah was assigned a room with no windows. The shahbanou's room had windows, but she was forbidden to open the drapes that covered them. When she did so anyway, she discovered the windows were barred outside the glass. Her door also had no handle on the inside. Farah became claustrophobic within minutes and immediately started demanding to know if Carter had put them in jail. Were they now prisoners about to be auctioned off to the ayatollah?

After three hours of the shabanou's frantic complaints, she and her husband, their dogs, and their retinue were moved out of the psychiatric wing to a nearby facility usually occupied by visiting officers. The building looked like an Econo Lodge or a Red Roof Inn. The three-room apartment the shah and shahbanou were given was the best available, but it was small and decorated with garish drapes and a vinyl couch on which the enormous dogs occasionally slept. All the surrounding area was swarming with air force security troops at high alert.

The royal couple and their dogs would live in this Lackland apartment for almost two weeks while Jimmy Carter searched the world for a country willing to take the shah off his hands.

Panama was the most recent addition to the list of possibilities. The Central American republic had been suggested when the shah was being evicted by the Bahamas six months ago, but His Majesty had rejected that idea so strongly then that no one had returned to it until late in the first week of December. Then, just as Cy Vance was about to leave for Europe to consult with the allies about "the Iran situation," he heard from the embassy in Panama City that the Panamanian military strongman, General Omar Torrijos, might be prepared to revive his previous invitation for the shah to take refuge there. Vance dispatched Warren Christopher to the president with the news. What was required, State and the president agreed, was the right person to ask Torrijos to step up.

Carter thought he knew just the man for the job.

The next morning, Hamilton Jordan began getting messages from the White House when he was still waiting for his driver to fetch him to work. The president wanted to see him as soon as he arrived. In case that wasn't clear, the same message was delivered twice more by radio during the chief of staff's post–rush hour trip through Washington to 1600 Pennsylvania Avenue. Jordan was on edge when he finally reached the Oval Office shortly before 10:00 a.m., having long since concluded that anything the president was so anxious about couldn't be good news.

Carter started their meeting by kidding with Jordan about why he showed up so late every morning, then raised the subject of Panama. Although doing so might have seemed odd to outsiders — Jordan, after all, was anything but a diplomat — no one in the administration felt odd about it. Indeed, Jordan had at one point been jokingly referred to among them as "the secretary of state for Panama." During the Georgians' first year in office, Carter had negotiated a treaty that scheduled the eventual end of American possession of the Panama Canal, and during those negotiations, Jordan had developed a friendship with Torrijos that was close enough for the Panamanian to call Ham "my son," and for Ham to call him "Papa General" in turn. Papa General, in his fifties but still handsome, had a reputation for drink and chasing women, and didn't really trust anyone who didn't share his predilections. Among the Carterites, only Jordan came close to fitting the bill, and he and Torrijos had bonded quickly. Carter expected the Panamanian would be hard-pressed to turn Ham down now.

Jimmy asked Jordan if he would fly to Panama City and make the request face-to-face. It would be too easy for Torrijos to say no over the phone.

Jordan said he would give it a try.

After a brief stop at his apartment to pack a bag, Ham caught a government executive jet at Andrews Air Force Base and headed south. The cockpit crew was sworn to secrecy about his presence on the flight, and after a refueling stop in Florida, the president's chief of staff landed in Panama at 9:45 p.m. He was met by the American ambassador and driven straight to Torrijos.

The general had more than a dozen residences that he occupied at random as a security measure, often only deciding where to sleep after midnight. "You can't overthrow a leader if you can't find him," he once explained to Ham. That night, he was in a modern, Spanish-looking mansion in the heart of Panama City. The place was surrounded by troops from his National Guard. Ham and the American ambassador were ushered into a room where Torrijos, in white slacks and a traditional Panamanian shirt, jumped up off the couch to greet Ham with a big hug.

Papa General ordered up several bottles of the local Balboa beer and the two of them drank and reminisced while the ambassador and others listened. "I couldn't just rush in and blurt out my request," Jordan explained later, "so I tried to disguise my fears and waited for the proper moment."

When Jordan reached his second Balboa, Torrijos tired of waiting and asked just what was up that Ham would fly in to talk to him in the middle of the night.

Jordan explained that the president had sent him and asked if he and the general could be alone for a few minutes.

The two of them and Torrijos's trusted interpreter went out on an enclosed porch, leaving the American ambassador and Torrijos's staff behind, out of view and earshot. Jordan began by describing in English the fix the president was in, pausing for translation to Torrijos. Ham said Jimmy Carter could not solve the Crisis as long as the shah was in the United States and there was now nowhere else for the shah to go. All of the places in Europe the shah knew and wanted to live in refused to have him. Egypt was an option, but Carter was afraid that would significantly undercut Sadat.

Torrijos agreed with the president about the danger to Sadat.

Jordan then dropped his punch line. He had scripted the request he was about to make over and over on his flight down. "We don't want to take advantage of our friendship by asking you to do something that ignores your own country's interests," Ham said, "but the president wanted me to ask if you would be willing to accept the shah in Panama until the hostage crisis is resolved."

Papa General took a long time to answer, drawing deeply on his Cuban cigar. Then, after a short speech about Panama living up to its international responsibilities, he said yes.

Jordan wanted to cheer. Instead, they returned to the room and informed the American ambassador. Then the chief of staff asked to use the phone to call the president and let him know.

It was close to 2:00 a.m. in Washington, but Jordan had the president woken to get the news. Jordan spoke in a spontaneous code because Torrijos had warned him that the line was probably tapped. "I'm with our friend down south," Jordan told Carter, "and he's willing to accept that gift."

"Thank God," Carter answered.

Jordan reminded his boss that the shah still had to be convinced to accept the invitation. In pursuit of that end, Ham said he was going to get back in his jet and fly to Lackland. He asked the president to dispatch the White House counsel to meet him there in the morning to help sell the shah on the idea.

Jordan spent another half hour with Papa General, drinking Balboa beer and discussing what the shah would need if he came. Finally Ham excused himself and said he had to fly to Texas. He gave Papa General a big hug good-bye.

Then, as the car with Jordan and the ambassador pulled away from the National Guard post at Torrijos's Panama City house, they heard the general shouting for the gringos to stop. He was running after them.

The Americans' car screeched to a halt.

Torrijos caught up, thrust a paper bag through the window, slapped the fender, and told his "son" to travel well and give his best to the shah.

The bag was full of ice-cold Balboas.

Eight hours later, Jordan and the White House counsel were ushered into their audience with the shah.

First, however, the two briefed Bobby Armao, to whom Ham took an almost instant dislike. "He was a snake," Jordan later remembered, "a sorry slinky son of a bitch in an expensive suit and a sculpted hairdo." At the moment, however, the White House chief of staff was his polite best.

Ham hadn't seen the shah since his visit to Washington in the fall of 1977. This time, His Majesty was seated on the vinyl couch, in what Jordan noted resembled "a $75-a-day Holiday Inn 'suite' in Peoria," wearing a robe with USA stenciled on its back. He tottered to his feet to shake hands. "He was kind of a pathetic figure," Jordan remembered. "You see all these pictures of him in his regalia and on the Peacock Throne and all that rigmarole, then here he was in this military building in this little room with tacky blue-and-green drapes and rug, wearing a borrowed bathrobe. He was still proud, though, and he still had those black eyes that could look right through you. His feelings were obvious. He thought the only reason he had fallen was because of the United States' flawed policy and probably because of Carter personally. I could feel his disdain and contempt."

The shah said he had noticed that the American government only came by to see him when they had something they wanted him to do. Just what was it this time?

Jordan was frank. There was no possibility of getting the hostages back as long as His Majesty was in the United States, he answered.

The shah responded that he wasn't all that sure of Jordan's reasoning. These people who had taken the Americans prisoner were "crazy communists who have been my enemies for years." It would be a mistake to treat them as rational. That said, he pronounced himself "grateful for my thirty-seven-year friendship with the American people." He was prepared to do whatever he could to help them out.

Jordan immediately raised the possibility of Panama.

The shah wondered why not Switzerland or Austria, as he had requested. White House counsel Lloyd Cutler now stepped in and informed His

Majesty that both countries had turned him down and both had reaffirmed their position in the last twenty-four hours.

The shah went silent for a long time and then told Jordan he didn't know much about Panama except that this man Torrijos seemed to be "a typical South American dictator." It seemed an odd remark to Jordan, but he let it slide and began an enthusiastic description of the country and its leader.

At this point, Bobby Armao interjected himself into the discussion. He said he knew Panama well and it was unsuitable for a number of reasons. Torrijos couldn't be trusted. If the price was high enough, he would sell the shah back to the Iranians. On top of that, security was a nightmare. This was the kind of country where you could buy passports for a dime a dozen.

The shah told Armao to be quiet and let Jordan and the counsel continue.

The Americans did so for a few more minutes and then suggested they leave the room to give the shah and Armao a chance to talk. Once alone, Bobby started arguing against Panama, but again the shah stopped him. It was the only option, His Majesty told Armao.

When the Americans returned, Armao stated the shah's position. Before agreeing to the move, he had three conditions. The first was a consultation with his doctors to verify that proper medical facilities were available in Panama. The second was an inspection tour by Armao and His Majesty's security experts to ensure that facilities there were indeed acceptable. And finally, he wanted assurances that the shah would be able to reenter the United States "in a medical emergency." Jordan agreed in principle to all of them and arranged to fly with Armao to Panama the next day.

As Jordan was leaving the meeting, he ran into Princess Ashraf in the hallway, on her way to see her brother.

Ham stopped, held out his hand, and began introducing himself.

Princess Ashraf ignored the hand and the introduction, brushing right on past without a word or even a pause.

Ham Jordan was back at Lackland with Bobby Armao in tow less than two days later. Armao had now reluctantly signed off on the deal, and the White House counsel had also worked out an understanding with the shah's doctors. The shah was to be allowed the full services of the American-run Gorgas Hospital in the Canal Zone for an operation that the shah's doctors anticipated having to perform in the next few months; His Imperial Majesty's spleen was problematic and would have to be removed sooner or later. The American government also agreed to provide transportation for all the principals of the operation who would have to travel from the United States.

The final condition set by Armao at Jordan's first session with the shah had been the right to return to the United States in the case of a "medical emergency." Cutler and Jordan again pledged to honor this. That promise would be known as "the Lackland agreement" and it would eventually become an issue.

As soon as the president got word from Texas that the arrangements were set, he called the shah. It was their first direct contact since Carter had phoned from Camp David in September 1978, when the shah was still on his throne facing the Revolution. This December 1979 call to His Majesty's Texas apartment would also be the last time the two ever spoke.

The exchange was short. "He warmly wished me good luck," His Imperial Majesty remembered, "and reiterated the assurances of his aides."

Early the next afternoon, a receiving line made up of General Omar Torrijos, a number of Panamanian National Guard officers, several dignitaries, and the American ambassador to Panama assembled on the tarmac at Howard Air Force Base in the American-controlled Panama Canal Zone as the shah's plane taxied to a halt. The shah disembarked, followed by his traveling party, causing Omar Torrijos to turn to a friend standing nearby.

"Imagine that," the Panamanian strongman whispered. "Twenty-five hundred years of Persian Empire reduced to ten people and two dogs."

· 20 ·

———————

BACK IN IRAN, AS THE RELIGIOUS FRENZY OF
Ashura ended and December began, chaos was still the order of the day.

Out on the streets, there were assassinations, including one of the imam's closest associates. Demonstrations for an entire pantheon of causes and issues were now so frequent and so disabling that the Revolutionary Council had to make a public appeal for a temporary halt. The army had almost evaporated as a political force. Close to ten thousand officers inherited from the shah, including all of those ranked above brigadier, had been released from the service. Of the shah's eighty-some generals, more than seventy had been executed, along with two hundred other lesser officers. Reports of a foiled air force plot to bomb Khomeini's residence were in wide circulation. The Kurds were already up in arms, and many of the country's other tribal and ethnic enclaves were in a state bordering on revolt, especially in the northwest Azeri city of Tabriz. There were also reports that Iraq, Iran's immediate neighbor to the east, was preparing to invade the oil-producing regions along Iran's southeastern border. To outside observers, the country seemed to be coming apart.

And Iran was choosing a constitution along with everything else. On December 2, the forty-eight-hour election period began. Voters were given a choice between a green card or a red card. Green, the Islamic color, signified "yes"; red, the satanic color, signified "no." In a number of locations, casting this ballot was a public act, observed by clergymen. Opposition to the proposed constitution took the form of election boycotts, particularly in the provinces of Kurdistan, Khuzistan, and Azerbaijan, as well as other Turkoman areas. Boycotts were also proclaimed by the secular forces surrounding the former provisional prime minister and those mustered by the leftists. In the previous referendum last spring, held on only the vague notion of an Islamic republic, almost all of Iran's 18 million eligible voters had participated. This time around, with a constitution of almost two hundred articles up for scrutiny, only 10.6 million Iranians voted, 99.4 percent of them casting green cards.

When news of the outcome reached Tabriz in eastern Azerbaijan Province, followers of a dissident ayatollah there seized the radio and television station and most of the other public buildings in protest. They would paralyze the city for several weeks, with more than a dozen people killed in armed skirmishes.

The constitution, however, stood. The Islamic Republic was now codified and could begin instituting a formal government with Khomeini as its guide.

The day after the constitution was approved, Abolhassan Bani Sadr traveled to Qom to discuss the coming elections to select a president and a parliament with the imam. "I said there was no use in having elections right now," he remembered. "The country was in chaos. There was violence everywhere and anyone who gets elected would just be the hostage of the hostages. I said, let's wait and then have elections once things have calmed down a bit."

Khomeini answered that elections had been promised and some election would have to be held. He was, however, willing to hold only the presidential vote now; the legislators could be elected later, in the spring.

After their meeting, the imam announced that the vote for president would be held in the last week of January, with the election of a Majlis to follow a month and a half later. He also ruled that anyone who hadn't voted in the constitutional election or had voted against the constitution was ineligible to stand for president. Conscious of the suspicions in some circles regarding the mullahs' intentions, he also forbade clerics from entering this first presidential contest. Otherwise, anyone who wanted could enter their name — and most of those did. In total, 124 Iranians filed their candidacies for president. Bani Sadr was one of them. So was Sadegh Ghotbzadeh.

Bani Sadr knew that the office of president had been stripped of much of its power in the final draft of the constitution and at first, he later explained, "the prospect of working with only a fragment of power did not interest me." According to Bani Sadr, his advisers then changed his mind. They argued that his candidacy was necessary to preserve the original values of the Revolution. Without him, there would be no one to stand up to the mullahs. He eventually described his decision to enter the presidential race as "staunchly defending independence, democracy, progress, and an Islam compatible with these three essential values." It was also something he had dreamed of ever since he was a little boy.

Sadegh Ghotbzadeh made no similar pretense of ambivalence about the post, and his ambition was no less than his rival's. The issue for him, however, was whether he could muster anything close to the public popularity necessary to win it. Bani Sadr was a commanding figure in Iran, but Ghotbzadeh, though one of the Revolution's more powerful insiders, had no public following to speak of.

Ghotbzadeh, however, was convinced that he could be president if he became the man who brought the shah back to Iran. At first, he just treaded water in the Foreign Ministry, looking for an opportunity. But when the shah moved to Panama, Ghotbzadeh thought his opportunity had come.

Sadegh learned of the move from a BBC broadcast on December 15, barely an hour after the Light of the Aryans stepped unsteadily onto the Canal Zone tarmac and shook General Torrijos's hand. After a few moments of thought, Ghotbzadeh called his old friend in Paris, attorney Christian Bourguet. The Frenchman had been in and out of Tehran a couple times that fall working on a business deal with another old friend of Sadegh's from Paris, an Argentine expatriate businessman named Hector Villalon. Villalon was a former protégé of Eva Perón who would later be described by the press as a "mysterious figure" and an "international adventurer." He had made a small fortune during the several years he held the exclusive rights to market Cuban cigars, a deal he negotiated directly with Fidel Castro. Villalon had first met Ghotbzadeh through Bourguet, who was Villalon's attorney as well. Hector was as tall as Sadegh and had a large nose and receding chin that gave him the look of what one mutual acquaintance described as a "large, impressive squirrel."

Conveniently, at least from Sadegh's point of view, the object of the deal on which his two Paris friends were working was a commercial relationship between Iran and Panama. After noticing that Panama had a shortage of oil refining capacity and that such a shortage meant they did very little business refueling the ships plying the canal, Villalon had approached Torrijos with a proposal to build a new refinery. In turn, he wanted to package the refinery project with direct purchases of crude from Iran. Bourguet had flown to Tehran and secured Ghotbzadeh's support. On the day before the shah left New York, the Revolutionary Council had contracted to sell $32 million worth of oil to Panama at a price well below the world benchmark, as a gesture of Third World solidarity with Panama. Though no money had yet changed hands, that agreement was enough by itself to ensure a bank loan to begin refinery construction.

When Sadegh now told Bourguet that the shah had moved to Panama, Bourguet's first thought was that the oil deal would no doubt collapse as a consequence.

Ghotbzadeh was not, however, calling to talk about oil.

He wanted Christian to find out everything he could about the shah's arrangement in Panama, using Hector's connections there. Sadegh wanted to know who had invited him and what deal had been struck between them.

"Who knows?" the Islamic Republic of Iran's foreign minister told Bourguet. "Maybe I could go there myself and get him. Take him off their hands."

Afterward, Sadegh sent a formal letter to the Panamanian Foreign Ministry, announcing the Islamic Republic's intention to file the appropriate papers seeking the extradition of Mohammad Reza Pahlavi, whose "reign represents more than 25 years of organized terror, of murders, of tortures, of pillages of the national wealth and betrayal of the people." Iran wished him returned to stand trial for his transgressions. To act on its behalf in this matter, the Islamic Republic formally retained Bourguet. The foreign minister instructed his old friend to collect Villalon and leave for Panama on the next plane.

Over at the Den of Spies on Taleghani Avenue, the Muslim Students Following the Line of the Imam responded to the shah's move to Panama by once again threatening to place the hostages on trial. They did not, however, take any steps toward that end other than their steady compilation of dossiers on their "guests." Although the prisoners were still banned from speaking to one another, the rules about blindfolds and bound hands began being waived. It soon became somewhat common for the hostages to be able to see and move their arms when they were at rest in their quarters. Whenever transported, however, they were bound, blindfolded, and usually covered with a blanket.

And they were still moved around with some frequency. Over the first two weeks of December, Robert Ode was bundled out of the embassy compound to a house in Tehran, then back to the embassy and the ambassador's residence. His room there was then switched every few days. On day forty-one, he was allowed outside in a small courtyard, where he received twenty minutes of exercise time. The fresh air made him feel faint. Several days later, one of the students returned Ode's wedding band, seized along with the cameo ring from his parents during the first days of the takeover. "You can't imagine how grateful I was to have it on my finger again," Ode noted in his diary.

Barry Rosen was moved back from a house in north Tehran to the ambassador's residence as well. He was glad for the times he was now unbound and without blindfold, but he could feel himself losing his grip nonetheless.

"I thought of little beyond the fact of captivity," Rosen remembered. "It seemed that [it] was pushing me toward some kind of limit. The recognition was sinking in that we were prisoners, with no real hope of ending the condition. It wasn't an adventure but a seemingly permanent pushing of our noses in dirt. [My] preoccupation with indignity drained my concentration. . . . I could not adjust to loss of control over my life. . . . Ordinary sounds began to affect me strangely. The opening and closing of our door cut through me like a rusty blade; the slight creak — which the others whispered was all it was — made me jump. . . . It was as if some relentless internal growth were putting pressure on my skin from the inside. . . . I was also having trouble sleeping. I wasn't really afraid, yet couldn't shut off a motor that generated a growing current of anxiety . . . about nothing specific; anxiety it seemed, for the sake of anxiety. . . . During the day, I ran in place as much as I could. But this didn't satisfy my craving to get up, get out, and move. It was as though my need to [free myself] had been compressed into a black hole that sucked the rest of me into its vortex."

Each of the hostages processed that same experience in different ways. Perhaps the most active response came shortly before Christmas from Bill Belk, an embassy communications officer being held in the residence's maid's quarters. The night shift guard who was constantly posted in the room he shared with one other hostage was in the habit of falling asleep, so, seizing his opportunity, Belk slipped out past the sleeping student and into the hallway. His plan was to take the stairs down to the kitchen area, exit through the kitchen door, and make his way across the compound to the back wall, which he planned to scale. Once on the other side of it, he hoped to hot-wire a car and flee to the British, Swiss, or Australian embassy.

When the communications officer got down the stairs to the kitchen, however, he heard the sound of conversation coming from there and when he peeked in, found it full of students. He retreated back up the staircase and went out an upstairs window onto the kitchen roof. It was cold outside, and the compound was brightly lit, so Belk climbed down to a wooden alcove on the side of the building and hid there for a while, watching students come and go through the guard post at the gate in the chain-link fence that sealed the courtyard from the rest of the compound. Finally he decided that he had no choice but to try to fake his way past the guard. As a group of students headed out of the kitchen for the gate, chattering away, he fell in behind them, pulling his sweater over his head as though he were just coming outside so he couldn't really be seen. To his surprise, he walked right through the gate without being stopped.

There was, however, another chain-link fence between him and the back wall. Belk decided to squeeze through a rusted-out section of the fence rather than try for another gate. He was just through it when his luck ran out. He looked up and found a woman student there, pointing a rifle at him and yelling for him to stop. He then jumped her and wrestled over the gun, which discharged twice before he fled toward the parking lot.

Now, however, the alarm had been sounded, and students were swarming all over the compound, most of them armed. The fleeing Belk made it to the back wall, but when he mounted it, two policemen on the other side fired their rifles at him. Thrown off balance by ducking the shots, Belk fell back into the compound and turned his knee. Unable to run, he hid in a water barrel for several minutes until the searching students discovered him. The injured but still defiant communications officer was carried back to the Mushroom Inn and kept in solitary confinement for the next two weeks.

Before the hostages had been taken, more than 70 percent of Americans told pollsters that Jimmy Carter could not be reelected. The Crisis, however, changed the political landscape dramatically. By the first week of December 1979, when the president made the official announcement that he would be running for reelection in 1980, his approval ratings, hovering around 20 percent in September, had ballooned past 60 percent. The country was standing behind its president. Seventy-one percent thought he was doing all he could to free the hostages. Sixty-eight percent did not want him to send the shah back to Iran. Sixty-six percent agreed with him that the United States ought to launch a military attack if the hostages were physically harmed or placed on trial.

He now also had official opposition. Despite his gaffes on *60 Minutes* the day the hostages were seized, Edward M. "Ted" Kennedy, forty-seven, the youngest brother of the assassinated John F. and Robert F., senior senator from Massachusetts, had announced his intention to contest the Democratic Party's primary elections. Kennedy was a formidable opponent — if for no other reason than possession of what was then the premier name in American politics — and Jimmy Carter was on unfamiliar turf. For all intents and purposes, Carter had never before run as an incumbent. He had been re-elected once as a state senator, but that race had been uncontested. Otherwise, Jimmy Carter, the peanut farmer from Plains, Georgia, had always run as a challenger and an underdog.

Incumbency or not, the campaign Ham Jordan was crafting looked much like its predecessors. As usual, Carter would be aggressive from the get-go and quickly make his opponent the issue. Ham's idea was to reinforce the public's doubts about Kennedy by indirection and accent the senator's political missteps when they occurred. One of the first of those concerned Iran.

Until early December, Kennedy had declined to make any comment on the Crisis other than to assert that all of America was "one nation indivisible" when it came to demanding the hostages' return. Then, two days after His Imperial Majesty left New York for Texas, Kennedy made stops in Reno, Nevada, and San Francisco on a western campaign swing and went after the shah and the decision to let him into the country in the first place. The result was what the *New York Times* called "the first major controversy of the Presidential campaign."

Ted Kennedy had been a major Senate critic of the shah's regime when it was still in power, and his remark to the audience in Reno was far milder than many he had made about HIM before the takeover. "We all support our country's efforts to end the crisis in Iran," Kennedy declared. "But our firm national commitment to the safe release of the hostages does not and cannot mean that this nation must condone the Shah and the record of his regime. . . . The Shah . . . ran one of the most violent regimes in the history of mankind, [engaging in] fundamental violations of human rights in the most cruel circumstances. . . . Few things could more seriously undermine our efforts to secure the release of the hostages than for the United States to condone the repressive dictatorship of the Shah."

Ham Jordan jumped on the statement and had presidential surrogates offer immediate comment. The chairman of the Democratic National Committee deemed the senator's remark "counterproductive" and "ill-advised." The State Department commented that Kennedy was endangering "delicate" negotiations. In addition, according to the *Times*, Kennedy's other "political opponents in both parties denounced him sharply for injecting the Iranian crisis into the political campaign."

Kennedy had to answer questions about the episode for the next week, usually on the defensive, reasserting his condemnation of the ayatollah and his support of the hostages' return.

Carter's campaign also used the high ground the Crisis provided to deny Kennedy political traction. In the second week of December, the president's office announced that he was canceling a previous commitment to debate Kennedy in Iowa during January. To the public, the White House cited all the same reasons it had already offered for his canceled trip to Canada and several other junkets. To Ham in private, Carter noted that if he went to Iowa as planned, he would go in as president and come out as just another politician. Kennedy protested that this Rose Garden strategy was denying democracy a chance to function, but to no avail. The president's challenger would never get to share a stage with him at any point in the primary process. In the language of political insiders, Kennedy had been cut off at the knees.

In the meantime, the president stayed in the White House, above it all. During the third week of December, he declared National Unity Day, asking all Americans to fly the flag as a demonstration of concern for the hostages. He also appeared on national television from a park near the White House, dedicating the national Christmas tree. Carter surprised everyone at the ceremony and the television audience by leaving many of the tree's lights off, explaining that he wouldn't illuminate the tree completely until all the hostages were home.

Perhaps the most watched video of that American holiday season was provided by Iranian National Television. It was called "The Hostages' Christmas."

Halfway through December, in response to a suggestion from the imam himself, the students had invited a group of Christian clergymen, including two Americans, to celebrate the religious holiday with the students' American "guests." For the event, they decorated a Christmas tree in one of the chancery's largest rooms. They also arranged for Iranian television to video-tape parts of it and put the edited tape up on the satellite link as "a goodwill gesture to the American people."

The festivities started shortly after 2:00 a.m. on Christmas morning. After being awoken, the hostages entered their party unbound and without blind-folds, though they had been transported there in their usual trussed and blinded state. Groups of a half dozen at a time were brought in and taken away before the next group was brought in, so no hostages had contact except with those with whom they had been transported. The successive interdenomina-tional services were short. Everyone attended except the seven hostages who were either in solitary confinement or had refused the invitation. Some of those who did attend were given a Christmas card with a message from Ayatol-lah Khomeini. "Our youth treat the spies in a Godly way because Islam orders us to have mercy on our captives," he declared, "even if they are oppressors."

On the American home front, the most disturbing aspect of the brief snippets of the embassy Christmas party released on the satellite feed was the head count. The three hostages being held at the Foreign Ministry were accounted for, but the visiting ministers and the State Department con-firmed that of the fifty captives at the embassy, only forty-three had ap-peared for their holiday celebrations. Almost immediately, State was deluged with calls from the media demanding comments about "the seven missing hostages." Receiving no answers there, the media in Tehran then besieged Foreign Minister Ghotbzadeh, and he had to admit that he had never been able to get a count of the captives from the students and had no idea exactly how many hostages there were.

The State Department Operations Center was eventually able to satisfy it-self that there were still fifty Americans being held at the embassy. The pro-gram of random calls to various embassy extensions by State's Farsi speakers, hoping to draw whoever answered into conversation, had continued since day one. The responses from the random Iranians included enough refer-ences to the number fifty that State reassured the press that the captives were all still there. The "missing hostages" story reverberated for another week nonetheless.

American policy toward the Crisis continued to be bipolar but with an obvious drift. By the third week of December, Brzezinski was telling the SCC that they ought to begin to develop military options, using the huge armada the United States had cruising within striking distance of Iran. He predicted there was no chance of getting the hostages released while Khomeini was in power. Three days before Christmas, Brzezinski sent his weekly report to the President, advising Carter that he was rapidly reaching the point where he would have "to make truly difficult choices." By the day after Christmas, according to Brzezinski, "the trend was towards more and more serious consideration of military action." As one administration insider noted, "The American people were not going to put up with statements from the Rose Garden forever. Something was going to have to be done."

That policy drift, however, was stopped in its tracks before New Year's. On December 27, the Soviet Union dispatched almost one hundred thousand troops into Afghanistan to prop up the teetering Marxist government there, effectively occupying the country that abutted Iran's western border. Jimmy Carter denounced the move as "the most serious foreign policy crisis since World War II," calling into question the entire basis for détente with the Soviets. There was much immediate speculation that the Russian troops would keep coming, into Iran and through it to the Persian Gulf — precisely the breach-of-containment scenario that had led the United States to support the shah in the first place.

Suddenly the geopolitical situation demanded that the Americans encourage Islamic resistance to the Soviets and avoid taking any actions that might alienate that religious resistance. All of the administration's foreign policy factions, including Brzezinski, agreed almost immediately that as long as the Soviet invasion continued, the option of a punitive military strike on Iran was off the books.

Inside those new parameters, both poles of the Carter administration's foreign policy team headed in separate directions.

For his part, Cy Vance returned to the UN, hoping to use his close relationship with Secretary General Kurt Waldheim to leverage the situation. In their discussions in New York, usually at Waldheim's town house on Beekman Place, the two men spent a lot of time examining the Iranians' professed desire for an international tribunal to hear their grievances. Vance explained that the United States was amenable to the tribunal idea, but only if it took place after the hostages were released. Vance also urged Waldheim to insert himself into the situation however he could. The secretary general readily agreed and arranged to visit Iran to see if he might assist the process.

Waldheim arrived in Tehran on the first day of 1980. Many of Iran's newspapers that week had run file photos of the smiling secretary general standing next to the shah and Princess Ashraf on a state visit two years earlier, putting him on the defensive immediately. The UN, the Iranian media had pointed out, had done nothing about the shah's abuses, so one of the first things his hosts did was to expose the secretary general to just what those abuses looked like: He was taken to a reception of victims of the shah's SAVAK. The first to confront Waldheim there was a man who held up his child for the UN visitor to see. Both the child's arms had allegedly been cut off by interrogators trying to convince his father to confess. According to the *New York Times,* the secretary general "appeared shocked and moved by the victims, who waved crutches and artificial limbs and displayed stumps as they chanted support for the Ayatollah Khomeini."

Next, the UN's chief executive was taken to a cemetery reserved for martyrs of the Revolution so that he could lay a wreath there. Waldheim was driven to the graveyard in a limousine, past a small group of Iranians, some dressed in white shrouds, chanting "Death to Carter, death to the shah." As the secretary general was getting out of his limo, the crowd charged through the protective barrier of Revolutionary Guards and headed right for him. Waldheim's bodyguard shoved his boss back into the car and slammed the door, and the limo sped off before the crowd could reach it. The incident left the UN chief afraid for his life during the rest of his brief visit.

After three days in Iran, Waldheim flew back to New York, then on to Washington the next day, to meet with Carter at the White House. As Carter remembered the encounter, the secretary general "spent the first hour with me in a very emotional and excited recitation of his horrible experiences [on his visit to Iran], at times with tears in his eyes. [He had] found complete chaos in Tehran. Waldheim believed his life had been in danger on three different occasions and that he was lucky to be alive. He was convinced the Iranians had no government at all."

Waldheim's report sent Cy Vance back to the drawing board yet again. Meanwhile, at the other end of the new American policy spectrum, Zbigniew Brzezinski focused his attention on the much smaller military option that was still active. Brzezinski had been an advocate of preparing for a rescue mission from day two of the Crisis, and those preparations were still in motion.

Command of this possible operation had been given to Colonel Charlie A. Beckwith, known to the army command as "Chargin' Charlie." Beckwith, fifty-one, was a combat veteran of both Korea and Vietnam, where he had been seriously wounded. An aggressive commander, he had been an advocate of elite commando warfare since a stint with the British Special Air Service in the early sixties. He had finally won his argument just two years earlier and been assigned to build the unit that became known as Delta Force, a hundred or so commandos to act as America's designated "door kickers" in antiterrorist and other special operations. Delta Force had just finished training its first class when the call went out to Charlie Beckwith on November 4.

By the beginning of December, a rough plan had emerged. It would feature an extraordinarily long helicopter assault. Turkey would not give permission to launch the action from its territory, and the American command did not want to take either of the carriers on station in the Indian Ocean into the relatively tiny confines of the Persian Gulf, so Tehran was beyond the reach of even the longest-range helicopters. That meant the operation would have to be a two-day affair, with a stop somewhere in the vast eastern Iranian desert to refuel on the way in. After an actual assault on the embassy compound, the helicopters would lift Delta and the hostages to an abandoned military airfield halfway between Tehran and Qom, which would be seized long enough to shuttle in C-130 transports to carry everyone home, leaving the choppers behind. "Logistically speaking," Beckwith remembered, "it would be a bear. There were vast distances, nearly 1,000 miles of Iranian wasteland that had to be crossed, then the assault itself, against a heavily guarded building complex stuck in the middle of a city of 4,000,000 hostile folks."

From the beginning, Beckwith was sure that the mission would never happen and secretly thought of it as an elaborate training exercise. Beckwith's opinion of Jimmy Carter was "very low" and he figured that "this administration really doesn't have enough grit to do anything more."

Still, Delta trained as though the rescue had already been decided upon. Beckwith's commandos started out working with mock-ups of the embassy buildings on a secret training area in North Carolina and then moved to desert training in Arizona, where they could work on tactics with the choppers. Perhaps the most pivotal outstanding issue in the rescue plan was where in the Iranian desert to refuel. The commandos would need somewhere so remote that whatever went on there would be unobserved. It also had to be as flat as a landing strip, with firm enough footing that eight choppers and six C-130s hauling their fuel could all touch down and get off again. This spot was dubbed "Desert One" in the plan but wasn't actually pinpointed on Iran's alkaline flats until January. To confirm its suitability would require an on-site examination, but at this point Jimmy Carter was unwilling to authorize the necessary secret inspection flight into Iranian territory.

Part of Carter's unwillingness to launch a covert operation into Iran to check out a possible Desert One location was a new diplomatic option that had suddenly emerged in the second week of January. This one was from a completely unexpected source and had landed in the lap of a decidedly improbable diplomatic player.

On Friday, January 11, Hamilton Jordan was staying at Camp David in hopes of taking a weekend off. For the last month, he had been deeply immersed in the reelection campaign as well as playing chief of staff. The Iowa caucuses — now the opening round of the primary season — were only three weeks away, and a month after that was the New Hampshire primary, right in Kennedy's backyard. It was early, but Ham was already looking for a break. He was having dinner in Laurel Lodge, where the presidential staff was fed, when he was interrupted by a phone call from Panama. Papa General's chief aide was on the line with "urgent" business to discuss. Torrijos wanted his "son" to come to Panama to talk with him tomorrow.

Jordan did his best to beg off, trying to salvage his weekend, but the general's aide was insistent. He couldn't tell him what it was about, only that it concerned the Crisis and the general thought it was incredibly important. After checking with State and then the president himself, Jordan agreed that given all the favors the general had done for the United States, they had no real choice but to accommodate him. Jordan called Panama back to accept the summons. By then, the general had concluded that all the international press roaming around Panama since the shah's arrival made Jordan's coming there too potentially public. Instead, Ham would rendezvous at Homestead Air Force Base in southern Florida with a delegation of three Panamanian emissaries carrying the general's message.

On Saturday in Florida, the Panamanians explained that they'd had a visit over Christmas from a French lawyer and an Argentine expatriate businessman who also lived in Paris. The two had presented themselves as representatives of the Iranian Foreign Ministry. They had come to talk about the shah's extradition. The Panamanians reassured Jordan that extradition was not a serious option, but added that there was a Panamanian legal procedure to be followed, of which they had informed the Iranian representatives. The Panamanians had been impressed with the competency of these "two Frenchmen" and had accepted an invitation to accompany them back to Iran for further discussions with Sadegh Ghotbzadeh.

Jordan's eyes widened when the Panamanians said they had met with Ghotbzadeh. Such a direct contact had been one of the United States' principal goals since the Crisis began.

The Panamanians then went on to describe a total of four meetings for almost nine hours over two days, held immediately after the UN secretary general left Tehran for New York. According to them, Ghotbzadeh had quickly changed the subject from extradition to the Crisis itself. He said some solution to it all had to be found between then and the Iranian presidential elections. He never explained exactly why, but the Panamanians guessed it had to do with Ghotbzadeh's own election campaign.

Ghotbzadeh said there were three ways the Crisis could be solved.

The first of those was that the shah could die. The UN secretary general had brought medical reports about His Majesty with him on his visit, and Ghotbzadeh said he and the imam now believed Pahlavi was a dying man. Ghotbzadeh and Khomeini were doubtful, however, that he would die quickly enough.

The second was the UN channel. The secretary general had talked a lot about an international tribunal. Iran thought that if the tribunal materialized and if the UN recognized Iran's right to seek extradition from Panama without actually handing the shah over, then a hostage release might be arranged.

The third possible solution was a Panamanian one. Although Iran recognized that Panamanian law would not support an actual extradition, it was important to both Ghotbzadeh and the imam that the principle of extradition be recognized. If the Panamanians just initiated the process, Ghotbzadeh claimed that would be enough for the imam to go to the students and ask them to release the hostages. Ghotbzadeh said he wanted to come to Panama to serve the official extradition papers himself.

The Panamanians told Jordan that they thought the Iranians didn't really want the shah back; having him in Iran would cause them more problems, not fewer. The Panamanians also said that the Iranians distrusted the State Department and were convinced it was under the thumb of Kissinger and Rockefeller.

Then the Panamanians dropped their blockbuster.

Foreign Minister Ghotbzadeh had also said that he would like to meet secretly with Jordan, perhaps when he came to Panama to personally serve formal extradition papers on the Panamanian government. He had read an article in *Time* about the president's chief of staff and the role he had played moving the shah to Panama. Direct contact with Jordan would complete the circuit and perhaps make an understanding possible, outside of more formal channels.

The Panamanians then asked Jordan straight out if he was interested in a secret meeting with Ghotbzadeh. If so, the Panamanians wanted to help them make a direct connection.

Ham said he'd have to get back to them on that, after he'd consulted with President Carter.

The Panamanians warned Ham not to take too much time making up his mind.

PART FIVE

CRESCENDO

———————

ON FRIDAY, JANUARY 18, 1980, HAMILTON JORDAN caught the supersonic Concorde airliner to London, traveling under the assumed name Sinclair. His mission was secret from all but perhaps a dozen people inside the administration. Before leaving, Ham had told the president that he didn't expect much to come from this, but, as he crossed the Atlantic, he hoped fervently that he was wrong.

Jordan was with an assistant secretary of state he had requested accompany him, and the following morning the chief of staff and the assistant secretary were driven from their hotel through London to the home of the deputy chief of mission at the American embassy. In his study, they rendezvoused with two of the three Panamanians Jordan had seen in Florida and Hector Villalon. Jordan described the suave Argentine as a "Latin-looking man immaculately dressed in a light brown suit and expensive leather shoes." Villalon wore a small mustache under his large nose and his black hair slicked straight back. Ham, in a blue suit but without a tie, looked far too young to be the central player in such a big moment.

After some lighthearted joking with the Panamanians, Jordan kicked the session off by thanking Villalon for meeting with him. The Americans, he said, just wanted to solve this problem and were here to "understand the situation in Iran and to learn from you how this might be accomplished." Make no mistake about it, Villalon declared in response, "the Revolutionary Council has approved this contact [and] the Revolutionary Council does not conduct business without the approval of Khomeini."

Villalon then explained that perhaps the most important thing Jordan had said was his reference to the need to learn about the situation in Iran. To reach a solution to the Crisis, it would indeed first be necessary for the Americans to understand the Iranian Revolution, and he was prepared to act as their teacher. With that, the Argentine launched into what the assistant secretary of state later described as "the first of many sweeping sketches of political conspiracy and intrigue in revolutionary Iran."

His starting point was the politics of Ayatollah Khomeini. The imam guided the Revolution by evoking a kind of broad consensus. He approved or disapproved of actions as often after the fact as before. He preferred staying in Qom, removed from events and above daily political disputes. As a consequence, there was a constant jockeying among factions to capture his attention and approval, all claiming to be hewing to the Imam's Line.

Jordan wanted to know exactly what this "Imam's Line" was that Villalon mentioned.

Villalon grinned. The Imam's Line was, of course, the thinking and logic of Ayatollah Khomeini — although often no one was quite sure ahead of time what exactly that was. As a consequence, the political process amounted to an exercise in what westerners would describe as "trying to anticipate the wishes of one's superior." Villalon also gave lengthy personality sketches of most of the key players inside Iran. Altogether, it was an impressive display that, according to the assistant secretary, "showed a far more comprehensive and direct familiarity with the current scene than any other individuals we had talked to."

After two hours, Hector Villalon stopped and suggested they all take a break. He now had to go to the airport to meet his negotiating partner, Christian Bourguet, who was flying in from Tehran. The two of them would return for a second session that afternoon.

When the Argentine had gone, Jordan turned to the assistant secretary and asked what he thought. The man from State said he had an abundance of questions but no doubt that Villalon was "for real."

And Villalon was just the preface. The exchange between the two sides really began with the arrival of Christian Bourguet, fresh from Tehran. Though he and Villalon worked closely, the French lawyer was the lead dog of the team. Bourguet bore little physical resemblance to his partner. Jordan described the French attorney as "a stick-figure of a man with a thick dark beard, a mass of shoulder-length hair, and heavy black-rimmed glasses." A Paris journalist who knew him observed that Bourguet had "the appearance of a respectable attorney below the shoulders and a long-haired anarchist above them." The chemistry between Bourguet and Jordan would eventually bring this effort close to success, but it did not start off easy between the two.

The Frenchman had come straight to London from seeing Ghotbzadeh, who had instructed him never to identify himself as having the authority to speak for Iran. Rather, he was a private individual seeking to act as an intermediary.

In London Bourguet took up where Villalon left off, adding more elements to the portrait of Iran's current operations, sometimes respectfully disagreeing with his partner. Christian had decided that the Americans would need a blunt introduction to the realities of the Iranian situation and provided one right away on the issue of the shah. He began by declaring flatly that any hostage release discussion would have to await the Panamanian government's decision on extradition.

The Panamanians interrupted to declare that there was no way Panama would extradite the shah.

Bourguet then allowed that perhaps just beginning the extradition process coupled with other measures might be sufficient, but he did not let go of extradition as an Iranian bargaining position. The political realities inside Iran dictated as much. Bourguet told Jordan that though he personally abhorred the idea of hostage taking, the Americans had to understand that the Iranians thought the student action had been taken with good cause. The shah was an evil man. Bourguet then demanded to know what had happened to America the country of law? Why shouldn't the evil man have to face up to his crimes?

Jordan took a few breaths before answering. He told Bourguet that he was grateful for the meeting but he hadn't come here to debate whether or not the shah was evil. Jordan didn't know one way or another. He did know that Jimmy Carter would never countenance the return of the shah, period. The United States was, however, prepared to endorse an international tribunal on his rule, but only after the hostages were released.

Bourguet answered by saying that the release of the hostages for nothing more than the promise of a tribunal was not worth another word of discussion.

That remark was followed by a momentary pause while both sides assessed each other.

Bourguet had not anticipated Jordan's straightforward and earnest amateurism. Ham's tangible goodwill was not an attribute Bourguet had previously associated with the American government. He had expected to be arguing with diplomats and instead found himself warming to the Georgian's approach. For Jordan's part, the exchange about the shah had given him further appreciation for just how big an issue the former Light of the Aryans was for the Iranians. He also gained insight into the position from which Bourguet and Villalon were dealing. It turned out that the Revolutionary Council as an entire body had not been made aware of this initiative. Rather, Ghotbzadeh had the support of three of the eighteen council members. The foreign minister had also spoken with Ahmed Khomeini, so Bourguet thought that the imam himself was aware of what was going on. Still, it was obvious to Jordan that Bourguet and Villalon were representing Ghotbzadeh and not a whole lot else.

The meeting lasted for a total of twelve hours. "We explained clearly why it is necessary to have a scenario that begins with the release of the hostages," the assistant secretary reported by cable the next day. "They explained why the political situation in Iran makes it possible only to proceed in stages so as to prepare public opinion. Privately we concluded that some scenario combining some elements of both approaches — including early release of the hostages — might be necessary, but we told them we had no authority to go beyond our present position. They had no authority to present any new position [either]. We said it would be a sign of seriousness if [Ghotbzadeh] would designate someone to negotiate directly with [an official] U.S. representative. . . . If that is impossible, we said contact through a third party is better than no contact at all."

When the discussion was done, Christian Bourguet asked if he might use the house phone. Then, without explaining what he was up to, he sat down, dialed Tehran, and, with Jordan standing a few feet away, got Ghotbzadeh on the line. Bourguet gave Iran's foreign minister a shorthand report that was basically positive, and attempted to induce Sadegh to say hello to Jordan. Ghotbzadeh refused, reminding the lawyer that the imam had forbidden him to talk directly to the Americans. Instead, Sadegh sent a message through the Frenchman that he was pleased with Jordan's obvious seriousness. He also told Bourguet and Villalon to fly to Tehran the next day.

Jordan didn't at first understand what was happening on the phone because Bourguet was speaking French, but when the interpreter alerted him, he was startled. "I don't know if it was his intention to impress me [by dialing up Ghotbzadeh]," Ham remembered. "But he certainly did."

Both parties left having agreed that the ball was now in the Americans' court.

The day after Jordan returned from London — once he had given Carter an oral report of what had transpired and then tended to the reelection campaign's frantic stretch run in the Iowa caucuses — Jordan canceled his appointments, locked himself in his corner White House office, and put his thoughts on paper in a memo to the president.

After making several points about the campaign, Jordan argued that it was critical to find some solution to the Crisis in the next two months, if for no other reason than to free the president's hands to deal with the Soviet invasion of Afghanistan. In light of that, Jordan reported, he had concluded that there would never be a hostage release that occurred simultaneously with "the other steps we are willing to take." That meant Carter had to "at least consider taking some risks in obtaining their release that were neither feasible nor advisable before the Soviet invasion. . . . We are going to have to consider modifying our tactics."

What Jordan proposed was development of a joint scenario that included the early release of the hostages *after* "some steps that tested each other's seriousness of purpose." He didn't think Ghotbzadeh or some other future government could secure Khomeini's blessing of a scenario in advance. "Khomeini does not think or operate that way." That meant that the United States would need to commit itself to a series of steps that "would create the proper atmosphere for Ghotbzadeh or Bani Sadr . . . to go to the Ayatollah and say, 'We have won, and it is time to let the hostages go.'" The risk, of course, was that they would take such steps and then Khomeini would reject the plea and they would be back at square one, "having used up most of our bargaining chips."

As an example, Jordan included a possible scenario of nine steps, featuring a United Nations commission whose hearings in Tehran would be immediately followed by the hostage release. Though this might not be the right scenario, Jordan argued, "it is my opinion that some scenario like this will have to be worked out before our people are freed. . . . We . . . need a new approach that is inherently risky for both our country and for you politically. . . . I believe that U.S. public opinion would support our taking such a chance, although it would look bad if we failed."

Jordan took the finished ten-page document straight to the Oval Office. The president returned it to him within the hour.

"Good ideas," Carter had scribbled in one corner. The president instructed his chief of staff to schedule a meeting at which Mondale, Vance, and Brzezinski could join them in discussing the memo.

Hamilton Jordan did as he was told, half expecting the meeting would put an end to all his diplomatic freelancing. Someone would veto his idea, he told himself, on appearances if for no other reason. The prospect of his good ol' boy backwoods south Georgia self being the central cog in a diplomatic maneuver of this global significance made him queasy. On the other hand, he wanted very badly to do something important — even to the point of self-sacrifice — to bring the hostages home. In London, he had told Bourguet that if the situation required him to fly to Tehran, he would do it. The Frenchman pointed out that Jordan would no doubt be taken hostage if he did. Jordan said he was prepared for that.

When he, Carter, Mondale, Vance, and Brzezinski then discussed his assuming the lead role in these secret negotiations, no one rose up to tell him no. Brzezinski was skeptical of the "two Frenchmen" and whether they could deliver Khomeini but was not opposed to going forward with it. Mondale thought it was worth a try, as did Vance. The president admitted that Jordan was more inclined to trust the Frenchmen than he was, but he still didn't think there was much alternative to "proceeding along the lines suggested in Ham's memo."

Afterward, Jordan experienced a stark moment of sudden doubt. He had just proposed and won a critical change in the United States' approach to the most crucial issue in Jimmy Carter's presidency, essentially because his gut told him these two guys from Paris could be trusted. If this blew up in Carter's face, it would all be on Jordan's account. And that prospect scared him shitless.

Nonetheless, when Christian Bourguet returned to Paris after a brief consultation in Tehran, he found a message from Jordan, asking him and Hector Villalon to come to Washington on January 25 to talk some more.

The second meeting between the president's chief of staff and the Iranian foreign minister's two emissaries began Friday, January 25, and lasted through much of the next day as well. The assistant secretary who had been in London was again present, but the Panamanians were not. The negotiations took place in Hamilton Jordan's corner office in the White House.

Bourguet began the encounter by opening his battered briefcase and presenting Jordan with an audiocassette Ghotbzadeh had sent. It was, he told Ham, "a present from Iran," nothing less than the official recording of the Revolutionary Council's early January meeting with the UN secretary general.

Ham thought the Frenchman must be kidding. An actual tape of it? Someone was pulling his leg.

When it turned out this wasn't a joke, Jordan's last doubts about the intermediaries' Iranian connections vanished on the spot. This was the signal he had been looking for. If these guys weren't in very deep, they could not have come up with this sort of thing.

Bourguet and Villalon then reported about their trip to Iran, where they had closeted themselves with Ghotbzadeh almost as soon as they arrived. Bourguet and Villalon made a point of telling Ham and the assistant secretary that they had been motivated in their discussions with the foreign minister by the "seriousness and honesty" the Americans had revealed in London. They claimed to have told Ghotbzadeh that though Iran's point of view had to be listened to, international standards of human rights ought to come first. They also challenged Iran to now muster as much seriousness as the Americans had already demonstrated.

After four hours, the two emissaries explained, the foreign minister had left them so that he could report on what they were up to at a meeting of the Revolutionary Council. When Ghotbzadeh returned to them after midnight, he told his two Parisian friends that the council had listened to Ghotbzadeh's report about their mission in London and had then made several decisions. Perhaps the most important was that the council had designated Ghotbzadeh as "the only negotiator for Iran" on this issue. They also required him to "immediately report" all developments personally to the imam. The goal, according to the assistant secretary's report of the January 25 meeting, was to settle the hostage question "within the next thirty days before a new government took office. It was anticipated that Ghotbzadeh would remain as foreign minister and would be charged with handling the hostage crisis during this period."

Nonetheless, the two Frenchmen were honest that this was a limited window of opportunity. While the council's action might look like a victory for Ghotbzadeh on the surface, it was also a way for his enemies to make him a scapegoat. If these negotiations with the Americans failed, they would describe them as Ghotbzadeh's failure. And if they succeeded, his enemies would accuse him of making less of a deal than he could have. Fortunately Sadegh had always been a man willing to take risks.

After another hour's worth of Bourguet and Villalon's analyses of the Iranian situation, the meeting finally took up the issue of what to do next.

Jordan quickly made it clear that for the first time, the Americans were prepared to subscribe to a scenario that began with something other than the hostages' release. Nonetheless, Ham admitted, "if we are able to put this thing together, it is going to be like one of those trick billiards shots where you have to hit five sides before the ball goes in the pocket."

Their starting point was a scenario proposed by the Revolutionary Council and introduced by Bourguet. The Iranians wanted to initiate events by calling on the UN to form a commission to come to Iran to investigate their grievances against the shah. In order to give the move credibility inside Iran, the Americans would publicly oppose the formation but it would be established anyway. The commission would come to Iran for ten days, including an inspection of all the hostages, and report to the UN and to Khomeini as they finished that the hostages were being held in conditions that were unacceptable by Islamic standards. Then, in an act of religious charity, the imam would release the hostages. After their return, the commission would issue a report on Iran's grievances, and the United States and Iran would negotiate the remaining outstanding issues, like Iran's frozen American assets and weapons purchases.

Though this plan involved too much action before the hostages were freed, Jordan was nonetheless encouraged that the Iranians clearly wanted to negotiate. He, Bourguet, the assistant secretary, and Villalon spent another twelve hours whittling at the opening scenario, splicing, rewriting, and fashioning it into something both sides felt they could take back to their principals. "In London," Jordan explained, Christian and Hector "had seemed like our adversaries, but after this second session, they were more like comrades, working with us toward a common goal." Still, he also found himself regularly stunned by the assumptions the "two Frenchmen" made about America — and those assumptions paled beside the ones made by the Iranians.

The document they produced was five pages long and designed, according to Bourguet, "to lay out the ground rules of the process and a series of reciprocal steps, each step calibrated to add weight to the seriousness of the positions of each party." With this draft in hand by the end of Saturday, the four negotiators broke off to give Jordan and the assistant secretary a chance to confer with the administration's foreign policy team and, of course, the president. In the meantime, Bourguet informed the Americans, he would fly with Villalon to Panama for a quick visit as part of the extradition effort Iran was pursuing on a separate track from its secret dealings in Jordan's corner office.

The two of them returned from Panama City late Tuesday afternoon and spent the entire evening and into the morning working with Jordan and the assistant secretary to fine-tune their script before the intermediaries carried it back to their client in Tehran.

Their task was complicated by a new political brush fire. While Iran was focused on its presidential elections, the six American diplomats who had taken refuge in the Canadian embassy on the day of the takeover — and had stayed there ever since, unbeknownst to the Iranians — were smuggled out of the country on forged Canadian papers. Jordan and the others were at work when word of the daring escape organized by the Canadians without American knowledge reached the chief of staff; by then the story was already out on the newswires. Ham immediately informed Bourguet, taking time to explain that there had been no intention to embarrass the Iranians.

Bourguet was stunned by this development. He told Jordan he could understand why they had done it, but this would still make things "very, very difficult." He and Hector had been working hard trying to convince the Iranians that the Americans could be trusted. This would undercut them significantly. The Iranians would feel they had been tricked by the CIA. Bourguet told Jordan that he had to call Ghotbzadeh right away and spin this turn of events enough to keep it from doing damage to their negotiations.

Jordan thought about it a minute and then suggested Bourguet tell Ghotbzadeh that there was an election going on in Canada right then and that this was an electioneering ploy of the Canadian prime minister. Ham advised blaming it all on the Canadians.

Bourguet, citing the Iranians' penchant for conspiracy theories, thought Ghotbzadeh just might buy that.

The French lawyer then asked Jordan if he could use the phone on his desk and, receiving permission, dialed a number and got Iran's foreign minister on the line.

Christian Bourguet exchanged greetings and called Sadegh by his Paris nickname, Papa. Then the attorney launched into a long explanation in very rapid French. After a little back and forth, he hung up.

Jordan immediately asked for a report.

Bourguet told him that Ghotbzadeh was "very, very concerned." He was going to do his best to divert public opinion away from outrage at the Americans, but he didn't know what the students would do at the embassy. Ghotbzadeh had also said that Bourguet and Villalon should get back to Tehran as soon as possible.

By then it was after 1:00 a.m. Washington time. As Christian and Hector got ready to leave the White House, Bourguet told Jordan that they would be in Tehran by Thursday. They would call as soon as they had news.

For most of the Iranian presidential campaign, Sadegh Ghotbzadeh had remained convinced that he could win the election if he could succeed in some way in his attempt to extradite the shah from Panama. His hope was the Panamanian constitution, which specified that once a claim for extradition by a foreign government was filed, the defendant — in this case the shah — had to be placed under some form of arrest for the sixty days the foreign government had in which to file its full claim for adjudication. It was just an arrest, and likely of a variety no different than the shah's current status under the watch of the National Guard at a resort on Panama's Contadora Island, but Ghotbzadeh thought that might be enough to capture the Iranian public's imagination. Indeed, several of his fellow members of the Revolutionary Council who were also candidates for president told him they would pull out of the race in his favor if he succeeded in becoming the man who had the shah arrested. With little more than a week before the vote and Bourguet on his way to Tehran for his last consultations before the Washington meetings, Sadegh, acting as foreign minister, officially notified the government of Panama that the Islamic Republic intended to file extradition papers for one Mohammad Reza Pahlavi. Then he waited to see what the Panamanians would do.

The last night before Bourguet was to leave Tehran for Paris and then

Washington, Ghotbzadeh was sleeping in his Foreign Ministry office when a call came in at 3:00 a.m. He roused himself when he learned the Panamanian president was on the line. The president — the titular but not actual ruler of Panama, whom Torrijos used as window dressing — told Ghotbzadeh that Panama, in keeping with the provisions of its constitution, would place the suspect, Pahlavi, in a state of arrest at 7:00 a.m. While that meant little more than the posting of a piece of legal paper — the shah's daily life would not be at all affected except for his freedom to leave Panama — Ghotbzadeh was nonetheless jubilant.

He called Bourguet over at the Intercontinental Hotel Tehran in a manic state. The Frenchman had been working at the Foreign Ministry until just an hour earlier and had to leave to catch his plane to Paris in a couple hours. He was fast asleep and woke up just long enough to warn Ghotbzadeh not to make any announcement until he received a telex from Panama informing him that the arrest had been made.

Ghotbzadeh objected that he couldn't wait around. He was due to make a morning campaign appearance in Mashhad, considered by many the holiest site in Iran, and if he didn't appear, it would be considered an insult to Shiites everywhere. Bourguet said if that was the case, he had better leave precise instructions about how to handle the announcement behind at the ministry.

After hanging up, Bourguet went right back to sleep, but not Ghotbzadeh. Sadegh was completely wired. He could almost taste his election as president. He was drafting a press release about the arrest when the phone rang again. This time it was Torrijos.

Their telephone connection was very scratchy, and Torrijos was speaking through an interpreter. The general repeated what his window-dressing president had said earlier, only with more rhetorical flourishes about "the courageous struggle of the Iranian people" and the like. He too said the arrest was scheduled for 7:00 a.m.

Again, Ghotbzadeh called Bourguet to celebrate. Christian had only one more hour before he had to leave for the airport and awoke just enough to mumble three or four words of congratulation before hanging up.

Ghotbzadeh spent the rest of the night finishing his press release and leaving careful instructions at the ministry. His announcement was to be released at 7:30 a.m., after the arrival of a Panamanian telex confirming the shah's arrest. Then Ghotbzadeh was off to Mashhad and unreachable for the rest of the morning.

The episode became a blunder for the simplest of reasons: The Panamanians meant that the arrest would take place at 7:00 a.m. *Panamanian* time, eight and a half hours later than Tehran time. At 7:30 a.m. Tehran time, one of Ghotbzadeh's aides tried to reach his boss for further instructions and, unable to do so, he ignored the stipulation about securing a confirming telex and released the foreign minister's announcement of the shah's arrest. It was still the day before in Panama City, with the arrest scheduled for the following morning. The premature announcement flashed around Iran, provoking people to run into the streets in spontaneous celebrations, and accounts of those celebrations then flashed around the world. When the news reached Panama, Torrijos was furious at being upstaged. Calls from Washington also began ringing the phones off the hook, and the general backtracked as quickly as he could. The Panamanian government announced that nothing could be further from the truth than the Iranian Foreign Ministry's claim. Someone in Iran must have misunderstood. They had no intention of arresting His Imperial Majesty, either now or later.

The disappointment in Iran set off by Panama's denial was even more intense than the premature celebration, and all of it focused on Ghotbzadeh. The foreign minister was almost immediately saddled with a reputation as deception personified, and his enemies among the mullahs began calling him "the Charlatan."

When Sadegh next spoke to Bourguet, he admitted that his hopes of being president were now completely dashed, and within days the actual election confirmed Ghotbzadeh's fears in no uncertain terms. Among more than sixty candidates who stayed in the race to its end, Sadegh received only one-quarter of 1 percent of the vote. His rival, Bani Sadr, ran away with the field with more than 75 percent. Bani Sadr's closest competitor, a former admiral who was later identified as the recipient of secret funds from the United States, polled barely 15 percent.

For Bani Sadr, of course, it was a dream come true. One of those with whom he shared his ecstasy on election night was the reporter from *Le Monde* who had befriended him in the old days in Paris, buying the impoverished Iranian exile sandwiches and listening to his then laughable pronouncement that he would eventually be elected president of Iran. About 1:00 a.m., the *Le Monde* correspondent was at his Tehran hotel, working on his election story, when the phone rang. Bani Sadr was on the line.

He was ecstatic over the crushing victory he had just scored and told the reporter that he would like to see him "very urgently."

Smelling an exclusive, the man from *Le Monde* said he would be right there.

The address Bani Sadr gave him was in the heart of one of Tehran's poorer neighborhoods. The streets were narrow and littered, the air thick with the smell of tenements. The new president of the Islamic Republic of Iran lived up three flights of stairs in a building with no elevator and no light in its stairwell.

When he arrived, the French correspondent was led into a single large room full of more than two dozen people. It seemed Abolhassan's whole family was there celebrating, including his children and his sisters and their families, as well as his friends. Bani Sadr's old mother was at the stove on one side of the room, cooking up a midnight feast. Bani Sadr himself was dressed in pajamas and barefoot. He greeted the man from *Le Monde* profusely and then led him over to an oriental sofa where the two men sat, Bani Sadr with his feet drawn up on the cushions.

Bani Sadr asked if his old friend remembered the time in Paris he had first told him that he would be the president of the Islamic Republic of Iran.

The Frenchman claimed he didn't remember.

Bani Sadr laughed. At the time, the new president reminded his guest, the Frenchman had burst out laughing. Now, Bani Sadr chortled, "here I am the first elected president of Iran in the past twenty-five centuries."

The man from *Le Monde* recognized the jibe as good-natured. He offered in return that had he laughed back in Paris, it was only because from there even the Islamic Republic had seemed impossible, much less Bani Sadr himself in power. Now the laugh was obviously on him; even *Le Monde* could be wrong. That said, the correspondent congratulated the new president on his extraordinary success.

Bani Sadr accepted the congratulations with grace and announced that he had asked the Frenchman to come specifically because he wished to introduce him to the very first person to ever predict that Abolhassan Bani Sadr would become the president of Iran.

Then Bani Sadr took the *Le Monde* correspondent over to his mother, hovering at the stove.

She, he declared, had been the very first. It had happened when he was fifteen years old and seriously ill with some mysterious fever. The doctors had been worried that he might die. His mother had nursed him, wiping his brow, and when his illness was at its most grim, told him not to worry. Someday Iran would be a republic, she said, and he would be its president. Bani Sadr told the reporter that he had believed her vision of his future forever after.

With that, the president of the Islamic Republic hugged his mother as the rest of the room cheered.

Perhaps the greatest uncertainty facing Bani Sadr's historic presidency was the role that would be played by Khomeini. On the same day that Ghotbzadeh had mistakenly announced the shah's arrest, the imam's office in Qom issued a statement that the imam was feeling "a little sickness and fatigue" and was canceling his schedule. The winter had been a bitter one, and he must have picked up a bug. On a couple of previous occasions the imam had taken two-week breaks when he wore down and needed to recover, so the announcement created little initial stir. The next day, however, the imam was driven in an ambulance from Qom to a heart disease hospital that had been built by the Pahlavis' dowager empress shortly before the Revolution. There, he was checked into the intensive care unit, complaining of "mild" chest pains.

Almost eighty now, Khomeini had had heart trouble before, and speculation that he might be about to die was suddenly rampant. Six hundred faithful stood outside the hospital through a snowstorm to pray for him, and in Qom two thousand sheep and cows were butchered in rites of prayer in his honor. To reassure the public, the imam delivered a ten-minute television address on election day from his hospital bed, describing his physical condition as "not bad" and urging everyone to vote. Bani Sadr, on the other hand, privately described the imam as "very sick" and "near death" at the time. Bani Sadr claimed that everyone — including Khomeini himself — thought the imam was dying.

In any case, the imam's doctors considered him well enough to leave intensive care after a week and move into the hospital's VIP suite to undergo continued observation and testing. There, in the royal blue rooms that had once been reserved for the shah's highest officials, the imam administered the official oath of office to Abolhassan Bani Sadr as the first president ever of the Islamic Republic of Iran, a year and three days after the two men's return from almost a decade and a half of exile.

The combination of the moment and the debilitated presence of his "spiritual father" touched Abolhassan, and he openly wept when he kissed the imam's hand. He also couldn't help but wonder if the old man wasn't about to die and leave him the most powerful political figure in Iran. The bond between the two was still, in Bani Sadr's words, "genuine and deep," and the imam obviously still trusted and relied on his old acolyte. In addition to swearing him in as president, Khomeini wrote a sixteen-word order that day naming Bani Sadr commander in chief of the nation's armed forces.

In his brief speech on the occasion, the imam urged his spiritual son to avoid "egoism, excess of ambition, and seduction by the world." Bani Sadr responded by saying that he had been elected by the people and represented their sovereignty — and not, by inference, the sovereignty of the Islamic jurist that the imam represented. Much of the ceremony was filmed by a national television crew, but when the film was aired that evening, only Khomeini's statement was audible.

The Americans watched all this from a great distance. The relationship that interested them more than any other in the seeming chaos of Tehran as February began was the one between the new president and Ghotbzadeh. Ghotbzadeh was the best connection they had at the moment, and his fate, now that Bani Sadr had the presidency, was a subject of much discussion between State and the White House. Ham Jordan even spent a long phone conversation fishing for insights from a professor and Iranian specialist at the University of Pittsburgh who had taught Ghotbzadeh during his days in the United States and was still in regular phone contact with him. Without apprising the professor of any of their secret dealings, Jordan asked him to assess how he thought his old student would now behave, particularly around the issue of the hostages.

"First," Ham reported to Carter, the Pitt professor

said that Ghotbzadeh could decide to "go it alone" and . . . implement a plan, only informing Bani Sadr so late in the game that he would have no choice but to go along. . . . The hope [in that instance] would be that Bani Sadr would find it impossible to remove him from some position of influence.

A second possibility would be that he would go directly to Bani Sadr and try to "make peace" with him. With the Ayatollah's health so precarious, this would be much less risky than going it alone. [The professor] says that the history of their relationship is that they have never liked each other personally but have worked together before when it was in their mutual interest. [He] speculates that with Khomeini ill and Bani Sadr seeing the need to both resolve the hostage crisis and consolidate his support, it would seem an alliance for the next thirty days [before parliamentary elections] would appear to be to their mutual advantage.

The third possibility would be that Ghotbzadeh would go to the "turbaned members of the Revolutionary Council who will have to be the ones who ultimately convince Khomeini to bring the hostage issue to a conclusion." He could . . . gain their support and hope to co-opt Bani Sadr in a way in which he can not object. . . . While Ghotbzadeh is at the "top of everyone's [hate] list," no one — including Bani Sadr — is going to want to take him on directly during the thirty-day period before the new government is formed. He said that this fear/respect for Ghotbzadeh reflects the feeling that he is still one of the Ayatollah's favorites.

All of this American speculation obviously assumed that somehow Ghotbzadeh would be able to seize the initiative. In truth, the initiative belonged to Bani Sadr, and he met with Sadegh to exercise it shortly after becoming president. His original intention was to force Sadegh out as foreign minister. Bani Sadr told Ghotbzadeh that he was one of the reasons Iran was in this corner. He had coddled and boosted these students, pumping them up over the television and radio. He was the one who had pulled the rug out from under the deal Bani Sadr would have made at the UN when he was foreign minister.

Unable to convince Bani Sadr otherwise, Sadegh began to plead. Bani Sadr couldn't throw him out while he was on the verge of pulling off a deal that would make all his previous wrongs right. Why not make the most of this opportunity? And Ghotbzadeh was the only one who could. At his most desperate, Sadegh begged Bani Sadr in the name of their days as comrades and in the name of Iran itself. Tears ran down his cheeks.

Eventually Bani Sadr relented and let Ghotbzadeh remain at the Foreign Ministry. And once Ghotbzadeh had at least momentarily secured his role as foreign minister, he began promoting the scenario that Bourguet and Villalon had brought back from Washington as his highest priority. His relationship with Bani Sadr was obviously at another one of its low points, but he had the backing of most of the Revolutionary Council, and he thought his relationship with the imam was better than Bani Sadr's. He figured all that ought to buy him at least another month to pull this thing off.

His first stop with the scenario was the Revolutionary Council, where he arranged for Bourguet to make a presentation about the negotiations. The council unanimously supported the scenario, with one qualification: that it must also receive the support of the imam.

To secure that support, the document was presented to Khomeini in his hospital room, where he was recovered enough to deal with occasional pieces of business. As was usually the case when the Revolutionary Council forwarded him a unanimous recommendation, he offered his conditional approval but didn't completely sign off on it.

Bourguet and Villalon's last stop before returning to Europe was with Bani Sadr. Bourguet had been Bani Sadr's attorney when he was in Paris, and their familiarity allowed the Frenchman to get right to the point.

The Americans were insisting on some formal sign of endorsement, Bourguet and Villalon explained. Heretofore, Bourguet and Villalon had been acting only as friends of the Iranian government. They were providing a conduit, but they were not empowered to make a commitment. Now, understandably, the Americans wanted evidence that the new president had signed on and that the intermediaries could speak on his behalf.

After some browbeating, Bani Sadr agreed and gave Bourguet a handwritten note to show the Americans. It was addressed to Bourguet. "I have looked over the memorandum you submitted to me," it read, "and confirm to you my agreement for you to continue to develop it, until it is finally approved by both parties."

With that in hand, Christian Bourguet and Hector Villalon contacted the Americans and arranged to meet again two days hence. This time, the conclave was scheduled for Switzerland.

· 22 ·

———

THE ONE POWER CENTER IN THE TEHRAN POLIT- ical scrum with which Bourguet and Villalon did not make contact during the first week of February was the Muslim Students Following the Line of the Imam, the actual holders of the hostages the intermediaries were negotiating to deliver. At their outpost inside the Den of Spies, the students continued to play their self-proclaimed role as Islamic counterpoint to the machinations of the government and the Revolutionary Council. And they continued to be revered by a huge portion of the population. "We weren't politicians," Sister Mary explained. "We were standing for principles." Ghotbzadeh and Bani Sadr were both convinced the students would sabotage any deal with the Americans if they learned of it too soon in the process. The students thought of themselves as beholden only to the imam and the faith the people had placed in them. And they meant to use all their considerable leverage to keep the Revolution pure.

That intention took daily form in the Muslim Students' ongoing document show-and-tell. As their subcommittee continued to sort through the papers that had been captured with the hostages, Sister Mary and others appeared regularly on Iranian national television reading selected portions of what they had discovered and naming names of Iranians who had been mentioned in the American documents. All aspiring Iranian politicians now cringed at the prospect of being denounced at the embassy gate, as a number of them were, including members of the interim government.

Ghotbzadeh had been clashing with the students since he first became foreign minister. On two occasions already, he had called for or announced the actual release of groups of hostages, only to be contradicted and stymied by their captors. There had also been an attempt by the students to convince the imam to order Ghotbzadeh to turn over the chargé and two other American diplomats he was still holding at the Foreign Ministry. They had argued that they all belonged in one group, held at the Den of Spies, but Ghotbzadeh had refused, and the imam ruled in Sadegh's favor. Ghotbzadeh was further outraged at the students' possession of the American documents and the leverage that gave them over the political process. In late January he had commented to a friend that where he was once confident he could control the students, that confidence was fading fast.

"I had one telephone confrontation with Ghotbzadeh myself," Sister Mary remembered. "He had called to try to persuade us of the error of our ways, and specifically to stop releasing the compromising documents we had uncovered. His taste of power had made him even more arrogant than before. He was convinced he alone was correct, and that he could singlehandedly bring the occupation to an end. . . . He accused us of playing into the hands of the 'extremists.' [He said,] 'We have to solve the matter rapidly, it's not in Iran's interests. I'm just as revolutionary as you are, but you're going too far.' That's when I realized that it was useless. I was wasting my time. . . . Ghotbzadeh claimed to support the students, but he talked against us behind our back."

Bani Sadr's conflict with them, on the other hand, had been out in the open for a while. And on the issue of the documents, he also had a personal stake, though he didn't yet know it. His was one of the names the students had stumbled across, in a series of four reports filed under the code name SD LURE/1, documenting the failed CIA attempt to infiltrate a deep-cover operative into a commercial relationship with Bani Sadr. The students hadn't yet revealed the American reports about him, so he was still ignorant of SD LURE/1, but Bani Sadr sought to seize control of all the captured documents anyway.

That conflict with Bani Sadr only intensified now that he was president. "We were to realize soon enough that we had been over-optimistic in our estimate of Bani Sadr," Sister Mary remembered. "He had largely concealed his real convictions . . . until after he was sworn in as head of state. He then began to express open opposition to the views of the Imam, the students, and the nation on the hostage question." As February began, Sister Mary announced in one of her daily media sessions at the embassy's front gate that the students would follow an order from the imam to release the hostages, but they would not follow an order on that subject from anyone else.

The hostages themselves, of course, had no idea that their fate was being bargained over. They had no information about the current situation outside the embassy grounds, other than the howling of the crowd on Taleghani Avenue. Only the three hostages being held at the Foreign Ministry even knew that Ghotbzadeh was foreign minister and Bani Sadr was now president.

Thus, the fifty diplomats in the hands of the students could only fret about what was going on in the most abstract terms. Barry Rosen, for example, got his hands on a photo torn from a *Washington Post* that showed President Jimmy Carter praying for the hostages at the National Cathedral, and Rosen worried. "I wondered whether he knew that the worst he could do was let the Iranians feel he badly wanted what they were selling," he remembered. "Nothing lowers [the] price so quickly as walking away from an Iranian's stall. . . . I hoped the President was being advised by people who knew the Iranian mentality well. I hoped even more he was playing his cards close to his chest and the press was cooperating by not making this a big story in which they told their readers — and Khomeini's lieutenants — every little thought."

In the far more immediate world the hostages occupied, conditions had improved somewhat with the New Year. Blindfolds and binding had been largely abandoned again, except when under transport. The Iranians had also brought in chess sets and cards to help their prisoners pass the time. Many of the possessions taken from the hostages during November were returned. Those included consular officer Robert Ode's other ring, the cameo from his parents, causing him to burst into tears. All of the Americans who had been taken off the compound to other locations were now back at the embassy, but frequent moving between rooms and buildings remained standard procedure. This too, however, lessened through January. The prohibition against talking to one another remained in place but was often only selectively enforced.

Robert Ode had been moved into his current quarters, a fourteen-by-fourteen-foot room in the basement of the chancery, on the next to last day of December, before dawn, when it was bitter cold outside. The room's high barred window showed only the embassy wall and a few treetops along Taleghani Avenue. There was a washroom down the hall that the students rarely cleaned, and using it required permission from the guard. The bathroom sink was also the basement's laundry. Ode would stay in his chancery basement room for the next two months. He was joined there that first afternoon by Rosen. Altogether, four hostages were confined there together, sleeping on mattresses or huddling around the gas heater on the coldest days. There was also a student guard who sat at a desk, with the desk lamp on all night long.

By the time he reached Ode's basement room, Rosen had fallen almost completely apart. He was now subject to unfocused anxiety and chest-crushing tension twenty-four hours a day. He often didn't sleep at all or for perhaps an hour before dawn. At times, his anxiety became so great that he was convinced he was about to die. Loud or unexpected sounds made him jump and set his heart pounding. Rosen had circles under his eyes so deep and dark he looked in a mirror and thought he was wearing "horror movie makeup." Despite the prohibition against talk, Ode and Rosen managed to communicate in occasional whispers, and the older man tried to help Rosen as best he could, reassuring him that he wasn't crazy, that this horrible frenzy in his brain and chest and legs would pass someday, and that he wouldn't die here in captivity.

A student doctor who examined Rosen concluded that his heart was in fine shape and ordered the guard to give him occasional doses of Valium if he requested it, but that provided little relief. Perhaps the greatest palliative for Rosen was the daily exercise period. Right after breakfast, he was allowed to go down the hall to a room that housed printing equipment. All of the equipment had been pushed aside to leave a space about the size of an "average bathroom" in which to jog in place or use some of the exercise equipment seized from the marines' quarters. The relief the exertion gave Rosen was momentary, but it was relief nonetheless.

This familiar routine circumscribing life in the chancery basement was shattered around midnight on the day that Bourguet and Villalon made their presentation to the Revolutionary Council. Suddenly, without warning, a group of unfamiliar guards dressed in camouflage fatigues burst in, shouting and waving assault rifles around. The Americans were ordered into the hallway and, one by one, taken into an empty room, where they were strip-searched. Rosen was convinced they were about to be executed and could hardly hold his arms above his head as the guards demanded. Ode was tempted to mouth off but kept quiet instead. When they returned to the room, all their bedding and their meager stashes of personal belongings were strewn about. Only the drinking glasses and porcelain dinner plates were seized. Rosen later learned that one of the hostages had attempted to slash his wrists with a broken glass that evening but failed.

When the "two Frenchmen" met with the Americans for the third time, everyone now greeted one another as old friends. The setting was a luxurious suite at the ornate Bellevue Palace Hotel in Bern, Switzerland, where they were the secret guests of the Swiss government. Swiss security officers had convinced the hotel management to empty the rest of the floor of guests, so the meeting was isolated from observation and state security guards could set up checkpoints in the corridor. More guards were stationed undercover in the lobby. The three Americans were registered under fictitious names.

There were objections that had been raised on both sides, so they started reworking the scenario almost as soon as Bourguet and Villalon's flight from Tehran landed. They worked from 8:00 p.m. until past midnight on February 9 and straight through all of February 10 and then some, from breakfast until far past midnight, breaking only to eat. Jordan wore a sweatshirt and was often barefoot. Both Bourguet and Villalon chain-smoked, mostly cigars. The translator's voice became increasingly raw. At various points in the process, Jordan went into one of the suite's bedrooms and called President Carter on a secure line that had been rigged for the occasion.

The biggest surprise of the Bern meeting happened in an aside, during a break from the general meeting. At that point, Bourguet and Villalon took Ham Jordan off by themselves, without the interpreter. Bourguet then used his rudimentary English to deliver a message Jordan had not been expecting.

"We," Bourguet began, speaking slowly with a shrug in his partner's direction, "we think . . . We think it is time for you to meet with the Iranians."

Ham's eyes widened. Direct contact had been a goal of the American approach in these negotiations in the beginning, but when using Bourguet and Villalon proved to be as efficient as it had been, the goal had been allowed to fade. Now, all of a sudden, it was back in full view, standing right in front of Ham.

Jordan told them he would have to check with his boss, but he was sure Carter would want him to pursue it. Ham's only question was, why now? It seemed they had a scenario already worked out.

Christian Bourguet thought hard about his response, trying to shape the English in his head before attempting to say it aloud. He then described the proposed meeting as "an investment in the future." It might make the release of the hostages faster. It would also start a dialogue between the two countries that could grow into a new relationship.

Ham wanted to know who "the Iranians" were with whom he would be meeting.

Bourguet said he would tell Jordan only under the condition that he would promise never to reveal the name of his contact and promise to keep news of it out of the press.

Jordan responded that he had no power to keep anything out of the press. He could only promise never to reveal the contact's name personally.

Christian thought that was reasonable. He was long since convinced Jordan was a straight shooter.

The Iranian, Bourguet told him, was Sadegh Ghotbzadeh.

Jordan's eyes bulged again.

Bourguet assured him they would be in touch soon to work out the details.

When the scenario drafting was finally finished, Bourguet called Ghotbzadeh and read the document to him. By then, it was early morning, February 11. With business done, Jordan, Bourguet, and the others sat around laughing and talking for a while, so loudly at times that the front desk called the suite to ask them to tone it down, they were disturbing the floor below. The whole group was jubilant and felt they had written a script that was going to work.

The scenario was divided into three stages. The opening stage detailed how a Commission of Inquiry would be established. First, Secretary General Waldheim would notify Ghotbzadeh that he would be ready within a week to dispatch a commission to Iran at Iran's request. Then, after a series of actions — including Bani Sadr or the imam greeting the commission as an Iranian diplomatic success — the United States would regretfully assent to a fact-finding mission to Tehran whose purpose, according to the document's summary, was "to hear the grievances of both sides, to meet with each of the hostages, and to report to the Secretary General."

That American act would trigger the second stage, concerning the work of the commission. Upon arrival in Tehran, it would meet in private and receive Iranian evidence. It was also to visit the hostages "as soon as possible." The commission would then draft a report. When the report was ready, the UN group would notify the Revolutionary Council that "the credibility of its report would be seriously limited unless the hostages were released immediately or at least moved from the compound to a hospital." It would also inform the council that it was ready to return to New York to report to the secretary general.

The final stage of the scenario would then be triggered with either the transfer of the hostages to a hospital or the student evacuation of the embassy, leaving the hostages behind. The next day, the commission would return to New York and, the day after that, submit its report. That report would include the recommendation that Iran be allowed to sue the shah to recover lost national assets. Day four of the scenario's final stage would bring the release of the hostages and their departure from Iran. An hour after their plane cleared Iranian airspace, the secretary general would release statements from Iran and the United States. Iran would admit the "moral wrong of holding hostages," express regret, and pledge to respect international law. The Americans would express "regret for the grievances of the Iranian people, including the widespread perception of U.S. intervention in Iran's internal affairs" and affirm the Iranian people's right to "make decisions governing their political future." The scenario would end with the establishment of a joint body to "resolve all unresolved bilateral problems," such as impounded funds.

Their work in Bern complete, the negotiators flew an American air force plane to Paris, where Christian Bourguet and Hector Villalon departed. The Americans arrived back in New York in time to meet Cy Vance late in the morning eastern standard time, Monday, February 11, and brief him on the finalized scenario. Then he, Jordan, and the assistant secretary went to lunch at the secretary general's home.

When he learned of the scenario and the role to be played by a United Nations Commission of Inquiry, Waldheim wanted to help, but first he sought to be sure that the plan had the backing of Iran as well.

Jordan then launched into a long explanation of Bourguet and Villalon and their connection to Ghotbzadeh.

But what about Khomeini?

Jordan pointed out that, as the secretary general no doubt knew, Khomeini was not the kind of man to concern himself with the details of a plan. Jordan and the other Americans were, however, convinced that he had been informed that the Revolutionary Council had unanimously endorsed this scenario.

That satisfied Waldheim. The rest of the meeting concerned the makeup of the Commission of Inquiry. The negotiators in Bern had come up with a list of members, which they delivered to the secretary general. He pledged to notify all of those selected for the commission and give them a full briefing.

Vance and Jordan flew on to Washington together when the meeting on Beekman Place was over. Vance complimented Jordan along the way for having got far more on paper from the Iranians than Vance ever thought he would.

Upon arrival at the White House, where virtually no one knew how he'd spent his weekend, Jordan immediately closeted with Carter and briefed him on the scenario that was about to commence. The president voiced doubts about the statement the United States was pledged to make, but Jordan reassured him that they would be able to find language to satisfy both the American public and the agreement. Carter also gave the go-ahead for his chief of staff's proposed secret meeting with Ghotbzadeh, and by the end of the following day, Jordan and Bourguet had arranged for Jordan to fly to Paris on the weekend for the clandestine encounter.

There would be only two instances of direct contact between representatives of the American government and the Islamic Republic of Iran through the entire 444 days of the Crisis. This one would be the first.

Hamilton Jordan had no illusions about the risk Sadegh Ghotbzadeh was taking. It was well-known to the Americans that the imam had expressly forbidden any such face-to-face contact. Jordan correctly suspected that he, in effect, had the Iranian's life in his hands. No one other than a few people at the very core of the administration knew what Ham was up to, and even fewer knew the name of the Iranian with whom he was up to it. On Friday the president's chief of staff made a point of being very visible around the White House, to help ensure that no one would notice his absence over the weekend. To disguise himself while traveling, Ham had the CIA outfit him with a makeup kit that included a false mustache and a wig.

Jordan, interpreter in tow, arrived in Paris by the Concorde on Saturday morning. The meeting was scheduled for late that evening in Hector Villalon's luxurious Paris apartment. Jordan waited there for almost two hours before Ghotbzadeh arrived, after midnight. The Iranian foreign minister was in Paris on an official Foreign Ministry junket. Hector ushered the two men into a mahogany-lined dining room where place settings faced each other across a table. The room was candlelit. Sadegh Ghotbzadeh and Hamilton Jordan then shared what Jordan described as "a leisurely dinner." Altogether, their talk lasted three and a half hours.

Jordan began by expressing his appreciation for the contact. He knew how risky it was, but he couldn't resist asking just what would happen if this meeting were known about back in Iran.

Sadegh smiled. He would lose his job, at least, he joked. Maybe his head too. Both men laughed.

The first forty-five minutes of the conversation were devoted to a review by Ghotbzadeh, often at his most pedantic and self-inflated, of the history of American and Iranian relations. Jordan grimaced internally and sometimes squirmed at all "this anti-American crap" but largely held his tongue. When the subject focused on the shah, Ghotbzadeh went on at length, denouncing His Imperial Majesty and the Americans for how they had used him to control Iran. Eventually Jordan interrupted to remind Sadegh that they were here to try to do something to solve this situation.

That, Ghotbzadeh retorted, could be done simply and quickly.

How was that? Jordan asked.

All the United States had to do to solve the Crisis was kill the shah, Ghotbzadeh told him. Nothing obvious, just some kind of injection, perhaps, that made it look like natural causes.

Jordan reacted with outrage at the suggestion, so Ghotbzadeh dropped it.

They ended up discussing the scenario Jordan, Bourguet, and Villalon had spent the last month constructing. On the vagueness of how soon the hostages would be released, Ghotbzadeh predicted that it would be two or three weeks. He described in some detail all of the work he would have to do between now and then, with Bani Sadr, the imam, and the Revolutionary Council, to make sure the release came off. He also told Jordan that the "two Frenchmen" had his "complete faith" and "power of attorney." The hostages were all still alive and safe, he said. He then spoke at length about the difficulty of getting the hostages out of the embassy compound. Ghotbzadeh mentioned that he and Bani Sadr "had a plan" for doing so, but didn't say exactly what it was, though it would probably have to involve the imam personally. He implied that his forces also had surreptitious contacts among the students themselves, but, again, he wouldn't elaborate.

Jordan asked directly if Khomeini had signed off on the scenario.

Ghotbzadeh paused before launching into a description of the approval process. He then told Jordan that although there had been much argument over the details in the Revolutionary Council, the support for the scenario among the council had ultimately been unanimous. A council delegation then went to Qom for an audience with the imam. They had told him that "we had shamed the United States sufficiently and taught it a lesson, and now we needed to resolve this problem."

So how did he respond? Jordan pressed.

Sadegh chuckled. The imam did not respond directly to much, he pointed out. The imam had listened to their report, often nodding. If he had disapproved, he would have said so, and the imam had said nothing. After the report, he prayed with them for a while, and they went back to Tehran.

Sadegh told Jordan that he planned to return soon to Tehran to see the imam and redouble his efforts to resolve this. He also asked Ham to tell President Carter that "the things I have said personally about him were said either in frustration with the U.S. or for domestic political purposes. I hope he understands." He wanted Carter to know that he would do "his very best" to get the hostages home soon.

Before Sadegh left Villalon's apartment, Jordan gave the Iranian foreign minister his home and his office phone numbers and told him to call whenever he needed to, about anything.

The President's chief of staff waited at Villalon's apartment for an hour after Ghotbzadeh left, just in case the Iranian had been tailed to their rendezvous. Then Jordan caught the next Concorde for Washington.

The scenario began falling apart almost as soon as it was under way.

The first misstep was by Waldheim. When it came time to announce the formation of the Commission of Inquiry, the secretary general completely ignored the scenario's stipulations and proclaimed that he had established this commission at the insistence of the United States. This was precisely what the Americans and Iranians had not wanted him to do, and he never bothered to explain his unilateral reversal of the terms. Waldheim told the press he was now awaiting Iran's reply to the commission's request to visit and collect information.

Ghotbzadeh, still in Paris, was furious when he heard. The commission was supposed to have been formed at Iran's request, allowing Iran to claim a diplomatic victory. Instead, thanks to the secretary general, they were put in the position of acceding to the Americans. The foreign minister now had no victory with which to initiate the process. "The mistake could not have been bigger," Christian Bourguet remembered. "It immediately gave a whole different tone to the sending of the Commission. Waldheim's statement meant there was no way anyone in Iran could think anything other than that the Commission was in the pay of the Americans. So, even before it arrived, everyone in Iran was entirely suspicious of it."

The blunder was compounded when Waldheim sent his official request for the commission's visit — the next step of the scenario — to Tehran, though Ghotbzadeh was still in Paris. In Tehran the official UN message was given to Bani Sadr to answer in the foreign minister's absence. Bani Sadr figured that since the scenario had already been breached by the secretary general's announcement, he was now free to rewrite the commission's mission statement to make up for the lack of a diplomatic victory. As a result the Iranian president's note back to the secretary general made no mention of visiting the hostages at all.

That set off alarm bells among the Americans. The head of State's Iran desk, who had been included in the most recent negotiations, instantly complained to Bourguet in Paris. The French lawyer and his Argentine sidekick then huddled with Ghotbzadeh, who, still furious at Waldheim, wanted to cancel the scenario altogether. Bourguet and Villalon finally succeeded in pulling Sadegh back from this precipice, and instead he sent a second Iranian response to the secretary general, this one in keeping with the scenario's provisions. "It was a humiliation," Bourguet remembered, "but Ghotbzadeh decided to salvage what he could."

Despite all these difficulties, the scenario was still alive on February 20, when the five-member Commission of Inquiry mustered in Geneva before flying into Tehran. The original plan had been for the commission to stay in Geneva overnight and then proceed, but the wait there lasted three days. A few members of Bani Sadr's faction tried to delay the arrival even longer, feeling that Iran wasn't yet ready to make its case against the shah, but Ghotbzadeh and Bourguet appeared before the Revolutionary Council and persuaded them to approve it. On February 23, a week after Jordan's secret meeting with the Iranian foreign minister, the commission finally left Geneva.

While they were still airborne, however, the scenario further imploded. This time, the problem was a statement issued by the imam's headquarters. The context of the declaration was the campaign for the upcoming parliamentary elections, but the content was all about the hostages, and the imam's pronouncement seemed to contradict the scenario absolutely. "The Muslim and combatant students who occupied the Den of Spies have . . . dealt a crushing body blow against the world-devouring United States," Khomeini announced. "But since in the near future the representatives of the people will meet [as a parliament], the issue of the hostages will be up to the representatives of the people."

Jimmy Carter almost jumped out of his chair when Vance told him what the ayatollah had said. If this meant waiting for the initial parliamentary elections and the runoff election to follow, then waiting more while the parliament organized itself, selected a prime minister, and formed a government, it would be months before the issue of the hostages would even be considered, much less resolved. Carter immediately called Ham. The president was outraged that the Iranians had violated the scenario and demanded to know what was going on.

Jordan hadn't even heard what Khomeini had said until Carter told him about it, so he started scrambling and spent the rest of the day back and forth with Villalon, who was in Tehran. The Argentine relayed messages from Bourguet. Bourguet in turn passed on messages from Ghotbzadeh and Bani Sadr. The imam's remark had taken all of them completely by surprise. They thought this must be the work of Khomeini's son, Ahmed, trying to preempt them. In any case, Bani Sadr pointed out that the imam had said that the hostage crisis would be resolved by "the representatives of the people" and, as president, he was just that. Bourguet asked Villalon to tell Jordan that whatever the statement said, the imam was still in play and could still order the hostages released tomorrow. The commission was about to land in Iran. They ought to go forward with this and see what their mission would yield.

Jordan passed that recommendation on to the president at the end of the day. "He accepted it because we really had no choice," Ham remembered, "but I could tell that he didn't like it at all."

To make matters even worse, the UN commission's arrival in Tehran went poorly as well. For starters, the foreign minister kept the commission waiting for almost two hours. Then, when they were finally ushered into his sleek ministry office, expecting to find Ghotbzadeh alone, they found him flanked by two men — one French, the other Argentine — whom the commission didn't know. The commission chairman — a Venezuelan and, like all the other members, a professional diplomat — objected strongly to these strangers' presence. This commission had come to Iran on a matter of some importance and secrecy, he pointed out, and they had expected to meet with the foreign minister privately.

Ghotbzadeh stared at the chairman, incredulous.

In any case, the chairman continued, the commission needed to know immediately when their work here would be complete and when they would meet with the hostages.

Hadn't the commission been briefed by the secretary general before it left New York? Ghotbzadeh demanded.

Of course they had, the chairman answered.

Had the secretary general told them that the decision to create this commission was the result of an agreement between Iran and the United States, reached through the two intermediaries sitting on either side of him?

No, the chairman answered, the secretary general hadn't. The secretary general had said the commission's formation was at the Americans' request.

Ghotbzadeh ground his teeth.

Sadegh asked if they had seen the text of the scenario to which both sides had agreed.

The commission, it turned out, had no idea such a scenario even existed.

By then the foreign minister's face had darkened.

Did they know that all five of them had been chosen for membership in this commission by these two mysterious figures here with him, Christian Bourguet and Hector Villalon, to whose presence they had objected?

They didn't. In fact, all of the commission members were stunned to be involved in what they had thought was a diplomatic mission and to find two civilian foreign nationals steering the process.

Sadegh then guessed out loud that none of these five idiots had a clue that they had been sent to produce a report whose conclusions had already been written.

The Venezuelan denied as much strenuously. Their report, he insisted, would be their report.

Sadegh Ghotbzadeh was now breathing in angry gulps and staring daggers at the commission chairman. If Waldheim had been in the room, Ghotbzadeh would likely have strangled him. The head of the UN had fucked up every task he had been given.

Bourguet and Villalon leaned over to whisper in Ghotbzadeh's ear and try to calm him down. They could see he was on the verge of erupting.

Fortunately the commission left the Foreign Ministry to consult with the secretary general over the phone. They returned to Ghotbzadeh's office the next day, having finally been let in on the plan, and agreed to continue.

The commission's relations with Ghotbzadeh, however, never overcame their opening round. Within forty-eight hours, the antagonism between

Sadegh and the Venezuelan had become so intense that both sides asked Bourguet to act as an intermediary between them.

The commission's annoying style also carried over to its inquiry. Nowhere was this more obvious than in "the affair of the victims."

When the visit of the commission was announced on the Iranian media, there was also a call by both Ghotbzadeh and the imam for anyone who had been injured by SAVAK to come to Tehran to tell their story to the people from the UN. Almost two thousand showed up, all deformed in one way or another by alleged encounters with the shah's American-trained secret police. The government decided to house about half of those victims in a wing of the previously boarded-up Tehran Hilton, which had been reopened to provide quarters for the Commission of Inquiry and its support personnel.

The commission's annoyance at having to deal with these victims was obvious. The UN panel had not planned on having to listen to a parade of suffering and mutilation and refused to go out of its way to do so, outraging Iranian public opinion in the process. The commission insisted on holding its hearings at the small UN headquarters building, several kilometers from the hotel, meaning that the largely disabled group of Iranian witnesses had to make their way across town. Tehran was still in the midst of winter, and the line of waiting cripples arrayed in the snow outside the UN headquarters made a pitiful sight. Photos of the scene were all over the Tehran newspapers.

Not surprisingly, the commission's attitude was harshly criticized inside Iran. These men from the UN, it was said, were as arrogant as the Americans who'd sent them. Such a perception only made Ghotbzadeh's work more difficult, so, with the assistance of Bourguet and Villalon, he begged the commission to at least meet with the entire group of victims together in one place as a symbolic gesture of its concern for their suffering. The commission resisted for a while but finally gave in and attended such a meeting at the Hilton.

The sight from the dais on which the UN diplomats sat was stunning. Everywhere they looked were people missing fingers that had been chopped off one by one or dragging legs that had been mangled while attached to a dungeon wall. Some hopped in, others just slid on the floor. Some could not see at all, some could see only a little, others had just a spastic tic or a neck that no longer swiveled. A few had lost all their teeth, several had holes that had been cut in their bodies and never healed. The commission members could not help but weep, diplomats or not.

*   *   *

Ghotbzadeh had initially said he thought the commission's visit to the embassy would take place during their third day in town, but the students kept scheduling that inspection, then rescheduling, and rescheduling again, without ever actually allowing the UN delegation to see the hostages. Finally Jimmy Carter lost his patience with the sputtering scenario and summoned his chief of staff.

Ham started their conversation by congratulating his boss on his victory in the New Hampshire primary the day before, but Carter wasn't in a celebratory mood. He got right to the subject of the commission.

Carter was discouraged by its failure to visit the hostages. And he was tired of dangling here, helpless, getting "kicked around in the press" and able to do nothing but hold his breath. The time had come, he told Ham, to "take the initiative."

Jordan asked what the president had in mind.

Carter said he wanted Jordan to make contact with Bourguet and Villalon and "make it plain to them that my patience is growing very thin." He told Ham to tell the "two Frenchmen" that "if something doesn't happen soon, we'll reveal the contents of the scenario."

Jordan was a little taken aback and asked just what Carter meant by "reveal."

Carter snapped in response that he meant "publish them in the damn newspaper." That way, at least the American people and the world would know that he had been dealing in good faith and "the fault lies with Iran."

Ham started to analyze this move, but the president cut him short. He didn't want to talk about it. He just wanted Ham to do as he'd been ordered.

Jordan immediately drafted a statement reflecting the president's attitude. Then the White House placed a call to Hector Villalon's Tehran hotel room. The phone rang a long time before a very groggy Argentine picked it up. When he was awake enough to converse, the interpreter read him a Spanish translation of the statement of impatience that Jordan had drafted. It succeeded in irritating Villalon into complete wakefulness.

The Argentine began his end of the conversation by demanding that the Americans not call him at the hotel ever again. The situation here was dicey, and their communication had to be far more surreptitious. He and Bourguet could be thrown out of the country for such calls. And they did not appreciate the American threat to expose the process. He and Bourguet were in a difficult enough spot as it was, without having to be bullied from all sides. Already they were receiving Iranian death threats and now had to be accompanied everywhere by bodyguards. More arm-twisting from anyone, Iranian or American, and they would just go back to Paris and let the whole thing collapse.

Jordan did his best to smooth Hector's ruffled feathers, and Villalon then provided a summary of where they now stood.

While they faced "problems, problems, and more problems," he reported, they had been given a new date for the visit to the hostages, and the eventual transfer of the hostages out of student control had now "been approved at the highest level," at least in general terms. The struggle here was between the alliance of Bani Sadr and Ghotbzadeh on one hand and "the clerics" on the other, with Khomeini wavering in between. For its part, the UN commission was making trouble over deviations from the script. Their lack of flexibility was a problem. As a show of good faith, Ghotbzadeh had secretly taken the commission to visit the three hostages being held in the Foreign Ministry. Bani Sadr had also met personally with the commission and guaranteed that the scenario would be carried out. Now was no time to get fainthearted, Villalon advised. The deal still had forward momentum, and Ghotbzadeh was fighting for it like a lion.

Indeed, Christian Bourguet would remember the first week of March 1980 as one of Ghotbzadeh's finest hours. With the fate of the scenario hanging in the balance, the foreign minister now took on Iran's national icon, the Muslim Students Following the Line of the Imam. It required enormous political daring, but Ghotbzadeh felt he had no choice.

By Monday, March 3, two more appointments for the commission to visit the embassy had been broken by the students for a variety of reasons. The commission was now openly discussing abandoning their mission and returning to New York because the Iranians were not living up to their promise to let them see the hostages. And the pressure from the Americans, delivered through Bourguet and Villalon, was intense. Sadegh had been rewriting the scenario in different ways ever since it began, trying to make up for Waldheim's opening blunder, all the while making the Americans increasingly uncomfortable. There would be no commission report at all if the hostages weren't visited and then transferred to the government's control — that was the scenario Jordan had agreed on, and the Americans were not relinquishing it. Someone would have to loosen the students' grip.

Frustrated and angry, Ghotbzadeh now went into public attack, denouncing the students for trying to make themselves a separate government. Iran had finally succeeded in getting the United Nations to pay attention to Iran's grievances, he declared, and now these self-righteous students were sabotaging that opportunity. They had to obey the edict of the Revolutionary Council instead of acting as a law unto themselves. "The very act of his [criticism] showed a considerable amount of political courage," one State Department political officer noted, "at a time when exhibitions of political courage in Iran were extremely rare." More than a few Tehran observers suggested Ghotbzadeh was signing his own political death warrant, but he did not back off.

Perhaps Sadegh's most visible assault on the students was a television interview run that week on the Iranian national network. The foreign minister began by belittling the students' claim to having embodied the thinking of the imam. They were the guards of the hostages, he pointed out, and although that might make them heroes, it didn't give them the right to assume a political role and usurp the powers of the Revolutionary Council and the government. Ghotbzadeh attacked their use of the captured documents — which he intimated they were forging in order to intimidate anyone they chose, including ministers in the government. The Americans from the Den of Spies should be in the custody of the government. Anything less was an assault on the Revolution and the revolutionary process. Since the Revolution was Islamic, that meant their stance was irreligious as well, completely invalidating their claim to be acting in accordance with the precepts of the imam.

On Wednesday, March 5, when the commission's appointment with the hostages was put off yet again, Sadegh went straight to the Den of Spies to confront the students face-to-face. The meeting turned into a shouting match and ended with the students expelling the foreign minister out onto icy Taleghani Avenue.

By then, the UN Commission of Inquiry had reached the end of its string. The chairman spent much of Wednesday afternoon engaged in conversations with the secretary general in New York and the American negotiators in Washington, as well as Bourguet and Villalon. The commission's five members were all agreed that they could not stay any longer; their information gathering was done, and it was time to leave — perhaps as early as that evening. They had lost all confidence that Iran could or would live up to its end of the scenario. Much of the four-way conversation was devoted to figuring out what to say when the commission abandoned Tehran with its mission unfulfilled.

In a last desperate act to save the scenario, Ghotbzadeh hurried to the Tehran Hilton in person and begged the commission to stay just another day or two. The commission, the secretary general, and the Americans were all skeptical of Ghotbzadeh's ongoing claims that the situation was on the verge of transforming, but they granted Sadegh a stay for at least the next twenty-four hours.

And this time the foreign minister's optimistic prediction actually came true.

The next morning, Sister Mary and several other students appeared at the embassy gate to read an announcement that surprised almost everyone who heard it. After a rote restatement of their opposition to the commission's proposed hostage visit, the student communiqué asked, "What can one do when the officials and those who are in charge in the Commission have accepted that whatever the Commission wants must be done? We cannot bow to and comply with a view that we do not regard as being in line with the Imam's policy." Then the Muslim Students Following the Line of the Imam dropped a bombshell. "But," their announcement continued, "since those in charge of the government always regard our methods as a factor contributing to their weakness . . . we [call upon] the Revolutionary Council, in order to allay any misunderstanding, to take delivery of the hostages from us to do with them anything they deem appropriate."

Ghotbzadeh saw the move as a bluff and pounced on it. The students thought no one would dare to take the hostage responsibility away from them for fear of an enormous political backlash. In keeping with this strategy, the students were already exhorting the crowds out on Taleghani Avenue to resist any effort to move the American diplomats.

To shore up his position, the foreign minister immediately went to see the imam in Qom. Sadegh told Khomeini about his plan to take all the hostages into the control of the Foreign Ministry and explained why it was necessary. The imam made no objection. Ghotbzadeh then informed Bani Sadr that he had the imam's endorsement. Bani Sadr double-checked this news by calling Khomeini's son, Ahmed, and Ahmed confirmed the imam's support for Ghotbzadeh's move.

That afternoon, Ghotbzadeh went on television and announced that the imam had approved his initiative. The transfer of the hostages to the government's control — the last step in the scenario prior to the commission's return to New York — was now scheduled for Saturday, March 8, the day after the Sabbath.

· 23 ·

———

WHEN HAM JORDAN HAD FIRST LEARNED OF THE students' offer to transfer control of the hostages, it was all he could do to resist turning handsprings on the spot. Everyone expected that the transfer would be followed shortly by the hostages' release. Plans were even made with the Swiss for possible evacuation of the captured Americans. As word circulated, people stopped Ham in the White House hallways to offer congratulations. Only Carter remained aloof from celebration, saying he would believe it when it actually happened.

In Tehran, Sadegh Ghotbzadeh readied the Foreign Ministry to accept fifty more guests. Lockers and beds were hauled in, windows painted over for security reasons. He also approached Bruce Laingen, senior of the three hostages being held in his building, and asked the chargé to assist him in maintaining order among his fellow Americans when they arrived. Ghotbzadeh planned to use air force helicopters to ferry the hostages from the Den of Spies to the ministry and to dispatch several trucks as decoys in case there might be an attempt to block the movement. When Bourguet asked him if he thought the students would actually deliver, he said that if they balked this time, he would use the Revolutionary Council to force them to make good on their promise.

Over at the embassy compound, the students were begrudging at best about the transfer. Their dislike for Ghotbzadeh and Bani Sadr was now rampant. The pair was commonly referred to as "Double-dealing and Deceit." Still, the students, their bluff called, felt they had no choice but to follow through with the transfer as the imam directed. The most resentful of them, however, managed to make sure the compliance was accomplished with considerable foot-dragging.

The transfer process began on Saturday morning, when a delegation of three students arrived at the Foreign Ministry, where Ghotbzadeh, Bourguet, and Villalon were waiting. Their conversation with Sadegh was stiff and uneasy. The student spokesman began by saying they were prepared to make the transfer. But, he went on, before they would do so, they needed a letter from Bani Sadr confirming the Revolutionary Council's order.

Ghotbzadeh lost his temper almost instantly. What bullshit was this? They would transfer the hostages, letter or not.

The student dug in his heels. Ghotbzadeh was simply the man designated by the council to receive the Americans: He couldn't speak for the council itself — only Bani Sadr could, and they were not going to budge until they had it from him in writing.

Sadegh fumed and blustered but quickly realized that he had no choice but to procure such a letter. He called Bani Sadr's office, which promised the document forthwith, and then Ghotbzadeh waited. And waited. As the first hour passed, Sadegh could feel the scenario's momentum draining away. Timing was everything, and this delay would only benefit the obstructionists among the students. When the letter didn't arrive after two hours, Ghotbzadeh called Bani Sadr personally and screamed at him. The helicopters were ready, the air force was ready, but where was the goddamn letter? Bourguet would later attribute Bani Sadr's delay to the president's fears of putting his name on paper until he was sure Khomeini wouldn't change his mind. That inertia, however, gave way in the face of Ghotbzadeh's rage. Bani Sadr's office finally delivered the letter, more than three hours after it had been requested. By then, the window of opportunity was rapidly closing.

Emboldened, the students used the arrival of the letter to demand that the foreign minister also provide a roster of the names of all the Americans he wanted transferred.

No such roster existed, and after shouting his objections, Ghotbzadeh began a frantic search to try and find a complete list of the captured Americans. It was now early afternoon. The transfer should already have happened, and Sadegh anguished over continued delay. To succeed, he needed to seize the moment, but as he searched for a roster, Sadegh turned on the television in his ministry office and received even worse news. The Iranian network was running live shots from Taleghani Avenue outside the embassy, where what seemed to be huge crowds were assembling, screaming against any movement of the hostages at all.

Ghotbzadeh's heart sank. He knew his support from the imam was fragile and feared that news of a mass objection like this would send Khomeini scuttling for political cover.

And he was right.

At 1:30 p.m., the imam's son, Ahmed, phoned the Foreign Ministry. Ghotbzadeh had been wrong to assume that the imam's silence about the hostage transfer had meant approval, Ahmed declared. The imam had given no such endorsement as Ghotbzadeh was claiming. Shortly after informing Ghotbzadeh, Ahmed issued a public statement to the same effect.

All of Sadegh's remaining leverage with the students evaporated almost instantly. The Muslim Students Following the Line of the Imam began laughing in the face of Ghotbzadeh's continuing demands. The foreign minister spent the afternoon trying to summon the Revolutionary Council into an emergency session to force the students' hand, but most members refused to even meet on the subject.

When darkness fell in Tehran, replete with snow flurries, Sadegh finally ordered the helicopters to stand down and instructed Bourguet and Villalon to notify Washington that the transfer had fallen through.

The complete collapse of the scenario followed shortly thereafter. Ghotbzadeh succeeded in assembling the Revolutionary Council on Sunday — except for Bani Sadr, who skipped the meeting. "He didn't have the guts for it," Sadegh later explained to one of his friends. Even without his most significant ally, Ghotbzadeh waged a ferocious fight to get the scenario back on track, arguing that the council had to give the students an ultimatum and back it up with the use of force should they refuse. The best he could get out of the council, however, was an agreement to take the issue to the imam for resolution on Monday morning.

When they did, the imam completely dashed Ghotbzadeh's hopes for an immediate resuscitation. Khomeini announced that the UN commission could see the hostages, but only after they had issued their report. If they had indeed reached the proper conclusions, then a visit to the captives at the Den of Spies seemed appropriate. The imam's statement didn't even mention the possibility of transferring control of the hostages to the Foreign Ministry.

On Tuesday morning, March 11, the hostages' 129th day in captivity, the UN Commission of Inquiry caught a plane out of Tehran to New York. Ghotbzadeh escorted them onto the tarmac. They were accosted there by a student who had brought an armload of documents for them from the embassy, which he claimed would prove beyond a doubt the shah's crimes and the Americans' complicity in them. The commission refused to accept the papers. And as their plane lifted off, Ghotbzadeh and the student could be seen standing on the runway, screaming at each other.

Immediately after the commission's departure from Tehran, Zbigniew Brzezinski sent President Carter a memo. According to the polls, the national security adviser pointed out, most Americans thought the administration's Iran policy was a "failure."

Carter scribbled a brusque comment in the margin. "The polls are accurate," he wrote.

His Imperial Majesty the shahanshah had followed the episode from his rented home on Contadora Island off Panama's Pacific coast, where General Torrijos had American newspapers flown to HIM daily. The shah was not doing well.

Despite his move from the United States to the Republic of Panama, ultimate medical oversight of Mohammad Pahlavi remained in the hands of David Rockefeller's New York–based doctor, a tropical disease specialist. Rockefeller's doctor had visited his patient shortly after the royal entourage's arrival in Panama and had assigned daily on-site care to a Panamanian oncologist who practiced at Gorgas Hospital, the US Army–run Canal Zone facility made available to HIM under the terms of the Lackland agreement. Rockefeller's doctor had also selected a team of local surgeons to act in case of an emergency and arranged for regular blood tests, which were to be evaluated by the lab at Gorgas. All of this was done with the explicit approval of

General Torrijos's personal physician, who also acted as the general's medical liaison. As was customary, the shah's new Panamanian doctors were required to address him as "Your Majesty," to always ask his permission before touching him, and to remain standing whenever they were in his presence.

The shah had seemed to be prospering during his first two months on Contadora, but about the time the commission landed in Tehran, the gray returned to his complexion, weight again began falling off of him, and, according to Torrijos, the Light of the Aryans began looking like "a walking dead man." After a period of relative passivity, the shah's spleen had begun swelling again and by the beginning of March was significantly engorged and dysfunctional. Instead of filtering the blood as it should, the cancerous organ had developed a condition known as "hypersplenism," throwing his blood counts out of whack and requiring transfusions to counter. The treatment for this condition was the complete removal of the spleen — as the shah's doctors had originally hoped to do at New York Hospital. The surgical procedure was relatively run-of-the-mill under normal circumstances, but the degree of swelling the shah was experiencing added significantly to the complexity. Nonetheless, the shah's Panamanian doctor and the French physician who had initially diagnosed the shah's lymphoma agreed that the surgery should be done and done soon. At the end of the first week of March, Rockefeller's doctor returned to Panama to consult with them and Torrijos's medical liaison on the subject.

This consultation was held out on Contadora Island on the same day the students in Tehran first announced their willingness to transfer the hostages. When Rockefeller's doctor indicated that he agreed with the need for surgery and expected it to be done at Gorgas, the Panamanian physician objected in no uncertain terms. Paitilla Hospital — just ten minutes from Gorgas, inside Panama and owned by a medical group that included Torrijos's doctor — was a far better venue, he said. On top of that, the Panamanian announced, he also had "a message to deliver." General Torrijos had asked his doctor to let the others know that although the shah was free to go wherever he wished in his pursuit of treatment, if he left Panamanian territory for the Canal Zone in order to use Gorgas, His Majesty would not be allowed back into Panama. Gorgas was a long-standing symbol of American domination, and the general did not want to pay the political price inherent in allowing the gringo hospital to be placed in a position of officially acknowledged superiority. It was Paitilla or hit the road, one or the other.

Bobby Armao bridled helplessly at the demand. The avarice of the security forces with whom the American PR man dealt seemingly knew no bounds. They spent the shah's money freely, insisting on renting fifteen cars to patrol an island that had only a few miles of roads and on feeding the shah's guards on room service fare ordered up from the nearby resort — all, of course, on His Majesty's tab. The Panamanians billed the shah more than $500,000 for the first ten weeks of his stay, not counting several large tips that the head of Torrijos's security force insisted upon. The Panamanians also tried to sell him Contadora Island itself for $10 million and were constantly bringing other real estate "investments" to his attention. They not only listened to all of the phone calls made from the shah's house, but also insisted that His Majesty pay for the tape recorder the Panamanians used in the process. That they should now demand the shah use the hospital owned by the general's cronies fit right in.

And the Panamanian ultimatum was almost impossible to circumvent. "My staff was outraged," the shah remembered, "but at that moment it seemed there was little we could do." They tried feeling out the State Department about returning to the United States, but that went nowhere. "It was clear the U.S. wanted to keep us in Panama," His Majesty said, "in order to keep playing games with Iran using me as bait for the release of the hostages." So, after consulting with the shah and Bobby Armao, Rockefeller's doctor tried another tack. His Majesty would accept undergoing surgery at Paitilla, but it would be conducted by an American doctor. Though that too seemed likely to raise the Panamanians' hackles, Rockefeller's doctor's idea, as explained to Armao, was to select a surgeon who was not just American, but also "so famous and powerful" that the Panamanian doctors would fall in line behind him without raising any more fuss. The man he selected, Dr. Michael DeBakey, was a pioneer of open-heart surgery from Houston who had huge international name recognition and was a familiar figure even to readers of American tabloids.

This celebrity approach seemed to work at first. The Panamanians were atwitter at the famous doctor's inclusion and quickly granted DeBakey special permission to practice medicine in the Republic of Panama. The extraction of His Imperial Majesty's spleen was scheduled for Paitilla Hospital on March 16, five days after the UN Commission of Inquiry fled Tehran. In preparation, the hospital was surrounded with National Guard units, including machine gun emplacements. Two days ahead of time, the shah checked into room 353, where he kept the door locked, the windows closed, and the air conditioner turned off. His Majesty now shivered unless the room was kept like a sauna and he dripped sweat. He was also nervous and became even more so when, shortly after he checked in, the Panamanian doctors suddenly challenged DeBakey's right to operate on him as he expected. The famous surgeon had only been admitted to the country to watch, the Panamanians now claimed. The actual surgery had to be performed by one of their countrymen.

The battle over who would cut out HIM's spleen — an American surgeon or a Panamanian — reached a crescendo in the Paitilla Hospital library on Saturday morning, March 15. All the Panamanian and American principals were present, most of the Americans having arrived a half hour early and several of the Panamanians having arrived a half hour late. The discussion ran hot and heavy. The outcome was a unanimous decision to pursue a "cooling-off period" during which they would seek a compromise solution "with a view toward preparing for an operation in about two weeks." In the meantime, the patient would return to Contadora Island to "rebuild his confidence" and wait.

In fact, Bobby Armao had already decided his client would never see the inside of a Panamanian hospital again. Before the Saturday morning meeting, he told DeBakey to "play along" and agree to postpone. Armao also instructed him to go back to Houston and await instructions. Armao told the surgeon that he didn't yet know exactly where His Imperial Majesty was going, but the shah was "getting out of here" as soon as humanly possible.

In the immediate moment, the shah checked out of Paitilla and he, the shahbanou, and Armao returned to Contadora Island. There, Armao and his client sat down to discuss the situation.

Armao was insistent. He said the shah had to move. This interference in his health care was unacceptable, and it was obvious that they couldn't count on Washington to control Torrijos any longer. On top of that, Armao had been talking to a source in the intelligence business who told him that the shah was in great danger from the extradition process. The Panamanians, he had heard, were getting ready to sell HIM to the Islamic Republic. Armao told His Majesty that they were "down to their last card" and now had to play it. It was either Egypt or there would be hell to pay.

The actual arrangements were made by the shahbanou. Sadat's wife was one of Farah's best friends and they spoke over the phone regularly. The shah, the shahbanou, and Bobby Armao all went into the shahbanou's bedroom and sat on the edge of her bed while she called Egypt. First the shahbanou and Mrs. Sadat spoke, then Sadat himself got on the line, speaking to Farah and then to Armao. Finally the shah got on the line and confirmed the plans.

It would take the better part of a week to get ready to move, and Armao pledged to do everything in his power to keep His Imperial Majesty's intentions secret in the meantime, but Armao's secret barely lasted a day, if that.

Ham Jordan learned of the shah's intentions on March 19. At the time, Jordan was trying to steer the Carter reelection campaign through its run-up to the primary in Illinois, the first major industrial state in which the president and Ted Kennedy would compete head-to-head. Ham had already been back to Bern for another meeting with Bourguet and Villalon as well, trying to pick up the pieces of the demolished scenario.

The news reached Jordan through Zbigniew Brzezinski, his occasional tennis partner. Ham found a note from Zbig waiting when he arrived at the White House that morning, asking the chief of staff to come see him immediately.

Brzezinski told Jordan that they had received an "intelligence report" stating that the Shah was going to leave Panama for Egypt.

Ham was stunned. He immediately asked the national security adviser what they could do about it.

"Hamilton," Zbig said with a laugh, "Panama and the Shah are your specialty. I'm in charge of current leaders and big countries — you're in charge of former leaders and small countries."

Within twenty-four hours, Ham Jordan was on his way to Panama, intent on heading His Majesty off at the pass.

The first leg of Jordan's flight took him by air force executive jet to Houston, where he tried to recruit the surgeon DeBakey to help him convince the shah to stay in Panama for his operation. This time, Ham promised, the United States would run interference to ensure the spleen removal happened in Gorgas and that DeBakey conducted it. DeBakey said only that he would operate in Panama if he had to, but otherwise Jordan was on his own.

Ham next took another air force plane toward Panama. About an hour out over the Caribbean, in the vast dark above ten thousand feet, Jordan's conversation with his traveling party of three men from the State Department was suddenly shattered by a very loud explosion. Almost instantly the plane nosed over and lost altitude. The cabin began filling with smoke and, as Jordan remembered it, "the floor became so hot that I could feel it through my shoes." Apparently one of the engines was on fire. When the smoke cleared and the plane finally leveled off low enough to see whitecaps reflecting the Caribbean moon, Jordan went up to the cabin to inquire what was going on. The pilots looked very worried. They were working frantically, steering a course for New Orleans, the nearest airport. Jordan went back to his seat and ruminated on the irony of his dying over the already half-dead shah of Iran until they finally touched down safely in Louisiana to the cheers of everyone in the cabin.

Hamilton Jordan and his party eventually got a new air force plane and reached Panama City around 7:30 a.m. on Friday, March 21. Ham had already decided that if he couldn't convince the shah to stay in Panama, it was better to bring him back to Houston for his surgery rather than foist him on Sadat. Sadat was taking a lot of heat for the Camp David Agreements, and Jordan did not want to add the shah to the Egyptian's baggage.

On the ground in Panama City, Ham began making phone calls right away. One was to Bobby Armao, whom Jordan and Torrijos sometimes referred to as "the sissy" with great laughter. Jordan suggested to Armao that he come out personally to Contadora to talk this over with the shah.

Bobby said Jordan or anyone else from the White House could visit if he wanted, but that wouldn't change the fact that the shah and shahbanou were leaving Panama for Egypt. That decision had already been made. Indeed, Armao told Jordan, while he was standing here talking on the phone, packed bags were being carried past him and stacked in preparation for His Majesty's departure.

The other phone call Jordan made was to Lloyd Cutler, the presidential counsel who had negotiated the Lackland agreement. Ham was worried that his negotiating directly with the shah on his possible exit stood a good chance of sabotaging the talks he was having with Ghotbzadeh through Bourguet and Villalon. Jordan wanted the counsel to fly south immediately, perhaps to meet with the shah later that day in his stead, and Cutler was airborne within an hour.

Though Jordan didn't yet know it, his partner in the secret negotiations, Christian Bourguet, was also in Panama.

Iran's French lawyer had come the day before to deal with the shah's extradition. He had brought with him all the material developed by the Iranians to show the UN commission, to be filed as substantiating evidence as part of the process necessary to make a formal claim against the shah as a suspect fleeing

his crimes. In accordance with Panamanian law, the Iranians had been allowed sixty days from their late-January notification of intent to seek extradition. Within those sixty days, Iran had to file its charges and evidence with
the court. If Iran did not, the claim was officially dropped. The final deadline
for making this filing against the shah was March 24, the coming Monday.

According to Bourguet's later account, the shah and Armao had good reason to worry about the possibility of extradition.

When the Frenchman arrived in Panama City on this trip, he was met by
the Panamanian attorney and close friend of Torrijos whom he had engaged
to manage the case in front of the Panamanian courts. The Panamanian lawyer
told Bourguet that once this formal filing took place, there would be more
than enough evidence to require the shah's arrest in preparation for a trial at
which Iran's case would be formally argued. And, the Panamanian offered
knowingly, there was a good possibility Iran might win the trial, should it
eventually be held. This, of course, was assuming that Iran would be prepared
at some future point to compensate Panama for the potential economic price
the country would pay for crossing the United States like that.

Bourguet asked what kind of compensation Panama had in mind.

The lawyer told him one billion dollars.

The Panamanian lawyer added that in the immediate moment, however,
there were more pressing issues to deal with. First, he explained, extradition
law required that Iran's claim be filed by an authorized diplomat from Iran,
and, though Bourguet had standing as the country's legal counsel, he didn't
have standing to make the filing. Bourguet then spent several hours on the
phone finding the nearest accredited Iranian diplomat, who turned out to be
in the UN delegation in New York, a civil servant left over from the shah's
reign. Bourguet had hoped to get the diplomat to Panama in time to file before the courts closed for the weekend, but the diplomat missed two flights
and would not be able to arrive before Sunday. Much to its attorney's frustration, the Islamic Republic of Iran would have to wait until Monday morning to formally file its demand that the Republic of Panama return the
criminal Mohammad Reza Pahlavi to face the music.

Christian Bourguet did not learn that the shah was about to leave Iran
until Friday afternoon, when he was in Torrijos's office, having been summoned there by the general to talk about the extradition case. Torrijos made
no mention of the shah's plans, but then Ham Jordan walked in.

Jordan had already seen Torrijos once that day, enlisting his help in convincing the Panamanian doctors to make it easier for the shah to stay. Now Ham had returned to check on the progress Papa General had made.

"What the hell are you doing here?" Jordan asked, momentarily dumbfounded at the sight of Bourguet.

Bourguet was also taken by surprise. He explained he had returned to file the extradition claim, as he had told Ham he would when they spoke last. What was Jordan doing here?

Ham sighed and launched into the whole story. We've got a problem, he said. The shah wants to leave Panama.

Bourguet's eyes bulged. Leave? Where would he go?

Jordan said either to Egypt or back to the United States.

Now Bourguet jumped in his seat. The United States? he screamed. That would be a disaster. Jordan could not allow this. "They will kill the hostages!" Christian exclaimed. "They will kill the hostages."

Until this point, Torrijos had been sitting quietly. Now he interrupted.

He could keep the shah here, Papa General announced. And he could make him stay for his operation. But he would not do that unless the Iranians immediately transferred the hostages out of the custody of the students. He would give them twenty-four hours. Papa General instructed Bourguet to "tell that to your friends in Tehran."

Bourguet left Torrijos's office shortly thereafter to do just that.

Jordan said nothing through their exchange, "not wanting," he remembered, "to encourage the General's scheme or oppose it."

Bourguet's reaction, however, had a profound impact on Jordan. By the time the chief of staff met with the presidential counsel later that afternoon, he had changed his tune completely on the possibility of the shah's return to the United States. The best option, Ham still believed, was to keep His Majesty in Panama. But the second best, he now thought, was Egypt. That conclusion coincided with the feelings at the State Department, but the president still felt bound to honor the shah's right to reenter the United States as specified in the Lackland agreement.

It was Vance who finally solved the White House dilemma. Vance suggested agreeing to let the shah return, but only on the condition that he abdicate before doing so, ensuring that the visit would be obviously "nonpolitical." The shah would likely reject that option out of hand, but the offer would have been made.

That formulation was added to Cutler's brief when he finally arrived in Panama. (He, like Jordan, had lost a plane on the way south and been delayed.) Once prepped, the White House counsel was taken in a smaller prop plane to Contadora Island, where his meeting with His Imperial Majesty began at almost 10:00 p.m. and lasted perhaps an hour. The counsel insisted that Armao be excluded from the conversation, and he was, even though it infuriated him. The counsel would have liked to exclude the shahbanou too, but she refused to leave. The three of them sat outside in the dark, on the modest house's terrace, speaking English. This would be the last official contact between the Pahlavi dynasty and the government of the United States.

Cutler spent a long time reviewing His Majesty's options. The best one, according to the American, was to stay in Panama. The counsel argued that the Panamanians could be trusted. The Americans would ensure that His Majesty would be operated on at Gorgas by DeBakey and whoever else he wanted. Leaving at this moment might very well destabilize efforts to free the hostages. If he went to Egypt, the move might undercut his friend Sadat as well, at a time when Sadat was very vulnerable. The final option was that His Majesty could, as specified under the Lackland agreement, return to the United States for his treatment. In that instance, however, the United States wanted him to relinquish his throne first, making it clear that this journey was about his health and not about politics.

At that point, the shahbanou could not restrain herself and began speaking sharply to her husband in Farsi. "Don't you dare," she told him. "Think of our son and our people. Abdication would be a disgrace."

When the shah responded in English to the counsel, he declared that he didn't care for himself, but he would not strip that right from his son. Someday the people of Iran would call for the Pahlavis to return. He was not going to abdicate. He did not relish staying in Panama; he knew he was going to die, but he didn't want it to be because of some "accident" on a Panamanian operating table. He also thought Torrijos would eventually sell him to the highest bidder. He would at least prefer his exile in the company of friends, and Egypt, he said with obvious bitterness, was the only friend he had left.

His Imperial Majesty told the presidential counsel he would think about it overnight before giving him a final answer, though his conclusion seemed foregone. "I did not seriously consider the American offers," the shah later remembered. "For the last year and a half, American promises had not been worth very much. They had already cost me my throne and any further trust in them could well mean my life."

Cutler returned to Contadora the next morning for his answer. The house was in an uproar when he arrived, with everything in various stages of being packed, so the counsel — having obviously failed to keep the shah in Panama — now spontaneously switched roles and helped facilitate the Pahlavis' move to Egypt. He apparently felt that having discharged his official position, it was best to fall back on the unofficial strategy of assisting the shah's escape from the extradition process before escape became impossible.

His assistance turned out to be pivotal. Though privy to Torrijos's secret last-minute dealings with the Iranians and with Bourguet's plans to file the extradition papers on Monday, Cutler didn't directly inform the shah and his entourage of either; instead, he simply advised Armao to "get the hell out of here as fast as you can," without providing any specific reason. Armao explained that they planned to travel on Sadat's plane, which was just then being dispatched from Egypt. In all likelihood, it wouldn't be ready to leave Panama on a return trip for at least three days.

That, the counsel responded, was too long. A lot could happen in Panama in three days and, in the shah's case, most of the possibilities were bad. The counsel then got on the phone to the United States and in the space of several hours arranged a charter from an American company widely identified as a proprietary corporation controlled by the Central Intelligence Agency. The chartered jetliner would be waiting for embarkation at Panama City tomorrow morning.

In the meantime, Christian Bourguet was holed up there in the Continental Hotel, on the phone to Tehran. He located Villalon and Ghotbzadeh, and both were soon scurrying around Iran trying to round up the Revolutionary Council, but that was even more difficult than usual. The traditional Persian New Year celebration was under way, and most council members were impossible to find. Eventually Ghotbzadeh located Bani Sadr, but the president of the Islamic Republic at first refused to believe that the shah was going to leave Panama and then refused to attempt to do anything to gain immediate control of the hostages in order to meet Torrijos's deadline. Ghotbzadeh yelled at him to no avail. When Bourguet later phoned Bani Sadr directly in hopes of some last-minute move that would be sufficient to convince Torrijos to force the shah to stay in Panama, Bani Sadr would not even take his call.

Jordan spent that Saturday lying around the American ambassador's swimming pool, ducking interview requests from the press and fielding occasional calls from Bourguet and Torrijos. Ham was committed to staying in Panama until the shah actually left. Cutler, on the other hand, flew back to Washington once his morning business with the shah was done.

By late that evening, His Imperial Majesty's house on Contadora was all packed up and most of its public rooms filled with enormous piles of luggage. The shah had a high fever and low blood counts. The platelets in his blood — the element responsible for its ability to coagulate — were below 10 percent of normal, and the upcoming cross-Atlantic flight raised the risk of his bleeding to death should he accidentally cut himself at high altitude. At the moment, however, he was more worried that the Panamanians would kill him before he could leave.

His Majesty found sleep impossible, so he and Bobby Armao played cards to pass the time. The rest of the house was so still, Armao remembered, "you could almost hear a pin drop." The two of them were watched over by a single Iranian bodyguard armed with a submachine gun.

The shah told Armao that everyone else had left because they expected the Panamanians to kill him that night. He also told Armao that if he too was afraid, he could leave just as the others had done.

Bobby tried to reassure His Majesty that everyone else had just gone to bed. There was no conspiracy afoot.

The shah, however, insisted that his life was in serious danger. This was, he pointed out, the last chance "they" had to get him.

The two of them whiled away the night playing cards, with the feverish monarch sneaking occasional looks over his shoulder to detect anyone who might be sneaking up on him.

The shahanshah's departure from Panama began first thing the next morning, out on Contadora Island's airstrip, which was capable of handling only small propeller-driven planes. One such started ferrying the shah and shahbanou's luggage into Panama City at first light. The original plan had been to depart the capital early in the morning for Cairo, but it took the small plane a half dozen trips to get all Their Majesties' stuff back onto the mainland.

The last load off Contadora was the shah and shahbanou, along with Armao and the dogs. The Great Dane was sick, but Bobby insisted His Majesty not leave the beast behind with a Panamanian veterinarian. The house the shah vacated was, according to its owner, "a mess," the furniture ruined, the drapes torn and soiled. "All he left here," the owner pointed out, "was a lot of dog shit."

The American plane waiting in Panama City was not what the shah had hoped for. A DC-8, it arrived rigged to carry three hundred passengers, with narrow seats jammed together to give maximum hauling capacity. There had been no time to reconfigure the cabin and still reach Panama City at the assigned hour. The DC-8's heating system didn't work well either, so the shah was forced to ride with his legs pulled in to his chest and the rest of him wrapped in blankets. The rented airliner finally lifted off at a quarter to two on Sunday afternoon, Panama time, and was out of Panamanian airspace ten minutes later.

After a long refueling stop in the Azores, His Imperial Majesty, the King of Kings, Light of the Aryans, Shadow of the Almighty, and Vice Regent of God, Mohammad Reza Pahlavi, landed in Cairo — the place where his exile had begun and where it would soon end. The American charter company charged the shahanshah $275,000 for the flight.

Anwar Sadat was again waiting on the runway, standing in the bright sun of Monday afternoon, backed by a military honor guard. The Egyptian ruler hugged the shah when he finally made his way down the boarding ramp.

"Thank God you're safe," was the first thing Sadat said to him.

Zbigniew Brzezinski had been very skeptical about the dance Ham Jordan was doing with the "two Frenchmen" from the beginning, but had accepted it. After the scenario collapsed, however, he felt the time had come to reassert himself in the hostage policy discussion.

On March 11, the day the UN commission left Tehran, Zbigniew Brzezinski began attempting to steer Iran policy away from the strategy of negotiation. At that day's meeting of the Special Coordinating Committee in the windowless White House Situation Room, the national security adviser returned to promoting the military options he had stored in the SCC's policy closet since December. As usual, it was Brzezinski on one end of the discussion and Vance at the opposite.

Brzezinski thought the hostages wouldn't be released until Iran had been convinced it would pay a stiff price if it didn't let them free. His personal recommendation was that the United States seize Kharg Island in the Persian Gulf, a principal Iranian terminal for oil exports, and hold it until the hostages were released.

Vance countered that the Iranians would only surrender the hostages when Khomeini was convinced they had served their purpose in establishing the Islamic Revolution inside Iran. World opinion meant nothing to him, and military action by the United States would only enlarge his domestic power base. It was painful, Vance said, but the national interest and the safety of the captured diplomats must take priority. They had to wait this out.

The same argument had been repeated to the SCC by Vance's deputy, Warren Christopher. State had been under instructions from the president to come up with a proposed list of increased sanctions against Iran, but the list Christopher presented did not even include breaking diplomatic relations. Carter himself wrote the comment "Worse than nothing" in the proposed list's margin. Brzezinski agreed, calling State's timid sanctions a travesty, and proposed that instead, the United States set a deadline for the hostages' release. If the Iranians didn't meet it, then the United States should begin striking targets in Iran until they did.

Brzezinski couldn't get that option seriously considered by the rest of the SCC, but his point that the policy needed to be reassessed made headway with the president. After reviewing the report Brzezinski sent him about a March 18 SCC meeting, Carter ordered a full-blown National Security Council gathering out at Camp David for the following Saturday.

In the meantime, Brzezinski's military subcommittee began meeting regularly again. Most of its proposals were still abstract and largely hypothetical. The one project that was active and almost ready to roll was the rescue mission being mustered around Colonel Charlie Beckwith and his Delta Force. That possible rescue was the first item on the agenda at the Camp David meeting on Saturday.

The gathering convened at 10:45 a.m., with the arrival of most of the participants by White House helicopter. Eight people were present, including Brzezinski; Vance; Brown, the secretary of defense; and Turner, the director of central intelligence, most of them wearing jeans or khakis. Ham Jordan was still down in Panama.

The chairman of the Joint Chiefs' briefing on the possible rescue was long and detailed. Many of the previous blank spots in the plan had been filled. The rescue was, according to one of the NSC staff, "designed to be accomplished in a series of related steps, each of which would be reversible without escalation and with minimum casualties should something go wrong." The first of those steps entailed pre-positioning equipment and men around the Indian Ocean in order to avoid a last-minute rush that might alert watchers that something was going on. Once this step had been accomplished, the time between the decision to conduct the rescue and its actual launch would be greatly reduced.

The operation itself would be "grueling and technically difficult" and would take place over two successive nights. As soon as darkness fell on the first evening, eight RH-53D Sea Stallion helicopters and six C-130 transport planes would take off from different bases and cross more than five hundred miles of the Iranian desert, to rendezvous at the Desert One location, near the small town of Tabas in the midst of the great Iranian alkali flats. It was this initial insertion that might very well be the most daunting. Flying helicopters that far, in the dark, below radar, and in radio silence was, as one NSC aide put it, "a heroic achievement in its own right." The choppers would fly empty to Desert One, and the C-130s would bring in Beckwith and the Delta Force as well as fuel to replenish the helicopters. The C-130s would then fly back while the choppers dropped Delta Force at a location southwest of Tehran and proceeded to a hiding spot north of the city. By then it would be first light, and everyone would spend the day in hiding.

The actual assault on the embassy compound would take place on day two, once it was again dark. The Delta Force would be ferried into Tehran on trucks and then go over the walls. Everyone agreed that as long as all the hostages were, as American intelligence indicated, inside the compound, this would likely be the easiest part of the operation. They anticipated little difficulty subduing any resistance offered by the students. The helicopters would then retrieve Delta and the hostages at the soccer stadium up the block from the compound and ferry them all to an abandoned airstrip outside of the city. More C-130s would meet them there, take everyone on board, and fly to freedom. The choppers would be destroyed and abandoned.

In the ensuing discussion, Brzezinski harped on how many places along the way this mission could be exposed and undone. The chairman of the Joint Chiefs described the national security adviser as "pessimistic" about the plan's prospects. Vance wasn't even that. He pointed out that in complex operations like this, something always went wrong and this one would be no different. At the very least, it was almost a certainty that some of the hostages would be killed.

The president, as always, had the final word on the subject. Carter said he was not prepared to pursue the rescue until he had no other options and, at the moment, he felt that the negotiating track still had possibilities. Jordan, Bourguet, and Villalon were not yet done. Carter preferred to put off the rescue decision for another ninety days while other things played out. He was not, however, ready to reject the plan simply because some of the hostages might be killed. That was a possibility even without a rescue.

The chairman of the Joint Chiefs responded that one of the complicating factors to the president's wait-and-see approach was the arrival of summer in Iran, when the nights would get shorter and shorter. If they waited too much longer, they would have to redesign the operation for three days in order to maintain the cover of darkness, making it even more difficult than it already was.

Carter asked what he needed to do now to lay the base for his future decision.

The chairman had several preparatory actions requiring presidential orders and laid them out. Perhaps the most significant of those concerned the Desert One location. To make sure it was suitable, they needed to send a reconnaissance plane in to examine the site up close.

Carter had rejected taking this step in January and again earlier in March, but now he agreed.

Almost a week after the Camp David meeting, four days after the shah landed in Egypt, the reconnaissance mission was dispatched with the next full moon to a grid on the map thirty miles outside of Tabas, a virtual ghost town in Khorasan Province. Desert One was on the eastern verge of the Kavir Desert, a vast flat tract of wasteland at the heart of Iranian territory, baked and often windswept, with widely separated, tiny settlements connected by narrow threads of asphalt. "Go to Tabas" was a colloquial curse among Iranians, equivalent to "go to hell," and that miserable but flat spot was about to enter the American consciousness as the second most recognizable location in Iran.

The reconnaissance mission to Desert One was composed of two CIA pilots and an air force officer. As they flew in, the moonlight made the alkali flat shimmer like a dinner plate. The night was clear, the wind minimal, and their light plane landed without incident. If their aircraft had somehow been disabled, the three were under orders to begin walking toward the nearest border, carrying a radio beacon to guide the rescuers who would come after them. No one had bothered to tell the mission planners that one of the CIA pilots only had one leg and wasn't much of a hiker. The pilots just laughed about it with each other.

Once on the ground, the three collected soil samples, took photos, and tested the density of the surface. Convinced the desert floor would support the C-130s if it came to that, the three also erected a light beacon that could be switched on by remote control when American planes approached the area. They saw several vehicles pass on the road that cut through the salt flats nearby, but were undetected themselves. Once finished, the three Americans took off and were out of Iranian airspace with no one the wiser.

That evening, Washington time, the White House was notified that Desert One was good to go.

· 24 ·

————————

*I*N THE MEANTIME, THERE WERE STILL MORE NE-
gotiations to be pursued. Another scenario, known as the "Second Revision,"
had been constructed by the same cast of characters during thirty-six hours
of negotiation over three days at Bern's Bellevue Palace Hotel in the immediate aftermath of the first scenario's failure.

The starting point of this new scenario had been a promise from Bani
Sadr to Jordan, communicated by Bourguet and Villalon two days after the
UN commission left Tehran. In it, Bani Sadr had pledged that the hostages
would be transferred from the students to the government before the end of
the month. As planned, the change in custody would lead immediately to
the reactivation of the UN commission and resumption of the previous
failed scenario. Bani Sadr promised the hostage move would happen no later
than March 25, a week after Iran's first parliamentary elections. Ghotbzadeh
endorsed that date as well. But neither Iranian promise had proven anywhere near on the mark.

Instead, the Islamic Republican Party dominated the first round of Majlis elections, and the shah's escape from extradition in Panama was a lead news story inside Iran for days. Out on Taleghani Avenue, suddenly rejuvenated crowds swarmed in front of the Den of Spies, shouting "*Marg bar Amrika,*" in the first spontaneous demonstration there in weeks. A number of Islamic clergy used the occasion to revive the call for trying the hostages. Ghotbzadeh, Bani Sadr, and their backers on the Revolutionary Council tried to depict the shah's flight to Egypt as a victory for Iran, since it demonstrated he was little more than a criminal escaping the reach of the law, but the damage control was only partially successful. Instead of acting like a catapult, the Panama extradition attempt ended up acting like an anchor, making any change in status for the captive Americans even harder to pull off.

The situation could not have been more demoralizing for Christian Bourguet. He had hoped the arrest of the shah by Panama would set off a wave of Iranian jubilation, giving Bani Sadr and Ghotbzadeh the momentum they would need to take control of the hostages. Now he felt little but despair and expressed it openly to Ham Jordan over the phone before leaving Panama.

It was the first time Ham had heard this kind of negativity from Bourguet and he moved quickly to bolster his friend before he returned to the fray in Iran. Jordan asked him to fly through Washington on his way back to Paris and then on to Tehran. He told the Frenchman that he wanted him to meet Jimmy Carter.

When Bourguet arrived on March 25, however, the president was not in a patient mood. He was in the middle of losing the New York and Connecticut primaries and was very, very tired of being jerked around. The hostages were supposed to be in the government's hands by now and instead there was no sign whatsoever of any movement in Tehran.

Ham cautioned his boss that he was trying to buck Bourguet up, so the president slapped a smile on his face and met with the Frenchman in the Map Room, a small formal chamber on the ground floor of the White House residence that Carter used occasionally for meetings. Bourguet looked "haggard," according to Ham, and "clearly discouraged by events in Panama."

The president greeted Christian as "our hero" and delivered a warm handshake. He sat on a couch and motioned Bourguet onto the stuffed chair across from him. Jordan also stayed in the room, along with an interpreter. Carter told his guest how grateful he was for everything the Frenchman had done and in what high regard he held him. Carter was also sorry for what had happened in Panama and hoped it wouldn't complicate the larger picture of the hostages. Carter pointed out that they had tried to convince the shah to stay in Panama to no avail. The question now, however, was what to do next.

Bourguet had much the same immediately sympathetic response to Carter as he had when he first met Jordan. The French attorney almost instantly accounted the president a man who meant well. He also gave him a lot of credit and respect for having thus far refrained from military attack.

Carter then made it clear that as much as he appreciated Bourguet and what he had been doing, he was losing patience with all this. He was tired of dealing with a "comic opera in Tehran" that made promises but didn't keep them. They hadn't made any progress at all, he complained with an edge in his voice. The United States was in the same position it was four months ago.

Bourguet defensively launched a review of the history of Iranian-American relations by way of explanation, but Carter interrupted.

Again addressing Bourguet as "Christian," the president said he was going to have to go now — he had only a little time to spare him — but he wanted to give him something to take to Tehran. Carter then picked up a notepad and scribbled down a simple list of the three things the Americans wanted. They wanted the hostages returned, they wanted better relations with Iran, and they wanted an opportunity for Iran to air its grievances. He then tore the page out and handed it to the Frenchman. "You can turn this over to Mr. Bani Sadr and to the Ayatollah Khomeini," he said.

Then the meeting was over. Ham and Christian walked back to Jordan's office. Jordan thought it had been a successful encounter. Certainly Bourguet had sampled the president's irritability. And Bourguet was obviously energized. The Frenchman was now talking excitedly again about what he was going to do when he joined Villalon in Tehran.

As Bourguet was flying east, Jimmy Carter had the State Department dispatch a formal written warning to Bani Sadr through the Swiss embassy in Tehran. After praising the Iranian president's "principled position on the fundamental wrong involved in the holding of hostages," the message made it clear that the United States wanted the hostages transferred within the next week as proof of "real movement towards a prompt resolution of the Crisis." If not, there would be consequences. "In the absence of such a transfer by Monday [March 31]," the message declared, "we shall be taking additional non-belligerent measures that we have withheld until now." It was time to put up or shut up.

Carter reinforced that pressure by letting it be known that the White

House was preparing a new round of much tougher economic sanctions that would be announced shortly. That was followed a day later with another message delivered through the Swiss, putting Bani Sadr on notice that the United States hadn't been fooling about either the deadline or the punishment.

Jimmy Carter's growing pugnacity had emotional roots in the presidential election as well as in the Crisis. He was being called weak and passive by his critics and he bridled at it. Beneath his parsonage style, James Earl Carter Jr. was a southerner and a military officer, and weakness was an anathema to him. Carter had been stung by his losses in the New York and Connecticut primaries. Next Tuesday, the day after his deadline to the Iranians, he faced another primary in Wisconsin, where some early polls had placed Kennedy in the lead. The *New York Times* described the Wisconsin vote as "crucial." For his part, Jordan, the campaign strategist, was worried that the loss of a third state in a row would embed a trend that could be politically fatal. And, as always, his candidate came out swinging. Mondale, Carter's chief surrogate campaigner, was rescheduled to blanket the state, and the president himself managed to find room in his Rose Garden posture to fire several broadsides at Kennedy in a White House interview with Wisconsin's leading newspaper, timed for the weekend before the primary. That same weekend, other administration sources let it be known that changes were in the works for Iran policy, likely of a far more aggressive cast than anything yet seen.

Then, on Sunday, Bourguet and Villalon sent word from Tehran that Bani Sadr would be making a very important statement the next day. They said the president of the Islamic Republic was in the middle of trying to force the Revolutionary Council to take control of the hostages. On Monday, Bourguet and Villalon sent more information — this time that Bani Sadr's statement had been delayed by twenty-four hours, but that the council had voted to take control of the hostages. Once again, a floor at the Foreign Ministry was being prepared for them, and the Swiss were about to be approached to make potential travel arrangements.

The deadline for the hostage switch had been reached, however, and Jimmy Carter was in no mood to ignore it. On Monday, March 31, he convened the National Security Council to formally approve a new list of sanctions, including finally expelling all remaining Iranian diplomats from the United States. "Those present at the NSC meeting," one of Brzezinski's aides remembered, "understood very well that the issue was larger than the limited package of new sanctions. . . . It was the beginning of a new phase of coercion. Military actions were again under active consideration and no one could be sure where this new policy would lead once it had begun."

Secretary of State Cyrus Vance was the major dissenter, still cautioning patience. He'd also brought with him another message from Bourguet and Villalon in Tehran. They said Bani Sadr had reached an understanding with the students. He would reveal the details in a speech at the huge rally tomorrow in celebration of the first anniversary of the Islamic Republic.

At first, Carter refused Vance's approach out of hand. He had made a deadline and it was time for that to be enforced. He was not going to postpone one more time. His critics would eat him alive.

Vance did not, however, back off.

What could they possibly lose by waiting another twenty-four hours? he pleaded.

Carter just stared at Cy for a long while. Finally he asked when tomorrow this rally in Tehran was scheduled.

When Vance answered 4:30 a.m., Washington time, Carter told his secretary of state that he would expect to see Vance here tomorrow at 5:00 a.m. to finish this meeting.

The gathering at 5:00 a.m. on April 1 in the Oval Office included not only the president and Vance, but also Vance's deputy, Warren Christopher, plus the assistant secretary who had been the other half of Jordan's negotiating team. The National Security Council was represented by Brzezinski, his deputy, and another staff member. The president's press secretary and Hamilton Jordan rounded out the group. A fire was burning in the fireplace and they sat around it, drinking coffee and making small talk while they waited for word from Tehran. Ham grinned at his boss and said that this might be the one, but Carter was having none of it. He had heard all that before. He fully expected to announce the new sanctions later in the day, once this hope had fallen through like all the rest.

The waiting ended with a phone call from the Swiss embassy in Iran. The assistant secretary took the call and received a summary of what Bani Sadr had said in his speech to the crowd of almost a million at the Tehran celebrations. Buried in the midst of the lengthy and convoluted oration was a statement, as promised, about the Iranian position on transferring the hostages. "If the United States issues an official declaration," Bani Sadr had said, "and announces it will not, until the formation of the Majlis and its decision on the hostages, make propaganda claims, speak or instigate on the issue, the Revolutionary Council will accept to take control of the hostages." He also wanted the Americans to formally recognize the Majlis's right to resolve the hostage situation.

The ensuing discussion in the Oval Office lasted perhaps forty-five minutes as the group tried to evaluate Bani Sadr's declaration and design a response.

Jordan thought Bani Sadr's position was a legitimate effort to live up to the terms of the Second Revision and ought to be accepted as such. Though he found the insistence on the Majlis's role a little disconcerting, he felt that the prospect of getting the hostages away from the Muslim Students Following the Line of the Imam was worth finding a way around that issue.

Vance thought the Iranian president's announcement was an incremental breakthrough that required the United States to back off further sanctions in order to succeed. Even Brzezinski thought that the acceptance of responsibility for the hostages by the Islamic Republic's government ought to be endorsed by the United States.

The most positive of all about Bani Sadr's statement, however, was Carter. His cynicism of a half hour earlier had been transformed. He had held back from endorsing any of the previous counterfeit breakthroughs, but this time felt like the real thing. The clouds had parted and blue sky was suddenly visible. Jimmy Carter thought that the moment he had been waiting for had finally arrived.

"I was convinced we had an agreement," the president remembered. "The key phrases came through from Iran indicating that Bani Sadr had concluded the deal as outlined."

Gradually celebration crept into Carter's voice. He thought that this was Bani Sadr's strongest statement yet. Carter pointed out that the Iranian president was "gutless" enough that he wouldn't be saying this if he didn't have Khomeini's backing. Carter believed from his statement that Bani Sadr wanted to "resolve this." Carter did not, however, want to accept the Majlis's "right" to settle the situation. That granted them a kind of jurisdiction that, if turned around, might be used to justify trying the hostages.

Warren Christopher finally came up with wording to deal with that objection. They could accept the Majlis's "competence" to deal with the Crisis and leave it at that. This phraseology would be conveyed to the Iranians in another official but secret statement sent to Bani Sadr through the Swiss.

The rest of the Oval Office meeting was devoted to drafting a statement for the world's media about this "positive development" and deciding who should deliver it. The press secretary thought he should give out the news and wanted to avoid Carter's going on television personally to accept Iranian terms. Carter disagreed. This was good news and he wanted to be the one to give it out. He always did that when there was bad news, so why not now? The compromise solution incorporated them both.

First, around 6:30 a.m., the press secretary read a very brief, carefully crafted paragraph to assembled reporters describing Bani Sadr's move as "a positive step." Then, at 7:20 a.m., Carter himself invited a crowd of journalists into the Oval Office.

He was beaming one of the fuller smiles anyone had seen from him in months. "An elated President," the *New York Times* reported, "called in reporters and television cameras to describe Bani Sadr's speech as 'a positive basis' for a negotiated solution and to announce that he would delay the imposition of [the] sanctions he had threatened."

Thanks to the eventual outcome of this episode, the timing and content of Carter's early-morning press conference would soon become issues of some contention. His critics would call his announcement incredibly self-serving. But, at the time, Jordan remembered, "it seemed the natural thing to do." They had to respond to Bani Sadr as quickly as possible, he argued, before this window of opportunity closed like all the others. In any case, Carter's press session about Bani Sadr's message was the nation's biggest story that day. And, as news circulated, the president's early-morning elation proved catching.

Particularly in Wisconsin.

News of this breakthrough with Iran reached Wisconsin just as polls were opening. By the end of the day, Carter had carried the state primary with a margin the *New York Times* described as "a romp." Other observers called it "a tremendous victory" and "a dominant performance."

Abolhassan Bani Sadr, on the other hand, found himself in a very difficult situation. The endorsement of a hostage transfer that he and Ghotbzadeh had once again secured from the Revolutionary Council had not been unanimous. The three most influential religious members, all stalwarts of the Islamic Republican Party, had refused to sign on, and a number of others had abstained. That lack of unanimity gave Bani Sadr great doubts about the backing of the imam, without whom his cause was hopeless. Khomeini was often wont to refuse to even discuss something on which the council hadn't reached a consensus. Bani Sadr was particularly worried about the Americans' acceptance of the Majlis's "right" to settle this. Iran's president had traded that condition for support at the Revolutionary Council and it was now the standard by which the possible transfer would have to be judged.

When the first translations of the statements from Washington reached Bani Sadr very late in the afternoon, Tehran time, he was crestfallen. The Majlis acceptance he was looking for was not there; indeed, the issue was hardly even referenced. Carter's press secretary had devoted one sentence out of four to it, merely reporting that "the Iranian government has said that the hostage issue will be resolved when the new Parliament convenes." Carter himself didn't mention it at all. The State Department document that did address the issue and offered the substitute word *competence* had been transmitted to the Swiss after their embassy was closed for the night and would not be delivered to Bani Sadr until the next morning.

By then, however, he had long since lost his nerve. In the middle of the night, Tehran time, Iran's president decided to cut his losses and issued a public statement saying that the Americans had not met the conditions of the Revolutionary Council's offer to transfer the hostages. Therefore the offer was being withdrawn. Privately Bani Sadr sent word to the Americans through Bourguet and Villalon that he needed more time to work up a unanimous position in the Revolutionary Council.

But Jimmy Carter was not buying it. By late in the evening Washington time, when the president sat down to make his daily diary entry, his earlier euphoria had been punctured. The illusion of agreement had vanished. "I decided to go ahead and call an NSC meeting," he noted, "to impose all the sanctions, expel all their diplomats . . . and to act without further delay."

Actually Carter gave the Second Revision yet another day, as Bourguet and Villalon tried desperately to help Bani Sadr in his return trip to the Revolutionary Council. But on Thursday morning, Carter told Jordan that he was pulling the plug. He explained that Bani Sadr was a coward and had blown his chance to move the hostages because he was afraid to act when the opportunity was there. Carter's words implied disgust with the Iranian and an underlying disgust with himself for having thought they'd actually had a deal. Now, the president confessed, he didn't know what to do. He and Rosalynn had been talking wistfully the night before about how wonderful it would be to spend the coming Easter weekend at Camp David knowing that the hostages "were out of the compound and maybe soon on the way home." It was obvious Carter had abandoned that fantasy now.

Jordan tried to reinforce him, pointing out that Bourguet and Villalon hadn't yet given up. But Carter did not even hear him out. Ham, he said, "the only people who think we're going to get our people back soon are you and your French friends." The one outcome from all of this was that the president and the United States had been made to look foolish. The scenarios were now over. No more deals with people who couldn't deliver. "You've done the best you could," Carter told his chief of staff. "But it just hasn't worked and I don't think it's going to work."

When Ham left the Oval Office that morning, his secret two-and-a-half-month run as a diplomat and international negotiator was done.

It was hard to find anyone around the White House who didn't want to strike Iran after the failure of the Second Revision. Everyone was fed up. Belligerence was now an almost universally expressed sentiment in the hallways, and among the administration's inner circle, momentum passed to the swelling ranks of hawks, led by Zbigniew Brzezinski.

On April 10, the national security adviser sent his boss a memo titled "Getting the Hostages Free." In it, he argued that "the negotiating track had come to an end" and this approach now offered little but "the continued imprisonment of the hostages through the summer or even later." If the president rejected such passivity, he was left with a very difficult choice. Essentially his options were either the rescue operation or what Brzezinski called "the direct application of force," an outright military attack. Since the latter option would no doubt "drive Iran into the hands of the Soviets," Brzezinski urged Carter to pursue the rescue and to do so quickly, before the shrinking summer nights made the mission impossible.

The next morning, Jimmy Carter ordered Brzezinski to convene an urgent meeting of the National Security Council. The time had come to act.

The summons to meet with the president arrived as a surprise to almost all concerned. Ham Jordan had to be stopped at the airport on his way to Atlanta, where he was to be the featured speaker at a couple big weekend fundraisers for Carter's reelection campaign. He immediately turned back to Washington and arranged to fly south later in the afternoon. Despite the last-minute notice, the only one of the president's foreign policy insiders who was not present at the April 11 meeting in the Cabinet Room was Cyrus Vance, the secretary of state. Cy and his wife had left the day before for a long weekend in Florida. It was Vance's first vacation in forever, so no one moved to interrupt it. His deputy, Warren Christopher, sat in the secretary's place at the Friday meeting, but the balance of power shifted dramatically in Brzezinski's direction as a consequence of Vance's absence.

"There are relatively few behavioral absolutes in Washington," Christopher remembered, "but one widely recognized commandment is that it is rarely a good thing to be out of the loop. As I sat there, a surrogate for the Secretary of State, it could not have been more obvious to me that I had not even been within shouting distance of this particular loop. The subject of a rescue mission was so secret that, as I later learned, Vance had not been permitted to brief me." Christopher made numerous attempts in advance of the 11:30 a.m. meeting to find out what was on the agenda, but he was completely unsuccessful.

In any case, the president arrived, according to one of Brzezniski's aides, with "his mind all but made up." After calling things to order, Carter said a few very strong words. It was time, he said, "to bring our hostages home." The nation's honor and reputation were at stake. Action needed to be taken to save them.

The president wanted the room's suggestions and he began by asking Christopher what State proposed. Christopher laid out some negotiating options they were exploring, but it was obvious that the president and the rest of the room had little interest in them.

Next to take the floor was the secretary of defense, who rejected all State's strategies out of hand and began touting the rescue as the only worthwhile option. The chairman of the Joint Chiefs had brought a map and followed the secretary with a briefing on the plan's status. It was obvious from the president's body language that this was what he had called the meeting to hear.

Christopher and Jordan were sitting next to each other at the Cabinet Room table and held a whispered conversation during the briefing.

What do you think? Jordan asked.

Christopher was puzzled. Did Vance know about this?

Jordan said Cy had been aware of the rescue plan from the beginning.

But, Christopher asked, "does he realize how far along the president is in his thinking about all this?"

Jordan didn't know.

When asked for State's response to the rescue, Christopher could only say that he hadn't been briefed on the subject by the secretary and had no basis on which to take a position. That said, he thought that "diplomatic options should [still] be pursued before we undertook such a risky step."

He was the only one there who felt that way. Mondale supported the defense secretary. Enough was enough, the vice president said. Jordan also agreed, as did the press secretary. So did the director of the CIA. And Brzezinski not only agreed but argued that there ought to be an air strike readied for immediate use against Iran in case the rescue mission failed and the national honor still needed to be retrieved.

Just after 1:00 p.m., Carter summed the meeting up. He asked the chairman of the Joint Chiefs the earliest date the rescue could be undertaken.

The chairman said April 24, less than two weeks away. Carter told him to set that date in motion.

Cyrus Vance returned to Washington the next Monday, April 14, and Warren Christopher briefed him first thing on what had taken place at Friday's meeting in the Cabinet Room.

Vance could not have been less pleased. The normally mild-mannered secretary's response was "volcanic," the angriest Christopher had ever seen him. Vance remembered a conversation about the rescue plan with Carter, but the president had given him no hint at the time they talked that any sort of immediate military action was being contemplated. Vance had been consistent and unequivocal on this subject every time it had come up. He was angry at the decision, but he was even more furious that the decision had been made without his involvement. Cy called Jimmy Carter immediately and the two arranged to meet at the White House very early the next morning.

Their Tuesday morning conversation lasted some forty-five minutes. Vance remembered Carter calling this the hardest decision he'd had to make as president. Carter also offered Vance a chance to make his argument to the NSC meeting at 12:45 that afternoon.

Vance and Carter entered the lunchtime meeting together, five minutes late. Brzezinski remembered them both looking "grim." Jordan described them as "stony faced." Carter kicked things off by saying that Cy had serious objections to the rescue, which he had asked him to share with the group. Vance, looking through spectacles perched on the end of his nose, then began to speak, referring to a nearby legal pad for notes.

He was absolutely against this mission, he declared. He had been selling sanctions to the allies as a nonmilitary option, and for the United States to now "use military force without prior warning to them" would seem nothing short of deceitful. In Iran, the Majlis was finally going to be elected. This would be a major step closer to resolution of the Crisis and provide someone with

whom the United States could seriously negotiate. It was no time to break
off contact. The hostages, according to the results of a recent visit from a
group of Red Cross doctors, were in satisfactory health and under no immediate physical threat. A rescue, he declared, was only justified if the danger to
the hostages outweighed the risks posed to them by a military option, and
that was simply not the case.

Vance also expressed doubts about the rescue's possible success and impact. He had spent a long time working in the Defense Department in earlier administrations, he pointed out. He knew about this kind of mission.
This was an elaborate, complex plan in which something was bound to go
wrong. Even if the rescue was technically successful, this raid would almost
surely lead to the death of some of the hostages and some of the rescuers,
not to mention Iranians. And once those hostages were out, there were still
hundreds of American nationals still living in Iran. Those remaining nationals might then become a second generation of hostages. At that point,
Vance claimed, "we would be worse off than before and the whole region
would be inflamed. . . . Our national interests . . . would be severely injured,
and we might face an Islamic-Western war."

When Vance was done, Carter asked if anyone else had any comment.
Vance looked around the room from face to face, "his eyes," Jordan remembered, "begging for support."

None was forthcoming.

After an awkward silence, Carter took the floor himself and presented a
brief summary of why he found Vance's arguments unconvincing. Then he
asked again if anyone else had a comment.

Again, no one did.

Vance sat through this last silence staring down at his notepad.

In case anyone had any doubts, Carter announced that the rescue mission
would go forward.

Then the president and the group switched gears and began to discuss a
number of details of the rescue's final planning. The operation was now only
nine days away. Everybody around the table joined in except Vance. Instead,
he sat silently, just listening and not bothering to take notes. Later, back at
the State Department, Vance confided to Christopher that he was thinking
about resigning.

The same group and a few additional participants met again about the
rescue on Wednesday evening, this time in the Situation Room. The purpose
was to have a final face-to-face briefing from the commanders of the opera-

tion's various aspects. At this point, Carter remembered, "the plans and training had been completed. The necessary helicopters and transport planes on
American aircraft carriers had been stationed south of Iran or nearby, in
such friendly countries as Oman and Egypt. We did not [, however,] notify
the leaders of those countries about [the planes'] purpose."

The rescue mission's military command structure appeared for the
Wednesday evening meeting disguised in civilian coats and ties, figuring that
a raft of uniforms suddenly appearing at the White House would be a dead
giveaway that something military was in the works. Jordan showed up in a
pair of Levi's. The vice president was in a sweat suit and expensive jogging
shoes. Carter wore a blue blazer and gray slacks.

The president opened the meeting at 7:37 p.m. and turned the floor over
to the chairman of the Joint Chiefs to introduce their guests. The first of
those to speak was the general who was commanding the overall mission,
including the various airlifts and the seizure of the abandoned Iranian air
base from which to exit. Under detailed questioning from Carter, he explained that his biggest worry was about remaining undetected. His next
biggest worry was the reliability of the helicopters being used under these ar-
duous conditions.

The second military man to brief those assembled in the Situation Room
was the star of the show, Charlie Beckwith. Beckwith was introduced by the
chairman of the Joint Chiefs as the unanimous choice for this job, and it was
easy to see why: Even in civilian clothes he looked every inch the soldier —
twice wounded in combat, decorated for bravery, straight talking and close-
cropped. He was also a native of Ellaville, in Schley County, Georgia, practically
next door to Plains, so the president and Beckwith made small talk about
mutual acquaintances in south Georgia before getting down to business.

This was Beckwith's first trip ever to the White House, and behind his
tough veneer, he was wide-eyed at it all. He thought Jordan looked "awfully
young" to hold the job he did. He was amazed that the vice president would
show up to a White House meeting dressed like that. Beckwith was also surprised by Jimmy Carter, for whom the soldier had an ingrained political dis-
taste left over from the president's pardon of Vietnam War draft law
violators. Carter, however, "looked good," the colonel remembered, and had
a simple, no-nonsense approach that Beckwith instantly appreciated.

Beckwith's briefing covered the mission from the point Delta Force left
Desert One in the choppers to their eventual escape with the hostages more
than a day later. The spot fifty miles southeast of Tehran where they would

lay up under camouflage netting for the daylight hours was dubbed Desert Two. From there, once night fell, more than one hundred Delta Force troopers would be hauled into the Iranian capital in a half-dozen Mercedes trucks and a couple smaller vehicles that had already been procured by CIA operatives inside Tehran. One small task force would split off to grab the three hostages at the Foreign Ministry as the main body proceeded to the embassy, where the three regular Iranian sentries would be dispatched by snipers using silencers, and the wall would be scaled. Inside the compound, the attackers would divide into three elements: Red, White, and Blue. Red and Blue groups included forty men each and between them would secure the compound and collect all the hostages. White group, the smallest, would set off the attack by detonating an explosive charge against the wall, blowing a hole "big enough for an eighteen-wheeler" and shattering most of the windows in the surrounding neighborhood. Then White would cut off Roosevelt Avenue and seize the soccer stadium on the other side. The liberated hostages would be hustled out the hole and across Roosevelt to the stadium and from there they would all exit in helicopters.

Christopher asked what would happen to the student guards they encountered.

Beckwith responded that the mission's objective inside the compound was "to take the guards out."

Christopher found that answer less than clear. Did that mean they would wound them or tie them up or what?

"No, sir," Beckwith explained. "We're going to shoot each of them twice, right between the eyes."

Christopher was a little taken aback. Did the colonel mean that literally?

Beckwith affirmed that was exactly what he meant. "We were going to kill every guard in the four or five buildings and anyone who interfered with the assault," Beckwith later explained. "We would put enough copper and lead in them so they wouldn't be a problem. . . . A lot of Iranians were going to turn and run for help and when they did, Delta was prepared to hose them down [too]. No question about it. That was the plan. I did not believe that the Iranians in the Embassy would stand toe to toe and slug it out. Yes, there would be the odd person who would because of religion and beliefs shoot to the death. [But] we were prepared to help him reach his maker."

After almost two and a half hours of questions and answers, the president had heard enough. He told the meeting that he didn't want to undertake this operation, but he had no choice. The only thing that could derail it now was the sudden release of the hostages. And when the mission went forward, he told the military men, "you will run it." He expected to be kept informed through the secretary of defense, but the officers in the field would call the shots.

When Carter laid all that out, Beckwith almost collapsed in his chair. "I just didn't believe Jimmy Carter had the guts to do it," he remembered. "Before that meeting in the Situation Room, I wasn't a big Carter fan, but the man impressed me. He wasn't going to allow the mission to be run by a god-damn committee. . . . And the President was going to stay out of it once we got under way. It was a slick command and control setup. . . . I was full of wonderment. The President had carved some important history. I was proud to be an American and to have a president do what he'd just done."

At 9:55 p.m., the meeting broke up and Carter headed back to the Oval Office. Still moved, Beckwith called out, "God bless you, Mr. President," as he left.

Everyone else was charged by the portent of the moment as well. In the mingling immediately afterward, Ham Jordan sought out Cy Vance. Cy had sat through the meeting without comment.

Jordan asked the secretary of state if he felt any better about the rescue after hearing the military's plans.

Vance said he did feel better. But, he pointed out, "generals will rarely tell you they can't do something." He still thought it was an enormous mistake to engage in a military operation as long as there was still the possibility of a negotiated release. This meeting had changed nothing as far as that was concerned.

In the passion of the moment, Cyrus Vance's response disgusted Hamilton Jordan. He thought Vance's refusal to behave like a team player was putting Carter in a difficult position, though the president's chief of staff didn't express that out loud down in the Situation Room.

Ham kept his anger to himself and simply entertained the secret hope that "Cy was going to feel like a damn fool when the helicopters landed on the South Lawn and our hostages climbed out."

The day after Carter approved the rescue mission, he held a morning press conference to announce yet another round of sanctions. If these failed to bring about the hostages' release, he told the international media, "our next step will be some sort of military action." Afterward, Brzezinski worried that this public threat would convince the Iranians to go into a military alert. What was needed, he thought, was "a disinformation campaign that will relax the Iranians."

Jordan volunteered.

Ghotbzadeh was in Paris at the moment, Ham pointed out. What if Jordan met with him there to reassure him that "in spite of all this military talk, we want to keep negotiating." He could also use the opportunity to make sure the Iranians were not about to release the hostages, thus obviating the need for a rescue.

Carter signed off on the idea, and Jordan immediately called Bourguet and Villalon in Paris, saying he wanted to keep the Ghotbzadeh channel open and check on the status of the hostages. Arrangements were made for another secret meeting between Jordan and Ghotbzadeh the following day. This encounter would be the second and last face-to-face contact between officials of the Islamic Republic of Iran and the United States during the Crisis.

Again, the meeting was held in Villalon's Paris apartment. Ghotbzadeh arrived at 3:30 a.m., after Jordan had been waiting there several hours. Sadegh was friendly, but, Ham remembered, "the confident enthusiasm he had shown at our first meeting was gone."

Jordan noted that a lot of water had gone under the bridge since they last saw each other.

"We came so close," the Iranian foreign minister responded, wistfully invoking the now dead scenarios. "But close is not enough."

They talked for a while about what had already happened, disagreeing several times and interrupting each other.

Then Jordan asked for a straight, nondiplomatic answer to the hostage question. When would they be coming back? He wanted to know what Ghotbzadeh really thought.

That provoked the Iranian to rail at the political situation in Iran. The second and final round of Majlis elections was now scheduled for the middle of May, and all public policy seemed to be paralyzed in the meantime. "The hostages are not important anymore," he told Jordan. "If you traveled to Tehran, you would find no one concerned about them. They have become simply a political issue. A candidate who takes a soft position on the hostages can't hope to be elected."

So how long until they came home?

A long time, Ghotbzadeh answered.

How long was that? Jordan pressed.

Ghotbzadeh's voice got quiet. "Months and months," he finally said. The Majlis would decide the issue and they wouldn't be elected until the middle of May. Then it would take the new Majlis at least six more weeks just to get organized before they could even approach the issue.

Jordan's frustration at the assessment seemed obvious.

Ghotbzadeh was apologetic. He appreciated the Americans' impatience, but this long path was, he insisted, "the only way." Ghotbzadeh hoped that in the meantime, "your President doesn't do anything rash, like attack Iran or mine our harbors."

Jordan's mission was to convince the Iranian that nothing like that was in the wings, so his response to Ghotbzadeh's worry came without hesitation, having already been rehearsed by Ham in his mind.

Don't worry, the president's chief of staff answered, Carter would not do anything like that. "President Carter is not a militaristic man," he explained.

Jordan's response sounded convincing, and Ghotbzadeh seemed to swallow the line without hesitation.

Shortly thereafter, the Iranian foreign minister said friendly good-byes, arranging for the two to check in with each other in another month, and left.

Jordan again waited more than an hour until the coast was sure to be clear and then caught a military jet to Washington, his last diplomatic mission accomplished.

Back in the District of Columbia, Cy Vance's dilemma was coming to a head. "He looked worn out," one White House insider remembered, "his temper would flare up, his eyes were puffy, and he projected genuine unhappiness." Vance doubted he could honorably continue in the face of such a fundamental disagreement about such a central question, and over the next five days after his failure at the NSC, Vance approached several trusted confidants about the possibility of his resignation. On April 17, the day Ham Jordan left Washington to see Ghotbzadeh in Paris, Vance first let Jimmy Carter in on what he was thinking.

The president had initiated the conversation with a call to Christopher that morning. Carter had noticed how "despondent" Vance had seemed over the last few days and asked Christopher if there was anything that could be done. Vance's deputy suggested a personal meeting with Vance that afternoon, and the president scheduled it.

What followed was described by Carter as "an extended discussion." Cy told him in the course of it that if the rescue went forward, he felt he would have no choice but to resign. At the time, Carter didn't credit the statement completely. On at least three other occasions over the last three years, Vance had raised the issue of resignation and typically, Carter observed, "after he goes through a phase of uncertainty and disapproval, then he joins in with adequate support for me." At this April 17 meeting, Carter claimed, Vance finally said "he would stay on, but afterward would reserve the right to say that he disagreed." For his part, Vance remembered simply saying that his mind was not yet finally made up and arranging to revisit the issue soon.

By all accounts, Cy Vance had a lot more pushing him out the administration's door than his disagreement about the rescue. He was losing his grip on American foreign policy, and everyone in Washington knew it. "The rush of events in Iran, Afghanistan and elsewhere has thrown his conciliatory, deliberate methods into eclipse," *Newsweek* observed, "and pushed the President into an increasingly hawkish posture. And Vance has no stomach for another eight months of bitter bureaucratic infighting with Zbigniew Brzezinski, the President's increasingly assertive National Security Adviser. After months of preaching a hard diplomatic line, Brzezinski apparently has won the crucial battle for the President's mind." Cy's profound disagreement over the rescue gave him a chance to escape this diminishment sooner rather than later.

As close as the two men were, Carter was ready to part company with Vance as well. "I think he was quite dissatisfied with Vance toward the end," Brzezinski remembered, "and I think Vance was quite dissatisfied with him. . . . There was a mutual disenchantment. . . . I sensed the rupture coming quite independently of the rescue issue, somewhat earlier. I just had the feeling that that relationship was coming to an end." Carter himself never said as much to Vance, but he did admit to being very bothered by the stance Cy was taking about the rescue mission.

Their mutual unease came to a head on April 21, two days after Jordan returned from Paris. That morning, Vance, Brzezinski, and the secretary of defense met with the president to consider what to tell Congress about the coming rescue. The discussion went smoothly, but at the end, Carter mentioned that several officers of the Methodist Church were coming to the White House. Their intent was to encourage the administration not to take military action in Iran. The president told Vance he wanted him to meet with them as the administration's representative.

Vance said that he couldn't in good conscience do that. The deception involved was simply beyond his threshold.

His secretary of state's response shocked Jimmy Carter. This was the first time in his presidency that anyone had ever directly refused one of his orders. Without saying anything, the president stood up, signaling the end of the meeting, and Vance and the others withdrew.

Cy Vance immediately returned to his State Department office and handwrote a letter of resignation on his secretary of state stationery. This ongoing charade was now intolerable.

"I know how deeply you have pondered your decision on Iran," Vance wrote. "I wish I could support you in it. But for the reasons we have discussed I cannot. You would not be well served in the coming weeks and months by a Secretary of State who could not offer you the public backing you need on an issue and decision of such extraordinary importance. . . . Such a situation would be untenable and our relationship, which I value so highly, would constantly suffer. . . . I have the greatest respect and admiration for you and it is with a heavy heart that I submit my resignation. It has been a privilege and a high honor to serve you."

Cy took the letter to the White House personally that afternoon. He met Carter in the Map Room.

"It was one of the most painful days of my life," Vance remembered. "We had become close friends, and I was torn at having to leave him in his time of trouble." When he gave the letter to the president, Carter started to stuff it into his pocket, but Vance insisted he read it on the spot.

Cy then told Jimmy that he would not make his resignation public and would continue to man his post until after the rescue mission was over, but that he would resign however the military raid turned out. "It was clearly understood that my decision was irrevocable," he remembered.

The administration's only odd man out was now simply out.

In the three days that remained before the rescue was launched, all those in the know could only keep their mouths shut, behave as though nothing was going on, and hope for the best.

The United States government made only one known attempt to predict the outcome ahead of time. That was a secret two-page report put together by the Central Intelligence Agency. The CIA guessed that the most likely outcome was the death of 60 percent of the people they were setting out to rescue.

· 25 ·

———————

SURPRISE WAS ESSENTIAL TO THE RESCUE PLAN
and, judging from all of the information available to the Americans, they
would have it. Security at the Den of Spies, once bordering on the paranoid,
was now far more lax. The entries in Robert Ode's diary during the week
leading up to the rescue mission spoke to how mundane and relaxed the
routine there had become.

"Received some mail from home," Ode wrote. "Had about 30 minutes in
the fresh air and sunshine followed by a hot shower. Were about ready to go to
bed tonight when we were taken upstairs and shown some TV — one episode
of *Lou Grant* and two of *How the West Was Won* — really a late, late show performance as we didn't get back to our room until 1:30 a.m.! . . . Were served
fresh scrambled eggs, jam, and really fresh unleavened bread this morning
for breakfast! What a welcome change from the usual stale bread and insufficient jam. However, for lunch we had cold chicken (it was supposed to have
been warm!), a big glob of cold mashed potatoes and another huge glob of
cold spinach! So one can't win around here! Later in the day we were shown

a new exercise room on our floor with a better Ping-Pong table and told that our new hour (we now have been assigned a full hour) will be at 11:00 a.m. daily and if we want to play again we can do so after 10:00 p.m.!"

Outside, the crowds had diminished in both size and ardor. The state of relaxation inside the compound was verified by high-resolution satellite photos. The embassy compound was observed daily by CIA operatives and they were joined on April 21 by a trio of U.S. Army scouts, infiltrated under false identities through the Tehran airport. All reported that the Tehran end of things looked like "a piece of cake."

The Americans stumbled over their best piece of advance intelligence about the embassy on April 23, the day before the rescue was to begin. A cook who had been making meals for the hostages left Iran to visit relatives in Italy and coincidentally happened to be on the same connecting flight from Istanbul to Rome as a CIA agent, with whom he randomly struck up a conversation. It seemed that the cook had personally served the captive Americans their meals. When they landed in Rome, the agent debriefed him and received an up-to-the-minute account of each hostage's location. According to the cook, five were still in the residence and the remaining forty-five were in the chancery. Three more, of course, were being held at the Foreign Ministry.

The next day, April 24, early in the morning, the rescue began as scheduled in Qena, Egypt, at an air base built a decade earlier as part of a Soviet foreign aid program. Secluded in an isolated corner of the facility, the ninety-seven-man Delta Force stood for final inspection before embarking on two C-141 air transports. They were dressed in Levi's, scuffed GI boots, flannel shirts, and army-issue field jackets that had been dyed black. An American flag was stitched onto each jacket's right shoulder but covered with tape. The flags were to be uncovered when they crossed over the embassy wall. Many were unshaven, others bearded. They all wore navy watch caps, and no one displayed any insignias of rank.

After inspection, the rescue force gathered in one of the base's empty hangars, sand flies swarming everywhere. A major read out loud from the Old Testament First Book of Samuel, recounting the story of David and Goliath, then, according to Charlie Beckwith, they prayed "for guidance and strength." Afterward, the men of Delta spontaneously began singing "God Bless America." The words echoed off the hangar roof. Eyes were wet, hearts stirred, and the troops were higher than Beckwith had ever seen them. This, he thought, was a very good sign. They were "rarin' to go."

Everyone in the operation felt that if the mission was to be canceled, it would happen at Qena, before they deployed to their forward jump-off position in the nation of Oman. But no cancelation orders were transmitted. Instead, Delta Force saddled up, and the two C-141s ferried them and all their ammunition and hardware down the Red Sea and then east to Masirah Island in the Arabian Sea off the Omani coast along the far eastern end of the Arabian Peninsula. At an air base there, the Delta troopers lay down to catch a few hours' sleep in the sixteen-man tents erected for them. They would set off after their layover in a fleet of six smaller C-130 transports, including three to haul fuel for the choppers. Actual embarkation on the mission was set to begin at 6:00 p.m., timed so the sun would set before they crossed into Iranian airspace. Two hours later, the eight RH-53D Sea Stallion helicopters flying empty but carrying extra fuel tanks would lift off from the aircraft carrier USS *Nimitz* in the Persian Gulf, closer to the Iranian coast. If all went according to plan, they would rendezvous in a synchronized schedule at Desert One.

The first C-130 to leave Masirah Island carried various elements of Delta, including a detail to secure the salt flat where they would be landing and the road that ran through it. Also on that flight was Charlie Beckwith. The rest of the C-130s would leave an hour later and reach the secured strip shortly before the helicopters. Beckwith's plane crossed the Gulf of Oman at 2,000 feet but dropped to 400 when it reached the Iranian coast. "To fly through the seams and into the gaps of the Iranian ground radar," he remembered, "it was necessary to fly a lurching, stomach-tumbling route — hard to port, hard to starboard, up and down, sharp again to port, a sudden dip. It went this way, irregularly but constantly, for several hours."

The lead C-130 was more than halfway to Desert One when news was flashed to Beckwith that all eight helicopters had left the *Nimitz* and were on the way. The five other C-130s were already airborne. Everyone was on schedule. The troops flying with Beckwith were sitting elbow to elbow, with their equipment strung on the netting covering the wall behind them. The only light inside the fuselage came from small red bulbs. No one said much and few moved. Some were airsick from the ride and quietly barfed. Beckwith himself was strapped in but racing back and forth in his mind, chasing random details about what was to come next.

The advance elements of Delta Force finally set foot on Iranian soil at almost 10:00 p.m. Tehran time, just as planned. The C-130 switched on the faint runway markers set up earlier by the CIA scout, circled once, then landed on a crude, unimproved road, taxiing west to east.

Looking out over the vacant alkali flat, Charlie Beckwith felt as though the rescue was on a roll.

And then it began to come apart, slowly but surely.

First, while the road watch team assigned to securing the area was still unloading its jeep and several motorcycles from the C-130, a Mercedes bus with forty-five religious pilgrims rolled right up the road into the middle of their deployment. The bus was traveling east to west and bound for the shrine at Qom, outside of Tehran. The road watch team disabled the Mercedes's engine and herded the passengers and driver into an area where they were held under guard. Though unexpected, an encounter with Iranian civilians was a possibility that had been addressed in the plan. The pilgrims were to be flown out on the last departing C-130s, to keep them from reporting what they had seen, then returned to Iran the next day on the planes that would fly into the abandoned air base outside of Tehran to fetch the completed mission.

But the complications didn't stop there. No sooner was the bus dealt with than a tanker truck's headlights appeared in the distance, followed by a pickup. The driver of the tanker, likely smuggling gasoline, slammed on his brakes when he saw armed men ahead and began turning around. One of the Delta Force fired a handheld rocket to stop him, disabling the tanker and setting it afire. Its driver ran back to the trailing pickup, and it sped away before the Road Watch could start up a motorcycle to give chase. Soon, flames two hundred feet tall were rising out of the burning wreck.

Suffice it to say, the five incoming C-130s had no problem finding the place.

Once the planes were all on the ground, two were sent back right away and the other four lined up several hundred yards apart to wait for the helicopters. Delta Force began offloading equipment and staging it in order to quickly fill the choppers once they arrived. If all had gone according to plan, the helicopters would have been there fifteen minutes after the last C-130 landed.

But they weren't. Unbeknownst to Beckwith, his helicopter fleet was in serious difficulty. The eight RH-53Ds had last been heard from right after takeoff, when they were still together in formation, headed for Iran. Ever since, however, they had been under orders to maintain strict radio silence. And they had been having trouble almost the entire time.

The first problem arose about an hour in, when a warning light came on in the cockpit of chopper 6. The light was attached to a high-tech system designed to detect possible cracks in the craft's rotor blades. Forty-three such warning episodes had been experienced before in the collective history of this model Sea Stallion and, after inspection, none of them had revealed any verifiable crack. Nonetheless, peacetime navy regulations said that the chopper could be flown a maximum of five hours after the light came on. Chopper 6 was landed in Iranian territory and abandoned, its crew transferred to one of the other choppers.

Now down to seven aircraft, the group headed off across the uninhabited Iranian wasteland toward Desert One and hit even worse trouble almost immediately: a haboob, a sandstorm that filled the air for hundreds of miles with fine white dust whipped up to enormous heights off the desert floor. Haboobs were a regular part of the seasonal weather cycle in Iran, and the possibility had been included in the plan's weather appendix, but this particular one came as a complete surprise. The Iranian weather stations that normally reported on such storms over these deserts had been closed in the breakdown of services after the Revolution, and haboobs were invisible to American weather satellites. The possibility of running into one of these storms had in fact been considered unlikely enough that the pilots had never been trained how to fly through one. Vision was nonexistent, and the choppers flew by instruments only, at the lowest altitude, in continuing radio silence. Soon they were all separated and out of formation, constantly fearful of running into one another.

When the choppers regrouped after finally exiting the first haboob, they hit a second, even larger one that lasted until they were within a half hour of Desert One. Now the flight was scattered completely, and after almost two hours in this second haboob, one of the RH-53Ds encountered yet another mechanical failure. This time chopper 5 lost two of its essential navigation instruments and had to return to the *Nimitz*. Only six choppers now remained, the absolute minimum number necessary to continue the mission as planned.

And all six were now very late. Beckwith and Delta Force waited near the still-blazing tanker amid the roar of four idling C-130s, checking watches and wondering where the hell the choppers were. The first chopper to arrive was almost an hour behind schedule, and the last would be almost an hour and a half late.

Beckwith ran through the darkness to greet the first pilot to set down —

a man he knew and respected — and found him taking a leak on the other side of his aircraft. Charlie asked how he was doing. The pilot just looked at him for a while and then said that if they had any sense they'd just ditch the choppers now, load everybody in the C-130s, and go home. It had already been a "hell of a trip" and would probably get worse. He had no idea where the rest of the flight was.

Each subsequent helicopter to arrive came in from a different direction, and all of the pilots were clearly shaken, some already exhausted. Their state bothered Beckwith, but the timing itself was even more troublesome. Delta Force was now in danger of not making it to Desert Two before dawn. If they were caught out in the light of day, the risk of exposure would escalate exponentially. The helicopters would have to be loaded immediately, refueled, and got on their way. As Beckwith was hustling that operation along, however, the next piece of bad news arrived — and it turned out to be the straw that broke the camel's back.

Chopper 2 had a malfunction during the flight in, its pilot reported, and had burned out its hydraulic pump. All the equipment the choppers had brought along to fix such problems had been in chopper 6, abandoned before they hit the haboobs. Chopper 2 was now useless.

That report hit Beckwith like a two-by-four across the eyebrows. Not only was he so late his troops might well end up caught out in the open, but he had only five helicopters left. According to the plan, when reduced to that number, the mission would have to be scratched. Grinding his teeth, Beckwith got on the radio and notified the chain of command that they were facing an "abort situation."

Charlie Beckwith knew what he thought the moment required, but this was a decision that had to be made in the White House.

Back there, the day had been spent by those in the know attempting to hide their anticipation. Their orders were to maintain secrecy by pursuing business as usual, and they all did so. Because of the time difference, the mission thus far had roughly coincided with normal administration working hours. "It was an eerie feeling," Walter Mondale remembered. "We had been told the mission was under way, but almost everyone we dealt with had no idea it even existed. The curse on the country might have been about to lift and we couldn't let on, not the least little bit."

That went for Jimmy Carter just like everyone else. At 4:30 p.m., the president hosted a campaign meeting in the Oval Office with Jordan and a number of his re-election staff. Fifteen minutes into it, the phone rang and Carter took the call. He listened a moment, then hung up without saying a word. Quickly excusing himself from the meeting, the president went next door to his small private office, where Brzezinski was waiting for him. The secretary of defense had called, his national security adviser explained. There was a serious problem at Desert One. They were down to five helicopters and facing a decision to abort.

Carter picked up the red "secure" phone and spoke with his defense secretary. He was told that Beckwith and the rest of the chain of command all thought going forward was now impossible and recommended the rescue be called off. The president only hesitated a moment before telling the secretary to go with Beckwith's recommendation.

At 4:57 p.m. Washington time, twelve minutes after the secretary of defense learned of the last helicopter failure, orders were transmitted back to Desert One to abandon the rescue and return to base. The C-130s would fly back to Oman and the choppers back to the *Nimitz*.

At the same time, Jimmy Carter quickly assembled his inner circle in his private office. Brzezinski was already present. The defense secretary was on his way over. Carter called Jordan in the Oval Office and instructed him to find a way to leave the campaign meeting and join him next door. The president also told Jordan to bring along the press secretary and Mondale. Cyrus Vance was chairing a different meeting down in the Situation Room and was given a note saying to meet the president in his private office immediately. Warren Christopher eventually joined him there. Jimmy would have liked to invite Rosalynn as well, but she was in Texas acting as his surrogate campaigner. He did, however, make time for a phone call to give her a hint of what was going on.

When almost everyone had assembled, the president announced to them that he'd had to abort the rescue.

The room fell deeply silent for a long time, flooded with disappointment.

Finally the silence was broken by another phone call, again on the red phone. Carter answered, listened for a moment, and then turned whiter than anyone in the room had ever seen him.

Out at Desert One, disappointment had now turned into disaster.

Word that Carter had agreed to call off the mission reached Beckwith shortly after 2:00 a.m. Tehran time. By then, all of the serviceable choppers at Desert One had been refueled and were awaiting orders. The tanker truck was still burning but with far less ferocity. The order to abort spread quickly. Delta Force was to return in the C-130s and began removing its supplies from the choppers and reloading the transports. Worried that one of the C-130s would take off before he had all his men loaded, Beckwith was making his way from cockpit to cockpit to remind them to await his order before embarking. In the meantime, the chopper that had been the first to arrive began to maneuver toward one of the fuel transports to top off its tanks. This first chopper had been idling its engine, waiting for the others to arrive, and would need all the fuel it could carry for the return flight to the *Nimitz.*

Then all hell broke loose. The chopper had risen about twenty feet off the ground to move over to the transport, but its pilot misjudged the distances involved. Beckwith saw the helicopter tilt to its left and then heard a loud boom as the chopper's blade sliced into the fuselage of the C-130. A ball of fire erupted immediately, engulfing both aircraft. Flames leaped more than three hundred feet into the air. The stash of handheld missiles inside the C-130 started going off, exploding in a giant fireworks display. Beckwith tried to run to the burning planes, but the inferno made it impossible to even get close. Most of the men on the C-130 had escaped, but eight crew members from the plane and the chopper had been burned to death and four others seriously injured. Beckwith was worried that the .50-caliber ammunition on the helicopter closest to the fire would start to cook off from the searing heat and withdrew his men back to the undamaged C-130s as quickly as possible. Some abandoned everything, including their weapons, in their haste.

With flames leaping to the sky and explosions tearing through the night, Desert One was becoming uninhabitable. Beckwith notified the chain of command that he was abandoning the choppers and loading the orphaned flight crews into the C-130s. Standard operating procedure would have been to set thermite charges in the abandoned craft to make sure they were destroyed, but Beckwith deemed that far too dangerous if not physically impossible at the moment. As a consequence, five intact Sea Stallions were left behind, some of them carrying crucial intelligence papers about the failed mission, including indications that there were agents already in Tehran ready to assist the attack on the embassy.

Beckwith's C-130 was the last to lift off from Desert One. Behind it, pillars of fire lit up the salt flats bright as day, silhouetting the cluster of abandoned helicopters. The Iranian pilgrims stood by their disabled bus on the edge of the conflagration and watched the Americans retreat. Beckwith's plane rumbled down the makeshift airstrip, but just as it was picking up speed, the plane's landing gear hit a three-foot-tall berm, bounced into the air, and came back down with a thud. At that moment, Beckwith was convinced they had all "bought the farm." Somehow, however, the pilot managed to keep the plane's engines roaring, and the transport was able to rise shakily into the air and gain altitude.

Beckwith checked his watch. The evacuation was completed at almost 3:00 a.m., the time when Delta Force had been originally scheduled to be reaching Desert Two.

Back at the White House, Carter was stunned by the news of eight dead. At first, the president insisted that he would call the next of kin personally. He had to be dissuaded by the secretary of defense, who said that the military had an established system for passing on such news and that an additional call by the secretary of the air force or the navy would suffice. Watching the president's agonized insistence, Ham Jordan could see that somewhere down deep his boss thought that making those phone calls was a way to atone for the decision he had made to send those men into harm's way in the first place.

As a few others joined the original group in the private office, they all moved to the Cabinet Room and fell to the task of damage control. A public statement would have to be made — the debacle would be impossible to hide, and it was better to make the announcement themselves rather than wait to be exposed — but what to say and when to say it were open issues. The director of central intelligence was particularly worried about the timing. His agency still had men on the ground in Tehran who had been assisting in preparations for the rescue. Before any word from the United States government informing the world and, more important, the Iranians, of what the Americans had been up to, Turner wanted time to get his agents to safety. He insisted on having as long as possible to do so. The other side of the timing issue was framed by Vance. If anything that had gone on thus far at Desert One alerted the Iranians before an American announcement, they might consider the mission to be ongoing and take reprisal on the hostages. By that standard, the sooner the announcement, the better, a position that eventually carried the day.

The Cabinet Room group's deliberations were conducted in an agonized stupor that afflicted everyone to varying degrees, but no one more than Hamilton Jordan. The president's chief of staff could not keep from seeing the bodies of the dead men at Desert One in his mind. They were charred and in his imagination, he could smell them very clearly. Eventually he became dizzy, and he had to take a walk to clear his mind. Jordan stumbled through the empty Oval Office and outside onto the South Lawn. The night was so warm and muggy that it became hard for Ham to catch his breath. This chased him back into the air-conditioned West Wing, where he walked to his own office and then to the Oval Office. As he got there, he was seized with a paroxysm of nausea, rushed into the president's private bathroom, and vomited up everything in his stomach.

By the time Jordan returned to the Cabinet Room, the subject had switched to the public statement the president would make at 7:00 a.m. They had already drafted a first announcement to be released by the press secretary at 1:00 a.m. This announcement, as it turned out, was the first the Iranian government would learn of the American military penetration of its borders. The press secretary told the meeting in the Cabinet Room that once he had let the world know the brief facts, Carter had to then give the American people the rationale for attempting the rescue when he spoke tomorrow morning — "why we did it and why we did it now."

In response, Carter made his only attempt at humor of the evening. He looked straight at Cy Vance, the lame-duck secretary of state whose resignation would be publicly announced in another two days, with a hint of a smile. Perhaps, he suggested, Cy would draft such a statement for him, laying out the mission's rationale.

"The President's attempt at humor was his strange way of acknowledging that Cy's reservations about the mission had proven to be wise," Jordan explained. But "Vance, caught off guard and clearly uncomfortable, [just] looked down at the table." Jordan experienced a bittersweet respect for Vance in that moment. "If you examined Vance's demeanor through the long night," he remembered, "you wouldn't have suspected that he was any less responsible for the disaster than the rest of us. Given the kind of man he was, he would never have said, 'I told you so.'"

Vance stayed at the White House until well after 11:00 p.m., working on the president's fifteen-paragraph statement that would be broadcast live on the nation's radio and television outlets. Those involved in the drafting finally dispersed well after midnight, except, of course, Jimmy Carter. He had summoned Rosalynn home from Texas, but she would not arrive until the next day, so he was alone for what was very likely the longest night of his life. The president managed only a couple hours sleep before rising to practice his 7:00 a.m. address.

PART SIX

ENDGAME

· 26 ·

THE DIRECTOR OF CENTRAL INTELLIGENCE HAD told the president in the days before the rescue mission was launched that any other resolution than the commando raid would be at least six months in bearing fruit, perhaps nine. Sadegh Ghotbzadeh had told Hamilton Jordan when they met for the last time that it would be "many" months before a solution emerged. Hostage Barry Rosen had guessed back in January that the Crisis might keep him imprisoned until at least November 1980, when the Americans held elections. Former secretary of state Cyrus Vance had counseled patience to allow time to ease the impasse. The original State Department analysis on day five of the Crisis had predicted it would most likely be more than a year before a solution was found. And they were all right.

The first issue resolved in the remaining 270-day process was the fate of the shah.

When Mohammad Pahlavi landed in Cairo after escaping Panama City, he was feverish, his blood counts were in a state of collapse, and his spleen was so swollen it threatened to burst. Anwar Sadat had planned for the shah and shahbanou to helicopter with him and Mrs. Sadat to the presidential residence to chat some before he checked into Maadi hospital, Egypt's best, but the shah wasn't even up for that. Instead, he was flown straight to the medical facility. To receive the shahanshah, the fourteen-suite VIP wing on the second floor had been entirely emptied of its previous occupants — two paraplegic Egyptian army officers — and redone with new mattresses and color televisions. The shah's wing included a one-bed intensive care unit, space for all his retinue and security force, and suites for the shahbanou and his twin sister, Ashraf, as well as himself. A military hospital, Maadi was run-down by American standards and somewhat spartan, even on the high-rent second floor.

Three days after His Imperial Majesty checked in, Dr. Michael DeBakey flew from Houston to Cairo in a chartered Boeing 707, hauling a support team of American physicians, including Rockefeller's doctor, and several pieces of medical equipment to be installed for His Majesty's treatment. The medical workups on their patient were hardly encouraging. In addition to his fever and blood counts, X-rays revealed that his cancer had begun spreading to several other locations around his body. DeBakey recommended immediate surgery to extract the spleen — the same surgery he had set out to do in Panama City — explaining to the shahbanou that this would prolong her husband's life, perhaps for a few years.

The surgery took an hour and twenty minutes. The shahbanou and other members of the entourage watched it all on a video monitor, listening to a running commentary from Rockefeller's doctor. He noted that the spleen DeBakey removed, normally the size of a fist, was now, "one foot long, literally the size of a football." The extracted organ weighed almost five pounds. The liver, right next door, had turned a mottled white color from its normal dark red and was obviously riddled with cancer. The greatest danger in the operation involved the tail of the pancreas, which fits into the spleen. Damage to the pancreas in the course of extracting the spleen often led to a postoperative abscess, generating infection and fluid in the abdomen after the patient had been sewed up. To address this possibility, surgeons often installed a drain ahead of time so the location could be flushed if need be, but DeBakey was so confident of his work that he didn't bother installing a drain. Afterward, he announced that the splenectomy had gone "about as smoothly as you could make it" and said his patient "couldn't be better."

Sadat showed his appreciation to his friend's American surgeon by awarding him the First Order of the Republic, the highest Egyptian medal for which a civilian is eligible. The shah spent several weeks in Maadi hospital recovering, as well as beginning another regimen of chemotherapy. When he was deemed well enough, he left to convalesce at a palace Egypt reserved for visiting heads of state. The shah had stayed there when he was only the crown prince, honeymooning with his first wife, the sister of the then king of Egypt. The enormous house was located behind a tall wall, surrounded by a slightly shabby park of gardens and trees — easy to defend and imbued with stature. At first, the shah responded well to the surroundings. "This lovely home," he noted in his memoirs, "offered the first peace, quiet, and security we have known since leaving Iran." Those memoirs were his last attempt at serious work.

By the time the rescue mission failed, the shahanshah's pressing medical issues had returned. Stomach pains were plaguing HIM and, though he didn't complain much, they were too intense to ignore. He was also vomiting and feverish. The Egyptian doctors now responsible for his immediate care were the seventh set of physicians who had ministered to the shah in the last year. They identified a pocket of fluid collecting above His Majesty's diaphragm and then aspirated a sample, using a long needle inserted into his chest. The fluid was full of infection. The Egyptians said that an abscess had developed around the pancreas and that DeBakey should have installed a drain.

What to do next was up to the shah's family, as decisions were now pretty much beyond the shah himself. The shahbanou distrusted the Americans and called the French oncologist who had first begun treating the shah's cancer eight years earlier. When she described what was going on, the Frenchman agreed with the Egyptians' diagnosis of abscess. Princess Ashraf, on the other hand, relied on the Americans. She would normally have turned to Rockefeller's doctor for advice, but he had already told her before he returned to New York that he expected His Majesty would die within weeks and his care should simply allow him to do so with as little pain as possible. That outcome was unacceptable to Ashraf, so she hired an oncologist who had been on the shah's team at New York Hospital and brought him to Cairo. The oncologist wanted to administer an additional program of megadoses of chemotherapy to pull His Majesty back from the brink of death and made a preliminary examination of the shah with that in mind, though the rest of his plan did not proceed. He told Ashraf afterward that the Egyptian abscess diagnosis was right on the mark.

*   *   *

Meanwhile, as word spread in Iraq of what had happened out on the al-kali flat near Tabas, huge crowds had massed outside the Den of Spies, once again shaking the chancery to its foundations with chants of "*Marg bar Amrika.*" Inside, the students considered the sandstorm that had bedeviled the Americans — and likely saved many of their lives — a case of divine intervention, much like Allah's saving Mecca from the Yemenis in the year the Prophet was born. Nonetheless, they took immediate steps to close their own window of vulnerability. Within forty-eight hours of the aborted assault, the students had begun dispersing the hostages around Iran so there would be no possibility of a similar rescue attempt. They called friends, arranged to borrow cars, and solicited commitments of space in which to quarter their "involuntary guests." Worried about security — from the threat posed by their countrymen more than the Americans — the students kept their activities secret and moved their charges at night, often in vans whose side windows had been painted over.

Once the hostages reached places like Tabriz, Qom, Yazd, Jahrom, Mahallat, Khorramabad, Isfahan, and Tabriz, they were spread out among basements, local jails, safe houses, and confiscated estates. As a result, the Muslim Students Following the Line of the Imam were spread out as well, and that dispersal effectively stripped the students of their pivotal political position. Rather than continuing as a concentrated force, almost all of them now disappeared for guard duty in parts unknown. Only a skeleton student crew occupied the Den of Spies, watching just a half dozen hostages who had stayed behind. The students' document section continued to sort through their captured paper, but their televised revelations disappeared from the airwaves. The scene out on Taleghani Avenue was no longer the world's, or even Tehran's, most electric venue. Henceforth, the role of the young men and women who had seized the American embassy and its occupants on November 4, 1979, was largely custodial.

DeBakey was the only physician involved in the shah's care who refused to accept the idea that the splenectomy had left an infection behind, but at the end of April, under pressure from both Egypt and New York, the surgeon returned to Cairo to see for himself. He found the shah feeling slightly better than the week before, with no abdominal pain to which he would admit, no distention of the abdomen, nor any rigidity — all classic signs of an abscess. He told his patient's family that the Egyptian diagnosis was far off the mark, pointing out that "my publications on subphrenic infections and abscess are considered classics in this field." The shah, he insisted, was having a reaction to the conventional chemotherapy he had been getting steadily since leaving Maadi. So, with the family's concurrence, he gave orders to reduce and eventually eliminate the shah's chemotherapy almost entirely. Then DeBakey flew back to Houston, having examined His Imperial Majesty for the last time.

After a little more than a month of the American's program, the shah could no longer hold any food down and registered white blood cell counts at the floor of the scale. He had been given so many transfusions and intravenous meals by then, his wife remembered, "they couldn't find any more veins." By the middle of June, the shahbanou was sure her husband had to return to the hospital, but she could no longer get DeBakey on the phone. The shah's wife then turned to the French doctor and begged him to put together a team to come save her husband's life.

Treating the situation as an emergency, the doctor searched France to assemble a group of surgeons who could fly to Cairo on short notice during the summer holiday season and drain what he was still sure was an abscess. That surgery was conducted back in the Maadi hospital on the last day of June. Altogether, almost a half gallon of pus, fluid, and pancreatic debris was removed from the shah's abdomen. The abscess, according to the French, had been generated by damage to the tail of the pancreas, either by a nick from a scalpel or the pressure of a clamp during the earlier surgery. From Houston, DeBakey continued to deny that possibility and to blame the chemotherapy for suppressing the shah's immune response. He also pronounced himself "cautiously optimistic" about the state of the shah's health.

In Cairo the French surgeons had to go back into His Imperial Majesty's abdominal cavity twice more during the first two days of July to stanch outbreaks of internal bleeding. His infection was now somewhat controlled, but even he no longer believed that he would leave the hospital alive.

The shahanshah's deathwatch lasted almost all of the month of July. Sometimes he sat up, but mostly he lay flat on a stiff camp bed in Maadi's VIP intensive care unit. His wife and his sister often slept nearby in their suites and were daily visitors. Anwar Sadat stopped by regularly, and several of His Imperial Majesty's longtime retainers, including his former ambassador to the United States, were often present as well. Almost until the very end, the shah worked with one of Armao's assistants on last revisions to his memoirs, even when His Majesty's voice was so faint the assistant had to press his ear against the shah's face to hear. The last of the Pahlavi shahs kept a Koran under his pillow and seemed to have come to terms with his fate.

The French oncologist who had first treated the shah in 1974 was at the reins of his care when the final collapse came. His Imperial Majesty's system had simply lost its capacity to resist the infection that was raging in his bloodstream, and his body went into toxic shock during the evening of July 26. After administering transfusions for eleven units of blood, the French doctor gave up and let nature take its course. The shah lasted through the night, surrounded by his grieving family and retainers. Among them all, Princess Ashraf was the most hysterical. At one point during the long vigil, having decided "I wanted to end our life as we had begun it — together," Princess Ashraf retreated to her hospital suite and downed a handful of Valium and sleeping pills. According to her own later account, the concoction hardly dented her and she was soon back at His Majesty's bedside.

The end came at 9:56 a.m. Cairo time, July 27, 1980.

After the shah's heart stopped beating, the shahbanou took the wedding band off his finger and one of the attending physicians took the last tubes out of his arms. Ashraf, in a grieving frenzy, began kissing her twin brother's corpse, from his head to his feet, until she finally felt his skin turn cold. She stood up, swooned, then quickly regained consciousness.

Two days later, Anwar Sadat staged a state funeral for his old friend. Only a few foreign notables attended. The American government had originally decided not to send anyone, but Zbigniew Brzezinski insisted that the United States ambassador to Egypt be dispatched and he was. Former President Richard Nixon attended as a private citizen and told the press at the airport when he landed that the Carter administration's treatment of his old friend and ally had been "shameful."

The funeral itself was a cortege from the Abdin Palace through the ferocious heat of some two miles of downtown Cairo to the Al Rifai Mosque, the same refuge where his father Reza's remains had once lain in exile. The shah's coffin was borne on a military caisson pulled by horses and escorted by a thousand-man contingent of Egyptian soldiers, with a phalanx of army helicopters patrolling overhead. The shahbanou, his children, and Ashraf, wearing dark glasses, walked behind. At several points during this march through the Cairo slums, crowds had to be pushed back by security police using electric crowd-control prods.

At the mosque, the final remains of His Imperial Majesty, Mohammad

Reza Pahlavi, King of Kings, Light of the Aryans, Shadow of the Almighty, and Vice Regent of God, were laid to rest in a crypt next to those of his former brother-in-law, the last king of Egypt, and not far from the crypt that had once housed the shah's father, Reza the Great, founder of the Pahlavi dynasty.

The original cause of the Crisis was now rendered moot. What remained was disentangling the two sides, from themselves as well as each other.

The Islamic Republic's official news agency responded to the shah's passing with an announcement that "the bloodsucker of the century has died at last." Several small celebrations gathered in the streets when word was first released. Otherwise, Iran seemed to react with widespread indifference. It was thought bad form to get too happy over anyone's death — even the shah's — and Iranians had a lot else on their minds in any case.

That summer, according to the National Security Council's Iran expert, "the sense of siege and paranoia in Tehran became intense. . . . The regime seemed to be on the verge of political, economic and military collapse." Iran's oil revenues had now shrunk to half of the level necessary to keep the government operating, inflation was in triple digits, unemployment was officially estimated at 40 percent, and the gross national product had been reduced by at least a quarter from prerevolutionary levels. The Kurds were in an open uprising, fighting regular skirmishes with the debilitated Iranian army. Sabotage in the oil fields was now a daily phenomenon. The revolutionary tribunals were still arresting people and imprisoning them in one of five different prison systems then functioning in the Islamic Republic — all controlled by different political elements and all being put to rampant use. At the same time, tensions along the border with Iraq escalated, including a couple minor military actions. "To the West," one Tehran observer noted during this four-month stasis, "the hostage issue comes first; to the Iranians [however], it has slipped down the list."

And the government was still in no position to grapple with much. A Majlis had finally been elected, with a commanding majority from the Islamic Republican Party, but at the time of the shah's death, the IRP was locked in a rearguard struggle with President Abolhassan Bani Sadr. Furthermore, the Majlis had not yet organized itself or finished selecting a prime minister and cabinet. The once broad-based Iranian Revolution was breaking into factions, and, emboldened by their control of the new parliament and Khomeini's endorsement, clerical forces began launching open attacks on all the others. The imam called for a cultural revolution to return Iran to the days of the Prophet and began insisting that all aspects of Iranian life meet Islamic standards and that women wear the encompassing chador. Opposing demonstrations broke out among women, doctors, and *bazaaris*. The imam ordered the universities closed until they could reopen in a more Islamic incarnation. The clerics denounced the "technicians" who used their expertise to manage society. The dissident press was often either shut down outright or pressured into self-censorship. The leftist mujahideen organization fought street battles with the clerical "Partisans of God." Revolutionary Guards fired into a leftist demonstration massed on Taleghani Avenue in front of the Den of Spies, killing five and wounding many others. Secular politicians were denounced as satanic. Almost everyone anticipated the outbreak of either civil war or another revolution.

There were several attempts at the latter during late June and early July, when the government identified four different coup attempts from various military elements, some thought to be working in cooperation with the Iraqis. Bani Sadr publicly denounced the largest of these schemes during the first week of July. An air force general had planned to seize control of seventeen fully armed US manufactured F-4 Phantom jets from a base in western Iran. This insurgent squadron would then destroy Khomeini's home in Tehran, Bani Sadr's presidential office, a seminary in Qom, and a number of other targets. The plot had also developed a list of seventy revolutionary leaders they intended to arrest and execute, including, of course, Khomeini, Bani Sadr, and Ghotbzadeh. It was the rebels' intention to install a government headed by the shah's last prime minister, now in Parisian exile. Instead, one of the pilots involved gave the others up, and more than six hundred were arrested.

In the midst of this turmoil, the imam still cast the largest political shadow by far. His popularity, though no longer universal, continued to dwarf any other's and often constituted not just acclaim but religious devotion. The Islamic Republic's supreme guide had checked out of the coronary hospital in late February and had been regaining his physical strength ever since. That summer, however, the possibility of his death continued to unsettle the political system despite his improvement.

After leaving the hospital, the imam moved into a home in the village of Jamaran, a suburb in Tehran's northeast foothills that adjoined the village of Niavaran, where the shah and his court had lived. Jamaran was known for its large number of sayyids in residence. Ruhollah Khomeini's new home was a gift from one of the faithful, fulfilling the 20 percent tithe required of all good Muslims. More buildings around it would also be donated en masse until the imam, his immediate family, and the brigade of people now devoted to keeping him safe took over the entire village. At that point, Jamaran would be surrounded with a wall and armed with antiaircraft batteries to protect its most precious resident.

In his Jamaran house, the imam held audiences, often televised, and made pronouncements, many of which generated shock waves throughout Iran. One of the latter came when the imam broke the fast of Ramadan at a public ceremony and, in his address for the occasion, dropped the ideology of consensus with which he had imbued the Revolution upon moving to Paris and making common cause with the exiles. Now the imam took sides. The Islamic Republic, he declared, "cannot tolerate those people who have been educated in Europe."

The final struggle between the Occidental and Oriental wings of the Iranian Revolution was now under way.

The imam would continue to hedge his bets on that combat, as he often did with touchy subjects, making declarations that each faction could venerate, but his drift was obvious to everyone concerned — especially his two self-anointed spiritual sons, Abolhassan Bani Sadr and Sadegh Ghotbzadeh. For the remainder of the Crisis, much of what was about to change inside the Islamic Republic would be reflected in the imam's relationship with the two younger men who had managed his exile in the land of the Franks. That three-cornered relationship would end with one of them in power, one back in Paris, and one dead.

Bani Sadr's battle with Khomeini's shadow, while often spirited, had been conducted in a constant state of retreat since May 15, when the final round of Majlis elections was held. Of the total 238 seats in the new body, more than 130 were directly controlled by the Islamic Republican Party, and only a handful were pledged to the president. Through June and July, Bani Sadr nonetheless managed to prevent the IRP from forming a government. The constitution gave him approval rights over the prime minister, and he considered the IRP's candidate and the candidate's choice of ministers unfit for their positions. He finally bowed to pressure from Khomeini and withdrew his objections in the first week of August, as the Majlis was beginning to officially function. Bani Sadr would later regret having done so but also point out that he really had little choice. His own powers as president were steadily being whittled away, and he, increasingly, just played the little Dutch boy with his finger in the dike.

The Crisis and the issue of the hostages had fueled the IRP's rise to power over the course of the spring, keeping alive an active state of national hysteria that placed a premium on religious devotion and anti-American fervor. Though the mullahs had used the hostages to tarnish Bani Sadr for being pro-West in the process, he still advocated a resolution to return the captive diplomats as quickly as possible. His most compelling argument came from his perspective as commander in chief of the Iranian military. Because of the American embargo, he pointed out, hundreds of millions of dollars' worth of military hardware that Iran had already paid for was frozen in American possession at the same time that the armed forces were disintegrating for lack of spare parts and replacement weaponry. Bani Sadr believed that Iraq would soon take advantage of Iran's strategic disrepair and demanded that it be remedied immediately. The only way to do so was to return the hostages.

The mullahs, one of whose goals was to replace the army with the Revolutionary Guards, ignored the president's pleas until after Bani Sadr had finally allowed the IRP to take over the administrative arms of the government. Then, on August 20, Bani Sadr attended a meeting with a number of the leading figures in the IRP, including the ayatollah who was its most recognizable voice. Bani Sadr brought up "the hostage problem," the military's desperate need for spare parts, and the dangers of an Iraqi assault on their weakened forces. They had to prepare for the possibility of war, he insisted, and to do that they had to get the American blockade lifted by releasing the diplomats.

At this point, the ayatollah interrupted. If Bani Sadr wanted the IRP to solve this Crisis, he demanded, Bani Sadr had to promise not to criticize them for doing so.

Bani Sadr asked why he would criticize them if they were working in Iran's interest.

The ayatollah ignored the question and told Bani Sadr to write down on paper that he wouldn't criticize them for the solution they might find and then sign it, like an official document.

President Bani Sadr found the IRP ayatollah's demand odd, and nothing immediate came of their contretemps, nor would anything ever come of their demand for a document.

The president, however, assumed henceforth that the mullahs, having milked the Crisis for all it was worth, were now looking for a way out, wherever they could find it.

All summer long, Bani Sadr's most visible ally on the hostage issue had continued to be the interim foreign minister, Sadegh Ghotbzadeh. One of the reasons was their mutual worry about Iraq. Ghotbzadeh had been the central figure in an incident that was often cited in the tabulation of tensions between the two countries. Sadegh had paid a foreign minister's visit to Lebanon, Syria, and then Kuwait during early May. In Syria, Ghotbzadeh had railed at what he characterized as the Iraqis' aggressive designs on Iran's Khuzistan Province along their mutual border, where most of Iran's oil industry was located. The foreign minister's last stop, Kuwait, was a former province of Iraq where the Iraqis were thought to still have a very active intelligence presence. Several dissident Iraqi exiles had been assassinated there in the week before Sadegh arrived. As Ghotbzadeh left a lunch with the emir of Kuwait, his limo was assaulted with grenades. Sadegh was unharmed, but three among his Foreign Ministry traveling party were seriously wounded. The assailants escaped but were assumed to have been in the pay of the Iraqis.

Ghotbzadeh thought it was criminal that the Crisis to which he had already devoted so much of his energy was still continuing and, on top of that, was about to make the country into easy pickings for Iraqi strongman Saddam Hussein. And Sadegh was increasingly alienated from the mullahs who were swarming all over the Islamic Republic's new government. "I don't want to collaborate with those people," he told Christian Bourguet that summer. "I don't share their ideas. I am against what they want to do in Iran. I am against their comprehension of Islam." He thought it might be better to just give the government over to the mullahs right away, so they could fail and be discredited accordingly.

By August 18, Ghotbzadeh had made up his mind to resign as foreign minister. First, however, he wrote an open letter addressed to the Majlis in which he devoted himself almost exclusively to the issue of the hostages. Sadegh walked over to the parliament and delivered it personally.

"I feel it is my religious obligation to do whatever is necessary and say what I know about our cause," Ghotbzadeh wrote. "I shall follow this course regardless of what people say about me, even openly. In this critical time it is not proper to be indifferent, remain silent, and be negligent." The soon to be ex–foreign minister then began describing the students' and all the other various positions around the hostage issue. First he praised each approach and used his description of it as an opportunity to rail at the evils of the shah and his American backers. Then he reviewed all the possible options other than an immediate release of the hostages, dismantling each in turn. After that, he went on for a while about what the Crisis was costing Iran — including at least $500 million thus far in lost interest on the money the Americans had frozen in their banking system.

"Releasing the hostages will deny Imperialism any excuse for direct interference in our affairs," Ghotbzadeh concluded. "Ending the Crisis . . . will help us embark on a new policy in the interest of our Revolution and in the interest of revolutionary peoples throughout the world. [This is a] course of action in compliance with our Revolution and it is our obligation to follow it. . . . If we leave this issue unsolved, our new government will be constantly under pressure. . . . It is better to settle this Crisis. . . . I know that by sending this letter I will receive unfavorable responses, insults and accusation. I have had such denunciations thrown at me before, but since I am a disciple of the Imam, I should tell the truth regardless of the consequences and I am prepared for martyrdom."

The same day he delivered his letter, Sadegh Ghotbzadeh went up to see the Ayatollah Khomeini in the imam's new quarters in Jamaran and submitted his resignation as foreign minister. Khomeini did not want to accept it, but Ghotbzadeh refused to change his mind. He told the imam that he could not work with these mullahs anymore. They were all "liars" and "traitors."

The imam told him to mind his tongue. The people he was talking about were "my brothers."

Brothers! Sadegh roared. Brothers! They just lied to the imam and then went on destroying Iran in the name of Islam. They weren't worthy of the title brother.

The imam, glowering intensely, forbade Sadegh to keep talking like this.

Ghotbzadeh was now furious himself. The imam, he answered, great as he was, had no right to forbid him to talk. Sadegh still believed in the imam and the imam knew that. But now was the time for the Revolution's guide to stand up to those who would soon destroy it.

The imam said nothing more on the subject, but he was not pleased.

Though it took them out of the political picture, the students' strategy of dispersing their captives was certainly successful in concealing them from American eyes. The White House spent much of the summer complaining to the CIA about the absence of any intelligence at all about the hostages' location. Otherwise, however, the effort and manpower necessary to maintain security at dozens of tiny locations spread all over the Iranian map were more than the students could really manage. By the middle of June, they had already begun to secretly move the hostages back to Tehran, and by the end of August, they had finished the process, despite two escape attempts, a foiled suicide, and a serious automobile accident in which one student, but no hostage, was killed.

Though back in Tehran, the captive Americans weren't returned to the embassy. All but a few were secretly moved into a prison built by the Germans during Reza's reign. The facility was by far the most manageable and easily defended option. At the request of the new government, the students, rather than the regular prison guards, continued to watch over the hostages there.

The most disturbing aspect of the stay in prison for many of the Americans was the sounds. Barry Rosen and a number of others were on a cell block where one of the cells was used by the regular Iranian security forces for interrogation of suspects, and the racket often echoed out of there twenty-four hours a day. "We could hear a tremendous amount of screaming," Rosen remembered, "and it was obvious that these people were in a great deal of pain. The screams would pierce right through me. While this was going on, we had a [student] guard named Ahmed who . . . liked to play classical music while these people were being tortured. He was trying to cover up the screams with music, but the music only made the torture that much more eerie."

The students reassured their "involuntary guests" that none of what they were overhearing had to do with them, so they should ignore it. The students also made an effort to give the Americans as many western amenities as they could arrange. A VCR was set up in one cell, and at least once a week each hostage was allowed to go in and watch tapes of American television sitcoms and dramas. When the hostages viewed the relatively risqué *Charlie's Angels,* they were often joined by the student brothers, who liked the show a lot.

In August one of Barry Rosen's cell mates was given a crossword puzzle torn out of an American newspaper for his amusement. Unbeknownst to the students, however, the back of the newspaper puzzle contained a fragment of a television schedule that included a program described as a documentary history of American intelligence from the Bay of Pigs to "the aborted attempt to rescue the hostages on April 24."

"A bomb seemed to have exploded in the cell," Rosen recalled. "The conclusion hit us like searing shrapnel. *That's* why we had been rushed out of Tehran in such a panic. . . . Crushing disappointment followed our shock: We concluded that if not for the rescue attempt, we might have been home by now. Any attempt to negotiate for us must have been obliterated by the [rescue] attempt. Since it had obviously failed, we had been stashed away in provincial hideaways and jail cells. . . . We felt certain that the attempt had brought us much closer to death than to rescue, that we had been saved by its failure — but also pushed much farther from real salvation. . . . Now when would we be freed?"

Rosen also learned of the death of the shahanshah that summer, about a month after it happened. Apparently one of his fellow prisoners had made the discovery. When Rosen was taken from his cell to the communal shower in the morning, he found a message scratched by someone's fingernail in the bar of soap there.

It said simply, "Shah dead."

The most significant public development of the summer involving the students was the release of one of the hostages from the embassy group, though none of the others with whom he had been held knew about it. The man had developed symptoms of a neurological disorder unrelated to his captivity, and the students sent him home in July to get serious medical attention.

With his departure, the total number of American captives was now down to fifty-two. And, with most of them gathered together in their Tehran prison, they were now, in effect, under the government's control for the first time ever. The Americans had no idea, but the stumbling block that had derailed their scenario six months ago had been bypassed and the students' grip on the situation had been broken.

· 27 ·

$\mathcal{B}$ACK IN WASHINGTON, JIMMY CARTER WAS EN-
during another of his political nadirs. The 75 percent approval rating in the
immediate aftermath of the embassy takeover in November had been reduced to 60 percent by January and then to 40 in the days just before the rescue mission. Now it was barely 20 percent.

That dive in public opinion had not kept Jimmy Carter from finishing off
Ted Kennedy, however. After the rescue failure, the president abandoned his
Rose Garden strategy and began to hit the political stump personally. He lost
more primaries than he won during the last month of the nomination campaign, but, added to his earlier successes, the effort was sufficient to give
Carter the delegates he would need to carry the Democratic Convention.
The president appeared at his victory rally in Washington during the first
week in June "smiling but not looking very happy," according to one of the
reporters there. He told his campaign workers that his heart was full of
"thanksgiving to all of you who turned what eight months ago was a prediction of absolute defeat into a wondrous victory." The sigh of relief from the

Carter campaign was audible though brief. "I felt like the long-distance runner who [reaches the finish line and] falls across the tape," Hamilton Jordan remembered.

Unfortunately the poll numbers offered Ham and Jimmy little respite. With the nomination in hand, the president's chief political operative dropped his job as White House chief of staff in order to concentrate solely on the fall campaign. Jordan's worries were amplified by the first head-to-head poll taken after the Republicans nominated former Hollywood actor and California governor Ronald Reagan at their convention in the middle of July. Reagan began the race 28 percentage points ahead.

Jimmy Carter remained confident nonetheless. "Reagan and I have perhaps the sharpest divisions between us of any two presidential candidates in my lifetime," he noted in his diary. "His policies are a radical departure from those pursued by [Republican presidents] Ford and Nixon. I also am convinced that on the major issues . . . we're on the right side, and if we can present our case clearly to the American people, we will win overwhelmingly in November."

Jordan, however, was anything but sanguine. And the factor that worried Ham most about his boss's reelection prospects continued to be the one over which they still had no control. The presidential vote that year fell on November 4, the first anniversary of the takeover of the Tehran embassy. If nothing changed on the hostage front, half of the nation's news programming over the final forty-eight hours before the vote would focus on the anniversary, magnifying voters' distress and humiliation. Under those circumstances, even if Ham was able to frame the race exactly as he hoped, Carter was going to be a hard sell.

On top of that, Jordan recognized that the Reagan campaign that was about to take the field against him was well led. William Casey, Reagan's campaign manager, would eventually become a Washington legend whose notoriety would dwarf anything Jordan ever generated, though for far different reasons. In the summer of 1980, however, Casey was still something of an insider figure. Bill Casey, sixty-seven, son of an immigrant Irish street sweeper and small-time New York City Democratic politician, was a big-time Wall Street lawyer and major Republican Party player. Among his accomplishments were authorship of the very first "tax shelter" ever approved by the IRS and a tour as chairman of the Securities and Exchange Commission in the Nixon administration. He had also been a hero in the Office of

Strategic Services — the Central Intelligence Agency's predecessor — during World War II, eventually running all the American espionage activity inside occupied Europe. Bill Casey still maintained strong informal connections with the agency. A tall man with a frog face who walked with a stoop, he was famous for speaking with a mumble so thick that he was often virtually incomprehensible. Whatever he was involved with, he always seemed to have his hands on the steering wheel.

Bill Casey had learned presidential politics as a partisan of Richard Nixon and had taken over as Reagan's campaign chief in late February, after the Californian stumbled somewhat in the New Hampshire primary. It was a tribute to his political mastery that he had quickly made himself indispensable to the campaign, despite being the new kid on the block. Casey brought formidable skills to his task. He was as erudite as he was Catholic and possessed an obsessive devotion to taking America back from the Democrats. "He wasn't a wild man as he's sometimes painted," one longtime friend observed, "but he was a risk taker. He would act on his hunches. He was a political animal, don't forget. . . . He had a very sharp mind, very quick. . . . And he understood how politics worked. . . . He had an enormous capacity for work. He wanted to make things happen. . . . And he could see through the fog."

One of the first conclusions Bill Casey reached about defeating Jimmy Carter involved the same factor that worried Ham Jordan. Casey was sure the Crisis over the hostages would be the key factor to deciding the election and fully expected Carter and Jordan to use it against the Republicans to their maximum advantage. Normally a behind-the-scenes figure, Bill Casey felt this strongly enough to momentarily emerge out of the background and say as much, on the record, to a reporter. This brief interview occurred in the middle of July, on the floor of the Republican Party National Convention in Detroit. The reporter was from the *Washington Star*. Casey told him that Carter was sure to pull some kind of "October Surprise" to steal the election, probably around the hostages. Look at what Carter had done in Wisconsin back on April Fool's Day, Casey pointed out. Carter had called that press conference and manipulated the Crisis in order to carry a critical state. The Republicans weren't going to let that happen to *them*. Casey said he had already begun to develop an "intelligence operation" to make sure they weren't taken advantage of, as Kennedy had been in Wisconsin.

This possible "October Surprise" that would snatch the election was one of Bill Casey's obsessions. Using a mainframe computer at Brigham Young University to sort input from some three hundred very skilled interviewers, a Reagan pollster had assessed the race depending on possible events and the time frame in which they might happen. One of the variables evaluated was the impact of a possible resolution to the Crisis. What the program spit back had grabbed Casey's attention as soon as he saw it. According to this computerized projection, if Carter brought the hostages home before October, the effect on the election would be minimal and Reagan would maintain anywhere from a 5 to 7 percentage point lead. But if Carter brought the hostages back between October 18 and 25, his poll numbers went up by 10 points, potentially giving him enough margin to win the election. And that, needless to say, had to be prevented at all costs.

Casey quickly developed a strategy for dealing with an October Surprise, including organizing several task forces inside the Reagan campaign devoted to anticipating it.

The first of those was known as the October Surprise Working Group and made up of about a dozen of the campaign's foreign policy advisers whose assignment was to discern possible Carter options and what might be done about them. Through their professional connections, its members also collected as much information about what the White House was up to as they could. At least one also met with Iranian exiles who approached the campaign to help. The most controversial of the Working Group's activities, later investigated by a congressional committee, was its chairman's admitted possession of several classified internal governmental documents slipped to him by someone working in Carter's National Security Council.

The second Republican campaign implement devoted to a possible October Surprise was known as the Skyline House Group, named for the building in suburban Falls Church, Virginia, where they met every weekday morning at 6:00 a.m. Its members included Casey and a half-dozen other campaign officials. According to the congressional investigation, "they assessed the latest hostage information and rumors, and planned what to do."

There was also a third Republican arrangement that used several operatives to further develop information. One of the operatives recruited several retired military officers to monitor domestic air bases from which any spare parts that might be traded to Iran as part of a hostage exchange would likely depart, providing early warning of an impending resolution of the Crisis. Another October Surprise operative became something of a mystery figure around the campaign's Washington headquarters, known for keeping his office door closed and decorating the wall above his desk with a huge map of Iran stuck full of colored pushpins.

All of these efforts were part of the larger "intelligence operation" Bill Casey had mentioned at the Republican Convention. When it hit its full stride, Casey's network included informants in the CIA, the Defense Intelligence Agency, the NSC, the banks holding the frozen Iranian cash, and even the White House Situation Room. If something indeed happened in October, Bill Casey wanted to be sure that whatever it was, it did not come as a surprise.

The presidential race that was about to begin was remarkable for its "volatility and uncertainty" from beginning to end. Even during its last forty-eight hours, one out of every five respondents to the polls would still be changing their minds. The Gallup Poll would admit that it had never seen a campaign like this in forty-five years of presidential political polling. The shifts were constant and often quite large.

Jimmy Carter's August was a case in point. Reagan's enormous lead at the end of July had been generated by the Republican National Convention, but the Democrats now had their turn, in the middle of August in New York's Madison Square Garden. Jordan and the president hoped to make the most of their opportunity, but nothing in Carter's reelection campaign was ever easy.

Ted Kennedy was still a problem. The defeated challenger had announced on the first day of the convention that he would endorse Carter, but the two sides continued to struggle with each other nonetheless. Kennedy partisans pushed a fight over economic policy in the platform committee, the Carterites escalated in response, and for two days relations between the two organizations were very tense. As a peace gesture, Kennedy was given the third day's evening session for a speech to the convention, broadcast on prime time. The address was what would eventually be described as "Kennedy-esque," full of rhetorical flourishes, liberal principles, and verbal chest beating. The convention loved it and interrupted him time after time with applause. Afterward, the Garden echoed with shouts of "Ted-dy, Ted-dy."

Jimmy Carter took the podium a day later, again in the middle of prime time. His appearance was preceded by a speech from Mondale and a film of Carter's accomplishments. Then, when the lights came on, Jimmy Carter entered to the strains of "Hail to the Chief," a musical ritual he had once banned from his appearances as too pretentious. The Garden shook with applause until Carter finally motioned for it to cease and began his address.

Jordan, seated in the audience, was on the lookout for things going wrong and he didn't have to wait long. Carter's teleprompter malfunctioned, so when he began to speak, he couldn't read the text.

"It seemed that the President lacked confidence as he began," Jordan remembered, "speaking in broken phrases without any rhythm or cadence. . . . He seemed to settle down once he got to the meat of his talk, but I was still nervous. . . . Perhaps he sensed that many in his audience were not really with him and that the speech of an incumbent President which addressed America's 'hard choices' was likely to be compared unfavorably to the fiery, emotional speech that Kennedy had delivered the night before. I was glad when he was finished, and I had no illusions about how it would be received. It was a solid defense and explanation of his policies and Presidency, appealing to their heads — but Kennedy had already captured their feelings."

When the president's speech was over, the official celebration of his candidacy was launched with the band playing "Happy Days Are Here Again" over and over, while the Carter delegates paraded around the Garden. A ceiling full of balloons was suspended in a net over the convention floor, but when someone yanked on the cord that was supposed to release them to descend onto the celebration, the mechanism jammed and nothing happened. The incident fed Jordan's nervousness. "That's not a good omen," Jordan remembered thinking.

Nonetheless, four days later, the polls indicated that Reagan's 28-point lead had been reduced to merely 7. Carter was pleased. The news came on Rosalynn's fifty-third birthday and the president described it as "a good present for Rosalynn from the people of the country." He also called it "a remarkable turnaround." The president would begin the fall campaign after Labor Day, within striking distance and with momentum.

The first sign that there might indeed be a breakthrough on the issue that mattered most in the race came at 8:00 a.m. on September 9. Edmund Muskie, the new secretary of state, a former senator who had replaced Cy Vance after the rescue attempt, received a call from the West German ambassador requesting an urgent meeting, though he would not say for what purpose. The secretary gave the West German an appointment an hour hence. For the actual meeting, the secretary was accompanied by several others, including Warren Christopher, who had stayed on at State as the deputy secretary.

The Americans were expecting to hear something pressing about Europe from the Germans, but, as it turned out, Europe never came up.

Instead, the West German ambassador explained that his government had been contacted by an Iranian who was close to Ayatollah Khomeini. This Iranian had been personally authorized by the imam to enter into secret negotiations with the government of the United States in order to arrange the release of the hostages. The imam's proposed emissary, Sadegh Tabatabai, had been in exile in Germany before the shah fell, was married to a German woman, and was fluent in German. The German ambassador to Iran had known him for a couple years. Tabatabai was also Ahmed Khomeini's brother-in-law and had told the Germans that only he, Ahmed, the speaker of the Majlis, and the imam himself knew that this contact was being made. Bani Sadr, for example, had no idea. It was a whole different group of characters than the Americans had dealt with before.

The West German ambassador gave the secretary a list of the Iranian terms. The emissary had insisted on a response to his invitation within forty-eight hours. It was the Iranians' stated goal to get the issue resolved quickly, before the takeover's first anniversary. The Americans told the ambassador that they would get back to him before the deadline, and as soon as the German left, the secretary called the president and told him what had just transpired. This was the first time in almost five months that they'd had any contact, direct or indirect, with the Iranians. The secretary and Warren Christopher would go to the White House that afternoon to discuss it.

In the meantime, Chris — as the president usually called Christopher — began assembling a small task force to assess the offer. The terms were simple. In exchange for the hostages, Iran asked for the United States to do three things: unfreeze Iran's assets, commit to a policy of nonintervention in Iranian affairs, and attempt to return the assets of the late shah to Iran. Noticeably absent was any demand for an American apology, which was a condition Carter had steadfastly refused to accept and, heretofore, the Iranians had always included. Unbeknownst to the Americans, the West German ambassador in Tehran had convinced the emissary to delete the apology demand from his original draft, knowing that it was unacceptable and that insisting on it would be self-defeating.

When the State Department team went to see Jimmy Carter at the White House, they had largely positive things to say about the invitation. They were wary, but there was also a sense of elation at this possibility that seemed to have just walked in the door out of nowhere. Iran's terms were certainly a place for negotiations to begin. Mondale was also present at the meeting, as was Brzezinski. The latter made the most cautionary comments. He warned that it could be a trap, concocted by the Iranians because they were afraid the United States might be preparing to act against them. Once they had derailed any action, they would then sabotage the negotiations, humiliating the president again.

Carter himself didn't seem worried about that possibility. He told the meeting that he wanted to pursue the negotiations on the schedule the emissary proposed. And he wanted Chris to do it personally.

Christopher's response to the Iranians went off to the Germans that evening. The United States accepted the Iranian invitation and agreed to come to Germany to negotiate, but wanted some assurance ahead of time that this man was indeed empowered by the imam.

The Germans got back to the deputy secretary shortly thereafter and told him that the next day, the ayatollah would be giving a speech. The imam's emissary urged them to listen to it. Sure enough, the next day Iran broadcast the ayatollah's sermon to a group of religious pilgrims. Like most of the imam's speeches these days, it was written by him and then read by an announcer. And there on the back end of the text, out of context and obviously just pasted in, were the points of negotiation.

This emissary was the real deal, and the president's selection of Warren Christopher to manage what remained of the Crisis signaled the end of the internal warfare surrounding Iran policy. Henceforth, Brzezinski backed off to focus on other issues and left the process to the deputy secretary. "My own role during this last phase . . . became quite secondary," the national security adviser explained. "I did not involve myself in these negotiations in any detail. . . . My main responsibility was to make sure we did not agree to a negotiated settlement that would tarnish our national honor." After September 9, Christopher did much of his work in direct consultation with the president himself, serving as what amounted to secretary of state for hostages.

Many Washington observers were surprised that Warren Christopher was still part of the Carter administration at all. After Vance's resignation, Christopher had been most pundits' choice to be given the secretary's post for the eight months remaining in Carter's first term. Vance recommended him and Chris was half expecting it himself. Carter, however, needed the help with

Congress that adding a respected senator and party leader like Muskie would give him and passed Christopher over. On the basis of that rejection, many had expected Christopher to resign, but the president had told Chris personally what he was going to do and asked him to stay. After thinking about it for a night, Chris agreed. "The chance of a lifetime is not necessarily the next rung up the ladder," Christopher later explained. "It may be the one on which you already stand."

Warren Christopher was described by some of those who disliked him as "Cy Vance without the charisma," a personality the opposite of what was commonly expected of Californians. Taciturn to a fault, thin to the point of looking gaunt, with blank eyes that peered out through layered folds of skin and eyelid, Christopher, fifty-five, looked and acted like the major-league corporate lawyer that he was. The son of a banker who'd lost his fortune and his health in Depression North Dakota and then moved his family to Southern California, Christopher went from Stanford Law to Supreme Court clerk to Los Angeles' largest and most powerful law firm. He'd turned down an appointment to the California Supreme Court while still in his thirties and served in the US attorney general's office during the Johnson administration. As deputy secretary of state, he was known as a nitpicker who once sent a proposed speech back to the department speechwriters thirty-three times for further revisions. He believed in negotiation and practiced it with great patience, a quick mind, and a poker face. Carter trusted him a lot.

Christopher set about his assignment by assembling an interagency task force of a half dozen or so from not only State, but also Treasury and Justice. "It consisted of officials just below the top levels of the cabinet departments," the deputy secretary explained. "Cabinet secretaries occasionally joined our meetings, but usually did not." The task force drafted negotiating positions in response to the Iranian opening gambit. That included the three original conditions and a fourth that Khomeini had added in his speech, demanding that the United States cancel all legal claims against Iran. Over the next two days, the task force constructed Christopher's rejoinder. "Though it can be more difficult negotiating a position within the U.S. government than with a sworn international adversary," Christopher observed, "this group managed to produce bureaucratic progress at unheard-of speed. By September 14, the date of my departure for my meeting with Tabatabai, I had in my briefcase a set of responses that passed muster with every involved arm of the U.S. government."

Warren Christopher traveled to Bonn accompanied by almost all the regular members of his task force. To conceal the true purpose of the trip, the State Department announced that the deputy secretary was flying to Europe to consult with the German foreign minister in Bonn, the British prime minister in London, and the French president in Paris, all on a variety of subjects. Christopher and his party flew on a regular government flight to Germany, in an air force jetliner full of others traveling on government business, and fit in as just one routine mission to Europe among many.

The American delegation landed at a West German air base on the morning of September 15 and were ferried from there to the countryside outside of Bonn, to a restored palace set in an expansive private park. The building was employed by the Germans as an official guesthouse, and the Americans would use it as their headquarters. Christopher had barely settled in when the Germans notified him that Sadegh Tabatabai was in Bonn and ready to meet. As part of security procedures, none of the Americans referred to the emissary by his given name but instead used a code name, "the Traveler." The Germans pointed out to the deputy secretary that the Traveler was by himself and had asked that Christopher bring only one aide along and that the German foreign minister sit in on their session. Christopher agreed, and in an hour, the two met face-to-face in a cottage out in the palace's surrounding park.

The Traveler did not look at all like Christopher expected. Rather than turban and robe, the Iranian had the same taste in dress as his friend Sadegh Ghotbzadeh. Clean-shaven in his French silk suit, Sadegh Tabatabai could have easily passed for a prosperous European businessman in his early forties. One journalist described him as "self-assured and handsome in an Atlantic City sort of way." Another portrayed him as "a sharp-witted, well-heeled young man about town, a bright bon vivant with a ruthless streak." In the days of the shah, the imam's emissary and Ghotbzadeh had helped organize the original Islamic Students Association while at the University of Tehran. Tabatabai had served as the organization's secretary general before fleeing to Germany, where he earned a PhD in biochemistry from the University of Karlsruhe. He saw his old friend Ghotbzadeh a lot during the sixties, often on trips to Beirut together to visit the Traveler's uncle, who was the leader of Lebanon's Shiites. Tabatabai joined the imam when Khomeini came to Paris and returned with him after the shah fell. He had served for a while as deputy prime minister in the provisional government. Now he and Ahmed Khomeini were partners in a lucrative export-import business.

With Christopher, the Traveler immediately reiterated that Iran wanted to solve the Crisis quickly and that the hostages would be returned almost instantly if they reached a deal. The emissary ascribed the sense of urgency to the imam's questionable health, but this was a ruse; Khomeini was better than he had been in months. A more likely explanation was that Tabatabai, like Ghotbzadeh and Bani Sadr, was worried about a possible attack by Iraq. Indeed, according to his own later explanation, this was the factor that had led him to go to the imam with this idea in the first place.

In their discussions, the deputy secretary concentrated on the Iranians' four points. The first of them, the demand for an American declaration of nonintervention, was not an issue; the United States accepted as much out of hand. The question of Iran's frozen assets was more complicated under American law because of outstanding claims against the Islamic Republic, but Christopher said that perhaps as much as $5.5 billion was in a position to be released immediately after the hostages were. As for the imam's desire for a renunciation of all legal claims against Iran, the United States could not accept that option but would be willing to accept an international arbitration tribunal to sort through all potential lawsuits.

The most difficult demand to address as far as Christopher was concerned was Iran's claim to the shah's assets. In part that was because the Iranians had inflated notions of the amount of money the shah had kept in the United States. Christopher did not know how much of the shah's wealth was actually in the United States, but he expected that the shah and his heirs had been sophisticated enough not to have tied up much there, for precisely the reason they were now discussing. He told the Traveler that the notion that the Pahlavis had billions squirreled away in the United States was very likely pure fantasy. In any case, Christopher explained, American law would not permit a seizure of private property like that, even if it was in the interests of the state. The American government would help Iran go to court to make its claim, but that's as far as they could go.

The imam's emissary found this latter point hard to accept and disputed it until the German foreign minister interrupted and pointed out to the Iranian that what Christopher was offering them in that regard was more than German law would have allowed.

The only other point the Traveler raised was about spare military parts. He wanted to know if the material already destined for Iran in the American military pipeline would be part of the asset release.

This too was a ticklish subject. Carter wanted to avoid any appearance of trading guns for hostages. Christopher told Tabatabai that such hardware was a sensitive issue for the Americans and ought to be resolved outside of this agreement, in bilateral negotiations about the larger relationship that might follow. There was, however, some $50 million worth of nonlethal spare parts that would be released once the rest of this agreement had been implemented. Tabatabai nodded and dropped the subject.

After two hours, both men were pleased with the discussion. Christopher suggested they meet again after a day's pause, just to review each other's positions after consulting with their respective governments.

This second meeting was held at 7:00 a.m. on September 17, over breakfast in the same small house in which they had first met. It was clear that the imam's emissary had contacted Tehran in the meantime and received positive feedback. Using a classic Farsi phrase, Tabatabai explained that the American response to the Iranians' four points was "not an unwelcome position." The Traveler had to stay in Germany for a few more days to fulfill the speaking engagements that were the cover story for his trip to the West, but on September 22 he would fly back to Tehran to consult. Whatever transpired next would depend on those consultations, but the Traveler was confident enough to tentatively schedule another meeting with Christopher for the last week of September, back here in Bonn. "I was very optimistic," Tabatabai later said.

Christopher flew straight back to Washington afterward and was at the White House to report to the president the next day. He ran into Hamilton Jordan in the hallway outside the Oval Office. Jordan had never seen the normally methodical and cautious deputy secretary this excited. "I think we have something," he told Ham. "The man I met with was realistic and obviously ready to resolve this thing." Jordan assumed that for someone of Christopher's normal demeanor to be this optimistic, he must really have hit pay dirt.

Christopher was in a hurry and had no time to tell Jordan anything more before reporting to the president, but Ham got the details from the president himself when Christopher was done. After running through all the details of the Bonn negotiations, Carter told Jordan that they "might be only days away from having the hostages home." Jordan was given the task of figuring out the best way to welcome the captives back and wrote the president a memo on the subject before the day was out. For a moment, it felt like all Ham's Election Day fantasies were about to be realized.

But nothing in this story was ever quite that simple.

Before dawn Tehran time on September 22, the day the Traveler was scheduled to fly home for what Christoper and Carter both hoped would be his final consultations, outright war broke out along Iran's border with Iraq. An Iraqi invasion force, fifty thousand troops spearheaded by tanks, crossed the Shatt al Arab waterway dividing the two countries and plunged into Iran's Khuzistan Province. The Iranian border outposts, surprised, under-manned, and ill equipped, were easily overrun. The Iranian air force, short of both maintenance technicians and spare parts, was unable to put enough planes into the sky to immediately stem the advance but avoided being de-stroyed on the ground. All the loyal army troops and Revolutionary Guards that could be mustered were thrown into the breach to slow the Iraqis down. In the meantime, Iraqi air force planes bombed targets throughout Iran, in-cluding Tehran's Mehrabad International Airport.

When Sadegh Tabatabai checked in at Bonn International for his trip home, he was told that Tehran was under attack and that all flights into or out of Iran had been canceled. It would be almost two weeks before the imam's emissary could return to make his report.

· 28 ·

---

*H*AVING MADE QUICK WORK OF IRAN'S BORDER
guards, the Iraqi invasion encountered little resistance as the Iranians made
a strategic retreat to defend the population centers deeper in Khuzistan. The
Iraqis' most notable success was setting fire to the Iranian oil refinery at
Abadan on the Shatt al Arab — the largest refinery in the world. Its loss
would deprive Iran's economy of more than half its domestic supply of re-
fined petroleum products. Having struck such an opening blow, the invading Iraqis expected the Iranian forces to disintegrate and the population to
welcome them as liberators. On the afternoon of September 22, the Iraqi
dictator, Saddam Hussein, held a press conference in Iranian territory before
a horde of international press he had lured to Iraq with subsidized fares and
hotel rooms and then bussed out to the front on this excursion. He said that
in a week he would hold another press conference, this time in Tehran. Two
days later, when another diplomat asked the Iraqi ambassador to the UN
how much longer it would take them to finish their military business, the
Iraqi said two or three days.

The Iranians, however, responded with fervor and ferocity. Even the shah-banou, in a statement from Cairo, urged her countrymen to defend their nation while also fighting against Khomeini. Thousands reported to government offices and mosques to volunteer for the front. Some would reach Khuzistan in just a matter of days, to be formed into Revolutionary Guard units and sent to plug gaps in the Iranian line. Overnight, the forces that had seemed about to pull the Islamic Republic apart concentrated instead. The state media played rousing hymns and even old prerevolutionary marching songs. The imam issued an immediate statement calling the Iraqis "godless."

Within days of the initial assault, *Le Monde* would report from Tehran that "the morale and combativeness of the Iranian population have reached a level comparable to that prevailing during the uprising against the Shah." Defending the homeland now became the issue that trumped all others, giving the victors of the Revolution's opening round all the momentum they would need to entrench their version of the Islamic Republic against what had been growing opposition. The IRP's prime minister even stated that "this war is a blessing from God" and hoped out loud that it would last "a year or more."

Most Iranians saw the Americans' hands in this invasion, even though Carter made an immediate statement that the United States had no side in an Iran-Iraq fight. Bani Sadr thought it inconceivable that the Iraqis would have acted without a green light from the United States. For proof he pointed to a meeting between Brzezinski and Saddam Hussein in Jordan in July — a meeting Brzezinski, his colleagues, and White House records claimed never happened. For most Iranians, however, the assumption was reflexive and irresistible. Even twenty-five years later, they would cite that alleged meeting in Jordan.

During the war's first days, the Muslim Students Following the Line of the Imam were among the leaders in the chorus of blame directed at the Great Satan *Amrika*. They described the Iraqi attack as an attempt to force Iran to free the hostages. Their spokeswoman Sister Mary appeared at the gate of the embassy and announced that in order to foil any possible plot, they had moved the hostages they had earlier dispersed around the countryside to other, even more remote locations. In fact, the hostages were still in their Tehran prison and were never moved after war broke out.

On September 23 the Majlis addressed the issue of the hostages after a debate provoked by an Iraqi radio broadcast claiming Iran had already released the American diplomats. The speaker of the Majlis, one of the quartet of Iranians aware of the Traveler's mission in Bonn with the Americans, was among the most outspoken. "We consider the Iraqi attacks to be part of a large U.S. plot," he announced. "These events will have their impact on the destiny of the hostages." The Majlis then voted to "freeze" any resolution of the fate of the captives from the Den of Spies until further notice.

Bani Sadr, though politically weakened, was still, by constitutional provision as well as the imam's directive, commander in chief of the Iranian armed forces. In that role, he had already been attacked by the IRP for taking too kind an attitude toward the army, which, to the clerics' minds, was secular, pro-shah, and a breeding ground for treason against the Revolution. The mullahs still hoped to replace the formal institution of the armed forces with the populist, guerrilla-oriented Revolutionary Guard, and over the next few weeks their approach seemed to yield at least two different military hierarchies trying to make strategic decisions. The mullahs tried to replace Bani Sadr with a military council under their control, but the president pointed out the move's lack of constitutional foundation and forced them to back off. Then they hoped the army's failure against Iraq would take Bani Sadr down with it.

Instead, the desperate and ill-organized Iranian resistance gained traction. After four days during which the Iraqis pushed farther into Khuzistan, Iranian lines finally stiffened and held. After three weeks, the Iranians had destroyed almost six hundred Iraqi tanks and one hundred aircraft, a third of Iraq's effective force. Though the war was years from being over, the Iraqis were as close to Tehran as they would ever get, and the president's initial success as commander in chief made Bani Sadr more of a threat to the mullahs than ever.

For the hostages themselves, the Iraqi attack was one of the few news events they learned of almost immediately. Their prison was near the flight path for Tehran's international airport, and a number of the Americans being held there were eyewitnesses to the air strike that had ended up stranding the Traveler in Germany.

"We heard this loud roaring *wa-woosh*," captive military attaché Colonel Leland Holland remembered. "I'd been on the ground before when attacking jets came in and dumped stuff. . . . That was just what this sounded like. We heard the *wa-woosh*, and then we heard the electric cannon on the plane burping away. Immediately I knew a bombing raid was going on. . . . Then we could hear the bombs. We heard a loud *boom!* Then right after that we'd hear secondary explosions ignite — it was *boom-kaboom!* One right after the other."

Everyone on the cell block heard it. "Some of the bombs landed pretty close," captive marine Corporal William Gallegos remembered, "and the entire prison was shaking. We could see the Iranians shooting their antiaircraft guns into the air. It was lighting up the sky, and I was getting excited. At first I thought it was Americans, and I was ready to go. I jumped up and was waiting for them to come bursting through the door."

When the hostages asked their student captors what was going on, the students insisted it was just Iranian troops going through their drills. "I just laughed," Bill Belk, the communications officer who had unsuccessfully attempted to escape the previous winter, said. "It was uncanny how those guys would lie. They'd come in and say these totally ridiculous things, and then expect us to believe them. What made it even more absurd was those guys were scared to death. . . . This one guy who came into the cell was so frightened he was actually shaking — his hands, his lips, everything was trembling. And he kept saying, 'Do not worry. It is only practicing.' "

Barry Rosen, the captive press officer, eventually figured out that the bombing was being done by Iraq. During the first few days of the war, he noticed that the students had added something to the chants they engaged in before their evening prayers. These were a regular occurrence in the prison courtyard, which the hostages usually overheard from a distance, through the thick walls. Usually the chants were "*Marg bar Carter; Marg bar Amrika.*" After the bombing raids, a new phrase was added that Rosen could not at first discern. Then, by capturing the rhythm of the different syllables, he figured it out. The students were now also chanting "*Marg bar Saddam Hussein.*"

The Iraqi air assaults became a regular part of hostage life. "It got to the point where we would actually look forward to the bombing raids," Joe Hall, a captive warrant officer, recalled. "If Tehran didn't get hit for several nights in a row, it would just depress the hell out of us. We liked the idea of them getting bombed. When the fighter planes came screaming in . . . we'd jump up and start clapping and cheering. . . . Hostages would be shouting, 'Give 'em hell!' 'Flatten Tehran!' or 'Buy Iraqi war bonds!' Things like that. We'd practically shake the prison with all our cheering and clapping. . . . When it didn't happen for a few nights in a row we really missed it."

Needless to say, their student captors felt much the opposite. The Muslim Students Following the Line of the Imam immediately added military training and drill to their daily routine, and they were not alone. Over the course of the Iraqi invasion and the war that followed, more than 60 percent of Iran's university students would volunteer and serve in the defense effort, and many of the Muslim Students Following the Line of the Imam were on this cutting edge. Several joined up in the opening days and were quickly mustered into a Revolutionary Guard unit and thrown into the struggle for the Iranian port city of Khorramshahr. There, the fight was door to door, block to block. In the ebb and flow of strategic retreats and advances, one of the Iranian army units involved claimed that it notified the students' Guard outfit, which they were supporting, that the army was pulling back. If they indeed sent such a warning, the word never got through. As a consequence of the army's withdrawal, these Revolutionary Guards were surrounded by the Iraqis and massacred, giving the student volunteers the martyrdom many had been expecting when they first went over the gate at the Den of Spies in November.

On the last day of September, with the fight over Khorramshahr still raging, the Iranian Majlis dropped its previous resolution to "freeze" the hostage question and began a three-day debate over what to do to resolve it. The debate was angry and occasionally verged on fisticuffs. It was also broadcast live on Iranian radio. Many Majlis members began their speeches by calling for the "spies" to be tried before a public tribunal, but many others cited the military necessities that demanded they escape from under the Americans' international embargo. Ultimately the Iranian popular assembly decided by a slim majority vote to establish a seven-man commission, headed by an Islamic revolutionary who had spent five years in the shah's prisons and now oversaw the prison where the hostages were being held. The commission was charged with "devising a pragmatic plan to end the impasse" but forbidden from engaging in direct negotiations with the Americans.

Several days after that, Sadegh Tabatabai was finally able to fly back to Iran and report on his mid-September meetings with Warren Christopher in Bonn. Included in the group to whom he first reported were Ahmed Khomeini and the speaker of the Majlis — who had both been in on the plan ahead of time — as well as the IRP's leading ayatollah and the new head of the Majlis's hostage commission, who had not. Tabatabai also spoke separately to Bani Sadr, informing him of the negotiations for the first time. At his backers' recommendation, the Traveler then sent an optimistic message to Christopher via the Germans on October 9.

The deputy secretary, who spoke with Carter every day to update him on any hostage developments, called the president during his campaign appearance at the Dixie Classic Fairgrounds in Winston-Salem, North Carolina, to give him the news. The Traveler's message was that "the American proposal has fallen on fertile ground." According to Christopher, they would push for "some sort of understanding, not later than early next week."

Tabatabai's October 9 message through the Germans was followed by another on Friday, October 10. This second message made it seem that the Iranians were down to simply haggling over the final terms.

Tabatabai now wanted the United States to send Iran an inventory of all the nonmonetary items in the United States' possession that Iran had already paid for and that would be released to them as part of any exchange. Though Tabatabai's request didn't specify as much, this would largely amount to a list of military hardware, since the only other goods of any significance the Americans had frozen in the pipeline were a jetliner and various items of oil industry equipment in which Tabatabai had never expressed any prior interest. Christopher and the rest of the White House team interpreted the message as an attempt to enlarge the $50 million package of military spare parts the deputy secretary had offered in Bonn.

Almost everyone saw the Iranian's request as a positive sign. Back in Washington from his North Carolina campaign foray and about to retreat to Camp David for the weekend before returning to the campaign trail, Carter told his Friday morning foreign policy breakfast about Tabatabai's second message. He noted, with an air of relief, that the Iranians were finally "making sensible inquiries" about the nuts and bolts that would have to be worked out before any deal could be consummated.

A core group of administration advisers, including both Christopher and Brzezinski, took up the question of exactly how to respond to the inventory request at a more than three-hour meeting later in the day. The Americans surmised that Iran had no independent inventory of the goods in question and the White House group consequently wanted to play their hand very carefully. The group did not want to return everything to the Iranians. Christopher's task force had prepared an inventory of military equipment before the Bonn meetings and, for the purposes of discussion, had organized the goods into three subdivisions. The least controversial was the "nonlethal" materiel included in the initial $50 million offer Christopher had already made. The most controversial was some $150 million worth of "highly lethal" supplies, including rockets, torpedoes, and sophisticated targeting systems. In between was a "gray" area of some $100 million worth of aircraft spare parts that one NSC aide described as "almost a random selection of items that happened to be [frozen] in the pipeline," some of which "would be of little value to the Iranian air force, but others could potentially be quite important."

On Saturday, the group faxed its recommendation out to Camp David. The consensus was that the president ought to now include the entire "gray" category in response to the Traveler's request, offering a total package of $150 million worth of goods, most of which were spread around the United States at various military bases. Carter agreed, so on October 11, Warren Christopher wired the new offer to the Germans for transmission to Tehran, along with an inventory of all the hardware being offered.

There was no immediate response from Iran, not even an acknowledgment of receipt, but an air of optimism had already infected almost everyone in the administration connected with the process. Reports of an imminent "breakthrough" soon appeared in the *Washington Post,* and some sources, speaking anonymously, were even more enthusiastic.

"My private conviction," one Carter insider declared, "is that something could happen at any moment — at 2:30 this afternoon or in the middle of next week. It's going to come as a bolt out of the blue because Iran now appears to have decided to liquidate this Crisis. Of this I am sure. It is not going to come as a result of any particular initiative of ours."

Just three weeks before Election Day, once again, all Jimmy Carter could do was wait on Iran.

As did the Republicans. It would never be clear just how much Bill Casey and his Republican Party "intelligence operation" knew about the details of what Christopher and Tabatabai were up to that fall, despite several eventual congressional investigations, but the Republicans' interest was full-blown. Casey pushed his operatives for more information but had thus far declined Carter's offers to be officially briefed on the Crisis for fear that this would handcuff the Reagan campaign when it came time to respond to any October Surprise. In any case, the Republicans spent the fall behaving as though a hostage deal were about to be announced, whether they knew as much or not.

Though his party had been thumping their October Surprise theme since June, Reagan himself had thus far shunned any comment on the issue because he did not want to "politicize" the hostages. Nonetheless, Bill Casey had Reagan kick off a campaign-stop press opportunity on the first of the month by observing that he would not be surprised if Iran released the hostages before Election Day simply because it was obvious the Iranians supported his opponent and would want to do whatever they could to help him. The day after that, Reagan's vice presidential running mate, George H. W. Bush, confessed to the press that he was worried about Carter pulling an October Surprise in a desperate attempt to overcome the fact that people no longer had any faith in him. By the middle of the month the phrase October Surprise was so familiar that no one covering the Republicans had to ask what it meant.

Having established the October Surprise idea, Casey's intelligence operation then attempted to fill it out with disinformation. One White House aide remembered that "it was an unusual day that passed without a columnist — usually one who supported the Reagan candidacy — providing a convincing story of plane loads of military equipment moving from the United States to Iran [in] a sudden breakthrough in the hostage situation. . . . None of the reports had the slightest basis in fact." Bill Casey's thinking in this instance was that, like the boy who cried wolf, if he stirred people up with false reports that the October Surprise was actually happening, when the real moment arrived, no one would pay it a whole lot of attention.

Two very visible examples of the technique's application would stand out in the congressional investigations to come. One was a column by Rowland Evans and Robert Novak, one of the nation's most widely read pundit collaborations. On the basis of what Novak later described as "an impeccable source in the Reagan campaign," they ran a report during October that the White House counsel had successfully negotiated the release of the hostages and that they were about to return. The second example was a report on a Chicago television station run just three days after Christopher's response to Tabatabai's inventory request, when the White House was still waiting for an answer from the Iranians. The station claimed that five navy cargo planes full of combat hardware would arrive in Iran within the next forty-eight hours and that the captive Americans had already been assembled in the embassy, from which they would be released gradually, in a step-by-step process. Although the Chicago station refused to further name its source, the substance of the report would eventually be identified by a congressional investigation as identical to one laid out in an internal Republican Party memo just a few days earlier. Both stories drew a brief spurt of national attention before disappearing into the escalating background noise of the campaign.

The instigation for the coming congressional inquiries would be the eventually widespread suspicion that under Casey's guidance, the Republicans had surreptitiously intervened with the Iranians to make sure the resolution of the Crisis was timed to Ronald Reagan's advantage rather than Jimmy Carter's. In the decade following the 1980 presidential election, this allegation would be repeated in dozens of magazine stories and several very visible books, eventually generating sufficient pressure to force Congress to form an October Surprise Task Force to investigate, a dozen years after the fact.

Although each version of the theory would have different twists, the various claims would all share the same outlines. Supposedly the Republicans had begun reaching out to possible Iranian contacts almost as soon as Casey took over the reins of the Reagan campaign in the spring of 1980. By late July, that outreach had borne fruit and Casey himself traveled secretly to Spain, where he had a series of meetings with envoys from the IRP mullahs. That conclave was followed by more secret meetings in Paris during mid-October that allegedly included not only Casey but George Bush as well. At both, the two issues discussed were the timing of any hostage release and what Iran could expect in return. The alleged end result was a deal in which the mullahs agreed to delay the hostage resolution until after Election Day, thereby denying Carter his October Surprise. In compensation, Iran would receive a much larger package of military hardware from the new Republican administration than Carter was offering.

Needless to say, Casey and the Republicans would dismiss the entire account as pure fantasy. Most of the evidence to substantiate these charges consisted of statements from various, often shady, characters involved in international arms dealing, some relying on second- or even third-hand information, and there was virtually no documentary evidence. The congressional October Surprise Task Force would issue a final report in January 1993 saying that it could not find sufficient corroboration to credit any of the charges.

In any case, the American discussion of this alleged scenario would come long after the fact, and charges of Republican collusion to undermine American foreign policy were never raised in the campaign between Jimmy Carter and Ronald Reagan. The same was not true inside Iran, however. There, a possible deal between the Islamic Republicans and the American Republicans was widely discussed in the fall of 1980. The most visible public proponent of the allegations about Casey and the mullahs was Sadegh Ghotbzadeh. "We know that the Republican Party of the United States," Ghotbzadeh declared in his open letter of resignation to the Majlis in August, "in order to win the presidential election, is working hard to delay the solution of the hostage crisis until after the U.S. election. . . . Some people [in the Majlis] suggest that the hostage crisis be settled a few months later [than my call for an immediate resolution]. This suggestion must be pleasing to the ears of the [American] Republican Party."

Ghotbzadeh, still notorious and available to the international press, followed these remarks with more of the same in several early-September interviews with the French media, all asserting that Ronald Reagan, David Rockefeller, Henry Kissinger, and the other Republicans were doing everything in their power "to block a solution" to the Crisis. In private, Sadegh included more specifics, saying that the IRP mullahs were actually in negotiations with a representative from the American Republicans and that those meetings had been held in Madrid and Paris.

Less visible in his conclusions on this subject but just as adamant was Ghotbzadeh's old rival, Abolhassan Bani Sadr. According to Bani Sadr, he first became aware of what was going on during July, when he had a conversation with the imam's nephew. The nephew told Bani Sadr that he'd had discussions in Spain with "Reagan's envoys." He also said that these American Republicans wanted to "make a deal" with Bani Sadr, but if Bani Sadr wasn't interested, they were prepared to make a deal with his enemies in the IRP instead.

Bani Sadr declined the offer, concluding it was just idle talk, but then thought differently in August, after his conversation about the hostages with the IRP ayatollah, in which the latter had asked him to sign a formal statement promising not to criticize the IRP if it solved the Crisis on its own. The Iranian president stewed over that request for a while and then confronted the ayatollah about it. Bani Sadr demanded to know with whom the ayatollah was going to solve the Crisis. If he was talking about solving it with Carter, then he was way out of bounds, because such negotiations were the prerogative of the Islamic Republic's president. In response, the IRP ayatollah refused to say who he was thinking of dealing with, and that refusal convinced Bani Sadr that the IRP was dealing with the Republicans. "I realized that there was another agreement in the works," he remembered, "and that it had nothing to do with Carter."

At the time, both Bani Sadr and Ghotbzadeh also made no secret of their feelings that the mullahs were picking the wrong side in the American election. Ghotbzadeh even went on television during October and warned

Americans against voting for Reagan. Bani Sadr made no such public statement, but took the question straight to the imam.

"I constantly mentioned [to Khomeini] the danger Reaganism would pose if the hostages were not released very quickly," Bani Sadr remembered. "I explained that Reagan's arrival [as president] would signify a change in the American mentality. From a post–Vietnam War mentality of everyone deciding his own fate, there would be a shift to the concept of intervention in the affairs of others. We should not contribute to Reagan's election. Khomeini said, 'So what if Reagan wins? Nothing will change. . . . He and Carter are both enemies of Islam.'"

By the middle of October, it was apparent to all observers of the American presidential race just how critical the possible resolution of the Crisis was going to be. There was now virtually no distance at all between the two candidates in the polls. Jimmy Carter had climbed all the way back from 28 points down. The Reagan campaign's own poll on October 14 showed Carter actually ahead 41 to 39, with the rest of the sample split between either undecided or Congressman John Anderson, the race's one independent candidate. It was a truly remarkable comeback, but the Carter campaign had little time to celebrate. The polls continued to fluctuate on an almost daily basis.

Meanwhile, behind the scenes, Carter, Christopher, Jordan, and everyone else in the know were still secretly waiting to hear back from the Traveler. Their wait went on and on and on. The "early next week" target for having a deal done, which Christopher had mentioned on the phone to the president at the Winston-Salem fairgrounds, came and went without a word from Tabatabai or anyone else. "In mid-October," an NSC aide remembered, after a period of "almost daily reports from Tehran through a variety of sources, describing new political developments and various plans that were being floated for a settlement, [suddenly] everything seemed to stop. . . . For five days . . . there were no new pronouncements, public or private, from the leadership in Tehran." The White House could only content itself with speculation about what was going on, but it didn't seem good.

In fact, the deal that had seemed on the verge of being done on October 9 had been referred to the Majlis by October 20, for official approval of its terms. Henceforth, for the Americans' purposes, Tabatabai was out of the picture, disappearing from sight as suddenly as he'd appeared. And, unlike Tabatabai, with his insistence on speed, the Majlis, consumed by the war and daily reports from the front, gave the task low priority. "We are not in a hurry to release the hostages," one of the members of the Majlis's seven-member commission charged with resolving the issue announced. "We have no intention of helping Jimmy Carter in his Presidential campaign."

Whatever the motive behind the stall, it finally eased on October 27, more than two and a half weeks after Christopher had sent the Traveler the requested parts inventory. That day, the Majlis debate finally began, again broadcast live on national radio. The gallery was full of international press. One Paris-based reporter described the scene:

"As they filed into what had once been the Imperial Senate, the deputies offered a vivid cross-section of the components of the revolution. Some checked their pistols in the cloakroom. Others were accompanied by ferocious-looking bodyguards carrying machine guns. The members of the religious community in their black-and-white turbans seemed anachronistic next to the young people in sport shirts, the bourgeoisie in their three-piece suits and women wearing veils. All the deputies sat in luxurious garnet armchairs arranged in a semicircle, underneath crystal chandeliers hanging from a graceful dome. The walls, alternating green marble and beige leather, offered a final, incongruous touch."

That day's session involved a lot of back-and-forth with what seemed to be a slight edge toward accepting Tabatabai's terms, but the proceeding eventually became sidetracked by fervor about the war. The result was a postponement for two days.

Word of what had happened at the Majlis reached the White House, eight time zones away, on the morning of Monday, October 27, eight days before the election. Jimmy Carter got the news just as he was leaving for Cleveland, Ohio. He was scheduled to debate Ronald Reagan there the next day, for the first and only time, in what would be the paramount event of the 1980 presidential campaign. Christopher, Secretary of State Muskie, and Brzezinski met with the president very briefly.

Carter listened to their report without comment. Then, Brzezinski remembered, he "gave us a wave, and abruptly terminated the meeting."

The Carter campaign had not particularly wanted the debate for which Carter was headed. Indeed, the president's pollster pointed out that such events always favored the challenger and predicted that Carter had at best a 25 percent chance of winning it. No one disagreed with him.

And the odds were even worse than they seemed. The briefing books the

Republicans used to prepare Reagan were copies of one of barely a dozen sets that had been produced by the Carter campaign in order to prepare the president. Republican procurement of the highly secret books was part of Bill Casey's "intelligence operation." They had been stolen and photocopied by someone inside the White House and then sold to the Republicans through an unidentified "informant" for $2,860. Casey denied all knowledge of the books, but according to the congressional committee that later investigated him for it, he had received the books personally and authorized the payment. All of this, however, remained secret until long after the debate itself. In the meantime, Reagan's natural actor's advantage in stage presence was multiplied tenfold by his secret possession of his opponent's battle plan.

On the day of the debate, Carter got up early and jogged through the Cleveland rain. His afternoon had been scheduled empty so he could relax and do a little last-minute practicing, but things came up that only he could deal with, so by the time Ham Jordan saw his boss, Carter was in a foul mood. "He tried to assure me he was relaxed," Jordan remembered, "but I could see tension written on his face."

Not surprisingly, behind his podium on national television that evening, Carter stumbled a bit out of the block and never quite got ahead of things for the whole ninety minutes. The Crisis and a possible October Surprise only came up briefly once under questioning from a panel of journalists, when the shah's old friend Barbara Walters asked the president about press reports that he was negotiating an arms-for-hostages swap with the Iranians. Carter responded that he had no plans to sell Iran anything more, but there was some military hardware Iran had already bought and paid for that would be delivered whenever the hostages were released and the American freeze on Iran's assets lifted. Reagan said he would never deal with terrorists, that the whole affair had been a national humiliation, and that there ought to be a congressional investigation into how Carter had handled it.

Afterward, Jordan congratulated the president and told him he had won, but Ham knew it was a lie at the time he said it.

· 29 ·

————

THE POLLS DURING THE LAST WEEK BEFORE THE
election continued to flutter, but Carter emerged from the debate 3 points
down and more or less stayed there. That gap was still within most polls'
margin of error and hence considered too close to call, but a dark cloud settled over the president's reelection prospects nonetheless. "Toward the end
of the campaign," one Washington journalist observed, "candidates take on
the look of what may be their fates — somewhat as dogs take on the look of
their masters — and for the past couple of days Reagan has been looking
like a winner (confident, buoyant) and Carter like a loser (strained, dispirited). Carter looks as if something has gone out of him."

There was also little doubt among observers about which issue had undone the president's reelection campaign more than any other. "The hostages
were seized . . . one year ago," the Washington journalist continued, and
"Carter has been trying to ride the crocodile [ever since]. Sometimes he has
been able to manipulate the problem to his own temporary advantage, but it
has always been there as a menace to him. The hostage Crisis became to

many a symbol of what they saw as a decline in our power. And it has added to an impression of Carter as hapless."

Jimmy Carter's hopes of resolving the Crisis before the presidential votes were cast continued to rise and fall according to the news from Tehran. On Thursday, October 30, the Majlis was scheduled to convene at 8:00 a.m., to resume its consideration of the fate of the hostages. According to reports the White House was receiving through the Swiss and other foreign embassies in Tehran, the forces supporting an endorsement of the Traveler's terms had at least a twenty-vote majority and were expected to carry that day's floor fight. Once again, however, they never got a chance. By 8:30, the old Imperial Senate chamber's plush seats were less than half full, a situation quite out of the ordinary. The deputies were usually punctual, but this morning a crowd of them refused to leave the antechamber and assume their seats. The international reporters already seated in the gallery were abuzz with rumors about what was going on. Finally the speaker of the Majlis gaveled for order and announced that the absent members were in the halls of the building but refused to be "formally present," hence the body had no quorum with which to proceed. The speaker said he had no choice but to declare another postponement.

The announcement set off a flurry of yelling and accusations hurled in the direction of the absent deputies until the speaker again hammered for order. He said that Iran had been close to a solution to the Crisis before "*Amrika* and its allies set off the war," so it was understandable that these deputies were angry about having to settle it now when Iranian soldiers were dying along the Khuzistan front. The Islamic weekend was about to begin, the speaker explained, but when business resumed on Sunday, November 2, the Majlis would vote on the question first thing.

When the news reached Hamilton Jordan, he figured that if something dramatic happened by Monday, Carter could beat Reagan by a nose. If something bad came out of Tehran on Sunday, though, it would mean Reagan's election.

Jordan was waiting in the president's Chicago hotel when the word from Iran was passed on in a 3:45 a.m. Sunday morning call to him from Christopher. The president was asleep in a suite down the hall. Chris told Ham that the Iranian Majlis had finally voted and he was about to report on it to the boss. The text of the Iranian resolution included the same four points laid out by Khomeini back in September, but there was a lot of language now wrapped around them that could prove problematic. The deputy secretary thought it essential that the president deliberate with his advisers about it as soon as possible.

Ham went down to Carter's suite to let him know and found the president awake and already on the phone with Christopher. When Carter got off the line, Jordan advised him to return to Washington to sort this out. Carter then called the secretary of state and the vice president, and both of them agreed with Ham. That was enough for Carter. The president ordered up *Air Force One,* and he and his entourage took off for the District of Columbia at quarter to six that morning. The Sunday events planned for Chicago were canceled, even though Jordan and Carter both knew he stood no chance of reelection unless he carried the city — and thus Illinois — by a healthy margin.

Carter would later say that he would never forget that November 2 flight from Chicago to Washington, with darkness to their back and the rising sun dead ahead. The president took in much of it from the cockpit, over the shoulders of the flight crew. The tableau of towering clouds embraced by the first light was "one of the most beautiful sunrises I have ever seen," he remembered. The president found himself praying in response. "My prayer was that the Iranian nightmare might soon be over and that my judgment and decisions might be wise ones. In a strange way, I felt relieved. It was out of my hands. Now my political future might well be determined by irrational people on the other side of the world over whom I have no control. If the hostages were released, I was convinced my reelection would be reassured; if the expectations of the American people were dashed again, there was little chance that I could win."

As always, Carter was ferried to the White House from Andrews Air Force Base in a helicopter that landed on the South Lawn. Brzezinski and Mondale were waiting for him on the grass, and Zbig immediately handed Carter the full translated text of the Majlis resolution, the first time he had seen it. The television news cameras caught the president striding with a serious face across the lawn for the White House, preoccupied with reading the document as he walked. "Very commander-in-chief-looking," one of the watching journalists observed.

Carter and his advisers immediately assembled in the Cabinet Room. By that point, the president had read enough of the two-page Majlis document to make up his mind.

"Until that time," Carter remembered, "I had hoped that we could reach an agreement in principle — with details to be worked out later — that would have permitted the hostage release before November 4. [But] that was unrealistic." Much of the new language in the Iranians' four points was over the top. The Majlis's terms called for the president to annul any court decisions encumbering Iran's assets, to grant Iran immunity from any other American legal actions, either public or private, and to seize "the assets of the cursed Shah" — all of which abrogated the United States Constitution and were hence out of the question. Carter told the group in the Cabinet Room that although there was very likely the basis for a negotiated settlement in the Majlis document, there were still significant differences to be worked out, too major to allow them to resolve the Crisis today or tomorrow or the next day.

"No one said anything," Ham Jordan remembered, "but every single person in that room knew at that moment that the hostages would not be free by Election Day."

The rest of the conclave was spent figuring how to tell the Iranians and the American public. Word of the Majlis action was all over the American media, most of which were treating it somewhat angrily as a bald-faced effort by the Iranians to influence the American elections.

The meeting was joined briefly in its deliberations by Rosalynn Carter. She had just flown in from one electioneering swing, was about to leave on another, and looked tired and drawn from weeks of continuous campaigning. She sat near the door and didn't say much. Finally Rosalynn and Jimmy walked out into the Rose Garden by themselves and could be seen holding hands as they talked. After a kiss good-bye, she walked out on the lawn to meet her helicopter. He returned to the drafting process.

Finally, at 6:23 p.m. Washington time — after a national media day spent in anticipation, televised analysis, and endless informed speculation — the president stepped to the podium in the White House briefing room and made his announcement to the press corps that had been on the move with him since 4:00 a.m. Chicago time. The statement was fed live onto the evening news.

"The Iranian parliament today has finally taken a position on the release of our hostages," he explained. "This is a significant development. We have long been aware that there would be no resolution to this problem until the new Iranian government was in place and the parliament had acted. . . . As we understand the parliament's proposals, they appear to offer a positive basis [for potential settlement]. We are pursuing the matter through diplomatic channels. . . .

"I wish I could predict when the hostages will return. I cannot. But whether our hostages come home before or after the election, and regardless of the outcome of the election, the Iranian government and the world community will find our country, its people, and the leaders of both political parties united in desiring the early and safe return of the hostages . . . but only on a basis that preserves our national honor and our national integrity."

Afterward, Ham Jordan put the best face he could on things. He argued that his candidate would get a boost for having a breakthrough, if not the hostages' actual release, and that Carter's "statesmanlike" performance under duress would gain him points as well.

Mondale, the other half of the ticket, didn't buy it. He thought their only chance to pull out a victory had just evaporated.

Jordan learned that Mondale was right thirty-one hours later, at close to 2:00 a.m. on the morning of Election Day, Tuesday, November 4. Jordan was asleep in his Washington apartment until the phone woke him; he finally managed to corral the receiver in the dark. The campaign's pollster was on the line. Jordan had asked him to call as soon as he had the results of their final poll, taken on Monday evening, after all the prime-time news broadcasts. The results were in.

The first thing the pollster said was "It's all gone."

It's all gone?

"The sky has fallen in," the pollster explained. "We are getting murdered. All the people that have been waiting . . . have left us. I've never seen anything like it in polling. Here we are neck and neck with Reagan up until the very end and everything breaks against us. It's the hostage thing."

The pollster predicted Jimmy Carter was about to lose the election by 10 percentage points.

Jordan and the pollster told Carter what was in store for him two hours later. The president had just finished the final event of his campaign, a midnight stop in Seattle after a day in Detroit. They reached him by phone. He was on *Air Force One*, as it was loading up for the cross-country night flight to Plains, Georgia. There, the president would rendezvous with Rosalynn and they would vote together as they always had. The press secretary knew what Jordan was calling about but had not yet had the opportunity to inform the president and soften the blow, so Carter got the information out of the blue.

The president said nothing after the pollster told him about the looming electoral massacre. Just silence.

Finally the pollster continued with an explanation. He said the hostage stuff, including the flood of first-anniversary stories that had been running in the press, had triggered a large outpouring of pent-up frustration with Carter's presidency. Almost all of those previously showing up in the campaign's polling as undecided were choosing Reagan. A lot of traditional working-class Democrats were going to wake up in another few hours and cast a Republican ballot for the first time in their lives. It would likely be a landslide against Carter.

Carter, in a voice Jordan described as "notable only for its lack of emotion," cautioned his aides not to tell Rosalynn, but leave that task for him. In the meantime, he was going to get some sleep.

Jimmy and Rosalynn voted the next morning in Plains, and during the brief remarks the president made there, his voice broke, but that was the only sign he ever gave the public of what he knew awaited him. The Carters were back at the White House by the afternoon and spent it talking with Ham and a number of others in their inner personal circle, all waiting around for the other shoe to fall.

Then returns finally started coming in, and they didn't have to wait any longer.

The networks called the election for Reagan at 7:15 p.m. eastern time, and Carter himself publicly conceded his defeat long before most of the polls west of the Rockies closed. The final tally was 51 percent to 41 percent, with the independent Anderson pulling 7. Only 52 percent of registered voters had bothered to vote. The popular-vote margin of Carter's loss was less than those Eisenhower had run up over Stevenson or Nixon had run up over McGovern, but the Electoral College tally was embarrassing. Carter carried only his home state of Georgia and Mondale's home state of Minnesota, plus Rhode Island, West Virginia, Maryland, Hawaii, and the District of Columbia. The electoral vote numbers were 489 to 49. Exit polls showed that half of those voting for Reagan explained themselves as voting against Carter more than anything else.

It was indeed all gone.

This story, however, was still not quite done.

With remarkable synchronicity, the final resolution of the Crisis began in the exact moments that Jimmy Carter's reelection was coming apart. On November 3, the day the polls began to turn on Carter, the Iranian prime minister met with the German ambassador in response to a request from the Americans drafted in the Cabinet Room the day before. The Iranian announced that henceforth, for the purpose of negotiating a solution to this situation, the linkage between the Islamic Republic and the United States would be through Algeria. According to the Majlis's stipulation, the Algerians would be acting as intermediaries, talking to first one side and then the other. On the Iranian end, negotiations would be handled by a committee of three, chaired by the same man who had headed the Majlis commission. "This was the kind of news we'd been awaiting for nearly a year," Warren Christopher said. "The Iranians had officially turned to a third party for help."

On the American end, these negotiations were Christopher's show, and he pulled them off with a deft touch and characteristic inconspicuousness. "Christopher was a highly disciplined man who, by instinct and conviction, shunned personal publicity," an NSC aide remembered. "If ever an official in an exposed position displayed a passion for anonymity, Christopher's performance in the hostage negotiations would have to be regarded as a classic example." Chris respected the Algerians as first-rate diplomats and set about constructing a document about the American position to present to them. His goal was something short, in language that a layman could understand, capable of surviving translation into French for the Algerians and then into Farsi for Iran. He sent back several drafts from the State Department lawyers until he got what he wanted. Then, on November 9, he flew to Algiers.

The meeting there, with the Algerian foreign minister and three of the country's foremost diplomats, was held in a Moorish palace outside of town, across a table covered in green baize, Algerians on one side, Americans on the other. Christopher had company from the State Department but did almost all the talking for the United States himself. His goal was to give the Algerians a deep feel for the American position, both substantively and politically. The latter he spelled out in no uncertain terms. Jimmy Carter was a lame-duck president, Christopher explained. He would be out of office by the afternoon of January 20, and after that the fate of the negotiations would be in the hands of Ronald Reagan and the Republicans. Christopher told the Algerians that, quite frankly, "the Iranians would be better off dealing with me rather than taking their chances with the new administration." All parties understood from the very beginning that the clock was ticking.

On November 12, after Christopher had flown back to Washington, the Algerians flew to Tehran and began the task of informing the Iranians of the

American response. On November 20 the Iranians delivered a written rejoinder to the Algerians, which, once the intermediaries had digested and discussed it, was delivered to the Americans in Washington on November 26.

The Iranian paper carried a note of irritation. It accused the Americans of not being to the point. The Majlis position had been presented to them with a demand for yes or no answers, and Iran still wanted a yes or a no on each of the four points. All of the American note was about "unrelated" matters that the Iranian negotiators had no mandate to address.

In the White House discussions on how to treat this Iranian approach, Brzezinski dismissed it as "insulting" and proposed rejecting it out of hand. Christopher, however, proposed a softer strategy. This was just the Iranians' opening gambit, so there was no point to using it as an excuse to cut off the process. Carter backed Christopher, so State spent two very long and intense days putting together a document carefully structured to sidestep the Iranian position. The new American rejoinder featured brief, positive responses to each of the Majlis's four points, treating them as abstract principles as opposed to specific guidelines. Each of those abstract positives, however, referred to a detailed codicil that addressed "procedural steps" necessary to realize those points. In those footnotes, Christopher laid out the American case, rejecting the language in which each of the four points had been couched, articulating possible solutions that fit inside American legal parameters.

The Algerians took the American document and, after discussing it in detail with Christopher, flew to Tehran. There, the intermediaries were again dealing with a different cast of Iranian characters than the Americans had ever dealt with before. Bani Sadr, though still president of the Islamic Republic, was rarely directly informed about any of the negotiations' details and was never asked to approve the deal when the time came — even though both were part of his office's prerogatives according to the constitution. And Ghotbzadeh, the man most associated by the Iranian public with previous attempts to resolve the Crisis, was not only out of the loop but drifting into deeper and deeper trouble.

After he left the government, Sadegh and several friends had decided to found a newspaper and use it as a base from which to criticize the IRP. The mullahs controlling the Ministry of Information, however, refused to issue him a publication permit. He fumed, but had no choice except to abandon his plans. He would not, however, be silenced. When the Majlis finally acted and launched these negotiations with the United States, Ghotbzadeh quite smugly pointed out that the four points they proposed were the same ones of which he had convinced the imam months earlier. He had also offered himself as a source for a long televised interview via satellite uplink with an American journalist in Paris on the subject of possible deals for the hostages. The interview had been scheduled for the day after the American presidential election, but when Ghotbzadeh went to the state media headquarters, the technicians there had refused to connect the uplink and effectively prevented the interview.

Then, using one of his remaining relationships inside the television and radio monopoly, Sadegh struck back at his IRP tormentors. He taped an interview as part of a larger program for Iranian television about broadcasting and the Revolution, and, once on camera, Ghotbzadeh, according to a Canadian journalist who watched the performance, "lashed out at the IRP and its . . . Prime Minister and at its subversion of all democratic process. He denounced the oppressive censorship of the regime and its rigidly controlled programming on the state radio and television. [He said] it was at best unbearably dull fare that an alienated population sneered at as 'mullahvision,' and at worst was propaganda and dangerous lies disseminated by power-hungry clerics." Sadegh also urged people to take to the streets against it.

On November 7, the day the tape was broadcast, Ghotbzadeh's ally at state television called him from Bani Sadr's house and warned Ghotbzadeh to make himself scarce. His ally was staying away from home in order to avoid possible arrest and recommended that Sadegh do likewise.

Sadegh did not, and the next day the religious police, carrying a warrant signed by two IRP public prosecutors, searched his living quarters and placed him under arrest. The charges were never specified. The former foreign minister was taken to the same prison where the hostages were being held. Those who saw him at the arrest scene said he seemed to have been expecting it and had only asked for time to fetch his Koran and his prayer shawl when they took him away.

Word of Ghotbzadeh's arrest reached Bani Sadr almost immediately. As many differences as he had with Sadegh over the years, they were revolutionary comrades, and at this point he thought they had no option but to make common cause. Abolhassan called for public outcry against Ghotbzadeh's imprisonment, and large demonstrations took the streets for several days running, all of them covered by the state media. Bani Sadr had his wife call Khomeini's wife as well and tell her that to imprison Sadegh simply because of what he thought was the grossest disloyalty. This was a man he had worked with for twenty years. Khomeini's wife called back after talking to her husband. He had told her that it would do Sadegh good to spend a little time in jail to think about things.

A furious Bani Sadr then went straight to the imam himself, to chastise his "spiritual father" for what was going on. When he threatened to go to the prison and join Ghotbzadeh, thus throwing the government into even more crisis, the imam relented and promised to have Sadegh released.

That release finally happened on the day after the Algerians arrived in Tehran from their first session with Christopher. Shortly after leaving prison, Ghotbzadeh went by the president's office. He told Bani Sadr that he had been sure all along that the imam wouldn't let the IRP get away with arresting him.

At that, Bani Sadr blew up. The imam? The imam? Didn't Sadegh get it? It was the imam who'd had him arrested in the first place. Bani Sadr was the one who got him out. If it had been up to the imam, Sadegh would have still been there next spring.

When he was finished talking to Bani Sadr, Ghotbzadeh went out to Jamaran to confront Khomeini. It was apparently a fiery encounter.

Sadegh told his spiritual father that although he loved him, the imam had no right to shut him up. Islam did not give him the right to total censorship.

Khomeini answered that he had the religious right to order him to shut up and he was doing it. The imam's command was necessary to save the Revolution and preserve Islam. And Sadegh, he ordered, would obey him.

Ghotbzadeh begged his father not to let the mullahs lead him into destroying everything for which they had struggled all those years.

Khomeini did not back off and continued to insist that Sadegh promise him that he would stop his attacks on the IRP. The Revolution needed time and it had many enemies. Ghotbzadeh had to trust him and obey.

Sadegh finally agreed, but he didn't mean it. On the contrary, Ghotbzadeh was now convinced that he and the man he had worshipped were on opposite sides. And he was already thinking about the need to behave accordingly.

On December 19 the Algerians delivered the latest Iranian note to Washington. The document threw everyone on Christopher's team for a loop. They had spent the last three weeks whittling down the Iranians' position to something closer to American realities, and now Iran suddenly leapfrogged all that and delivered a demand that seemed even more impossible than the one with which they had started.

In total, the Iranians now suddenly asked for some $24 billion to be placed in escrow with the Algerians before any hostage release — a figure almost three times the one the Americans had been proposing and twice anything the Iranians had mentioned before. Of this, $14 billion covered frozen assets — a figure close to the one used by the Americans, before claims against those assets were subtracted — and the other $10 billion was to be a guarantee against the future American seizure of the shah's wealth. They also still demanded that the Americans immunize Iran from all potential civil claims against it, including almost $3 billion in current outstanding actions for broken contracts, confiscated property, and unpaid debts.

At first, this exorbitance seemed to the White House like the last straw. Carter and his foreign policy advisers seriously considered simply abandoning the negotiations where they stood and handing the problem over to the incoming Republicans. "The Iranian message," one of Brzezinski's aides later remembered, "appeared so far removed from the reality of what was possible for the United States — legally or morally — that it appeared to be a calculated insult. . . . It seemed that the negotiations had broken down totally and irrevocably." Only Christopher raised a contrary voice in the White House inner circles. He reminded the president that they were dealing with people "grounded in the bazaar tradition, where the making of outrageous demands and haggling up to the last minute are routine."

Instead of automatically rejecting the Iranian note, Christopher and his team tried to get past the insult and scrutinize the contents at arm's length. When they did so, Christopher pointed out, it became clear that the document contained several clear and major concessions hiding behind its rhetoric. The Iranians had accepted the use of escrow to handle financial questions, Iran's obligation to bring current the loans made to Iran by American banks in the time of the shah, and the use of an international arbitration process to deal with claims. The most obnoxious part of their response had been the demand for financial guarantees. However, this was designed, according to one of those involved in the discussions, "to cover themselves politically and avoid the appearance of being taken in by the Americans . . . and not be seen as relying solely on the word of the Great Satan. . . . It was possible to see the

Iranian response as a rather far-reaching effort to accommodate the U.S. position, but with some protective factors built in to ensure that they would not be cheated by an enemy they hated and distrusted."

Christopher recommended going forward, and Carter ultimately agreed. They would simply ignore the disagreeable Iranian proposals and concentrate on the breakthroughs.

The deputy secretary then spent most of the rest of December structuring a new approach, first with his State Department team and then with the Algerians. Until now the Algerians had simply been acting as "postman," carrying each side's positions back and forth to each other. Now Christopher proposed that they begin "accelerating the negotiations by breaking this cycle" and focus on creating "a new form of document that set out a series of mutually dependent promises that would be made to Algeria by both the United States and Iran." Each country would sign a declaration to the Algerians that included the terms of the deal. This way, the Iranians would not have to sign the same physical document as the Americans — something they had steadfastly refused to do — but the parties could nonetheless concentrate on creating a single text to which they would both adhere, rather than throwing position papers back and forth.

The other thing Christopher now added to the mix was an absolute deadline. If there was no agreement in place by January 16, 1981, he warned the Algerians, the Carter administration could not guarantee to deliver on its end of things before its term ran out.

That the Iranians themselves were expecting to soon make a deal was apparent to the hostages before the Americans even proffered their new approach. On December 17 the American captives were moved out of the prison and into new, far more comfortable housing.

"After half an hour's drive as the usual blindfolded sardines in back of a van," Barry Rosen remembered, "we stopped in a place that smelled of snow and the country. Delicious warmth greeted us inside the building. . . . When my blindfold was removed, I was in one of the handsomest offices I had seen in Iran, without a trace of warping wood or makeshift carpentry. Grasscloth wallpaper and fine contemporary furniture matched the fine construction, and the adjoining bathroom was clean, modern, and pleasantly heated. Five others were installed [with me] in the same large room. . . . Almost the entire wall opposite the door was a sliding window leading to a balcony. We were ordered not to part the curtains until morning. When we did, we made out a countrylike panorama broken by a road, tin roofs tipped with snow. . . . We assumed this pastoral district was in northern Tehran, near the [shah's] palace. The building itself might have been an office in the shah's imperial court, perhaps even on the palace grounds. . . . The view of the outdoors and the privilege of looking out without restriction until the 6 p.m. curfew put us in good spirits. The first day, we gazed for hours at snow falling on fir trees."

On Christmas Eve some of the hostages used their new panoramic window to watch an Iraqi bombing raid conducted against the city below, with huge explosions and flurries of antiaircraft fire lighting up the early-evening sky, easily the largest such bombardment these hostages had ever witnessed. The Iraqi planes didn't just attack and go, but circled to attack again and again. About twenty minutes after the air raid was finished, the Americans were taken to their Christmas festivities. The drill was the same as the year before, with everyone celebrating in separate groups of a half dozen or so. A tree had been erected and presents were distributed, mostly jogging clothes that had been donated by an American manufacturer earlier in the year, many the wrong sizes for the people to whom they were given.

Christmas, the next day, brought the biggest treat. The Algerians came calling on the captives. "Two well-suited men with briefcases," Rosen recalled, "introduced themselves as the Algerian ambassador to Iran and a member of the Algerian Foreign Ministry. Checking our names against a list, they also checked our condition visually. . . . They explained that Algeria was 'helping with negotiations concerning you' and confirmed that the chief point of issue [between Iran and the United States] now was money. At the moment, they said, there was a deadlock. They were leaving for Washington that very night with an Iranian counterproposal. . . . Negotiations had [clearly] acquired a momentum, and we could almost taste the result." Before their departure, the Algerians collected mail from any of the hostages who wanted to send something to their families.

"The Algerian ambassador appeared to be very sympathetic to our plight," Robert Ode noted that night in his diary. "Surely hope that something good will happen this time!"

Certainly the pace of the exchanges between Iran and the United States accelerated with the New Year, and on January 7, Deputy Secretary of State Warren Christopher moved his base of operations to Algiers to facilitate the Algerian mediation. He brought with him a troop of State Department lawyers and was soon joined by another troop from the Treasury Department. The document they were drafting would be characterized by the *New York Times* as "one of the most complex international agreements in recent history." The freeze of Iranian assets was no small matter to untangle, as was simply generating an accurate accounting of the monies involved. There was also a separate negotiation, which had been ongoing since the previous June, between the Islamic Republic and the American and European banks from whom Iran had borrowed some $3.6 billion under the shah. In order for any deal concerning Iran's potentially attachable assets to be consummated, the banks would have to sign off. At the very least, that would require bringing those outstanding loans "current" by making good on missed payments and interest.

Despite the hard work of his lawyers and of the Algerians, progress on resolving the bank loans was so slow that by January 14, two days before the deadline he had posted back in December, Christopher did not believe the negotiation would be finished before Reagan's inaugural.

Then, once again, the Iranians surprised him.

Out of the blue, on January 15 the Islamic Republic's negotiators sent word to the Algerians that they were prepared to take the whole bank loan issue off the table by paying those loans in full. The Americans were stunned. The Iranian move amounted to a reversal of enormous magnitude. The Americans had considered asking for such a $3.6 billion payoff early in the negotiations, but thought that it ran so counter to Iran's obvious financial interest that it would never be acceptable. To almost all the Americans involved, that the Iranians now proposed such a solution on their own was a clear sign of how desperately Iran wanted to get this deal done, though the exact reason for their urgency remained unclear.

The new arrangement required the troops of lawyers and bankers to spend ninety straight hours redrafting what would eventually be officially referred to as the Declaration of Algiers, racing against the clock. Unforeseen disagreements over implementing mechanisms threatened to stall progress on several occasions, but each was sorted out. Finally, during the last full remaining day of the Carter administration, the deal was set: When $7.955 billion was placed in escrow for Iran at the Bank of England, the fifty-two American captives would be released. All but $2.2 billion of that money in escrow would be held to pay off the banks and cover possible judgments against Iran in the American courts. The Americans also agreed to refrain from intervention in Iran's internal affairs and agreed to facilitate any claims Iran wished to make in the American courts against the estate of the shah. The $2.2 billion net from escrow would be transferred to Iran as soon as the Algerians certified that the captive American diplomats were out of Iranian airspace.

After receiving Carter's approval, Warren Christopher signed the Declaration of Algiers on behalf of the United States at a small official ceremony in Algiers on January 19. Christopher appeared in the same suit of clothes he had worn for the last forty-eight hours straight. One of his assistants standing in the line behind him at the ceremony fell asleep on his feet and had to be caught as he collapsed.

Back in Washington, Jimmy and Rosalynn Carter had returned to the White House from their very last trip to Camp David to await the final news from Christopher.

By this point, the president remembered, getting the hostages released during his watch "had become almost an obsession with me." Carter waited in the Oval Office, where he would end up spending almost all of his final forty-eight hours as president. He was dressed in a cardigan sweater and slacks, and his mood matched his wardrobe. About 2:00 a.m. on Monday morning, he took his shoes off, had the stewards fetch him a blanket, and lay down on the couch facing the fireplace. He was resting, not sleeping, and every now and then got up to place another log on the fire. He also invited the White House counsel and Ham Jordan to join him, and they lounged by the hearth, discussing what lay in store for the country when this was all over.

Finally, at close to 4:00 a.m., Chris called from Algiers and said they had a deal. The three men cheered and Jimmy immediately got on the phone to Rosalynn upstairs and let her know. She came down to join them, and they all broke out champagne to toast their success.

"To freedom," Carter declared, hoisting his glass in the air.

At 4:44 a.m. on Day 443, the president went into the White House briefing room and informed the press, shying away from discussing the details of the deal or from claiming any victory.

It had been his original plan to fly to Germany to greet the hostages when they were ferried to an American air base there and then return in time for Reagan's inaugural, but Christopher called back in a bit and disabused him of that idea. There were still difficulties to be ironed out, the deputy secretary explained. The latest was a roadblock that had been thrown up by the

Iranian Central Bank. No hostages were going to be released until these final glitches were straightened out. There would be no way the president could fly to Europe, greet hostages, and be back for the ceremony at noon tomorrow. To be honest, Christopher only hoped that the hostages would indeed be freed while Carter was still president. Right now, that looked like a questionable proposition.

Even in the end, down to his last hours in office, Jimmy Carter had to wait some more.

On January 20, 1981, James Earl Carter Jr.'s final day as president of the United States, sometime after 3:00 a.m. Washington time, long complex telexes to a dozen and a half banks in five different countries began being dispatched from Algiers, instructing them to commence their various roles. The telexes themselves would take several hours to send and be verified. Carter and his inner circle were camped out in the Oval Office all night. Jordan fell asleep on a couch sometime early in the morning and had to be awoken at close to 6:00 a.m. and told that the actual fund transfer had begun. Almost $8 billion was now being shifted from the twelve American banks holding Iranian assets to the escrow account in London. In Algiers the Americans kept a line open to the Bank of England and tracked the running total on a calculator as each of the banks transferred its funds.

At 8:09 a.m., Christopher called. The Bank of England had certified the transfer, he reported, and Iran was being notified accordingly by the Algerians.

A significant crowd of staff and insiders had now gathered in the Oval Office and they all expected that now that the Americans had fulfilled their part of the bargain, the hostages would be released at any moment. The room throbbed with a celebration that was about to break out, but by then they should have known better. At 8:39, Carter was notified that American intelligence in Tehran had reported two Air Algeria jetliners were on the ground at the airport, off on a far corner of the runway. That was soon followed by a report that the hostages had been loaded onto the planes.

Then everything froze in place. The Algerian airliners did not move.

When Zbigniew Brzezinski came in to give his final national security briefing at 9:00, the president was in the midst of the gathering, still in his jeans, on the secure red telephone trying to find some news to explain the delay. One of those present described him as "fidgety and impatient." He stayed on the open red phone line for the next hour, interrupted by side talk and by increasingly insistent requests from Rosalynn that he get dressed. The Reagans were going to be there soon. Around 10:00, Jordan emptied the Oval Office so the president could have a few minutes alone. By this point, Brzezinski had concluded that it was "clear that the Iranians were deliberately holding [the release] up so that the transfer of hostages would not occur while Jimmy Carter is President of the United States." Finally, at 10:25, Carter went upstairs to put on his suit.

Jordan and another aide now took over monitoring developments in Tehran. They set up in the Situation Room and used one of its televisions to watch the president welcome his successor out on the White House portico. Carter called in for news as soon as he was off camera, but they could only report that the Swiss ambassador in Tehran had been called by the Iranians at 11:00 Washington time and told to come immediately to the airport to witness the hostages' embarkation. Nothing else had happened.

Close to 11:30, after Jimmy and Rosalynn had left the White House in the motorcade to the inauguration ceremony, word came from Tehran that the state media there had announced that the hostages would be leaving in the next half hour. Carter was given the word over his limo's phone. If any more news came while he was up on the reviewing stand, transferring power, Carter had an aide on a secure open phone line under instructions to bring him a note.

In the meantime, Ham Jordan and the other Carterites had to leave the White House to make room for the new administration. All the pictures of Jimmy Carter in the offices were being changed to pictures of Ronald Reagan as Jordan left the Situation Room and made his way outside. Ham then caught his limo for Andrews Air Force Base, where he was to rendezvous with the president and fly to Georgia together in an air force transport. After a short layover, they would then fly to Germany to welcome the hostages.

Jordan arrived at Andrews before Carter, still without news of the hostages, so he used a secure phone there to call the Situation Room to see what had happened. After an awkward delay, Ham was told by the duty officer with whom he'd been dealing all morning that he could not receive the information for which he was asking. It was now past noon and, since 11:57 a.m., Ronald Reagan had been president of the United States. As a consequence, Hamilton Jordan was no longer on the list of those cleared to learn the answer to his question.

As it turned out, the report Jimmy Carter had been given shortly before

9:00 a.m. Washington time saying the hostages had been loaded onto the Algerian airliners, was in fact, baseless. Almost 9:00 a.m. in Washington was almost 5:30 p.m. Tehran time, and at that hour, the forty-six hostages being held at the North Tehran palace — now including the three from the Foreign Ministry — had not yet moved. Nor had the half dozen still in the chancery building at the Den of Spies.

But they had all been told they were going. In the chancery building, Robert Ode remembered being informed of his pending release by a student guard "who I thoroughly detested and I always referred to as 'Shovelface' because of his rather flat facial structure. . . . Shovelface spoke English well and, with a newspaper before him, informed me that 'some' of the hostages were to be released . . . and that I was 'one of the candidates'! While I couldn't seriously believe that our government would permit or accept the release of some but not all of the hostages, the thought raced through my mind. . . . 'If I am one of the "candidates" — how do I win this election?'"

Ode and the others at both the chancery and palace waited all afternoon, expecting imminent release. It was already dark when the call to evening prayers went out. By that point, some hostages had given up for the day and returned to their normal routines of exercise and activity. Out at the palace, Barry Rosen remembered, "minutes passed like weeks."

Finally, shortly after six, Rosen and others there were told to prepare to leave. They were instructed to take one small plastic garbage bag of personal possessions. Everything else would have to be abandoned. For security reasons, the student guards had previously taken away a number of the captive diplomats' shoes. Those without footwear were guided to a room downstairs in which there was a huge pile of shoes that had been seized earlier or confiscated when the students searched the apartments of their captives. The barefoot hostages were told to find a pair that fit.

At the chancery, Robert Ode's final hurdle before leaving was a video-taped interview with Sister Mary, for the students' archive. "Several TV cameras were focused on us," Ode remembered, "and Mary asked me to describe my daily activities while being held hostage. I related how I did calisthenics each morning; then, following breakfast, I would [pace] rapidly across my room for approximately 1,200 times to equate two miles of walking; write letters to my wife . . . read, play Scrabble and other games with hostages in my room, and study Spanish. Mary queried me as to whether I had been well treated, to which I replied, 'There was much room for improvement in our treatment.' Then she asked me whether I felt there was any justification for having been taken hostage. I replied, 'There was absolutely no justification . . . there never was.' With that, Mary said, 'The interview is over!'"

The captives at the palace began being moved around 7:00 p.m. Tehran time. "Blindfolded," Barry Rosen remembered, "we groped downstairs from the third floor, carrying our bags. The motor of a bus — surely it was a bus, and a large one — ran and ran. Platoons of [student] guards were scurrying again. [The leader of the guards] directed the operation as if it were the embarkation for the Normandy invasion. Under his orders we handed over our bags, which were tossed aside. Somehow I knew they wouldn't be going with us. Six months later, most of the contents were sent to me in Brooklyn via the Red Cross."

The only incident came when Mike Metrinko, an embassy political officer who was suspected of being CIA, got into a shouting match with one of the students. Metrinko had spent much of his captivity undergoing long interrogation sessions. As they were loading, he called the student a "son of a whore" in Farsi —"an insult he knew would infuriate," Rosen explained. "I could hear him being taken off the bus. Slaps and punches sounded over the grumble of the motor." Then Metrinko was put back on, and the bus headed for the airport. It was now approximately 7:30 p.m. in Tehran, about the same time Jimmy Carter and Ronald Reagan were being photographed together on the White House portico in Washington.

The captive diplomats' trip through the city was eerie. As air raid protection, all buildings and street lamps were entirely blacked out, so the ride was like sailing through ink. The bus never stopped on its way to the airport, an unheard-of phenomenon at any hour in ordinary Tehran traffic. Once there, it was driven out to a spot on the far end of the tarmac, perhaps thirty yards from the Algerian airliners, and parked.

"We sat there at the airport, motionless, for what must've been thirty minutes," embassy budget officer Bruce German recalled. "Maybe more. I don't know how long for sure, but it seemed like a long time. The goons were waiting until it was twelve noon in Washington, so that Carter would no longer be president. That meant it would have to have been 8:30 at night in Iran. So they were waiting for the official word that Reagan had in fact been sworn in before they said, 'Let's move 'em.'" Several who peeked out from under their blindfolds could see the student guards just standing there, looking at their watches.

When the word to disembark eventually came, it was sudden. One by one, the captives were guided to the door of the bus, where their blindfolds were pulled off without warning and they were shoved into the glare of movie lights. The students were filming them one last time as they emerged. To reach the waiting Algerian airliner, the hostages were forced to run a gauntlet of some sixty or seventy students, all shouting "*Marg bar Amrika*" over and over with great ferocity. "This was no ritual," Barry Rosen remembered, "but an expression of fury. . . . I had never heard [these chants] laced with more venom." Some of the Americans were jostled or spat upon during their walk between the rows of Iranians. One captive communications officer went through the line shouting "*Marg bar Khomeini*" and flipping the students the bird. "They were shouting right back at me," he remembered, "and spitting and swinging at me."

When they reached the planes, the hostages were greeted by an Algerian security detail and the Swiss ambassador. Once the ambassador had certified that all fifty-two hostages were on board, the Air Algeria airliners taxied away from the Muslim Students Following the Line of the Imam and took off.

For his part, Jimmy Carter did not hang around the scene of his last moment as president of the United States any longer than he had to. Immediately after Reagan finished his inaugural address, Jimmy and Rosalynn gathered up the Mondales and bundled into their limousine for the ride to Andrews Air Force Base. At 12:38 p.m. — just after 9:00 p.m. in Tehran — as the capital was disappearing in the former president's rearview mirror, the phone in the limo rang.

Carter answered it, received a quick message from the Situation Room, and then hung up. He turned to Mondale.

"They're out," he said.

WELCOME
BACK TO
FREEDOM

EPILOGUE

EPILOGUE

THE AMERICAN HOSTAGES FLEW WITH THE ALGE-
rians from Tehran to Algiers, where they were greeted by Warren Christopher, then transported in American planes to a medical facility at a NATO
air base in Germany. There, the former captives were welcomed by former
president Carter and, later, by former secretary of state Vance. Upon their return to American soil after medical examination and debriefing, they were
greeted by President Reagan.

They didn't act as a group again until the year 2000, when all the former
hostages or their heirs joined in a class action lawsuit filed in Washington
DC Federal District Court against the Islamic Republic of Iran. The suit
sought damages under provisions of 1996 federal antiterrorism legislation
that created a legal cause of action for American victims of state-sponsored
terror. The Islamic Republic refused to respond to the suit, and the hostages
won a default judgment in August 2001. A hearing on damages was scheduled for that October, with a number of hostages to testify about their experience, but at the last moment, the United States government intervened and

asked the court to dismiss the matter entirely. It argued that any such lawsuit by the hostages had been specifically precluded in the Declaration of Algiers. The hostages' attorney responded that the Declaration of Algiers had never been ratified by the Senate, was literally a deal made with a gun to America's head, and had been superseded by the 1996 statute and its subsequent amendments. The hostages' attorney also argued that the declaration had unfairly singled the hostages out — detailing the intricacies of adjudicating commercial claims against Iran but specifically barring Iran's captives from seeking similar redress for their pain and suffering. While sympathizing with the plaintiffs, the district court agreed with the government, denying the hostages' claim as a matter of law, and the District of Columbia Circuit Court of Appeals affirmed that judgment. The hostages petitioned the United States Supreme Court in February 2004 and await a response.

Barry Rosen, the press officer threatened at gunpoint and eventually overwhelmed with anxiety attacks, reluctantly retired from the Foreign Service, "for the good of my family," a year after the hostages' return. He went to work at Columbia University in the public affairs office, then to Brooklyn College CUNY as an assistant vice president, and finally back to Columbia in 1995 as vice president and executive director of external affairs for Teachers College. Rosen resigned his post in February 2004 to head up a Columbia University project in Afghanistan, engaging in teacher training and textbook development. It is his first return to the region and to his original career path since his release from Tehran twenty-three years ago. In 1998 he arranged a highly publicized meeting in Paris with a former Muslim Student Following the Line of the Imam. Rosen had hoped this initial overture would lead to more extensive meetings, but the former student with whom he met was subsequently imprisoned in Iran. Rosen's anxiety disorder has not disappeared, and he continues to treat it with medication and therapy.

Robert Ode, the consular officer who was the oldest American diplomat taken hostage on November 4, 1979, retired to his home in Sun City, Arizona, where he died in September 1995.

John Limbert, the political officer who attempted to negotiate with the invading students in the embassy hallway outside the locked second-floor door, went on to Foreign Service postings in Algiers, Conakry, and Dubayy. He eventually spent three years as ambassador to Mauritania and is currently serving as president of the American Foreign Service Association, the Foreign Service labor union.

Don Hohman, the army medic who was displayed at the embassy gate during the first days of the Crisis, continued in the army until he retired in 1990. He currently works as a civilian physician's assistant at the Army Community Hospital in Fort Knox, Kentucky. He has not slept well since being taken captive and now keeps a loaded gun under his pillow. Talking about his captivity brings back bad memories, so he rarely does, but, he admits, "it always wanders around in the back of my mind." The Veterans Administration finally granted him a 30 percent disability for his post-traumatic stress disorder but has refused to credit the cardiac arrhythmia that began during his imprisonment, even though it led to a coronary in 1995 and the subsequent installation of a pacemaker. The VA claims there is no proof the condition began during his days as a hostage. Hohman sees the government response to the hostages' lawsuit as part of a pattern. "We did our duty," he says, "yet we're the ones getting dumped on." Hohman was abused physically throughout his imprisonment and vows he would only return to Tehran armed with an M16. "You can't ever forgive and forget," he explains, "if they don't admit to being wrong."

Bill Belk, the communications officer who attempted to escape in December 1979, retired from the Foreign Service in 1986. After a brief stab at the restaurant business in Washington state, Belk moved to Florida "to play golf," and has been doing so ever since. He harbors no animosity toward the Iranians but still believes that "what they did to us was absolutely wrong." Now sixty-eight, he calls the government's opposition to the hostage lawsuit "a slap in the face."

Colonel Leland Holland, the military attaché who immediately recognized the sounds of the Iraqi aerial bombing run from his prison cell, died in 1994 from prostate cancer.

Corporal William Gallegos, who mistook the Iraqi attack as the leading edge of an American rescue, left the Marine Corps shortly after his return to the United States. Unable to find work, he went back to school and received a degree in criminal justice and criminology from Metro State University in Denver, Colorado. He eventually hired on at the Denver sheriff's office and then transferred to the Denver Police Department, where he now works as a metropolitan patrol officer. Imprisonment like the one he endured, he points out, "stays with you no matter what you do."

Joe Hall, the army warrant officer who sat in his cell cheering the attacking Iraqi aircraft, stayed with the army until retirement in 1988, serving in

Washington DC as a congressional liaison officer. Since then he has worked as a lobbyist for a high-tech communications company doing contracting with the FAA. He too is frustrated by the government's decision to block the hostages' lawsuit, calling it "the screwing we get for the screwing we got."

Mike Metrinko, the hostage political officer who was slapped around by his captors while waiting to board the bus for the airport, is currently on assignment with the Department of State "somewhere in Afghanistan."

The Muslim Students Following the Line of the Imam assembled at the Den of Spies to consider their future shortly after the hostages' release. There was much discussion about whether or not to continue as an active organization, and the group eventually decided against it. That was their last official meeting. Since then they have only assembled for reunions, having gone their own separate political ways. Some seventy of them were killed in the Iran-Iraq War.

Ibrahim Asgarzadeh, the engineering student who first proposed seizing the American embassy and helped found the Muslim Students Following the Line of the Imam, went on to work at the official *Kayhan* newspaper and with the Ministry of Culture and Islamic Guidance, as well as serving a six-month tour in the Iran-Iraq War. From 1988 to 1992, he was a member of the Majlis and acquired a reputation as a critic of the mullahs' restrictive policies, so much so that the Guardian Council banned him from running for reelection and sentenced him to a month of solitary confinement. In 1996 he was one of the founders of the reform movement that sought to loosen the mullahs' grip. That movement succeeded in electing the current Iranian reform government headed by Ayatollah Khatami. Asgarzadeh himself won election to the Tehran city council, one of the few bodies whose elections were not under the Guardian Council's control. On the nineteenth anniversary of the embassy takeover, in November 1998, Asgarzadeh publicly invited the former hostages to come to Tehran for a visit. Shortly after issuing the invitation, he was waylaid by Islamic vigilantes and seriously beaten. In the 2003 Tehran municipal elections, Asgarzadeh's bid for reelection failed.

Massoumeh Ebtekar, a.k.a. **Sister Mary,** the students' spokesperson to the foreign press, became the editor in chief of *Kayhan*'s English-language edition and returned to school, where she eventually earned a PhD in immunology. In 1995 Dr. Ebtekar was named an assistant professor at Tarbiat Modarres University. By then, she had already established herself as a leading advocate for the rights and status of women and was a frequent Iranian representative to international conferences on the subject. She also played a significant role in the founding of the Iranian reform movement and the election of the Khatami government. Since 1997 Ebtekar has served as a vice president of the Islamic Republic and head of Iran's Department of the Environment.

The chancery building of **the American embassy** on Avenue Taleghani continued to be occupied by the students' documents subcommittee for another three years as they finished sorting the captured files and preparing them for publication in a collected edition that numbered more than forty volumes. When the documents were done, the Revolutionary Guard Corps took over the property in its entirety. At first they used it as a training center for their troops, then as an educational center for adolescents who expressed an interest in the guard, and finally as a recruitment depot. It is currently largely vacant, awaiting possible transformation of the chancery into a museum about American imperialism. "We never gave in to the United States and this was the true path we have selected" is spray-painted on the wall out front. The anniversary demonstration, billed as a "National Day for Struggle Against World Arrogance," is staged by the Revolutionary Guard Corps. On that one day a year, the chancery building is opened to the public. Its innards long since stripped of all floor and wall coverings, the bare concrete is decorated with blown-up photos of American misdeeds along with explanatory text for the occasion.

William Sullivan, the last American ambassador to hold sway here, left the Foreign Service after resigning his post in Tehran and retired to Cuernavaca, Mexico. He has since suffered a severe stroke, reportedly leaving him without the power of speech, and now lives in a Washington DC nursing home.

Bruce Laingen, the chargé d'affairs who followed Sullivan as first in command and spent almost the entire 444 days held hostage at the Iranian Foreign Ministry, continued in the Foreign Service, serving as vice president of the National Defense University for five years before retiring. He became executive director of the National Commission on Public Service in 1987 and since 1991 has served as president of the Academy of Diplomacy, a private educational organization based in Washington DC.

*   *   *

It was the last wish of His Imperial Majesty, **Mohammad Reza Pahlavi, the shah of Iran,** that his remains be buried in Iran, but they are still entombed in the Al Rifai Mosque in Cairo on a "temporary" basis. His Niavaran Palace on the north slope of Tehran is now open to the public as a museum.

After years of exile in Greenwich, Connecticut, his widow, **Farah, the shahbanou,** now lives in Paris and Washington DC.

His son, the crown prince and heir to the dynasty, **Reza Pahlavi,** forty-four, lives in Potomac, Maryland. After existing in relative obscurity for two decades, Reza surfaced during 2001 as a commentator on National Iranian Television, a dissident satellite channel broadcasting to Iran in Farsi from a studio in Los Angeles. Until then, he was a virtual unknown to his native country. In his broadcasts, the crown prince called for a representative democracy in Iran, along with separation of mosque and state, and opening to the West. Any contact with him was officially banned inside the Islamic Republic, but during the large student demonstrations in Tehran that year, a few people carried his picture and shouted his name. He has never renounced his claim to the Peacock Throne.

Princess Ashraf Pahlavi, the shah's twin sister, lost her only son to an assassin in Paris while the shah was still living on Lackland Air Force Base outside of San Antonio, Texas. Ashraf now lives in New York City and the south of France, and still grieves over the loss of her brother and her son.

Richard Helms, the shah's schoolmate at Le Rosey, former CIA director and ambassador to Iran from 1973 to 1977, pled no contest to charges of lying to Congress about CIA activities, but served no jail time. Helms died in 2002.

David Rockefeller, the exiled shah's leading advocate with the United States government, retired from Chase Manhattan Bank in 1981 but continues to have an active involvement in a number of his favorite charities and causes.

Henry Kissinger, former secretary of state and the exiled shah's other leading advocate, has reportedly made a small fortune over the last two decades as a consultant to international businesses. He now keeps a home on Park Avenue in Manhattan and an office in Washington DC.

Robert Armao, the exiled shah's right-hand man, continues in the public relations business in New York City, servicing a small and select clientele.

Omar Torrijos, the military ruler of Panama whom Hamilton Jordan persuaded to host the shah between December 1979 and March 1980, died in a plane crash in the Panamanian jungle in August 1981, allegedly arranged by his own intelligence chief.

Anwar Sadat, the military ruler of Egypt who won the Nobel Peace Prize for his role in the Camp David accords and provided the shah his first and last refuge in exile, was assassinated by Islamic militants in October 1981. The assassins were members of an elite Egyptian military unit who turned their guns on Sadat when passing his reviewing stand during a parade.

Dr. Michael DeBakey, the shah's surgeon, continued his distinguished career without missing a step. He was eventually awarded the Lifetime Achievement Award by the United Nations and the National Science Medal, as well as the Presidential Medal of Freedom. Now ninety-five years old, he is the chancellor emeritus of the Baylor University College of Medicine.

The imam, Ayatollah Ruhollah Khomeini, continued as spiritual guide of the Islamic Republic of Iran until his death from prostate cancer in June 1989 at the age of eighty-eight. A shrine to him has been erected in the holy city of Qom and his memory is officially revered throughout Iran. February 1, the day he returned to Iran from his Paris exile, is now a national holiday.

His son **Ahmed Khomeini,** then forty-nine, died of unknown causes in March 1995.

Mehdi Bazargan, asked by the imam to be the provisional prime minister of the revolutionary government only to eventually resign, continued to serve in the Majlis for a number of years as head of the Freedom Movement of Iran. He and his organization described themselves as "loyal critics of the Clerical establishment" and were severely harassed for their accusations of mullah mismanagement during the war with Iraq. Bazargan died in January 1995 at the age of eighty-eight.

Ebrahim Yazdi, the provisional foreign minister who rescued the embassy from its Valentine's Day assault and then resigned after the hostage taking, was subsequently asked by the imam to act as his emissary to the rebellious provinces. He next ran a publishing company, again at Khomeini's request. He served in the Majlis for four years as a delegate of the Freedom Movement of Iran. Increasingly, Yazdi clashed with the clerical faction and in 1986 he left Iran and returned to exile in Texas in search of quality medical care for one of his sick children. During the 1990s, he moved back and forth between Iran and the United States and was named leader of the Freedom Movement of

Iran after Bazargan's death. In 1997 Yazdi was arrested in Tehran, but he was released after a public outcry. He finally moved back to Tehran from Texas for good in 2002 at the age of seventy-one to take a more active role in the opposition inside Iran. Suffering from cancer, he is currently under house arrest in Tehran.

Abolhassan Bani Sadr, the first president of the Islamic Republic of Iran, spent the four months after the hostage release using the Declaration of Algiers against the Islamic Republican Party, whose partisans had negotiated the deal. Bani Sadr attacked the agreement as a financial disaster for Iran that had failed to secure any of the wealth the shah had sucked out of the country or even retrieve all the money Iran had in the United States. Soon his fight with the mullahs led to physical battles between each side's loyalists in the streets of the capital. During that spring, Bani Sadr's security detail thwarted two assassination attempts aimed at him. As his battle with the mullahs became more desperate, he made an alliance with the leftist mujahideen guerrillas, who had pledged to lead an uprising if the mullahs forced Bani Sadr out. Bani Sadr urged Khomeini to hold a referendum between Bani Sadr and the IRP — promising to leave the government if he lost, as long as the IRP would do the same if they lost. He also claimed publicly that he was more popular than the imam himself. On June 15, 1981, Khomeini signed a nine-word order dismissing Bani Sadr as president of the Islamic Republic. Fearing arrest on treason charges, Bani Sadr went into hiding and, after shaving off his mustache to disguise himself, was smuggled out of the country by his leftist allies. There was no uprising to return him to power. He fled to France, where he still lives in exile outside of Paris in the suburb of Versailles, publishing a Farsi newspaper, *Enqelaab Eslaami,* and making plans for an eventual political comeback inside Iran. His house is still under twenty-four-hour protection by the French police and his private bodyguards.

Sadegh Ghotbzadeh, the imam's other spiritual son and the Islamic Republic's former foreign minister, considered exile but decided to stay in Iran and struggle against the mullahs instead. In April 1982 he was arrested after Iranian security forces intercepted phone calls by him to several Saudi Arabian agents in which he openly plotted a coup to overthrow Khomeini and his henchmen. After extensive "interrogation," Sadegh was tried and condemned to death. Khomeini offered to commute the sentence if Ghotbzadeh would only recant and ask to be forgiven, but Sadegh refused. Ghotbzadeh was executed in September 1982.

"Iran's lawyer," the French attorney **Christian Bourguet,** who conducted secret negotiations with Hamilton Jordan on behalf of Ghotbzadeh and the Iranian Foreign Ministry, continues to practice law in Paris. He has lost contact with his old negotiating partner, the Argentine expatriate businessman **Hector Villalon,** who at last report had left France for Belgium.

Kurt Waldheim, the UN secretary general who botched his assigned role in the plan negotiated with Jordan by Bourguet and Villalon, retired from the United Nations in 1982. In 1986 he ran for the presidency in his native Austria. Controversy attached itself to his candidacy when documents were discovered indicating that despite his claim to have spent most of his World War II service in the German army stationed in Vienna, Waldheim had actually served as the intelligence officer in a German military unit in occupied Greece that committed a host of war crimes before its withdrawal. Waldheim won the election anyway and went on to serve a single six-year term.

Sadegh Tabatabai, the emissary from the imam—code-named the Traveler—who opened negotiations with the Americans in September 1980, was convicted of attempting to smuggle almost four pounds of opium into Germany in 1983, but the sentence was quashed after the intervention of the German Foreign Ministry. He currently lives in both Europe and Iran, apparently still in the import-export business.

The **Iran-Iraq War,** set off by Iraq's September 1980 invasion, was finally halted by a cease-fire in 1988 and settled with a peace agreement in 1990. During the mid-1980s, Iran had seemed on the verge of conquering the Iraqi army, but the Reagan administration intervened on the side of Iraq with crucial military assistance, and the conflict continued. Much of the battlefield action featured trench warfare, human wave assaults, and the use of poison gas. Each side eventually lost well over a million troops in the fighting.

Saddam Hussein, the Iraqi dictator who started the war with Iran, went on to invade Kuwait in 1990, thinking he had American permission, only to be repulsed by his former American sympathizers. After a decade of international sanctions following the end of the first American war with Iraq, he was finally overthrown by a second American war and invasion in 2003. Saddam Hussein was captured by American troops after six months in hiding and is currently being held at an undisclosed location inside occupied Iraq, awaiting trial for crimes against the Iraqi people.

*   *   *

Jimmy Carter, thirty-ninth president of the United States, bears the brunt of the Crisis, even a quarter of a century later. There is a long list of "if onlys" that still haunts his one term in the White House, with different ifs for different sides: If only he hadn't backed the shah; if only he had backed the shah to the hilt; if only he hadn't visited Tehran and said what he did; if only he had endorsed the army and the iron fist; if only he had pursued a connection to Khomeini early rather than late; if only he hadn't admitted the shah; if only he had evacuated the embassy. History, however, allows few second serves, and Carter has never asked for any. He did his best, he explains; he kept the country out of a potentially disastrous war and he brought all of the hostages home alive with the national honor intact, despite the wrong they'd been done. Outside of that endless loop of speculation, perhaps the most knowing judgment of the Carter presidency was made in Washington DC by the then chair of the Democratic Party. He allowed that Jimmy had simply "used up all his luck just getting here."

Jimmy Carter went on to become the most active and influential former president in the history of the office. In addition to writing a dozen books since leaving the White House, he has acted as an international mediator, human rights consultant, and impartial election observer in countries throughout the world for more than two decades. In 2003 he was awarded the Nobel Peace Prize in recognition of his efforts.

As always, his wife, **Rosalynn Carter,** has acted as his partner in virtually all his ventures and initiated a number of her own.

Hamilton Jordan, Carter's legendary political operative and chief of staff, returned to Georgia to teach political science at Atlanta's Emory University and launch a successful career as a real estate investor and business consultant. He takes satisfaction in not having stuck around Washington to simply sell his services to the highest political bidder. After leaving the White House, he helped found the ATP professional tennis tour and the Jacksonville franchise of the National Football League. In 1985 he was diagnosed with a non-Hodgkin's lymphoma, the cancer that killed the shah. Jordan's malignancy went into remission following an intensive course of chemotherapy. In 1986 Ham ran unsuccessfully for one of Georgia's seats in the US Senate and in 1992 he briefly managed the presidential campaign of Independent candidate Ross Perot. In 1995 Jordan was diagnosed with prostate cancer, the disease that killed the imam. Jordan's second cancer went into remission following surgery. He now lives in Atlanta with his second wife and their three children.

Cyrus Vance, the secretary of state who resigned in disagreement over the hostage rescue mission, returned to his law practice in New York City. Though he assisted in several international negotiations as a private citizen, he never again served in the government. His January 2002 death from pneumonia and other complications was announced in a front-page story in the *New York Times.*

Lloyd Cutler, the White House counsel who helped President Carter sort out the shah's exile, returned to private practice until the next Democratic administration and then served as an adviser to Bill and Hillary Clinton during the Whitewater investigation. In February 2004 Cutler, eighty-six, was named to the presidential commission charged with investigating intelligence shortcomings leading up to the second war with Iraq.

In polling done at the end of the Carter administration, National Securitiy Adviser **Zbigniew Brzezinski** was decidedly the most unpopular of its members with the general public. Nonetheless, one of Jimmy Carter's last acts as president was to award him the Medal of Freedom, the nation's highest civilian decoration. Brzezinski returned to academia and is now counselor in residence at Washington's Center for Strategic and International Studies and a professor of American foreign policy at Johns Hopkins University's Nitze School of Advanced International Studies.

Jimmy Carter's vice president, **Walter Mondale,** was nominated for president in 1984 by the Democratic Party but was beaten handily by Ronald Reagan, the Republican incumbent. He then returned to his native Minnesota, where he practiced law, taught at the University of Minnesota, and served on more than a dozen corporate and charitable boards of directors. During the 1990s, he also served for four years as the American ambassador to Japan. He returned briefly to the US Senate in 2002 to fill out the few months remaining in the unexpired term of Minnesota senator Paul Wellstone, killed in a plane crash. Mondale has since resumed his Minnesota law practice.

Colonel Charlie A. Beckwith, commander of the aborted raid by the American Delta Force to free the hostages, resigned from active duty shortly after the failed mission. His last statement to his commander in chief, Jimmy Carter, was to let him know that whatever anyone else said, "me and my boys think you are tough as a woodpecker's lips." Beckwith retired to Austin, Texas, and was found dead in his bed from natural causes in June 1994.

Warren Christopher, the deputy secretary in Carter's State Department who negotiated the Declaration of Algiers, finally freeing the hostages, was awarded the Medal of Freedom by Carter before resuming his Los Angeles law practice. After the election of Bill Clinton in 1992, Christopher returned to Washington and served eight years as secretary of state. He is now back in Los Angeles again, practicing law.

Ronald Reagan, who defeated Jimmy Carter to become the fortieth president of the United States, served two terms before retiring to California, where he lived in Beverly Hills, disabled by Alzheimer's disease and no longer seen in public, until his death in June 2004, at age ninety-three. There is currently a Republican movement afoot to place his likeness on the dime, replacing Franklin Roosevelt.

Ronald Reagan's campaign manager, **William "Bill" Casey,** served as the director of central intelligence in the Reagan administration. Casey became a household name when it was revealed in late 1986 that he had been using the CIA to secretly wage war against the then Marxist government of Nicaragua, despite being explicitly forbidden to do so by Congress. Just as Casey was being called to testify about his activities to a congressional investigation, he was struck down by a brain tumor and rendered incapable of speech. He died in April 1987, without ever recovering sufficiently to face trial for his activities.

The Crisis itself has continued to reverberate along at least two distinct tracks in our geopolitical life:

The Islamic revolution against the United States, introduced to the world at the embassy on Taleghani Avenue, has proliferated among Sunni and Shiite alike during the quarter century since. The next major collision was in Lebanon, where again American hostages were taken and others were killed in the bombing of an American embassy, this one protected by an American expeditionary force. Sparks subsequently flew in Somalia, east Africa, occupied Palestine, along the Persian Gulf, and in Afghanistan, where the forces the United States had backed against the Soviets turned against the Americans and provided comfort to the attackers of the World Trade Center and the Pentagon in 2001. It is now a truism that Islam and America are at odds. The two forces may very well lock horns again in the current jockeying over the political outcome in American-occupied Iraq.

Relations between the Islamic Republic of Iran and the United States of

America continue to be defined by the Crisis. There is still no functioning American embassy in Iran, and American interests in Tehran are still watched over by the Swiss. Nor is there an Iranian ambassador in Washington. The old Iranian embassy there now functions as a consular office, handling only visa requests, largely from Iranian immigrants who still have family in the old country. If anything, the bitterness between the two governments has only increased. The Iranian outrage at the United States was reenergized by American policy in the Iran-Iraq War and even more so in August 1988, when an American naval cruiser in the Persian Gulf shot down a crowded Iranian airliner on a normal commercial travel route, killing all 290 aboard. Most recently, President George W. Bush reasserted the antagonism between the two countries by labeling the Islamic Republic of Iran a part of the international "Axis of Evil." A significant faction inside the Bush administration continues to argue for targeting Iran next in the administration's ongoing attempt to remake governance of the region into something more to its liking.

AUTHOR'S NOTE

_____

THOUGH ONLY MY NAME APPEARS ON THE TITLE page, I couldn't have produced this book without the assistance of a number of other people. I owe all of them my gratitude and appreciation.

First and foremost, I want to thank my editor, Geoff Shandler, whose editing skills and vision made this a much better book than it would have been otherwise. I am a more accomplished writer for having worked with him.

My agent, Kathy Robbins, also deserves being singled out. Her steadfast guidance and support have provided the underpinnings of my career for some twenty years. My respect for her is matched only by my affection.

I owe an enormous debt to my friend Sarah Crichton, as well, who, in her previous incarnation as a publisher, helped me conceive of this book and whose advice I relied on throughout the entire process.

There were also a number of people whose assistance in accumulating and sorting my research and other tasks was irreplaceable: Merrian Fuller, Chris Tyler, Peter Stair, Jason Rezaian, Peter Kornbluh, Abby Fosburgh,

Linda Richards, Elaine Harris, and Bob Zuber. In my travels to collect research, I was taken in by friends whose generosity and spare beds were a godsend: Helen Whitney, Alex Avery, Peter and Sally Dean, Whit and Abby Fosburgh, and Kent and Guillaine Hudson. As my writing progressed, I made use of a group of readers who reviewed drafts of this text and gave me invaluable feedback: Cheri Forrester, John Sullivan, Bob Zuber, and Neil Reichline. Finally, I would have been lost without the computer services provided by Will Kirkland of Computers in Plain English in San Francisco.

NOTES ON SOURCES

My HOPE THROUGHOUT THE THREE YEARS THIS book was in the making was to weave a compelling and seamless story out of the actual events of twenty-five years ago. In pursuit of that end, I constructed the narrative from five basic types of source material:

Firsthand accounts lead the list — including interviews conducted in the United States, France, and Iran, as well as oral histories and memoirs. The voices given to characters are derived from these sources. Some quotes come, in a few instances, from multiple sources, which I have bound together inside a single set of quotation marks when they were making the same point. If the different sources had slightly different versions of what was said, I have tried to determine, on a word-by-word basis, the most reliable version and have used the synthesis that emerges. For my interviews inside Iran, I am grateful for the assistance of the Resaneh Yar Foreign Media Guide Center, the Ministry of Islamic Guidance, the Revolutionary Guard Corps, and my interpreter. During my interviews in France, I was assisted by the interpreting of Kent Hudson. I am indebted to the oral history collections of the Carter

Presidency Project of the Jimmy Carter Library and those of Tim Wells in his book *444 Days*. I was fortunate that most of the major characters in this story — even those who would not or could not talk to me — wrote memoirs. I made good use of all of them, but Hamilton Jordan's *Crisis,* William Sullivan's *Mission to Iran,* Zbigniew Brzezinski's *Power and Principle,* Massoumeh Ebtekar's *Takeover in Tehran,* and Barbara and Barry Rosen's *The Destined Hour* were particularly important to me.

This story was also blessed with a huge underpinning of contemporary internal governmental documentation, including portions of the cable traffic between Tehran and Washington and a number of White House memoranda. Again, I made extensive use of collections that others had already amassed. I owe particular thanks to the National Security Archive of Washington DC and its senior analyst, Peter Kornbluh; to the Hoover Institute and Stanford University Libraries; to the Carter Library and archivist Albert Nason; and to the collection released by the Muslim Students Following the Line of the Imam under the title *Documents from the U.S. Espionage Den.*

The third element from which this story was woven was a series of congressional investigations and reports including "The Iran Hostage Crisis" by the Committee on Foreign Affairs of the US House of Representatives, "The October Surprise allegations and the circumstances surrounding the release of the American hostages held in Iran" by the Special Counsel to Senator Terry Sanford and Senator James M. Jeffords of the Committee on Foreign Relations of the US Senate, "Unauthorized Transfers of Nonpublic Information during the 1980 Presidential Election" by the Subcommittee on Human Resources of the Committee on Post Office and Civil Service of the US House of Representatives, "Iran's Seizure of the United States Embassy" by the Committee on Foreign Affairs of the US House of Representatives, and the "Joint Report of the Task Force to Investigate Certain Allegations Concerning the Holding of American Hostages by Iran in 1980" of the US House of Representatives.

The fourth element was the contemporary news coverage provided by the world's media. While I used a wide variety of publications, the work of the *New York Times,* the *Washington Post, Time, Newsweek,* and *Le Monde* were particularly useful.

Finally, I was able to piggyback my own reporting on top of that previously done by a number of writers in book-length treatments that covered either the breadth of the story or one particular aspect. Being the most recent,

I was able to boost myself to a commanding view of my subject by standing on top of what they had already accomplished. While I made use of a number of these accounts, I owe a special debt to the work of Gary Sick, William Shawcross, Pierre Salinger, and Amir Taheri, all of whose work provided me with guidance and information that were invaluable. I did not credit them by name in the text of the story, but that was only because of my desire to advance the narrative in the smoothest fashion, rather than a reflection of their importance to whatever I have accomplished.

BIBLIOGRAPHY

―――――――

Interviews
Robert Armao, 1/11/02
Ibrahim Asgarzadeh, 11/5/02
Paul Baltha, 3/7/02
Abolhassan Bani Sadr, 3/6/02
Bill Belk, 2/27/04
Christian Bourguet, 3/7/02
Jimmy Carter, 7/17/02
Bill Cofield, 2/6/04
Massoumeh Ebtekar, 11/4/02
Ali Mohammad Farzin, 11/4/02
Dr. Cheri Joy Forrester, 9/12/02
William Gallegos, 3/2/04
Sadegh Ghotbzadeh to BBC, 11/19/79
Joe Hall, 2/26/04
Don Hohman, 2/27/04

Hamilton Jordan, 1/30/02

Bruce Laingen, 1/29/04

William Miller, 5/16/01

Walter Mondale, 1/22, 1/23/02

Behzad Nabavi, 11/6/02

Taghi Rezaian, 3/22/02

Barry Rosen, 1/27/04

Eric Rouleau, 3/6/02

Ahmed Salmatian, 3/7/02

Mohammad Sept, 5/14/02

Hossein Shariatmadari, 11/3/02

Gary Sick, 11/13/01, 12/3/01, 1/21/02

Vafa Tabesh, 11/6/02

Ayatollah Mahdi Hadari Tehrani, 11/5/02

Ebrahim Yazdi, 11/4/02

Sayyed Ezatolah Zargani, 11/4/02

Oral Histories, Interrogatories, Diaries, Etc.

Cort Barnes, in *444 Days*

Bill Belk, in *444 Days*

Zbigniew Brzezinski, Carter Presidency Project, Jimmy Carter Library, 2/18/82

Landon Butler, Carter Presidency Project, Jimmy Carter Library, 11/6/81

William Gallegos, in *444 Days*

Bruce German, in *444 Days*

Joe Hall, in *444 Days*

Sgt. Kevin Hermening, in *444 Days*

Don Hohman, in *444 Days*

Col. Leland Holland, in *444 Days*

Hamilton Jordan, Carter Presidency Project, Jimmy Carter Library, 11/6/81

Malcolm Kalp, in *444 Days*

Cpl. Steven Kirtley, in *444 Days*

Sgt. Paul Lewis, in *444 Days*

John Limbert, in *444 Days*

Capt. Paul Needham, in *444 Days*

Robert Ode, in *444 Days*

Sgt. William Quarles, in *444 Days*

Richard Queen, in *444 Days*

Barry Rosen, in *444 Days*
Lee Schatz, in *444 Days*
Sgt. Rocky Sickman, in *444 Days*
Victor Tomseth, in *444 Days*

Interrogatory, Zbigniew Brzezinski, 4/15/02
Interrogatory, John Limbert, 2/27/04
Interrogatory, Princess Ashraf Pahlavi, 1/14/02

Speech, Ebrahim Yazdi, Metro State University, 10/18/00
Speech, Ebrahim Yazdi, Ohio State University, 11/3/00

Statement, White House, "Rescue Attempt for American Hostages in Iran,"
    4/25/80
Statement, President Carter, "Hostage Rescue Attempt in Iran," 4/25/80

Documents
Cable, AmEmbassy Tehran to SecState, "Understanding the Shi'ite Islamic
    Movement," 2/3/78
Cable, AmEmbassy Tehran to SecState, "Public Reaction to Shah's Inter-
    view," 5/21/78
Cable, AmEmbassy Tehran to SecState, "Rumors re Health of Shah," 7/26/78
Cable, AmEmbassy Tehran to SecState, "Shah's Constitutional Day Speech,"
    8/7/78
Cable, AmEmbassy Tehran to SecState, "Recommendations for President to
    Shah Letter," 8/29/78
Cable, AmEmbassy Tehran to SecState, "Situation in Iran," 9/10/78
Cable, AmEmbassy Tehran to SecState, "Political Report," 10/5/78
Cable, AmEmbassy Tehran to SecState, "Security Report," 10/16/78
Cable, AmEmbassy Tehran to SecState, "Political Security Report," 10/22/78
Cable, AmEmbassy Tehran to SecState, "Political Security Report," 10/30/78
Cable, AmEmbassy Tehran to SecState, "Situation Report," 11/6/78
Cable, AmEmbassy Tehran to SecState, "Political Security Report," 11/7,
    11/9, 11/10, 11/11, 11/12, 11/18, 11/21/78
Cable, AmEmbassy Tehran to SecState, "Thinking the Unthinkable," 11/9/78
Cable, AmConsul Shiraz to SecState, "Opposition to the Shah," 11/21/78
Cable, AmEmbassy Tehran to SecState, "On the Eve of Moharram," 12/1/78

Cable, AmEmbassy Tehran to SecState, "Political Security Report," 12/1/78

Cable, AmEmbassy Tehran to SecState, "Mood Among Tehran Rioters," 12/2/78

Cable, AmEmbassy Tehran to SecState, "Political Security Report," 12/2/78

Cable, AmEmbassy Tehran to SecState, "Political Security Report," 12/3/78

Cable, AmEmbassy Tehran to SecState, "Political Security Report," 12/5/78

Cable, AmEmbassy Tehran to SecState, "Political Security Report," 12/10/78

Cable, AmEmbassy Tehran to SecState, "Political Security Report," 12/11/78

Cable, AmEmbassy Tehran to SecState, "17 Point Opposition Program," 12/11/78

Cable, AmEmbassy Tehran to SecState, "Political Security Report," 12/20/78

Cable, AmEmbassy Tehran to SecState, "Political Security Report," 12/22/78

Cable, AmEmbassy Tehran to SecState, "Political Security Report," 12/23/78

Cable, AmEmbassy Tehran to SecState, "Security Report," 12/24/78

Cable, AmEmbassy Tehran to SecState, "Political Security Report," 1/3/79

Cable, AmEmbassy Tehran to SecState, "USG Policy Guidance," 1/10/79

Cable, AmEmbassy Tehran to SecState, "Political Security Report," 1/10/79

Cable, AmEmbassy Tehran to SecState, "Political Security Report," 1/11/79

Cable, AmEmbassy Tehran to SecState, "Political Security Report," 1/13/79

Cable, AmEmbassy Tehran to SecState, "Political Security Report," 1/14/79

Cable, AmEmbassy Tehran to SecState, "Shah's Travels," 1/16/79

Cable, SecState to AmEmbassy Tehran, "Sadegh Ghotbzadeh," 1/21/79

Cable, AmEmbassy to SecState, "Sadegh Ghotbzadeh," 1/23/79

Cable, AmEmbassy Tehran to RUEHC/SecState, 1/30/79

Cable, SecState to AmEmbassy Bern, 2/23/79

Cable, AmEmbassy Tehran to SecState, "Corruption Under the Pahlavis," 3/3/79

Cable, AmEmbassy Tehran to SecState, "Iran's New Constitution . . . ," 3/6/79

Cable, AmEmbassy to SecState, ". . . damages sustained during Feb. 14 Attack on Embassy," 3/11/79

Cable, AmEmbassy to SecState, "March 30th Referendum," 3/20/79

Cable, SecState to AmEmbassy Rabat, "Shah of Iran," 3/29/79

Cable, AmEmbassy Tehran to SecState, "Political Sitrep . . . ," 4/8/79

Cable, AmEmbassy to SecState, "Iran's Referendum . . . ," 4/14/79

Cable, AmEmbassy Tehran to SecState, ". . . Revolutionary Trials," 4/12/79

Cable, AmEmbassy Nassau to SecState, "Shah of Iran," 5/7/79

Cable, AmEmbassy Mexico to SecState, "Possible Residence in Mexico for Shah of Iran," 5/17/79

Cable, "Secret," Tehran to Director, "SD LURE," 6/7/79

Cable, AmEmbassy Tehran to SecState, "Iranian Constitution," 7/3/79

Cable, CIA, CITF Director to Priority Tehran, "WNINTEL RYBAT AJAJA SDLURE," 7/25/79

Cable, SecState to AmEmbassy Tehran, "Shah's Desire to Reside in the United States," 7/26/79

Cable, AmEmbassy Tehran to SecState, "Shah's Desire to Reside in the United States," 7/28/79

Cable, "Secret," Tehran to Director, "SD LURE," 8/24/79

Cable, "Secret," Tehran to Director, "SD LURE," 8/30/79

Cable, "Secret," Tehran to Director, "SD LURE," 9/4/79 (2)

Cable, "Secret," Tehran to Director, "SD LURE," 9/9/79 (2)

Cable, AmEmbassy Tehran to SecState, "Council of Experts . . . ," 9/18/79

Cable, SecState to AmEmbassy Tehran, "Shah of Iran," 9/29/79

Cable, AmEmbassy Tehran to SecState, "The Shah of Iran," 9/30/79

Cable, AmEmbassy Tehran to SecState, ". . . Iranian Human Rights," 10/15/79

Cable, AmEmbassy Tehran to SecState, "Shah's Illness," 10/21/79

Cable, SecState to AmEmbassy Tehran, "The Shah's Illness," 10/21/79

Cable, AmEmbassy Tehran to SecState, "Shah's Illness," 10/22/79

Cable, AmEmbassy Tehran to SecState, "The Shah in the U.S.," 10/24/79

Cable, AmEmbassy Tehran to SecState, "Shah in U.S.," 10/31/79

Cable, SecState to Swiss Embassy Tehran, 12/1/79

Cable, AmEmbassy Panama to SecState, "Iran-Panamanian Initiatives," 1/14/80

Cable, British Embassy Washington DC to SecState, "The Shah," 1/15/80

Cable, AmEmbassy Panama to SecState, "Iran Seeks Arrest of Shah," 1/16/80

Cable, AmEmbassy London to SecState, "Meeting with Panamanians and Iranian Emissaries," 1/20/80

Cable, AmEmbassy Paris to SecState, "Visit," 2/14/80

Cable, AmEmbassy Paris to SecState, "Visit," 2/15/80

Cable, SecState to AmEmbassy Algiers, "Press release on gold movements," 1/16/81

Diary, Jimmy Carter, 4/9, 6/12, 7/27/79, 3/30, 4/1, 4/17, 4/21, 7/31, 10/9, 10/31, 12/28/80

Diary, Robert Ode, 11/13, 12/6, 12/9, 12/12, 12/16, 12/24, 12/25/79, 4/17, 4/18, 4/19, 4/22, 4/24, 6/24, 12/25/80

Handwritten notes, Cyrus Vance, "Notes for talk w. Zbig," undated

Handwritten notes, Cy Vance, "Pat Caddell," undated

Letter, Richard A. Falk to Zbigniew Brzezinski, 5/19/77

Letter, Jimmy Carter to William Sullivan, 10/25/77

Letter, Jimmy Carter to His Imperial Majesty, 1/1/78

Handwritten note, Jimmy Carter to Shah, 9/28/78

Letter, Henry Precht to William Sullivan, 12/19/78

Handwritten memo, Jimmy Carter, 1/4/79, 6:15 p.m.

Handwritten memo, Jimmy Carter, 1/4/79, 6:45 p.m.

Handwritten memo, Jimmy Carter, 1/5/79

Letter, Jimmy Carter to Ambassador William Sullivan, 4/24/79

Letter, Ashraf Pahlavi to the President, 8/10/79

Handwritten note, Jimmy Carter, 11/13/79

Handwritten note, Jimmy Carter, 11/23/79

Handwritten note, Jimmy Carter, 11/27/79

Handwritten note, Cyrus Vance, 12/4/79

Letter, Hamilton Jordan to Mr. Bourguet and Mr. Villalon, 1/30/80

Letter, Hamilton Jordan to Abolhassan Bani Sadr, 3/13/80

Letter, Sadegh Ghotbzadeh to General Omar Torrijos, 3/21/80

Handwritten letter, Cy Vance to Mr. President, 4/21/80

Letter, Sadegh Ghotbzadeh to the Majlis, in Inquilab-i Islami, 9/11/80

Note, Jimmy Carter to Chris, 10/17/80

Memo, Hamilton Jordan to Jimmy Carter, "Personal and Confidential," undated, 1977

Memo, C. R. Vance, "Overview of Foreign Policy Issues and Positions," undated

Memo, Cyrus Vance to the President, "Visit of the Shah and Shahbanou," undated

Memo, "A Possible Scenario," undated

Memo, Hamilton Jordan to President Carter, "Eyes Only," undated

Memo, Hamilton Jordan to President Carter, undated (4)

Memo, "Points to Cover," typed, undated

Memo, Gretchen Poston to the President and Mrs. Carter, "Visit of the Shahansha and the Shahbanou of Iran," 11/8/77

Memo, Gary Sick to Zbigniew Brzezinski, "Human rights in Iran," 11/10/77

Memo, Warren Christopher to the President, "Your visit to Tehran . . . ," 12/13/77

Memo, Department of State, Bureau of Intelligence and Research, "Analysis," 1/29/78

Memo, CIA, "The politics of Ayatollah Ruhollah Khomeini," 11/20/78

Memo, Barbara L. Schell, "Audience with Shah, David C. Scott, Allis Chalmers," 11/25/78

Memo, CIA, Office of Central Reference, "Mehdi Bazargan," 12/8/78

Memo, Robert B. Mantel to Henry Precht, "Contact with Sadegh Ghotbzadeh," 1/17/79

Memo, CIA, "Iran — Prospects for Moharram," 11/29/78

Memo, CIA, Office of Regional and Political Analysis, "Opposition Demonstrations in Iran . . . ," 12/21/78

Memo to President, "Evening Reading Item: Iran," 2/22/79

Memo to President, "Evening Reading Item: Iran," 2/22/79 (2)

Memo, CIA, National Foreign Assessment Center, "Iran's Ayatollahs," 3/20/79

Memo, SecState, "Biographic Information . . . ," 3/26/79

Memo, John J. McCloy to Warren Christopher, 4/16/79

Memo, CIA, Special Analysis, "Iran: Six Months After the Revolution," 8/4/79

Memo, "President's Evening Reading Item: The Shah's Operation," 10/24/79

Memo, Hamilton Jordan to President Carter, "Eyes Only," 11/8/79

Memo, Office of the Under Secretary of State, 11/8/79

Memo, Iran Working Group, "Sitrep No. 21," 11/12/79

Memo, Henry Precht to Harold H. Saunders, "Seeking Stability in Iran," 12/19/79

Memo, Hamilton Jordan to President Carter, "Situation with the hostages," 1/15/80

Memo, Hamilton Jordan to President Carter, 1/22/80

Memo, author deleted, "Meeting with B and V . . . ," 1/25/80

Memo, Hamilton Jordan to President Carter, "Re: Telephone Conversation . . . ," 1/29/80

Memo for the record, Iran Working Group, "V & B Conversation with Ghotbzadeh," 1/30/80

Memo, "Message from [name deleted], LS No. 95090/JRF/French," 1/30/80

Memo, State Department, "Cottam-Ghotbzadeh Conversation . . . ," 2/4/80

Memo, Iran Task Force, "Bani Sadr's Foreign Policy Views," 2/5/80

Memo, Assistant Secretary of State, "Secretary Vance's Meetings at the UN . . . ," 2/18/80

Memo, Department of State to the Secretary, "Report from Tehran," 2/23/80

Memo, Lloyd Cutler, "Call from Robert Armao," 2/26/80

Memo, Harold H. Saunders to the Secretary, "Contacts with the Lawyers in Iran," 2/27/80

Memo of phone conversation, Hector Villalon / Stephanie Van Reigersberg, noon, 2/27/80

Memo of phone conversation, Hector Villalon / Stephanie Van Reigersberg, 2/28/80, 1:30 p.m.

Memo, Iran Working Group, "Sitrep No. 235," 2/28/80

Memo, Gary Sick to Dr. Brzezinski, "Iran," 3/5/80

Memo, Lloyd Cutler to Hamilton Jordan, "The Shah," 3/5/80

Memo for the record, Iran Working Group, "Conversation with Hector Villalon," 3/6/80

Memo of phone conversation, M. Bourguet / Henry Precht, 3/6/80

Memo, Henry Precht to HJ, 3/7/80

Memo of conversation, Henry Precht / Christine Villalon, 3/8/80

Memo of conversation, B. H. Kean / Dr. Dustin, 3/9/80

Memo of conversation, Iran Working Group, Sadegh Ghotbzadeh / Richard Cottam, 3/11/80

Memo, Iran Working Group, "Sitrep No. 255," 3/16/80

Memo, Iran Working Group, "Cottam-Ghotbzadeh Conversation," 3/18/80

Memo, Hamilton Jordan / Arnold Raphel to the President / The Secretary of State, 3/21/80

Memo, "Suggested Talking Points," 3/25/80

Memo, Bob Garrick to Bill Casey, "Presidential Itinerary," 10/23/80

Memo, Harold H. Saunders to the Secretary, "Iran Update," 10/28/80

Memo, Bob Garrick to Bill Casey, "Additions to Carter's schedule," 10/30/80

Press guidance, "Bani Sadr election," undated

Bio, US Department of State, Warren Christopher

Bio, US Department of State, Sadegh Tabatabai

Press release, Office of the White House Press Secretary, 4/7/77

Minutes, AmEmbassy Tehran, "Country Team Meeting," 10/25/78

Toast, Jimmy Carter, State dinner in Tehran, Public Papers of the Presidents, 12/31/77

Communiqué #1, Muslim Students Following the Line of the Imam, 11/4/79

Press release, Office of the White House Press Secretary, "Statement by the President on the Hostage Situation," 11/2/80

Telegram, AmEmbassy Tehran to SecState, "Serious Religious Dissidence in Qom," 1/9/78

Telegram, AmEmbassy Tehran to SecState, "Khomeini placed under house arrest, Liberation Movement of Iran (LMI) seeks further US contact," 9/25/78

Telegram, AmEmbassy Paris to AmEmbassy Tehran, "Ayatollah Khomeini Interview," 10/25/78

Telegram, AmEmbassy Tehran to SecState, "Political Security Report," 11/2/78

Telegram, AmEmbassy Tehran to SecState, "Political Security Report," 11/5/78

Telegram, AmEmbassy Tehran to SecState, "Political Security Report," 11/6/78

Telegram, AmEmbassy Tehran to SecState, "Iran Situation," 11/9/78

Telegram, State Department, "Current . . . ," 4/6/79

Telegram, AmEmbassy Paris to SecState, 11/30/79

Telegram, Secretary of State, 12/3/79

Telegram, State Department, "Current Foreign Relations . . . ," 12/5/79

Telegram, State Department, "Public backs current approach . . . ," 12/5/79

Telegram, AmEmbassy Panama to SecState, "Medical treatment of the Shah," 3/4/80

Telegram, AmEmbassy Panama to SecState, "Talk with Dr. Rios on Shah's Illness," 3/5/80

Telegram, AmEmbassy Panama to SecState, "Shah's Hospitalization," 3/6/80

Telegram, AmEmbassy Panama to SecState, "Hospitalization of the Shah," 3/7/80

Telegram, AmEmbassy Panama to SecState, "The Shah's Operation: Where We Are," 3/16/80

Report, Defense Intelligence Agency, "Iran: The Month of Muharram," undated

Report, State Department, "Human Rights Reports," March 1978

Report, US Embassy Tehran, "Royal Family Participation in Iranian Business," 6/20/78

Report, International Jurist Committee, "Preliminary report . . . ," 11/23/78

Report, WNINTEL, "Instructions from Ayatollah Khomeini to stage anti-government demonstrations during Moharram," 11/30/78

Report, State Department, "Human Rights Practices / Iran," 10/18/79

Report, Eben H. Dustin, M.D., "Medical Status of the Shah," 10/20/79

Report, "October 20 Summary of Medical Findings," 10/25/79

Report, CIA, National Foreign Assessment Center, "Iran: The Meaning of Moharram," 11/19/79

Report, Defense Intelligence Agency, "Iran: New Constitution," 12/21/79

Report, CIA, 3/16/80 in *America Held Hostage*

Report, Joint Chiefs of Staff, Special Operations Review Group, "Rescue Mission Report," 8/80

Report, Committee on Foreign Affairs, House of Representatives, "The Iran Hostage Crisis," 3/81

Periodicals, Etc.

AFP, 1/20, 11/23, 11/26, 11/29, 12/5/79

The American Spectator, 2/93

BAMDAD, 11/28/79

BBC World Service, 12/4/79

Boston Globe, 3/23/80

Christian Science Monitor, 6/24/63, 10/3/80

Current Biography, 11/79

(London) *Daily Telegraph,* 2/12, 4/2/79

Department of State Bulletin, 12/19/77

Economist, 8/7, 11/20/76, 11/19/77, 12/16/78, 2/10, 12/15/79, 2/2, 6/7, 7/19, 9/13/80

Figaro, 12/3/79

Financial Times, 4/11, 12/8/79

Foreign Affairs, Fall 1980

Iran Times, 11/23/79

Le Monde, 11/30/79, 10/19/80

Middle East Journal, Winter 1971, Fall 1976

National Geographic, 8/67

National Journal, 6/14/80

Newsweek, 5/3/76, 11/20, 12/18/78, 2/26, 4/23, 6/4, 8/6, 8/27, 11/19, 11/26, 12/31/79, 2/4, 4/7, 5/5, 5/12, 9/22, 12/29/80, 2/2/81

New York Times, 6/6/63, 10/13, 10/15/71, 11/16/77, 11/7, 11/8, 11/15, 12/8, 12/9, 12/10, 12/11/78, 1/14, 1/25, 1/26, 1/27, 1/28, 1/30, 1/31, 2/2, 2/3, 2/4, 2/6, 2/12, 2/21, 3/1, 3/5, 3/7, 3/15, 3/16, 3/17, 4/20, 4/21, 4/29, 6/17, 7/10, 8/4, 10/25, 11/6, 11/19, 11/21, 11/23, 11/27, 11/28, 12/1, 12/3/79, 4/1, 7/29, 8/12, 8/15, 9/23, 9/25, 10/3, 10/7, 11/3, 12/3/80, 5/13, 5/17/81, 7/7/83

New York Times Biographical Service, 4/80, 12/95

Paris Domestic Service, 12/3/79

PARS, 11/18/79

Playboy, 9/81

Policy Review, Spring 1980

Prologue, Spring 1990

San Francisco Examiner, 10/17/80

Saturday Evening Post, 11/6/54

Sixty Minutes, 3/6/77

Tehran Domestic Service, 11/11, 11/22, 11/26, 11/28, 12/3/79, 11/2/80

Time, 11/6, 11/13, 11/20, 11/27, 12/11, 12/18, 12/25/78, 1/1, 1/8, 1/15, 1/22, 1/29, 2/4, 3/5, 3/12, 4/23, 5/7, 5/21, 6/25, 7/16, 11/6/79

UPI, 3/11, 3/14/80

U.S. News & World Report, 8/2, 11/22/76, 9/4/78, 2/12, 4/2, 12/3/79

Wall Street Journal, 12/4, 12/7/79, 11/5/81, 5/24/84

Washington Post, 11/6, 11/8, 11/10, 11/15, 11/19/78, 3/2, 7/10, 8/25, 9/18, 10/14, 11/28, 11/29, 12/4, 12/7/79, 1/25, 3/14, 3/31, 4/3, 4/28, 5/1, 8/15, 9/24, 10/15/80, 11/13/82, 7/1, 7/7/83

Washington Star, 7/15/80

Yale University Library, "Biographical Sketch of Cyrus R. Vance," 1995

David Frost Productions, *The Crown Absolute,* 1978

Roper poll, 9/30/78, 12/11/79

ABC News poll, 3/27/79

Patrick H. Caddell, Cambridge Survey Research, "Of Crisis and Opportunity," 4/23/79

Books

Andrianopoulos, Gerry Argyris. *Kissinger and Brzezinski*. New York: St. Martin's Press, 1991.

Bani Sadr, Abolhassan. *My Turn to Speak*. New York: Brassey's (US) Inc., 1991.

Barrett, Laurence I. *Gambling with History*. New York: Penguin, 1984.

Beckwith, Col. Charlie A. *Delta Force*. New York: Avon, 2000.

Ben-Menashe, Ari. *Profits of War*. New York: Sheridan Square Press, 1992.

Bloom, Jonathan and Sheila Blair. *Islam*. New Haven: Yale University Press, 2002.

Bourne, Peter G. *Jimmy Carter*. New York: Lisa Drew / Scribner, 1997.

Brown, Harold. *Thinking About National Security*. Boulder, CO: Westview Press, 1983.

Brumberg, Daniel. *Reinventing Khomeini*. Chicago: University of Chicago Press, 2001.

Brzezinski, Zbigniew. *Power and Principle*. New York: Farrar, Straus & Giroux, 1983.

Carter, Jimmy. *Keeping Faith*. Fayetteville: University of Arkansas Press, 1995.

————. *An Hour Before Daylight*. New York: Simon & Schuster, 2001.

————. *Why Not The Best?* Nashville: Broadman Press, 1977.

Carter, Rosalynn. *First Lady from Plains*. Boston: Houghton Mifflin, 1984.

Christopher, Warren. *Chances of a Lifetime*. New York: Scribner's, 2001.

Cottam, Richard W. *Khomeini, the Future, and US Options*. Muscatine, IA: Stanley Foundation, 1987.

Deaver, Michael K., and Mickey Herskowitz. *Behind the Scenes*. New York: William Morrow, 1987.

Drew, Elizabeth. *Portrait of an Election*. New York: Simon and Schuster, 1981.

Ebtekar, Massoumeh. *Takeover in Tehran*. Vancouver, BC: Talon Books, 2000.

El Azhary, M. S. *The Iran-Iraq War*. London: Croom Helm, 1987.

Farmanfarmaian, Manucher, and Roxanne Farmanfarmaian. *Blood and Oil*. New York: Modern Library, 1999.

Grummon, Stephen R. *The Iran-Iraq War*. New York: Praeger / Center for Strategic and International Studies, 1982.

Honegger, Barbara. *October Surprise.* New York and Los Angeles: Tudor Publishing Company, 1989.

Ionnides, Christos P. *America's Iran.* Lanham, MD: University Press of America, 1984.

Jerome, Carole. *The Man in the Mirror.* Toronto: Key Porter Books, 1987.

Jordan, Hamilton. *Crisis.* New York: G. P. Putnam's Sons, 1982.

————. *No Such Thing as a Bad Day.* Marietta, GA: Longstreet Press, 2000.

Kaufman, Burton Ira. *The Presidency of James Earl Carter Jr.* Lawrence, KS: University of Kansas Press, 1993.

Kyle, Col. James H. *The Guts to Try.* New York: Orion Books, 1990.

Kreisberg, Paul H., ed. *American Hostages in Iran.* New Haven: Yale University Press, 1985.

Laingen, Bruce. *Yellow Ribbon.* New York: Brassey's (US), Inc., 1992.

Ledeen, Michael A. *Perilous Statecraft.* New York: Charles Scribner's Sons, 1988.

Lenahan, Rod. *Crippled Eagle.* Charleston/Miami: Narwhal Press, 1998.

Lowenfield, Andreas, Lawrence Newman, and John M. Walker Jr. *Revolutionary Days.* Record of a Conference Held at NYU School of Law, 6/99. Huntington, NY: Juris Publishing, 1999.

Marks, David. *An Election Held Hostage?* New York: Fund for New Priorities, 1991.

McFadden, Robert D. et al. *No Hiding Place.* New York: Times Books, 1981.

McLellan, David S. *Cyrus Vance.* Totowa, NJ: Rowman & Allanheld, 1985.

Morris, Kenneth E. *Jimmy Carter.* Athens, GA: University of Georgia Press, 1996.

Moses, Russell Leigh. *Freeing the Hostages.* Pittsburgh: University of Pittsburgh Press, 1996.

Nacos, Brigitte Lebens. *Mass-Mediated Terrorism.* Lanham, MD: Rowman & Littlefield, 2002.

Pahlavi, Princess Ashraf. *Time for Truth.* In Print Publishing, 1995.

Pahlavi, Farah. *An Enduring Love.* New York: Miramax Books, 2004.

Pahlavi, Mohammad Reza. *Answer to History.* Toronto/Vancouver: Clarke, Irwin & Co., 1980.

Parry, Robert. *Trick or Treason.* New York: Sheridan Square Press, 1993.

Pelletier, Jean, and Claude Adams. *The Canadian Caper.* New York: William Morrow, 1981.

Peress, Gilles. *Telex: Iran.* Millerton, NY: Aperture, 1983.

Persico, Joseph E. *Casey.* New York: Viking, 1990.

Queen, Richard. *Inside and Out.* New York: Putnam, 1981.

Ranney, Austin. *The American Elections of 1980.* Washington, DC: American Enterprise Institute for Public Policy Research, 1981.

Rafizadeh, Mansur. *Witness: From the Shah to the Secret Arms Deal.* New York: William Morrow, 1987.

Rosen, Barbara, and Barry Rosen. *The Destined Hour.* New York: Doubleday & Co., 1982.

Rubin, Barry. *Paved with Good Intentions.* New York: Penguin, 1980.

Ryan, Paul B. *The Iran Rescue Mission.* Annapolis, MD: Naval Institute Press, 1985.

Salinger, Pierre. *America Held Hostage.* New York: Doubleday & Co., 1981.

Scott, Col. Charles W. *Pieces of the Game.* Atlanta: Peachtree Publishers, 1984.

Segev, Samuel. *The Iranian Triangle.* New York: Free Press, 1988.

Shawcross, William. *The Shah's Last Ride.* New York: Simon and Schuster, 1988.

Sick, Gary. *All Fall Down.* New York: Penguin, 1986.

———. *October Surprise.* New York: Times Books, 1991.

Sickmann, Rocky. *Iranian Hostage.* Topeka, KS: Crawford Press, 1982.

Skidmore, David. *Reversing Course.* Nashville, TN: Vanderbilt University Press, 1996.

Smith, Gaddis. *Morality, Reason and Power.* New York: Hill and Wang, 1986.

Strong, Robert A. *Working in the World.* Baton Rouge, LA: Louisiana State University Press, 2000.

Sullivan, William H. *Mission to Iran.* New York: W. W. Norton & Co., 1981.

———. *Obbligato 1939–1979.* New York: W. W. Norton & Co., 1984.

Taheri, Amir. *The Spirit of Allah.* Bethesda, MD: Adler & Adler, 1985.

———. *The Unknown Life of the Shah.* London: Hutchinson, 1991.

Turner, Stansfield. *Terrorism and Democracy.* Boston: Houghton Mifflin, 1991.

US House of Representatives. Committee on Post Office and Civil Service, Subcommittee on Human Resources. *Unauthorized Transfers of Non Public Information During the 1980 Presidential Election.* 98th Cong., 2nd sess., May 17, 1984.

US House of Representatives. Committee on Foreign Affairs. *The Iran Hostage Crisis.* 97th Cong., 1st sess., March, 1981.

US House of Representatives. Committee on Foreign Affairs. *Iran's Seizure of the United States Embassy.* 97th Cong., 1st sess., February 17, 19, 25, and March 11, 1981.

US House of Representatives. Task Force to Investigate Certain Allegations Concerning the Holding of American Hostages by Iran in 1980. *Report.* 102nd Cong., 2nd sess., January 3, 1993.

US Senate. Committee on Foreign Relations. Report to the Special Counsel to Senator Terry Sanford and Senator James M. Jeffords. *The "October Surprise" Allegations and the Circumstances Surrounding the Release of the American Hostages Held in Iran.* 102nd Cong., 2nd sess., November 19, 1992.

US Senate. Committee on Foreign Relations, Subcommittee on Near Eastern and South Asian Affairs. *Whether the Senate Should Proceed to Investigate Circumstances Surrounding the Release of American Hostages in 1980.* 102nd Cong., 1st sess., November 21 and 22, 1991.

Vance, Cyrus. *Hard Choices.* New York: Simon and Schuster, 1983.

Wells, Tim. *444 Days: The Hostages Remember.* New York: Harcourt Brace Jovanovich, 1985.

Wilson, Robert A., ed. *Character Above All.* New York: Simon and Schuster, 1995.

INDEX

ABOUT THE AUTHOR

———

David Harris, formerly a contributing editor at the *New York Times Magazine* and *Rolling Stone,* has written eight previous books, including *The League, Dreams Die Hard, The Last Stand,* and *Shooting the Moon.*